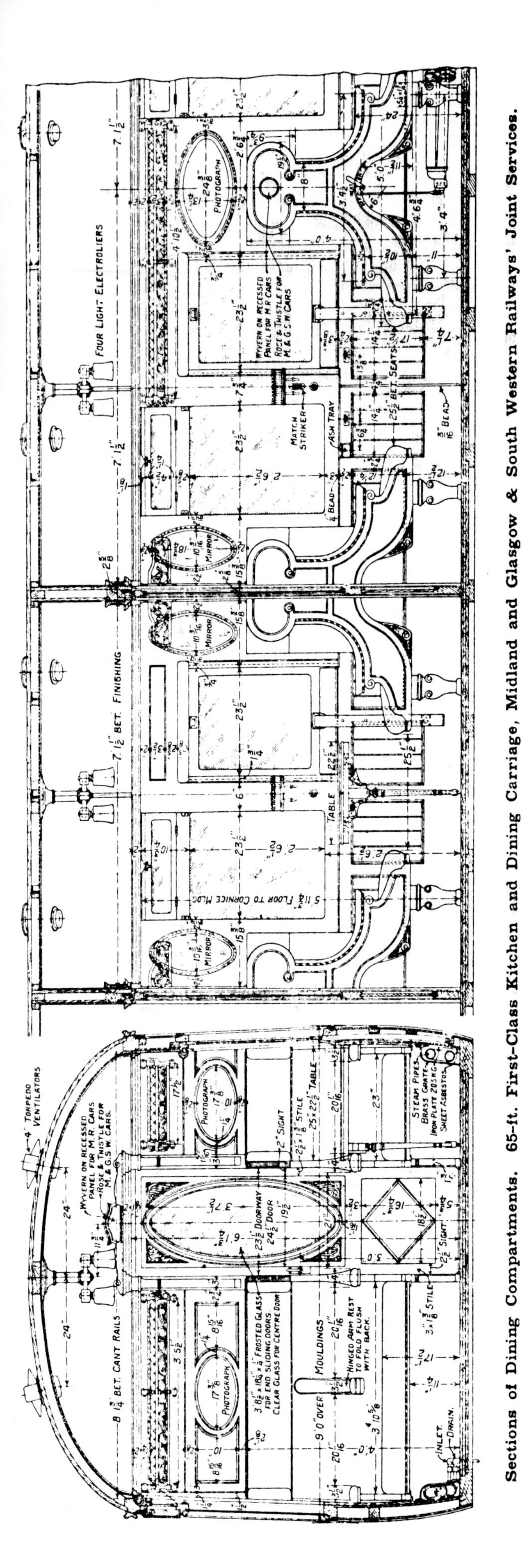

Sections of Dining Compartments. 65-ft. First-Class Kitchen and Dining Carriage, Midland and Glasgow & South Western Railways' Joint Services.

Of the relatively smaller number of ... carriages with kitchens, some, espe... D450 version, may have ope... site open coaches; bu... Railway third class ... diner to be regarded ... and to carry detachabl... the carriage mentioned ... Diagram 575, as preserv... ...useum, was built to a third cla... ...egarded as a 'common' dining carriage ... ...vice with detachable class boards and no class m... ...gs on the outside. It was not until LMS days that it was finally classified 'third' and the doors marked accordingly.

We have gone into some detail in this matter of operation because we feel that it helps in the understanding of the catering vehicle building policy of the Midland Railway and, when related to the summary of carriages appended below, should give a reasonably accurate summary of the situation.

It is interesting to contrast Midland Railway catering vehicle policy with that of the other major 'dining vehicle' constituent of the LMS, namely the LNWR. The London & North Western Railway built, almost exclusively, 'proper' dining carriages, i.e. with kitchen, for all its patrons and constructed them in considerable batches. It was, therefore, by no means unusual on LNWR lines to see two, or sometimes three, full diners in a train, often one each in separate parts of the formation.

LMS policy seems to have been to adopt a sort of amalgamated solution rather than to allow one of the two approaches to dominate. The LNWR practice of 'large builds' of one type was followed but the Midland Railway concept of diner plus open coach was the commonly adopted arrangement as far as train marshalling went. More often than not this was, as in Midland Railway days, first class diner plus open third. Less common, but quite numerous, was third class diner plus open composite. Composite dining carriages continued to be used mainly as single unit vehicles. This meant that the Midland Railway carriages frequently carried on, in terms of utilization, exactly as before, whereas the LNWR dining saloons often found themselves 'paired', in LMS days, with new LMS standard open stock of Midland Railway appearance. The end result could be quite interesting, visually!

Needless to say, after the Grouping, both Midland Railway vehicles and their LNWR contemporaries tended to migrate system-wide, especially into Scotland during the 1930s, where many of them supplemented, or replaced, the Pullman dining vehicles which had been the favoured Caledonian Railway solution to catering services. Ex-Midland Railway carriages also formed the bulk of the Highland line catering fleet during LMS days, in particular some of the 59ft. clerestories to Diagram 436.

Having started by giving this general overview of the subject, the rest of this chapter will follow a pattern which we shall use throughout the book, namely a more detailed look, via photographs and drawings, at some of the vehicles built, followed by a summary in tabular form *(Table 2)* of all the vehicles listed in the lot book which were built between 1877 and 1923, together with such amplifying details as are known to the authors. Where information is not known to us, or is of a speculative nature, we shall endeavour to make this fact clear and invite further information, via the publisher, from interested readers.

Clayton Clerestory Dining Carriages 1892-4

We start our detailed survey of types by attempting to unravel the mysteries surrounding the first generation of purpose-built Clayton dining carriages. Twelve vehicles were involved and we are concentrating here on the first nine, Diagram 440 (first class) and Diagrams 562/558 (third class). The last three were rather different (first class - D441) and are illustrated in *Plates 17, 27, 35 & 36.*

The first to emerge was Lot 278 of D440 - a one-off first class vehicle built for the Midland itself and unique, as far as we are aware, in carrying a representation of the Midland Wyvern on its central lower panelling *(Plate 46).* This vehicle was probably non-gangwayed at both ends. This was followed by two more (Lot 308) to the same diagram for the MSWJS, accompanied by three rather similar third class non-kitchen carriages to D562. These vehicles were featured in the *Railway Engineer* of 1893 and designed to operate as pairs *(Plate 47).* We incorporate plan views *(at Figure 9)* of the carriages as built.

As built, the carriages were gangwayed to each other, but not to the train, and were, in consequence, used for 'all the way' travelling when first introduced.

Contemporary interior views *(e.g. Plate 44)* clearly show seats across the full width of the outer ends. At a slightly later date, the Midland fitted gangways at both ends (also to Lot 278, we believe) and considerably remodelled the interiors of all six carriages. *Figure 9* shows the gangwayed version of D440 as rebuilt, in which it can be seen that the kitchen and pantry were completely rearranged and all five dining bays brought together by repositioning the central lavatory/luggage area to the outer end of the vehicle. Regrettably, we can locate no suitable illustrative material for the somewhat similar conversion of D562.

Around 1894/5, D558 appeared - the pioneer third class dining carriages with kitchen, also for the MSWJS. Externally very similar to the previous designs, these three carriages are represented by *Figure 10* and *Plate 48.* They seem also to have been built without gangways (at least at the non-kitchen end; probably at both ends) but were soon altered to the form shown with gangways at both ends. However, little other remodelling seems to have taken place, except for the fitting of corridor connections. In 1908, these three were split between the Midland and GSW, with the Midland taking two and the GSW one.

Bogie and underframe details for all vehicles are at *Figures 2* (bogie) *and 10*; and the interior finishes were walnut with crimson morocco leather upholstery (first class), and mahogany with crimson plush rep upholstery (third class). The carriages were gas lit and the first six at least were heated by circulating *hot water* from the locomotive supply according to contemporary accounts. We are inclined to think that this fairly rapidly gave way to conventional steam heat. An amusing contemporary comment states that there had been 'no lavish expenditure in useless decoration' - things were obviously different in those days!

We cannot give withdrawal dates for these pioneer carriages but they seem not to have survived the Grouping very long, if at all.

Plates 43 to 45 This magnificent set of contemporary pictures shows the first class, third class and kitchen interiors of the original twelve wheel clerestory dining carriages. Note the MR Wyvern in the luggage rack supports of the third class carriage - albeit a Joint Stock vehicle. The full width seating (at the non-gangwayed end) can just be discerned beyond the far door of the third class carriage.

(NRM)

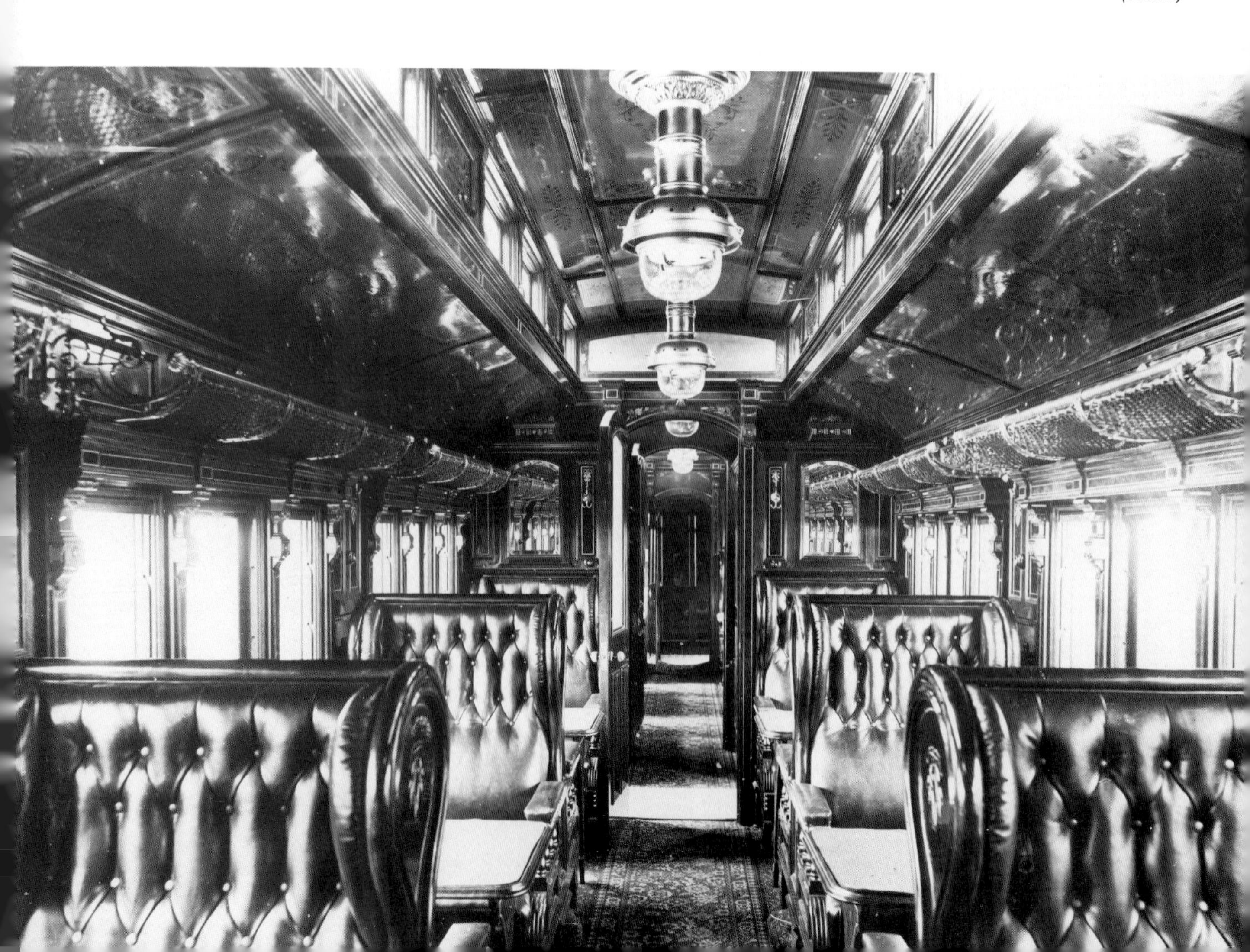

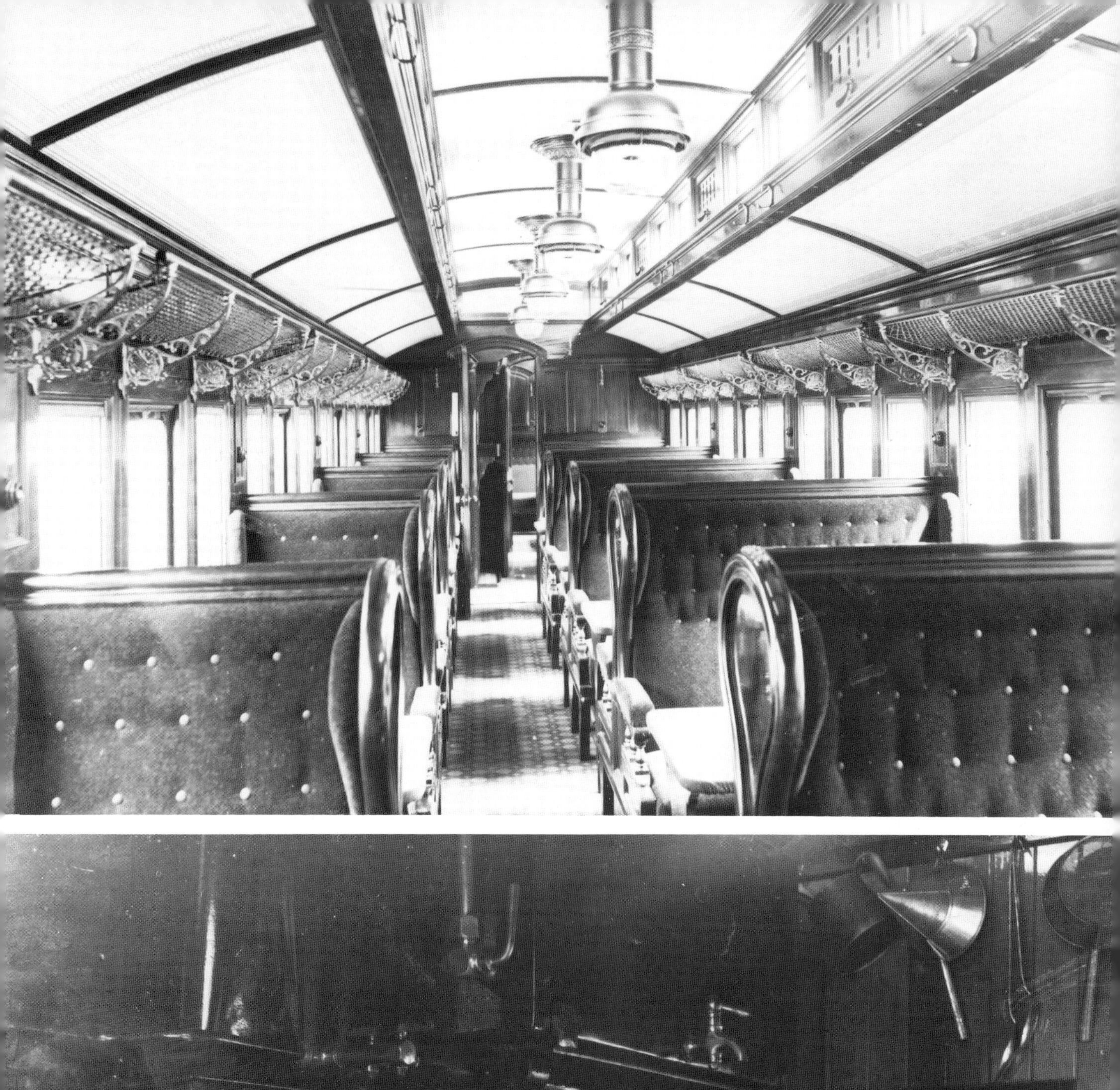

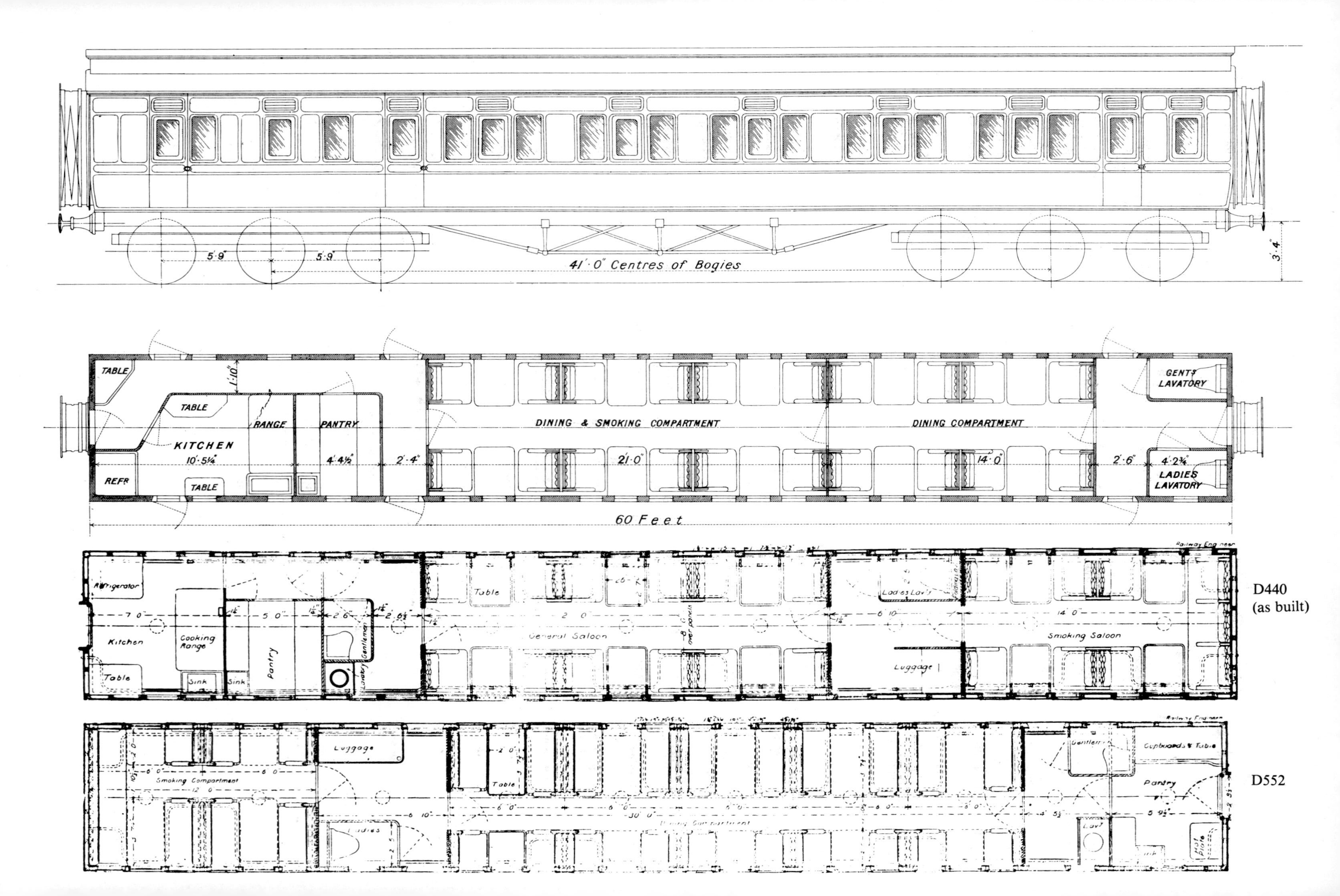

41' 0" Centres of Bogies
5' 9"
5' 9"
3' 4"
TABLE
TABLE
KITCHEN
10' 5¼"
RANGE
PANTRY
4' 4½"
REFR.
TABLE
2' 4"
DINING & SMOKING COMPARTMENT
21' 0"
DINING COMPARTMENT
14' 0"
2' 6"
GENTS LAVATORY
4' 2¾"
LADIES LAVATORY
60 Feet
Refrigerator
Kitchen
Cooking Range
Table
Sink
Sink
Pantry
Lavatory Gentlemen
Table
General Saloon
Ladies Lav's
Luggage
Smoking Saloon
D440
(as built)
Luggage
Smoking Compartment
Ladies
Table
Pantry
Cupboards & Table
Lav's
Hot Plate
D552

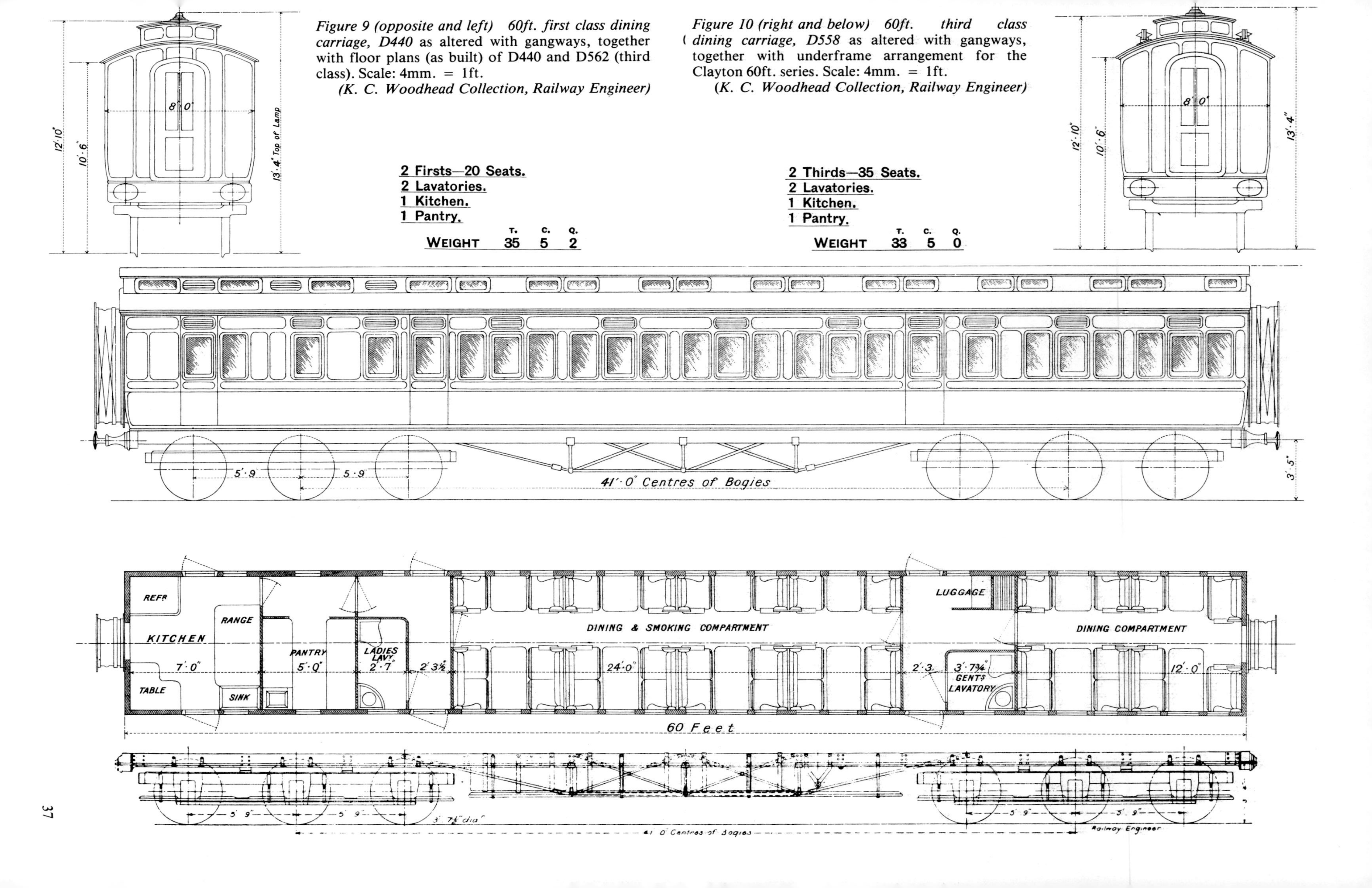

Figure 9 (opposite and left) 60ft. first class dining carriage, D440 as altered with gangways, together with floor plans (as built) of D440 and D562 (third class). Scale: 4mm. = 1ft.
(K. C. Woodhead Collection, Railway Engineer)

Figure 10 (right and below) 60ft. third class dining carriage, D558 as altered with gangways, together with underframe arrangement for the Clayton 60ft. series. Scale: 4mm. = 1ft.
(K. C. Woodhead Collection, Railway Engineer)

Plate 46 (above) An exterior view of MR No. 359 later No. 2752 (D440, Lot 278) as built. Note the lack of end gangway and the Midland Wyvern (below the MR in the waist panel). The two MSWJS examples to this diagram were, as far as is known, all but identical.

(BR/LMR)

Plate 47 (opposite, upper) The MSJS pairing of vehicles to D440 and D562. Note that both vehicles carry MSJS No. 1 - illustrative of the fact that separate number series were used for first and third class vehicles.

(NRM)

Plate 48 (opposite, lower) MSWJS third class dining carriage No. 4 to D558. This vehicle became MR No. 2256 after 1908.

(BR/LMR)

THIRD CLASS
No 1
DINING
CARRIAGE
M.S.W.J.S
FIRST CLASS
DINING CARRIAGE
No 4 M.S.W.J.S
DINING
CARRIAGE
M.S.W.J.S No 4

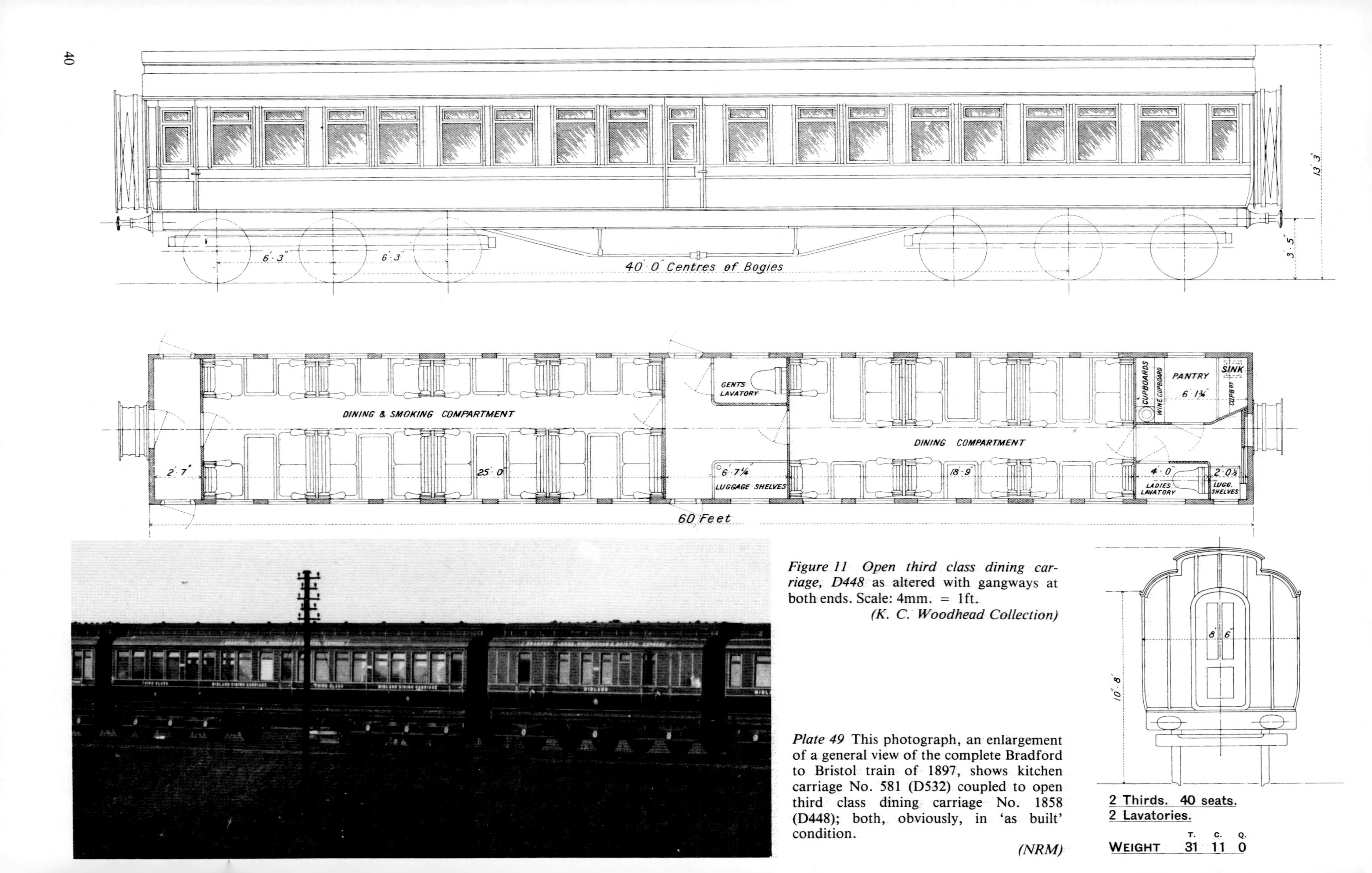

Figure 11 Open third class dining carriage, D448 as altered with gangways at both ends. Scale: 4mm. = 1ft.

(K. C. Woodhead Collection)

Plate 49 This photograph, an enlargement of a general view of the complete Bradford to Bristol train of 1897, shows kitchen carriage No. 581 (D532) coupled to open third class dining carriage No. 1858 (D448); both, obviously, in 'as built' condition.

(NRM)

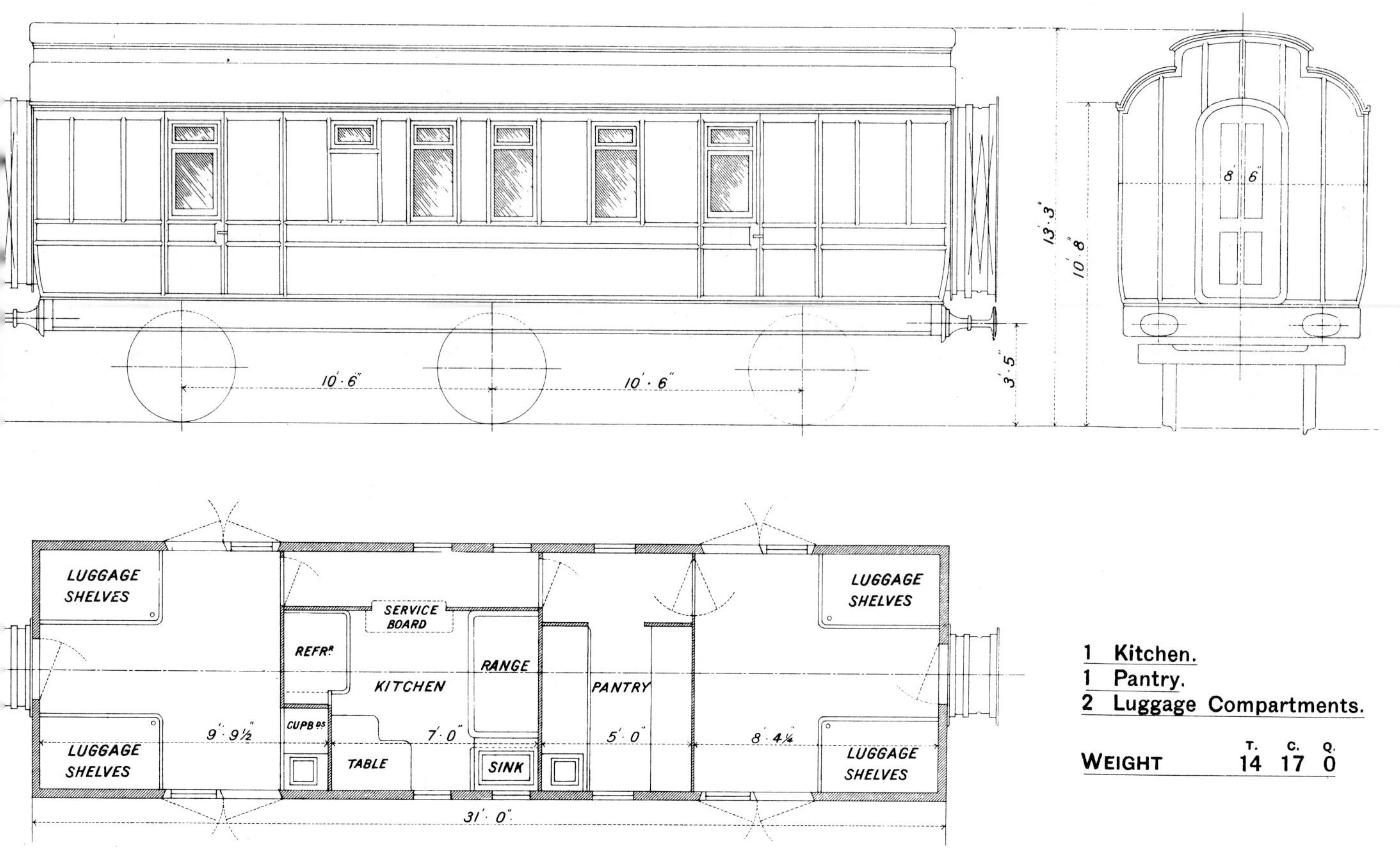

Figure 12 Kitchen carriage D532. Scale: 4mm. = 1ft.
(K. C. Woodhead Collection)

Kitchen Car and Third Class Open Dining Carriage 1896-7

The next featured types are two of the pioneer square-panelled clerestory designs for the Bradford to Bristol services. Ordered in 1896, the carriages did not actually commence operation until 2nd August 1897. The trains were the 1.25p.m. from Bradford and the 2.05p.m. from Bristol, with one of the three sets built standing spare. We have chosen to illustrate the six wheel kitchen car (D532) and the third class open dining carriage (D448). The only good photographs we can locate are of the full train. An enlarged portion of one of these views is at *Plate 49* and the full train is shown at *Plate 20.*

This set formation seems only to have lasted a few years and, early in the present century, the vehicles were split up for general service and some small modifications were made. A passage was added past the kitchen of the six wheelers, and gangways were fitted at both ends of the open thirds (hitherto gangwayed only at the kitchen car end), together with a pantry. This is the condition represented by the diagrams at *Figures 11 & 12.* Some time after 1906, the kitchen car roofs were lowered to clear the Metropolitan line gauge. All six vehicles appear to have reached the LMS but none survived to the 1933 renumbering.

Modellers should refer to *Figure 2* for bogie detail generally suitable for the open thirds and underframe detail generally applicable to the kitchen car. Detailed panel height dimensions for square-panelled clerestory stock will be found at *Figure 3.*

Bain Twelve Wheel Dining Carriages

The classic Bain Midland twelve wheel clerestory carriage is best exemplified by the kitchen/first plus open third pairing built in both square and round-panelled types. We have selected for illustration, on the next few pages, the diagrams of the square light kitchen first and round-panelled open third, but the basic dimensions of both were the same - as indeed were most of the underframe details so, with the photographs appended, a fairly comprehensive picture can be derived. The diagrams concerned were D571/D437 (first class) and D572/447 (third class). These pictures and drawings are relatively self explanatory but, regrettably, we cannot locate detailed underframe arrangement drawings. However the bogies are generally similar to the final MR 12ft. 6in wheelbase twelve wheel design *(Figure 7, page 24)* which became the basis of the LMS standard type, and most underframe features are tolerably clear from the pictures.

These carriages had a long and honourable life, all surviving into the 1940s *(see Table 2).* Although none survive, their general characteristics (save for the underframe truss rods) were not dissimilar to the preserved MR No. 3463 at the National Railway Museum *(see Plates 38 & 39).*

Plates 50 & 51 (above) Comparative views from the kitchen side of kitchen firsts to D571 and D437 respectively. The square-panelled type (D571) is represented by M&GSW No. 208 to Lot 576 (LMS Nos. 3907-85) and the round-panelled version by MR No. 2506 (second LMS No. 87). Panel styling apart, the almost exact correlation of detail between the two designs is readily apparent.

(BR/LMR)

Plate 52 (below) A corridor side view of D437 - MR No. 2509 (second LMS No. 88). Note the differences in class marking between this vehicle and No. 2506 *(Plate 51)* of the same Lot, demonstrating clearly that these vehicles emerged during the period of livery detail changes circa 1906 - *see also Appendix III.*

(BR/LMR)

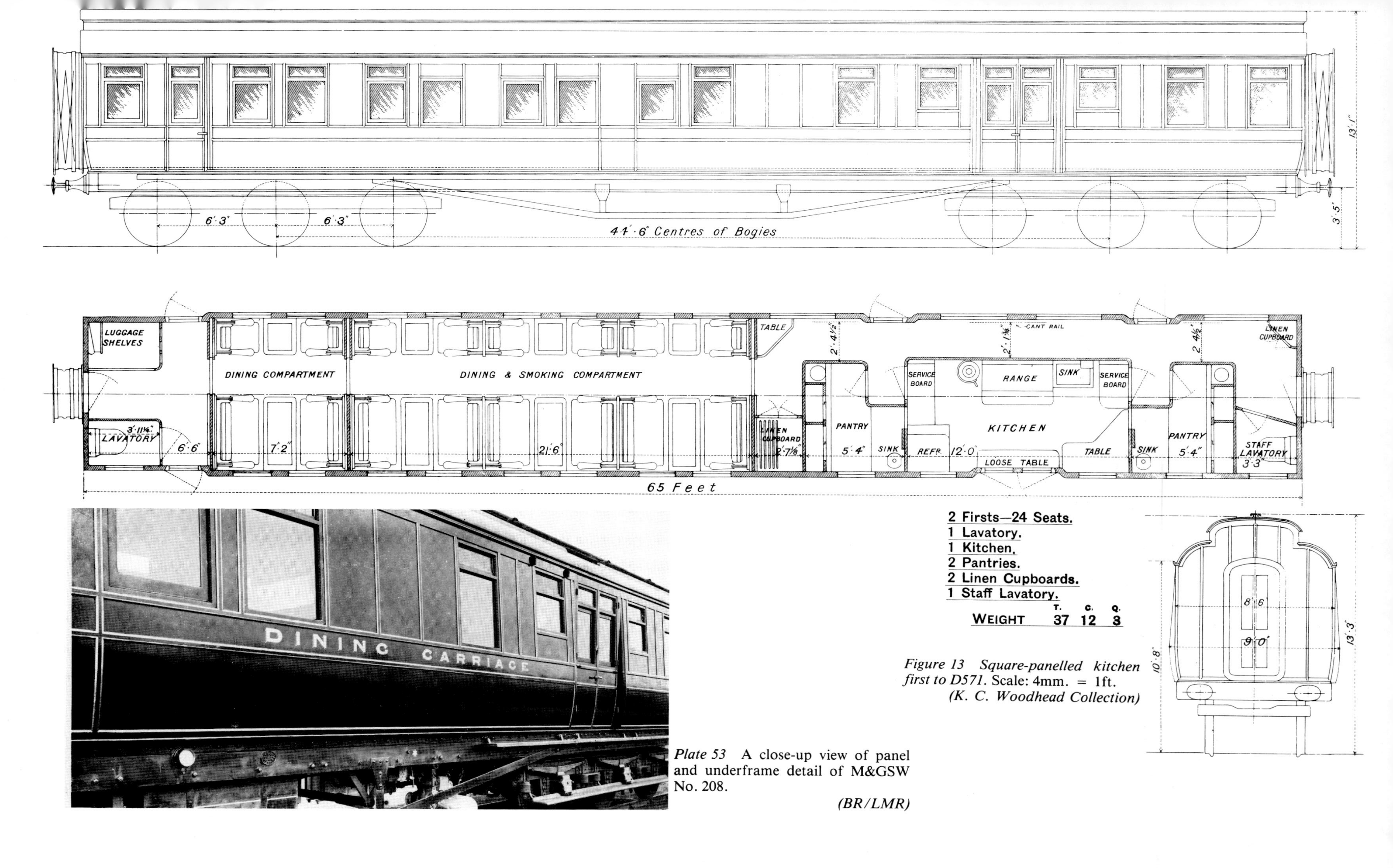

Figure 13 Square-panelled kitchen first to *D571*. Scale: 4mm. = 1ft. *(K. C. Woodhead Collection)*

Plate 53 A close-up view of panel and underframe detail of M&GSW No. 208.

(BR/LMR)

Plate 54 & 55 That interiors of the first class carriages to D571/D437 hardly varied is clearly indicated by the views of No. 2593 to D571 (second LMS No. 157 after downgrading) and No. 2509 to D437. The round-panelled version (D437) can be distinguished by the seat antimacassars and the laid-up tables.

(BR/LMR)

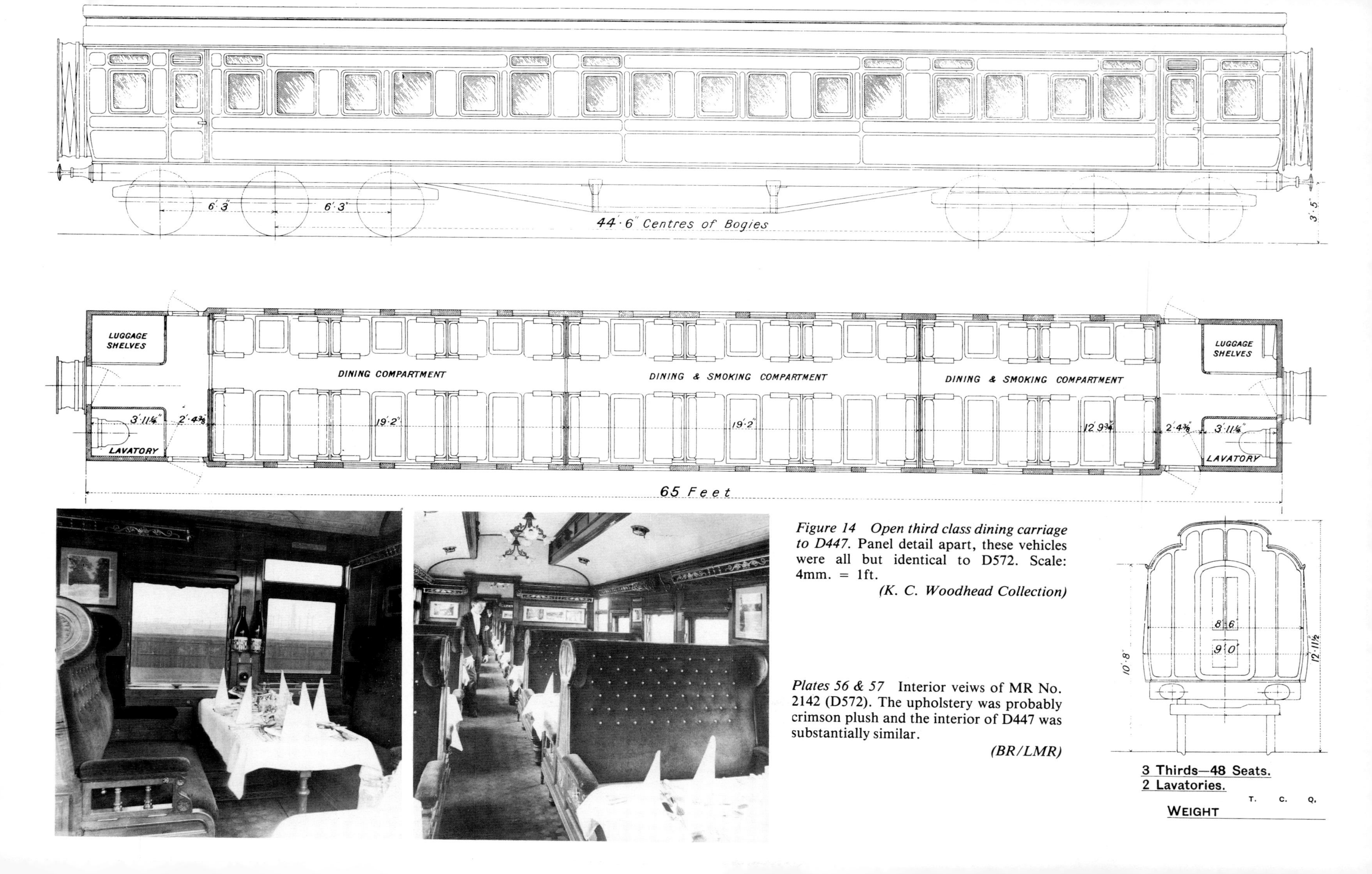

Figure 14 *Open third class dining carriage to D447.* Panel detail apart, these vehicles were all but identical to D572. Scale: 4mm. = 1ft.

(K. C. Woodhead Collection)

Plates 56 & 57 Interior veiws of MR No. 2142 (D572). The upholstery was probably crimson plush and the interior of D447 was substantially similar.

(BR/LMR)

Plates58 & 59 Opposite side views of open third class dining carriages MR No. 2139 and MR No. 2142 (second LMS Nos. 9621/4 respectively) to D572. Again note the difference in class markings, dating the pictures circa 1906/7.

(BR/LMR)

Bain 59ft. Kitchen First - D436

The existence of good official photographs of this design, together with the fact that one of the authors had already made detailed drawings, persuaded us to include a third type of Bain clerestory dining carriage in this detailed survey. We were additionally tempted by the knowledge that it was one of the more numerous MR diners, and that its survival into the 1950s *(see Table 2)* might make it a suitable modeller's prototype.

In essence, the design was a reduced length version of D437 *(above)* but with round bar truss rods and pressed steel four wheel bogies. They were originally designed (as were most of the Midland kitchen firsts) to operate with matching open thirds - in this case D446. However, for much of their life they ran as 'single unit' vehicles and, in LMS days (after 1933), many were renumbered into the third class series to run as 'common' dining carriages - being, inter alia, particularly associated with the Highland section of the LMS system. Although not, perhaps, the most famous of a celebrated 'breed', they do, in many respects, typify the classic Midland dining carriage more than any other single design.

Plate 60 Panel, underfran and pressed steel bogie det of MR No. 2793.

(BR/LM

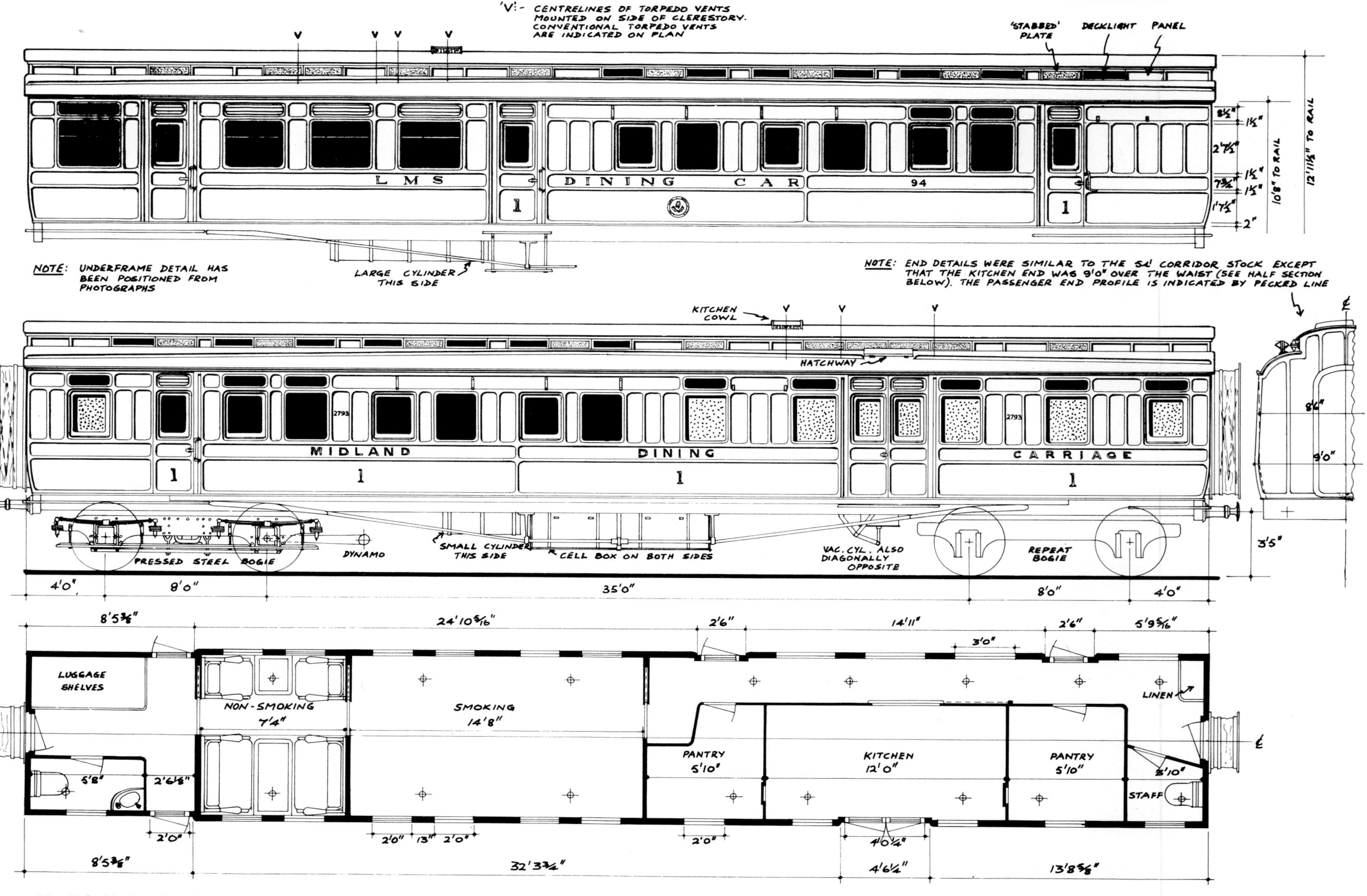

Figure 15 59ft. kitchen first class dining carriage to D436. Scale: 4mm. = 1ft. (D. Jenkinson)

Plates 61 & 62 Opposite side views of MR No. 2793 (second LMS No. 95, later No. 180) to D436. Note the general similarity to D437 *(Plates 51 & 52).*
(BR/LMR)

TABLE 2
Summary of Midland and Midland/Scottish Joint Stock Catering Vehicles

ag.	Lot	Qty.	Date of Order	Dimensions	Wt.	Style	MR	Pre-Group Numbering M&GSW 1st	M&GSW 2nd	M&NB 1st	M&NB 2nd	Post Group Data/Numbers 1st LMS	2nd LMS	Type Extinct	Remarks
rst Class Dining Carriages (RF/RFO)															
0	278 308	1 2	1891 1892	60' x 8' 0" 60' x 8' 0"		CC1 CC1	359, later 2752 –	MSWJS 1,2	MGSW 201/202						Pioneer 12 wheel diners. As built did not quite match details given on diagram (window positions, etc.).
1	365	3	1895	60' x 8' 0"	34½T	CC1	360–2, later 2753–5								Very similar to D440 but a change in window style and other minor details.
8	395	2	1897	60' x 8' 6"	33½T	CC2	3001–2, later 2591–2					2591–2		c1930	Originally RFO+T (ordinary) for Manchester sets. To RF in 1902 (kitchen replacing 3rd class area). Ran with Lot 398 (D449) originally.
9	441	2	1898	60' x 8' 6"	34½T	CC2									Built for Private Parties, possibly to 3rd class later.
2 O)	478	3	1899	48' x 8' 6"	24T	CC2	369–371, later 2762–4					2762–4			Original utilization not known but possibly paired with RT–D449, Lot 477.
1	555 576	6 3	1903 1904	65' x 9' 0" 65' x 9' 0"	37½T 37½T	BC3 BC3	2593–7 2598 –	– – 207–9	– – 209–11	– – –	– – –	2593–7 2598 3906–8	157–61 83 84–6	12/49 9/46 9/46	Originally built to operate with RTO (D572) and shown (incorrectly) as D437 in some sources. Most of Lot 555 downgraded to 3rd class/unclassed by mid-LMS period – hence different number series after 1933.
7	620	2	1905	65' x 9' 0"	38T	BC4	2506/9	–	–	–	–	2506/9	87–8	2/46	Round-panelled version of D571 and originally paired with RTO (D447).
6	662	8	1908	59' x 9' 0"	31T	BC4	2787–94	–	–	–	–	2787–94	89–96 (see notes) 180–182	5/50 10/52	Essentially an 18 seat version of D437 on 4 wheel pressed steel bogies. Initially paired with RTO (D446). Three downgraded by LMS in 1946 viz:- 90–182; 92–181; 95–180. One early casualty (LMS 91) at Little Salkeld (1935).
5	951	3	1920	65' x 9' 0"	39T	E	2652 –	– –	– 215/6	– –	– –	2652 3912–3	97 98–9	2/54 2/58	The only elliptical roof kitchen-diners and originally ran with RTO (D1197). LMS No. 98 reduced to 'common' status by 1936, possibly earlier, but not renumbered (c.f. D571).
mposite Dining Carriages (RC/RCO)															
4	438	5	1898	60' x 8' 6"	33T	CC2	3126–30	–	–	–	–	3128–9		c1930	Nos. 3126/7/30 later converted to 3rd Saloon – see D545, *Table 4*.
3	440	3	1898	60' x 8' 6"	34T	CC2	–	–	–	119–21	29–31	to LNER 32282;	32321/2		Virtually the MNB equivalent of D444 with slight extra seating capacity.
5 O)	479	9	1899	48' x 8' 6"	24T	CC2	939–47, later 3739–47	–	–	–	–	3739–47	–	c1931	Seem to have been built with D442 (RFO)– original utilization not known but possibly paired with RT – D449.
4	633	2	1905	65' x 9' 0"	38T	BC4	–	–	–	158 159	68 69	4091 to LNER	296 in 1928	10/37	The only Bain period composites, Central kitchen arrangement.

iag.	Lot	Qty.	Date of Order	Dimensions	Wt.	Style	Pre-Group Numbering MR	Joint Stock 1st	Joint Stock 2nd	Post Group Data Numbers 1st LMS	2nd LMS	Type Extinct	Remarks
hird Class Dining Carriages (RT/RTO)													
62 TO)	310	3	1893	60' x 8' 0"	32½T	CC1	–	MSWJS 1–3	MGSW 331–3				Very similar style to RF (D440) and possibly built to run with Lot 308 of this diagram as pairs.
58	335	3	1894	60' x 8' 0"	33T	CC1	2256/7 (after 1908)	MSWJS 4–6	No. 6 to GSW Stock in 1908	as MR (if not scrapped)	–	pre-1930	Pioneer 3rd class dining carriages with kitchens.
48 TO)	385	3	1896	60' x 8' 6"	31½T	CC2	1858–60	–	–	1858–60	–	pre-1933	First true 'Midland' Clerestory design for Bristol-Bradford sets (Lots 384–9). Built without gangway at one end and later given gangways both ends, plus pantry.
49	398 477	2 10	1897 1899	60' x 8' 6"	32½T	CC2	1864–5 2074–83	– –	– –	1864–5 2074–83	147 (ex 1865) 148–156 (not 2077)	11/33 12/33	Lot 398 built to work with D438 (RF) as originally built. Virtually withdrawn en bloc in 1933 as a result of new build of LMS standard 68ft. RT type.
50 TO)	399	2	1897	60' x 8' 6"	32½T	CC2	Believed 1866–7	–	–	as MR	–	pre-1933	Built for London-Bradford service and just possibly operated (initially) with RF (D439) – otherwise, where did the cooking take place?
72 TO)	556	6	1903	65' x 9' 0"	36T	BC3	2138–43	–	–	2138–43	9620–5	6/41	Built to operate in pairs with RF (D571). Final LMS numbers are in the non-dining open 3rd series.
47 TO)	577 621	2 2	1904 1905	65' x 9' 0"		BC4	– 1312; 1364	MGSW 231–2 –	MGSW 364–5 –	3998–9 1312; 1364	9626–7 9628–9	12/44 3/42	Round-panelled version of D572 and originally paired with RF (D437)
75	671	3	1907	65' x 9' 0"	38T	BC4	–	MGSW 246–8	MGSW 379–81	4013–5	162–4	9/46	Diagram annotated M&GSW but Lot 843 was purely Midland.
	843	2	1914				3432; 3463	–	–	3432; 3463	165–6	5/54	Lot 843 was regarded as RC/RU and No. 3463 (LMS 166) preserved at National Railway Museum.
46 TO)	663	10	1907	59' x 9' 0"	29T	BC4	2243–52	–	–	2243–52	9607–16	1948	Built to operate (initially) with RF (D436). Diagram shows later alteration to elliptical roof. Not known how many, if any, were rebuilt.
197 TO)	952	3	1920	59' x 9' 0"	29T	E	–	–	MGSW 394–6	4028–30	9617–9	9/59	Elliptical version of D446 to operate (initially) with RF (D1196).
ther Catering Vehicles													
32	388	3	1896	31' x 8' 6"	15T	CC2	579–81	–	–	as MR ?	–	pre-1933	Six wheel kitchen cars for Bradford-Bristol sets, later use not known.
59	481	3	1899	50' x 8' 6"	24T	CC2	–	MGSW Stock	–	–	–	–	Built as FK plus Kitchen, later to BFK (*see Table 6 for details*).
43	651	6	1906	54' x 8' 6"		BC4							Essentially BCK plus Kitchen. Described in lot book as Composite Dining Carriages – all to Ambulances in World War I.
44	Part 593	3	?	54' x 8' 6"	24T	BC4							Three vehicles from D476 (BTK) rebuilt temporarily with pantry in one compartment. Later reverted to BTK.

Compiled by D. Jenkinson, December 1983

Chapter Three

Sleeping Carriages

The Midland Railway was not a great user of sleeping carriages and the story of its vehicles in this category is complicated by the fact that, initially, its sleeping vehicles were Pullman-built and owned. They are, in consequence, strictly speaking outside the scope of this book, but we have given a basic outline in *Appendix I*. In this chapter, we shall, for the most part, confine our comments to the Midland Railway coaches which appear in the diagram or lot book.

During the 19th century, the only Midland Railway-built sleeping carriages described as such, were four vehicles, built one each to Lots 171-4 during 1887. They were of typical Clayton arc roof style and obviously experimental since all were different. No diagrams have been located for them but all four were officially photographed and are illustrated in this book.

After this mild flirtation with its own design of sleeping carriages the Midland Railway itself appears to have virtually ignored the type until early in the 20th century when, between 1900 and 1911, it put into service the whole fleet of its own conventional general service sleeping vehicles. However, this does not mean that the Midland Railway was unaware of the needs of overnight travellers during the latter part of the Victorian period. Although few of its own design of general service sleeping carriages were built, the Pullmans were still in use, now owned by the Midland Railway, and the Company did introduce a considerable number of Family Sleeping Saloons which, presumably, fulfilled much of the same function for the more well-to-do passengers of the time. It must be stressed, of course, that in those days, sleeping carriages were the preserve of first class passengers only and possibly the Midland Railway, which always carried a high proportion of first class passengers, felt that the semi-private saloon might be more acceptable to its patrons. These family sleeping saloons, along with all the other saloon vehicles, are covered in the next chapter.

Whatever the precise reasons, the Midland did not itself introduce conventional sleeping carriages until 1900 when four vehicles to Diagram 453 were put in service. By 'conventional', we mean a side corridor coach with transverse sleeping berths arranged in single or twin compartments - an internal layout very familiar to modern passengers and already widespread in Britain, particularly on the LNWR routes, by 1900. Even then, D453 was not wholly conventional as first built *(see Figure 16, page 54)* as it was still something of a maverick type since the clerestory bodies were pure Pullman and not built by the Midland Railway. In consequence, no lot number was issued. They were very elegant and stylish coaches with a mixture of Pullman 'sections' and transverse berth compartments when first built. Very soon afterwards they were converted to a wholly side corridor style.

After this final fling with Pullman-styled vehicles, albeit owned by the Company itself, the Midland Railway seems to have decided that its new clerestory style would be every bit as acceptable to overnight passengers as it was proving on the day trains, and all subsequent Midland Railway sleepers, less than thirty all told, displayed conventional Midland Railway clerestory features.

In spite of the small numbers, there were six separate diagrams and, essentially, five different types. As with catering carriages, the coaches were, for the most part, built in batches of four or fewer. Only the composite diagram (D456) was built in larger quantity and even then only to eight examples.

Two body styles were used, square and round light clerestory and, although the lot numbers of the first built examples (Diagrams 452, 455 & 456) were issued in 1901, the vehicles themselves exhibited the Bain modifications to the square-panelled style and it seems likely that the coaches did not appear until 1903.

For some reason, the Midland Railway chose to build both eight and twelve wheel sleeping carriages. The twelve wheelers were either 60ft. square-panelled or 65ft. round-panelled, and the eight wheelers were 50ft. square-panelled or 54ft. square and round-panelled. First class coaches contained exclusively sleeping accommodation but the one composite design was a mixture of first class sleeping, first class ordinary and third class ordinary. They were rather attractive vehicles. The two 65ft. round-panelled designs (Diagrams 451 & 601) were virtually identical but with some minor layout alterations in Diagram 601 - not, however, of a radical nature.

All sleeping carriages were originally Midland Railway-owned but several were later transferred to joint M&NB ownership. Strangely, none were ever in the M&GSW fleet as far as we can deduce.

Unlike the Midland Railway dining carriages, which achieved a high post-grouping survival rate, the broadly contemporary sleeping vehicles did not fare so well. The Midland Railway itself seemed rather prone to destroying them in accidents and none at all survived to the 1933 LMS renumbering *(see Table 3)*. This is superficially rather surprising since even the oldest Pullman-styled examples were only just 30 years old and the later clerestories between 20 and 25 years old. In the climate of the 1920s and 1930s, this was not particularly venerable - many older ex-LNWR twelve wheelers last much longer and we cannot give any confirmed reason for the early scrapping of the ex-Midland Railway sleepers. This early withdrawal means an absence of a logically-based 1933 LMS number series for the coaches and has made data checking rather difficult, for which omission we apologize.

The only reason we can advance for the early scrapping of Midland Railway sleeping carriages is that they probably did not really suit the overall LMS operating philosophy. We think it not without significance that sleeping cars were the one type of LMS standard coach where LNWR influences, both in style and layout, were dominant. Moreover, most of the older LNWR-built sleeping coaches had been extensively modernized, internally, at or about the time of the Grouping to bring them up to date, so were, presumably, considered more suitable than the ex-Midland Railway carriages for longer term retention.

We cannot really believe that the Midland Railway carriages were inferior to the LNWR as vehicles, although we must admit that it would have been difficult for them to have been any better in the sleeping car field. The plain fact is that the West Coast route operated far more sleeping vehicles than the Midland line and LMS policy reflected this. So the Midland Railway carriages had no real part to play.

As an aside, therefore, we feel we must point out that totally authentic railway modellers should not operate Midland Railway pattern sleeping carriages unless their layouts are pre-1933 in date! This has not prevented us, however, from including drawings and photographs of what we hope is a representative cross-section of what seem to us to be rather forgotten vehicles.

Plates 63 & 64 - Lots 171 *(above)* and 172 *(below)*. For full caption see overleaf.

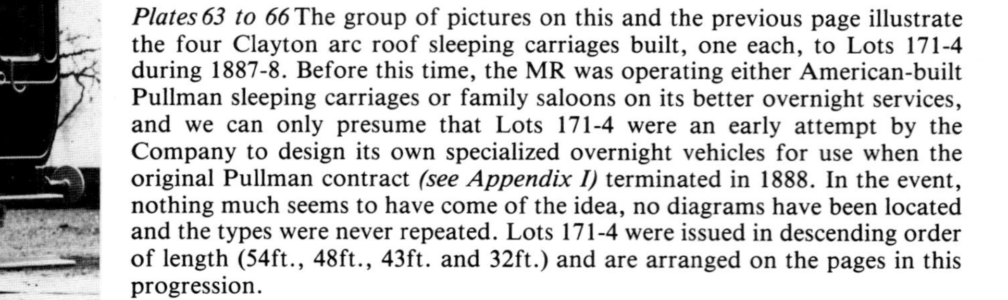

Plates 63 to 66 The group of pictures on this and the previous page illustrate the four Clayton arc roof sleeping carriages built, one each, to Lots 171-4 during 1887-8. Before this time, the MR was operating either American-built Pullman sleeping carriages or family saloons on its better overnight services, and we can only presume that Lots 171-4 were an early attempt by the Company to design its own specialized overnight vehicles for use when the original Pullman contract *(see Appendix I)* terminated in 1888. In the event, nothing much seems to have come of the idea, no diagrams have been located and the types were never repeated. Lots 171-4 were issued in descending order of length (54ft., 48ft., 43ft. and 32ft.) and are arranged on the pages in this progression.

(BR/LMR and NRM)

Although, in general, the Pullman contribution to the MR carriage story is covered in *Appendix I*, these four sleeping carriages form something of an exception, and it seems more logical to include details here. They were, like their predecessors, a joint venture between Derby and America, but stand as a transitional link from the purely Pullman earlier vehicles and the fully Midland designs which followed them.

On this occasion, the carriage bodies only were built in the USA and supplied to the MR in kit form. They were assembled at Derby using standard Midland design bogies, drawgear and auxiliary equipment. Self evidently 'American', they were, nevertheless, more modern looking than the earlier Pullmans *(see Appendix I)* and were finished externally in a 'Pullmanized' version of the Midland livery - i.e. crimson lake with much gold ornamentation.

As built, the vehicles had no gangways and the interior plan was a combination of side corridor 'state rooms' (believed to have been for ladies) and centre gangway Pullman sections *(see smaller plan on Figure 16)*. At a later date, apparently quite soon after building, gangways were fitted and the interiors remodelled to a wholly side corridor, transverse berth arrangement. There was one early casualty, No. 35 (other details not known) but, in rebuilt form, three survived to reach the LMS and lasted until circa 1930.

Contemporary photographs suggest that these carriages were elegantly and superbly finished. A good selection of views is given, along with the drawings, which cover most of the changes which took place.

Plate 67 The sumptuous interior of one of the D453 sleeping carriages, showing part of the original centre gangway section. We have also included some contemporary sketches at *Figure 16* from the *Locomotive Magazine* showing more details of the original interior arrangement.

(NRM)

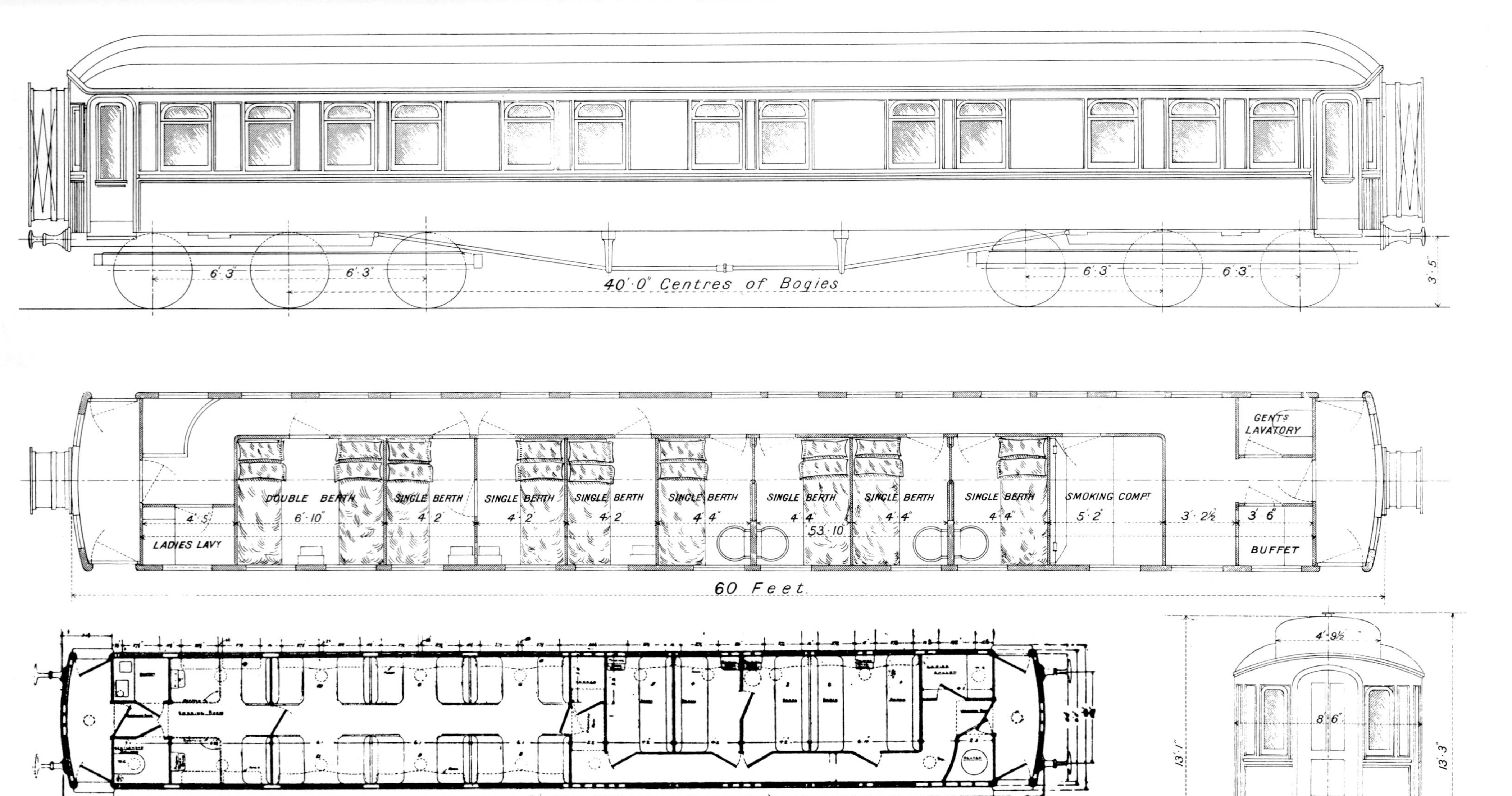

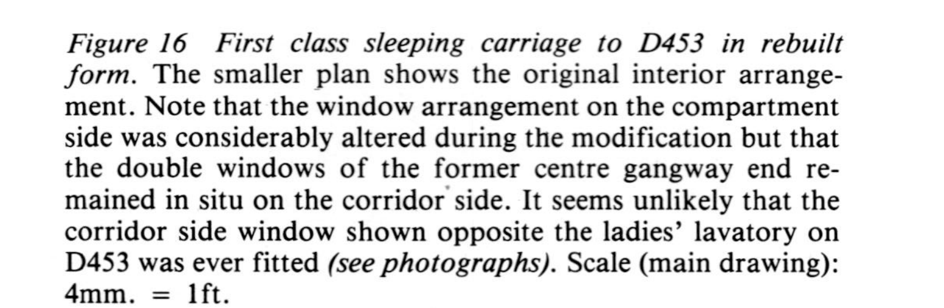

Figure 16 First class sleeping carriage to D453 in rebuilt form. The smaller plan shows the original interior arrangement. Note that the window arrangement on the compartment side was considerably altered during the modification but that the double windows of the former centre gangway end remained in situ on the corridor side. It seems unlikely that the corridor side window shown opposite the ladies' lavatory on D453 was ever fitted *(see photographs)*. Scale (main drawing): 4mm. = 1ft.
(K. C. Woodhead Collection and Locomotive Magazine)

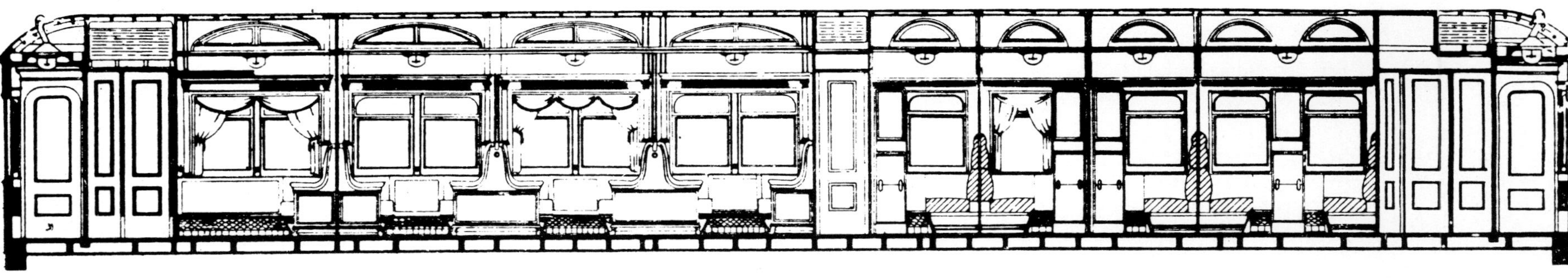

INTERNAL SIDE ELEVATION, SLEEPING CAR, MIDLAND RY.

SIDE FINISH IN SMOKING ROOM

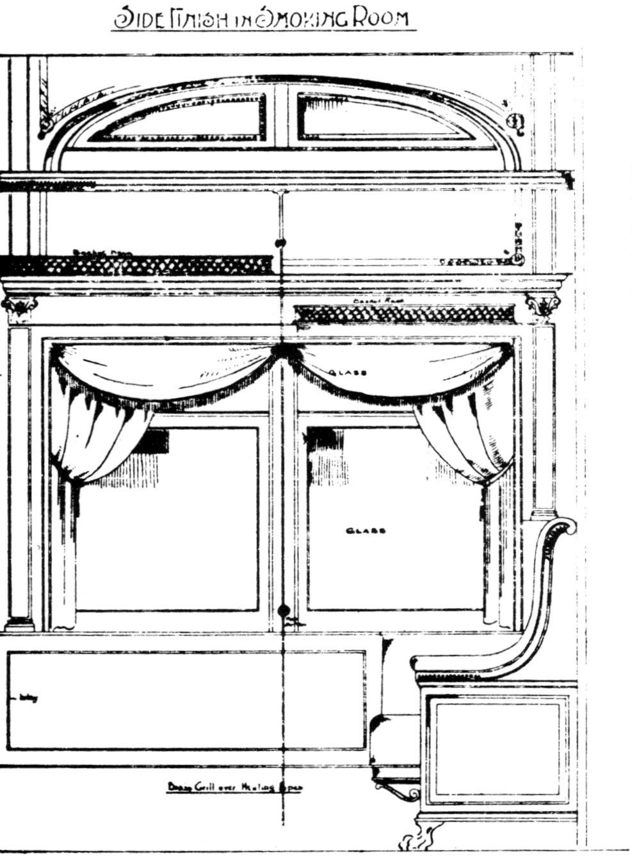

NEW SLEEPING CARS, MIDLAND RY.

CONTINUING our description of these new sleepers, we append drawings showing the internal arrangement and furnishings. The open saloon with six berths is divided up as shown in our perspective view when arranged for night, one partition being represented in position at the far end of the bunk, whilst the sections of the roof show how the curtain rod along the front is fitted. The interior woodwork is in mahogany with finely executed carved mouldings and decorations. Bevelled mirrors of elliptical shape adorn the central and end partitions, whilst the dividing doors have large upper panels of plate glass. The ceiling is handsomely decorated in gold and color, and the floor is covered with linoleum in the passage-way and Wilton carpet in the staterooms and saloon. Brass grilles are arranged in front of the heater pipes, and gilded baskets are pro vided for passengers' light articles.

Plates 68 & 69 Midland sleeping carriages Nos. 35 and 36 as built. MR No. 35 shows the corridor side (which remained largely unchanged after rebuilding) and MR No. 36 shows the compartment side. Comparison with *Figure 16* will indicate the extent of the structural changes at the right-hand end after the rebuilding.

(BR/LMR and NRM)

Plates 70 & 71 Comparative three quarter views of MR No. 36 as built and LMS No. 02773 (ex-MR No. 37) as rebuilt and from the opposite side of the vehicle. Note the LMS pattern buffers and the replacement of the transverse leaf bogie bolster springs by coil springs. Note also that the toplights above the double windows on No. 02773 are two separate units and not the double width type shown on MR No. 36. It is not known whether this modification was carried out on all coaches at rebuilding or whether No. 02773 (the last of the series) was built new with modified toplights. Finally note the disappearance of virtually all ancillary roof detail consequent upon the fitting of electric lighting, the dynamo for which being just visible beyond the nearer bogie.

(NRM and F. W. Shuttleworth Collection)

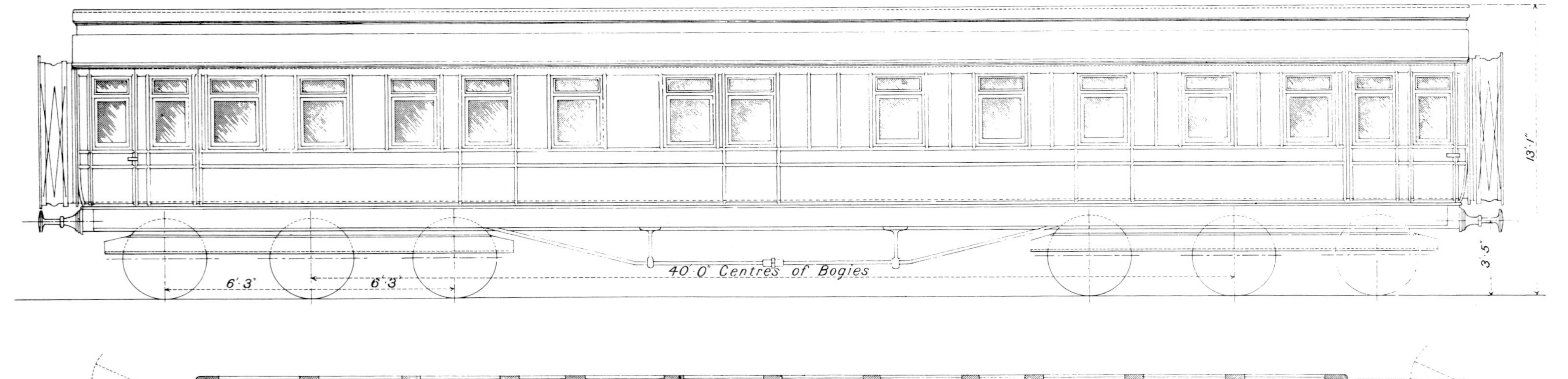

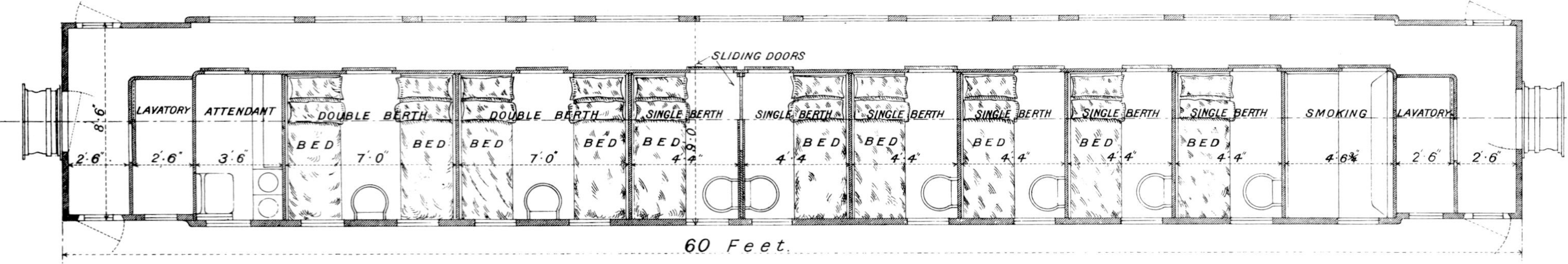

Square-Panelled Clerestory Sleeping Carriages

The first truly Midland clerestory sleeping carriages appeared circa 1903, before Bain had reintroduced the round-cornered panelling. Selected for illustration are the 60ft. twelve wheel first class coaches to D452 and the 54ft. eight wheel composites to D456 - the latter being the most numerous single design of Midland sleeping carriage. Contemporary photographs, indeed any photographs of these vehicles, seem hard to discover but the diagrams featured are very clear and standard practices were observed in the construction of the coaches.

It seems probable that these coaches were amongst the first Midland clerestories to display the 'clipper' profile between the entrances. At this time, the normal carriage width was 8ft. 6in. with an absolute maximum of 9ft. over projections. By confining the doors to the 8ft. 6in. wide area, it was possible to widen the passenger area to 9ft. without fouling the load gauge - an obvious benefit in a sleeping carriage with transverse berths, and an idea also adopted in the broadly contemporary dining carriages *(see Chapter 2)*.

Both batches had a somewhat chequered history and such details as are known are given in *Table 3*.

2 Double Berths.
6 Single Berths.
1 Smoking Compartment.
2 Lavatories.
1 Attendant's Compartment.

	T.	C.	Q.
WEIGHT	32	14	3

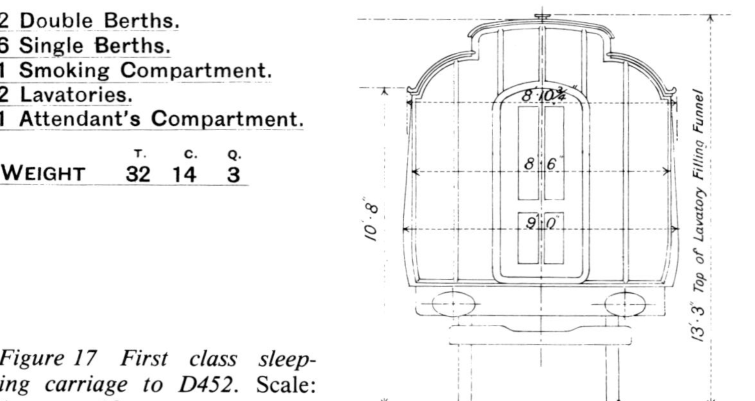

Figure 17 First class sleeping carriage to D452. Scale: 4mm. = 1ft.
(K. C. Woodhead Collection)

Plate 72 A corridor side view of No. 2765, the first to be built to D452. This is the only surviving official view of the square-panelled sleeping carriages but gives a very good impression of the corridor side window style adopted on all of them.

(NRM)

Figure 18 *Composite sleeping carriage to D456.* No official photographs can be offered for this type, but its general characteristics were similar to D452 and also to those of the 50ft. family saloons to D457 - *see Plates 90 & 91.* Scale: 4mm. = 1ft.

(K. C. Woodhead Collection)

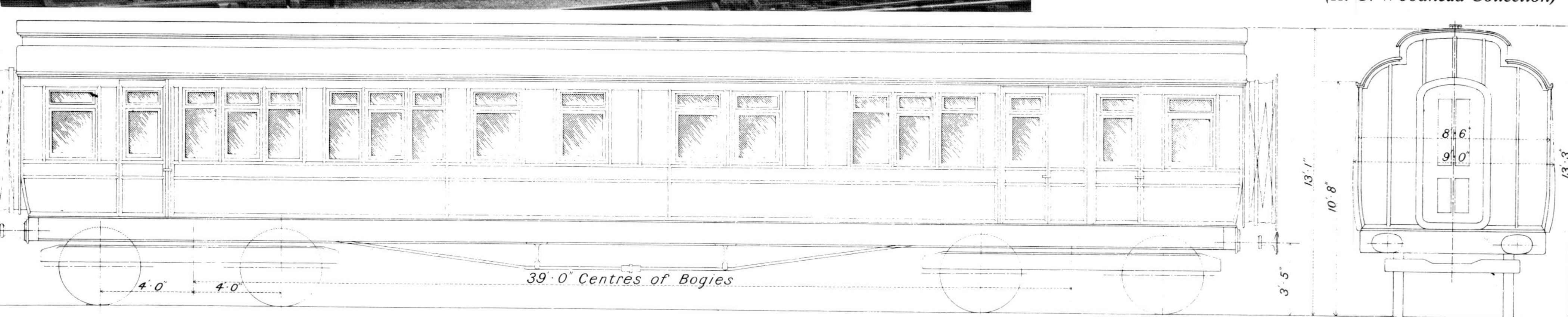

LUGGAGE
LAVATORY 3' 11¼"
8' 6"
2' 3½"
THIRD ORDINARY 6' 2"
THIRD ORDINARY 6' 2"
FIRST DOUBLE 7' 3"
0' 6
FIRST SINGLE 4' 6"
FIRST SINGLE 4' 6"
FIRST CONVERTIBLE 7' 3"
LUGGAGE 4' 1"
2' 2¾"
ATTENDANT
LAVATORY 4' 0"
54 Feet.

2 Thirds (Ord.)—12 Seats.
1 Double Convertible Berth.
1 Double Berth.
2 Single Berths.
2 Lavatories—1st and 3rd.
1 Attendant's Compartment.
1 Luggage Compartment.

	T.	C.	Q.
WEIGHT	28	5	3

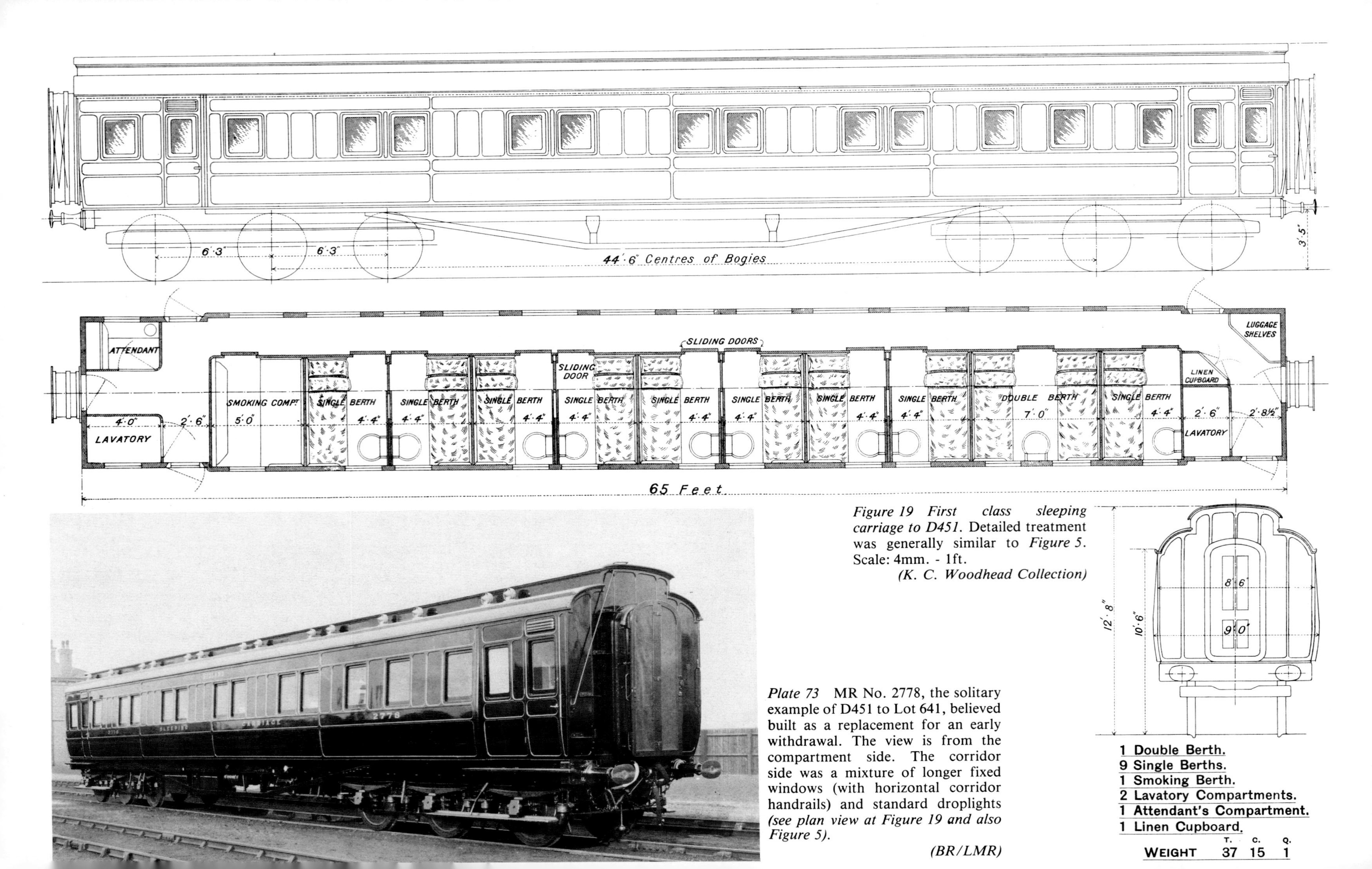

Figure 19 *First class sleeping carriage to D451.* Detailed treatment was generally similar to *Figure 5.* Scale: 4mm. - 1ft.

(K. C. Woodhead Collection)

Plate 73 MR No. 2778, the solitary example of D451 to Lot 641, believed built as a replacement for an early withdrawal. The view is from the compartment side. The corridor side was a mixture of longer fixed windows (with horizontal corridor handrails) and standard droplights *(see plan view at Figure 19 and also Figure 5).*

(BR/LMR)

65ft. First Class Sleeping Carriage to D451

Diagram 451 was a very typical Bain clerestory and, internally, displayed the layout of the traditional British sleeping carriage. Interestingly, the carriage height was reduced to 12ft. 8in. (which was the Metropolitan line height) but we do not believe that these coaches ever worked into the City. Of the first lot of four, only three numbers can be traced, the fourth, presumably, being an early casualty. The three survivors were soon transferred to M&NB ownership and the 'one-off' to Lot 641 *(see Table 3)* may have been a replacement for the withdrawn coach.

The M&NB vehicles lasted until the late 1920s when they were withdrawn in favour of new LMS standard types. Interestingly, two of these new LMS pattern carriages (M&NB Nos. 1 and 2) took, for a year or so, the Joint Stock numbers of the clerestory carriages which they replaced until the M&NB stock was divided between the LMS and LNER in 1928.

Two more Bain twelve wheel clerestory sleepers were built, also 65ft. long, but this time to D601. These were very similar to D451 but the double berth was almost exactly central in the vehicle, and there was a single recessed door on the corridor side opposite this double berth. An enlarged detail drawing of part of one of these later carriages is given at *Figure 5* and the detailed dimensions thereon are, generally, also valid for D451.

Plates 74 & 75 Two more views of No. 2778, showing additional details and the interior compartment arrangement.

(BR/LMR)

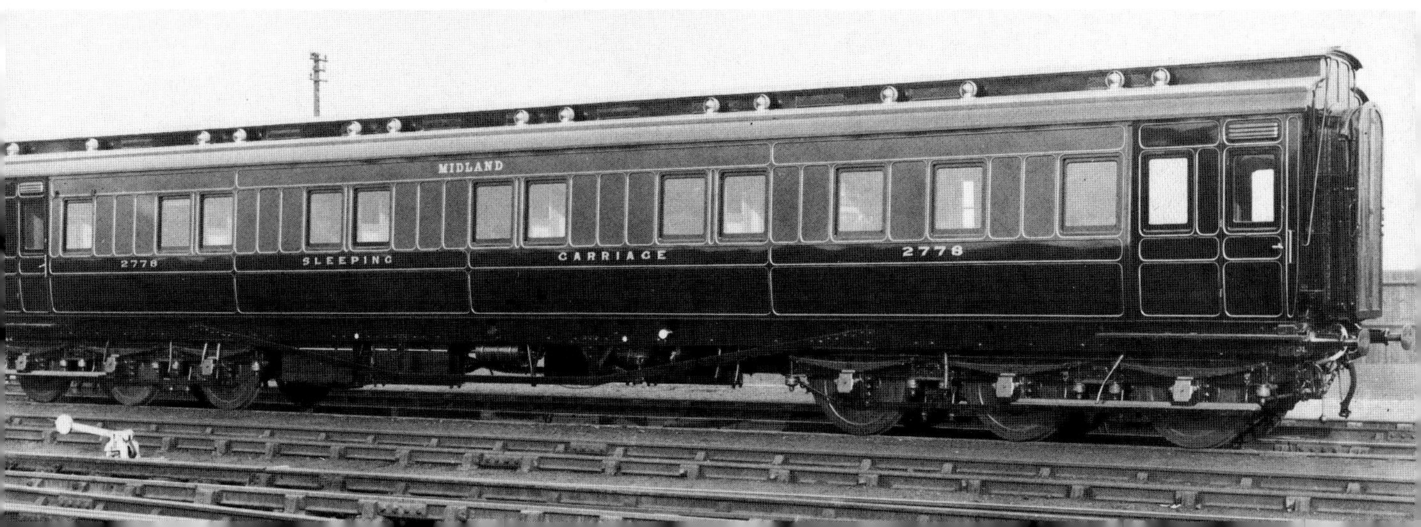

TABLE 3
Summary of Midland and Midland/Scottish Joint Stock Sleeping Carriages

Diag.	*Lot*	*Qty.*	*Date of Order*	*Dimensions*	*Wt.*	*Style*	*Pre-Group Numbering*			*Post Group Data/Numbers*			*Remarks*
							MR	*Joint Stock 1st*	*Joint Stock 2nd*	*1st LMS*	*LNER*	*Type Extinct*	
First Class Sleeping Carriages (SLF)													
	171	1	1887	54' x 8' 0"		CA	356				–		Experimental batch of 'one-offs', no diagram apparently issued.
	172	1	1887	48' x 8' 0"		CA	357				–		
	173	1	1887	43' x 8' 0"		CA	358				–		
	174	1	1887	32' x 8' 0"		CA	913				–		
453	Pullman	4	1900	60' x 8' 6"	34½T	Pullman	34–7, later 2771–3 (not 35)	–	–	2771–3, later 02771–3	– –	pre-1933	Typically Pullman and last Pullman built coaches for Midland system. No. 35 (the early casualty) had a somewhat different window style (see pictures). Not clear whether all were originally like No. 35, later slightly altered.
452	520	3	1901 (built c1903)	60' x 9' 0"	32½T	BC3	2765–7	–	–	2766 only	–	pre-1933	First essentially 'Midland' sleeping carriages. Nos. 2765 & 2767 seem to have been early casualties, replaced by D601 in 1911/12.
455	521	3	1901 (built c1903)	50' x 9' 0"	25T	BC3	2768–70	–	–	2768–70, later cyphered viz: 02770	–	pre-1933	Basically a short version (8 wheel) of D452 on standard 50ft. frame. Like D452, built with Bain modifications to panelling.
451	590 641	4 1	1904 1906	65' x 9' 0"	38T	BC4	2771–3 2778	M&NB 101–3 –	M&NB 1–3 –	 2778	 –	 pre-1933	Rather similar round-panelled version of D452, but longer. Only 3 numbers traceable for Lot 590 and all these to M&NB after a short period as MR. Lot 641 could be a replacement for an early casualty from Lot 590.
601	764	2	1911	65' x 9' 0"		BC4	2765/7	–	–	2765/7	–	pre-1933	Slight variant of D451 but basically the same type. Seem to have replaced two from Lot 520 (destroyed ?).
454	591 661	4 2	1904 1907	54' x 9' 0"	29½T	BC4	2774–7 2785/6	– –	– –	2774–7 2786 only			54ft. version of D451. No. 2785 scrapped by 1923 – destroyed in accident? (NB: LMS used first series Nos. 2768–78 again for new SLFs to D1705 in 1927).
Composite Sleeping Carriages (SLC)													
456/ 456A	522	8	1901	54' x 9' 0"	28T	BC3	3792–3 3794 3795 3796 3797–8 3799	– M&NB 171 (1908) – M&NB 154 (1906) M&NB 155–6 (1906) M&NB 157 (1906)	– M&NB 81 – M&NB 64 M&NB 65–6 M&NB 67	3792–3 disposal not known destroyed Cudworth 1905 4087 – 4090	– 3761/9 	pre-1933 pre-1933 1944 pre-1933	Originally all MR – essentially 1st (sleeping) plus 3rd (ordinary). D456A was for No. 3794 (MNB 171/81) with extra berth, modified from original design. The two which went to LNER in 1928 were converted to BTK. Like D452 & D455, these vehicles were probably built c1903, some time after ordering, and had Bain features to the square panelling.

Compiled by D. Jenkinson, December 1983

Chapter Four

Saloons

The Midland Railway owned, what seems to us to have been, by comparison with other railways, a disproportionately large number of carriages described as 'saloons'. They are all summarized in *Table 4* later in the chapter, but by way of introduction to the detailed drawings and other data, we have chosen to consider them by the three broad categories into which they naturally fell.

Special, Officers' and Departmental Saloons

The Midland Railway possessed relatively few saloons in this category, a total of seven in all, and two of these were rebuilds. It is, therefore, not quite appropriate to refer to a policy as far as the Company was concerned.

Pre-eminent amongst these vehicles was the special saloon No. 1910 (LMS No. 809 after 1933). This vehicle, happily preserved at Butterley, albeit (1984) devoid of much of its original interior, is a beautiful Bain clerestory (Diagram 597) which, in effect, formed the Midland Railway's 'Royal' Saloon. In fact, it is sometimes referred to as Queen Alexandra's Saloon and was, in its prime, in all respects comparable with perhaps more celebrated vehicles from other railways. It is illustrated in more detail in *Figure 20.*

The other vehicles were, essentially, for railway officers of various grades of importance. Four of them dated from the earlier Clayton period and were built between 1880 and 1891. One, built to Diagram 462, was a bogie saloon to the unusual length of 44ft. and had a clerestory extending part of its length. The others, to Diagrams 463 & 464, were six wheelers and one of them was, in 1908, extended in length to 54ft. and given a bogie underframe, becoming D543 in the process. All of these vehicles lasted well into LMS days *(see summary).*

The last two saloons in this group were also for railway officers but were of a rather more palatial nature. One was built in 1903 (Diagram 461, Lot 558) and may well have been the first Bain vehicle to carry the new style of round-cornered panelling. The vehicle itself was of clerestory type, but the ends of the clerestory were swept down to the lower roof level at each end giving the side elevation a sort of duck-billed appearance, rather after the style of some American and Continental clerestories of the time. It was classed as the Directors' Saloon and had a long life, eventually becoming LMS No. 45052, by which time it had been converted for locomotive testing purposes and numbered with the LMS dynamometer cars.

The last of the seven saloons, built to Diagram 478, still survives, but as yet unrestored, in the National Collection. It is a 60ft. square-panelled eight wheel carriage with arc roof and was converted in 1917 from the steam railmotor No. 2234, built to Diagram 479 in 1904. As a railmotor it was not a total success and the saloon conversion took the form of removing the prime mover and then refitting the vehicle interior for the use of the Superintendent of the line. It went into private ownership on withdrawal and was acquired by the National Railway Museum in the late 1970s. It is possible that it may be restored, at least cosmetically, to steam railmotor condition, since this type of vehicle no longer exists in any form in Britain. Details of No. 2234 as a steam railmotor are given in *Appendix II.*

Family and Invalid Saloons

This was quite a large group, numbering 73 vehicles in the lot book, to quite a number of diagrams *(see summary).* Apart from a small batch of 40ft. bogie clerestories of early Clayton type, built in 1877 to Lot 7, the vehicles in this category were either six wheel Clayton arc roof types or 50ft. Bain clerestories (both square and round-panelled examples).

For the most part they were classified as 'Family Saloons' or 'Family Sleeping Saloons', although each design period saw the limited building of broadly comparable 'Invalid and Family' saloons. All were considered as first class vehicles and it does seem that the sheer number of these vehicles available to the more wealthy patrons may have been one reason why the Midland Railway did not make more widespread use of the purely general service sleeping carriage.

The Bain clerestory examples of the genre were particularly nice vehicles, both visually and, one would assume, in comfort terms. One or two of them were subsequently modified, notably one of Diagram 542 (latterly LMS No. 932) which, in 1919, was altered to an equerries' saloon for Royal workings on the Midland lines. The Midland Railway did not have a full Royal Train as such, unlike the LNWR, GWR and East Coast routes, but could offer a very passable substitute from its more lavishly-equipped general service saloons and dining cars.

Other Saloons

For the most part, the remaining Midland Railway saloons were third class, and what would generally be recognized as picnic saloons with centre tables and mostly longitudinal seating. Again, there was a sizeable number of them, 91 in all, and as with the Family Saloons, there were two main groups; Clayton arc roof six wheelers and bogie clerestories.

The six wheelers were possibly unique in any Midland Railway carriage category, in that all were to the same diagram (D465 of 1884) and built to no fewer than five separate lots between 1884 and 1890, a very unusual thing for Midland Railway vehicles of such a specialized nature. The first lot was designated first class, but all vehicles to the diagram were identical, save for the actual seating capacity which was greater in the thirds.

The clerestories were also mainly of the 'picnic' type but Diagram 545 was a small group of 60ft. twelve wheelers, rebuilt from composite open dining carriages and rather more in the dining idiom than pure picnic saloons. They were third class after rebuilding and presumably classified 'saloon' because of the 'picnic' type layout adopted in the erstwhile first class area.

There was one diagram of a semi-saloon nature (D598), but much of its length was given over to conventional side corridor accommodation, and we have included it in the next chapter as a semi-corridor third.

Unfortunately, the authors are unable to make any very useful comment about the precise nature of operation of this multiplicity of Midland Railway general service saloons, save for the already mentioned beliefs regarding the family sleeping saloons; but, collectively, this whole group of vehicles must have played a fairly prominent part in Midland operations. The whole of the Midland Railway side corridor fleet was only some five times bigger than the saloon group on its own, a fact which we find astonishing, so it seems clear that saloons, in some form or another, were probably found quite often, if not regularly, on many of the principal trains. We would welcome more information from readers who may be able to help.

Plates 76 & 77 Exterior and interior views of Clayton clerestory family saloon No. 731 to Lot 7. Note particularly the American pattern equalized beam bogies - a common feature of early MR built bogie carriages, and undoubtedly copied from Pullman practice - *see Appendix I.*

(NRM)

'late 78 A family saloon No. 1932M (ex-MR No. 2934) to)542. This typical Bain ehicle, one of ten to this iagram, had a particularly nteresting life. It was altered or use by the equerries in ie Midland Royal Train circa 918 - *see Plate 27* and much ater (1946) became an inspec-on saloon. It is seen here in s final guise in early BR days nd was withdrawn in 1961.

(T. J. Edgington)

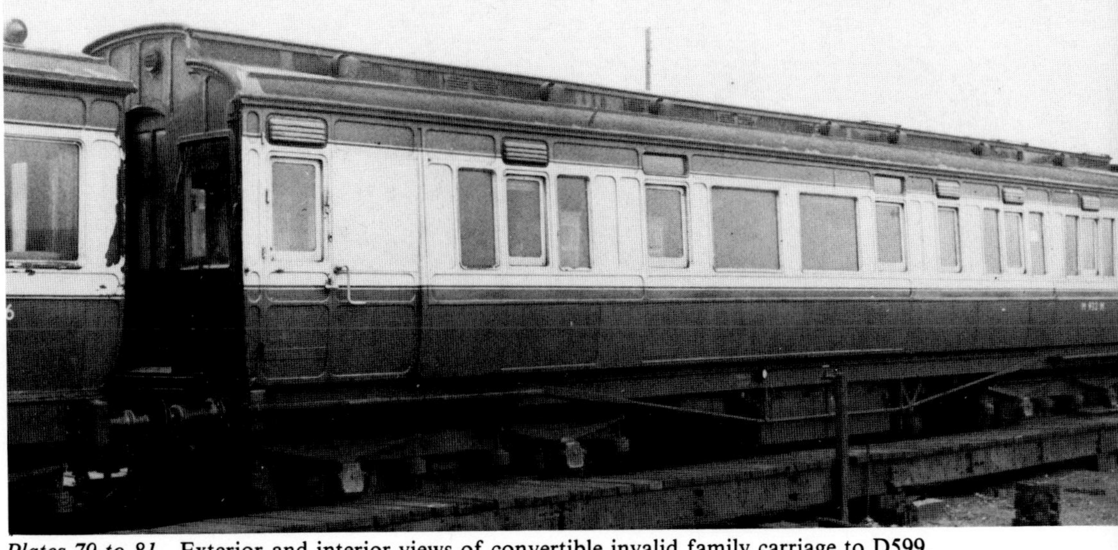

Plates 79 to 81 Exterior and interior views of convertible invalid family carriage to D599. No. 3639 (MR and first LMS series). The 'low' height clerestory is very apparent from the interior views (compare, for example, *Plates 54 & 55*, showing a normal height clerestory interior). One of these coaches, MR and first LMS No. 3638 (second LMS No. 993) was particularly long-lived, but the other three had gone by 1933.

(Authors' Collection and BR/LMR)

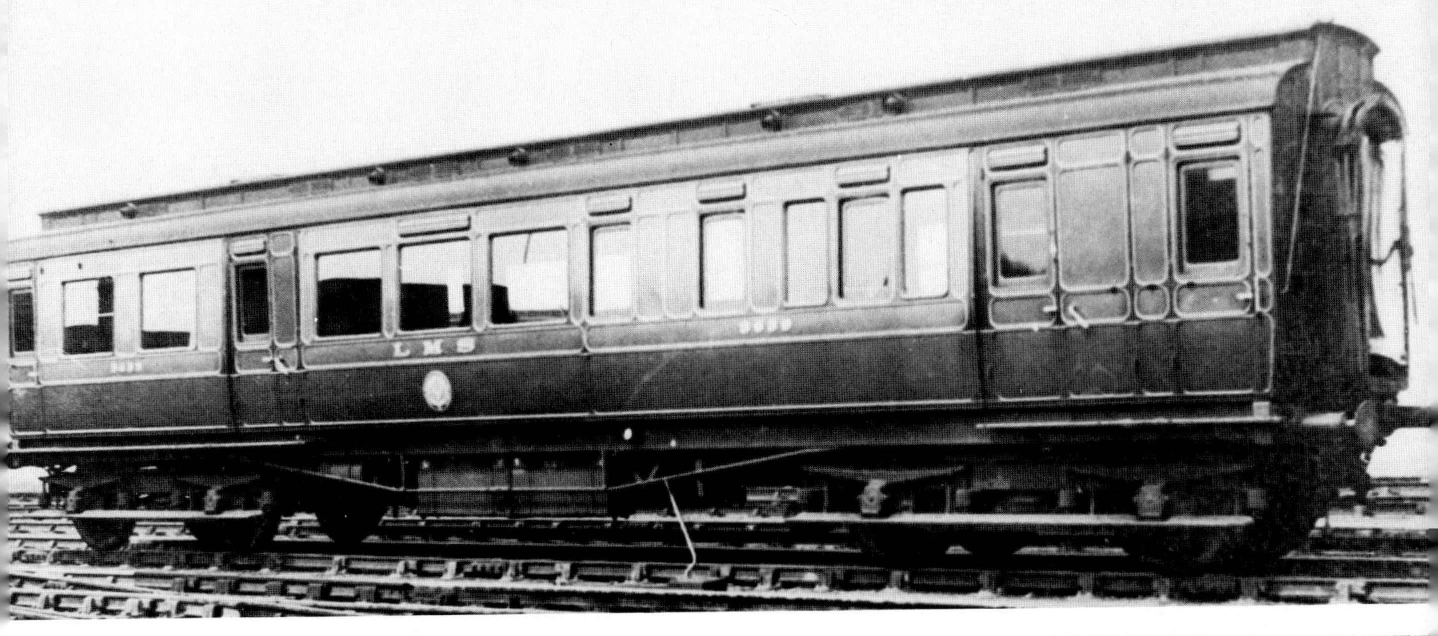

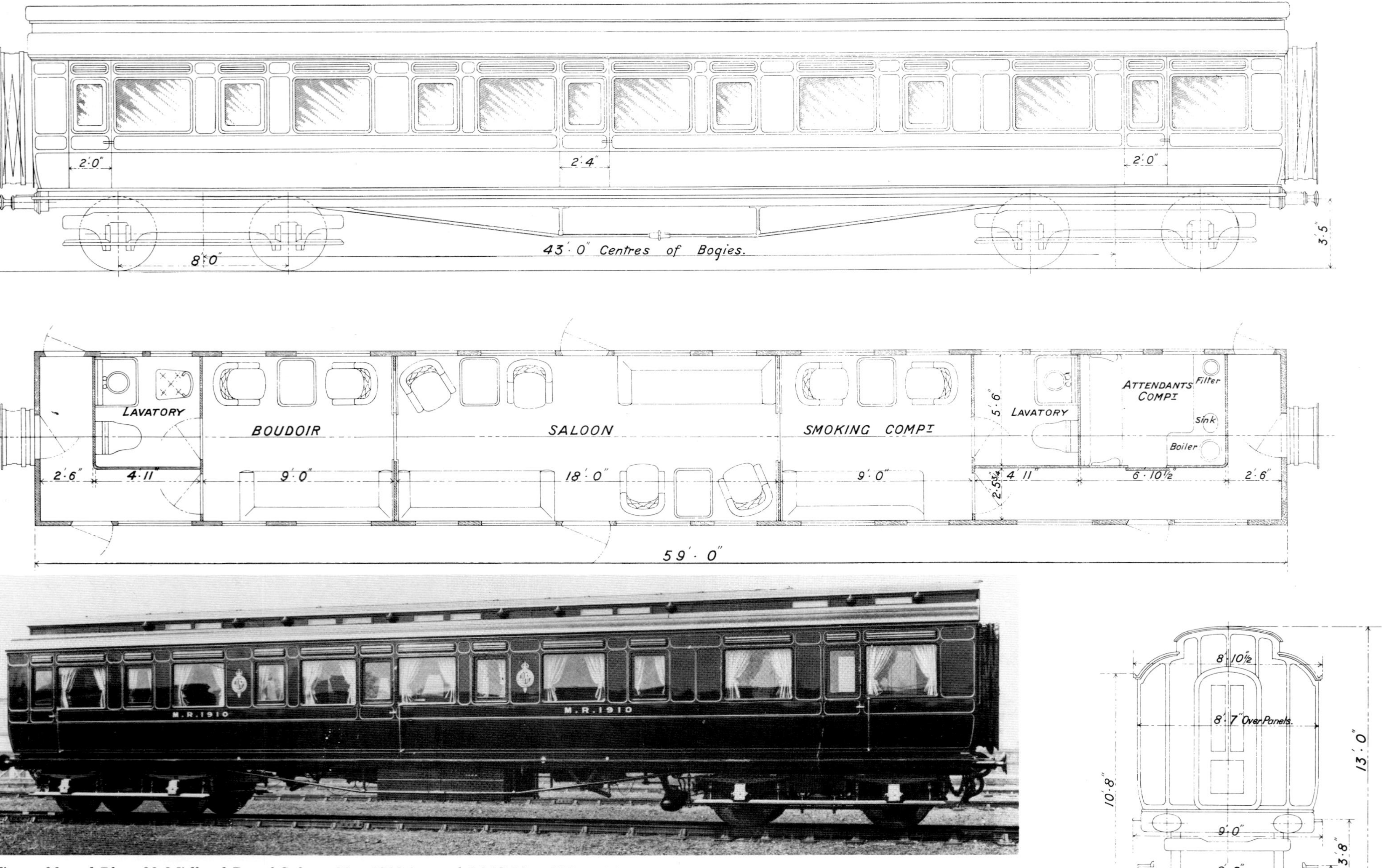

Figure 20 and Plate 82 Midland Royal Saloon No. 1910 (second LMS No. 809). The drawing shows the D597A version (i.e. in its final form) and the photograph shows it as built. There was no significant change save for alterations of furniture, etc. The number 1910 commemorates the year of building. Sometimes called 'Queen Alexandra's Saloon', the coach is preserved at Butterley and (in 1984) well on the road to restoration - but it has lost its original 'loose' furniture and it seems unlikely that complete interior rehabilitation to original state could be achieved. Prior to withdrawal from BR as No. M809M, it had acquired a sort of general use status and figured, amongst other vehicles, in the 'North Wales Land Cruise' trains of the 1950s. Scale: 4mm. = 1ft.

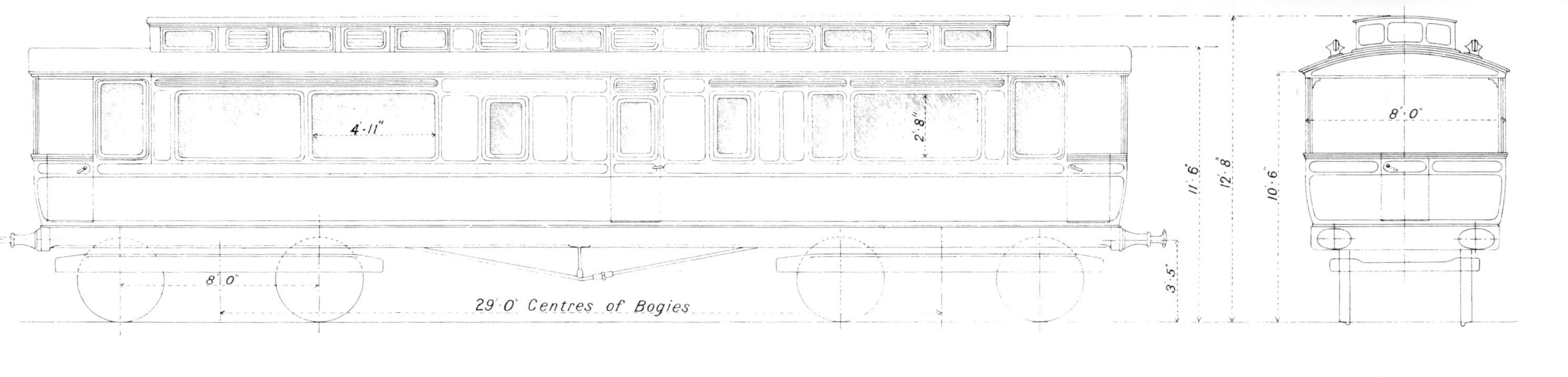

Figure 21 and Plates 83 & 84 Engineers' Inspection Saloon to D462. The drawing depicts this very long-lived saloon in its final MR configuration as running after 1903. The pictures show it as built with large open end verandas *(MR No. 1)* and as rebuilt to the later configuration *(see drawing)* as MR No. 02501 *(see also page vii)*. Note the change in bogie bolster springs and the addition of underframe truss rods. The kitchen was also added at this conversion. Scale: 4mm. = 1ft.

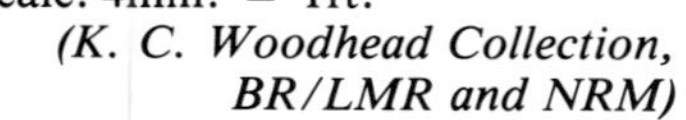

(K. C. Woodhead Collection, BR/LMR and NRM)

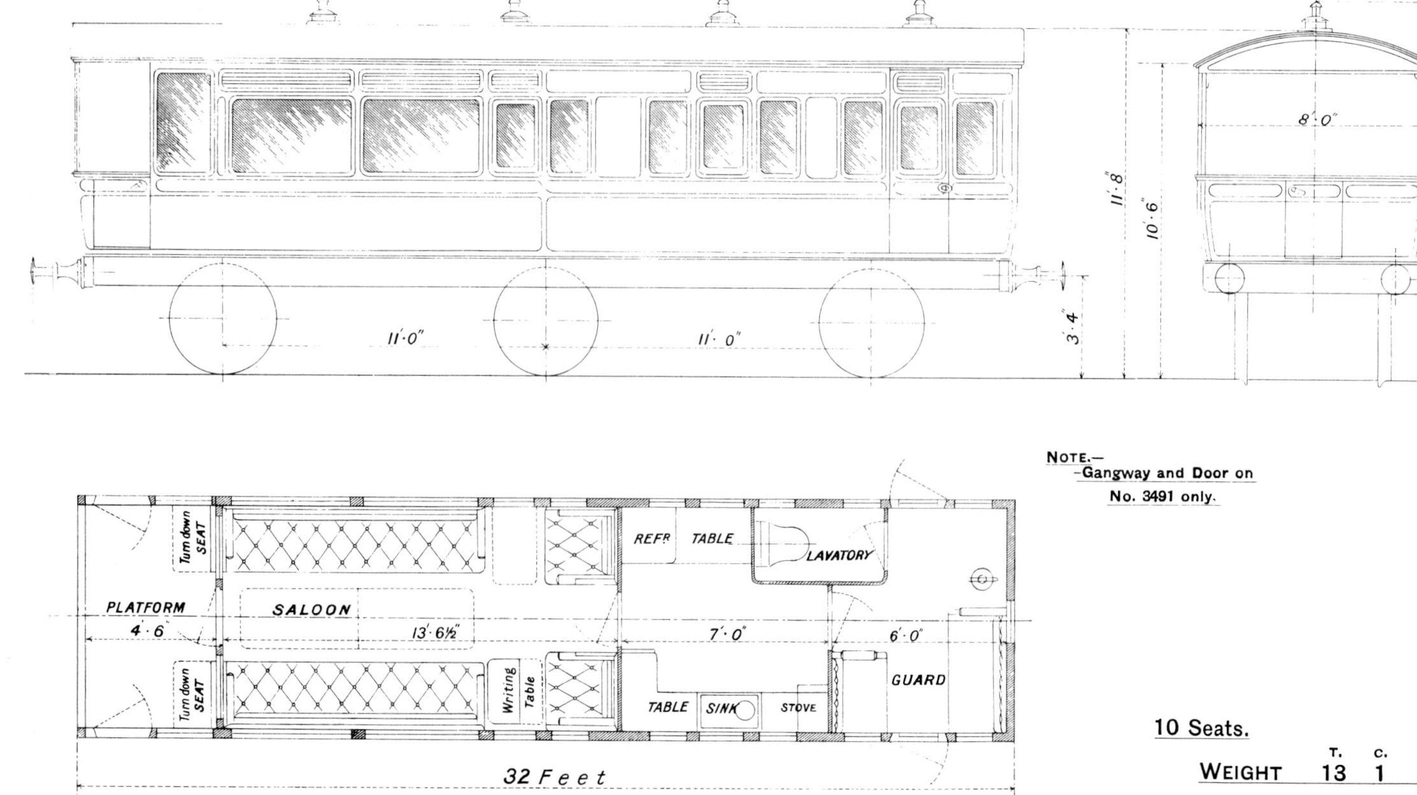

NOTE.—
–Gangway and Door on
No. 3491 only.

10 Seats.

	T.	C.
WEIGHT	13	1

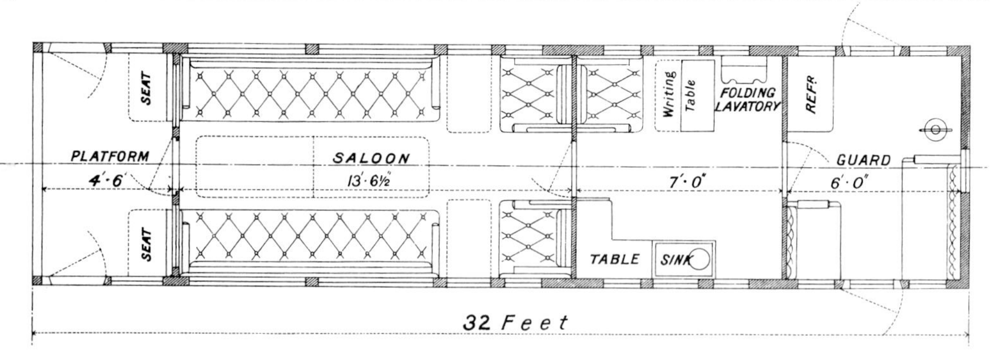

D463 (above)

D464 (plan only, left)

11 Seats.

	T.	C.
WEIGHT	13	4

Figure 22 and Plates 85 to 88 Officers' Saloons to D463/D464. Two vehicles were built to D463 as given and saloon No. 439, later No. 3491 *(opposite)*, shows the original arrangement. The photograph *(below)*, taken in early BR days, shows the second vehicle after conversion by lengthening to D543. As D463, it was MR No. 124, later No. 2552, and as D543 it was No. 2552, 02552 and finally 45016 as shown. Diagram 464, raised for saloon No. 400, later No. 3458 *(opposite)*, was so similar to D463 that it seemed worth featuring both variants. As can be seen, the external elevations were the same and both diagrams were actually built to the same drawing, the only difference being the lavatory arrangement. The photographs show both sides of the vehicle taken before and after renumbering. Scale: 4mm. = 1ft.

(K. C. Woodhead Collection, F. W. Shuttleworth and BR/LMR)

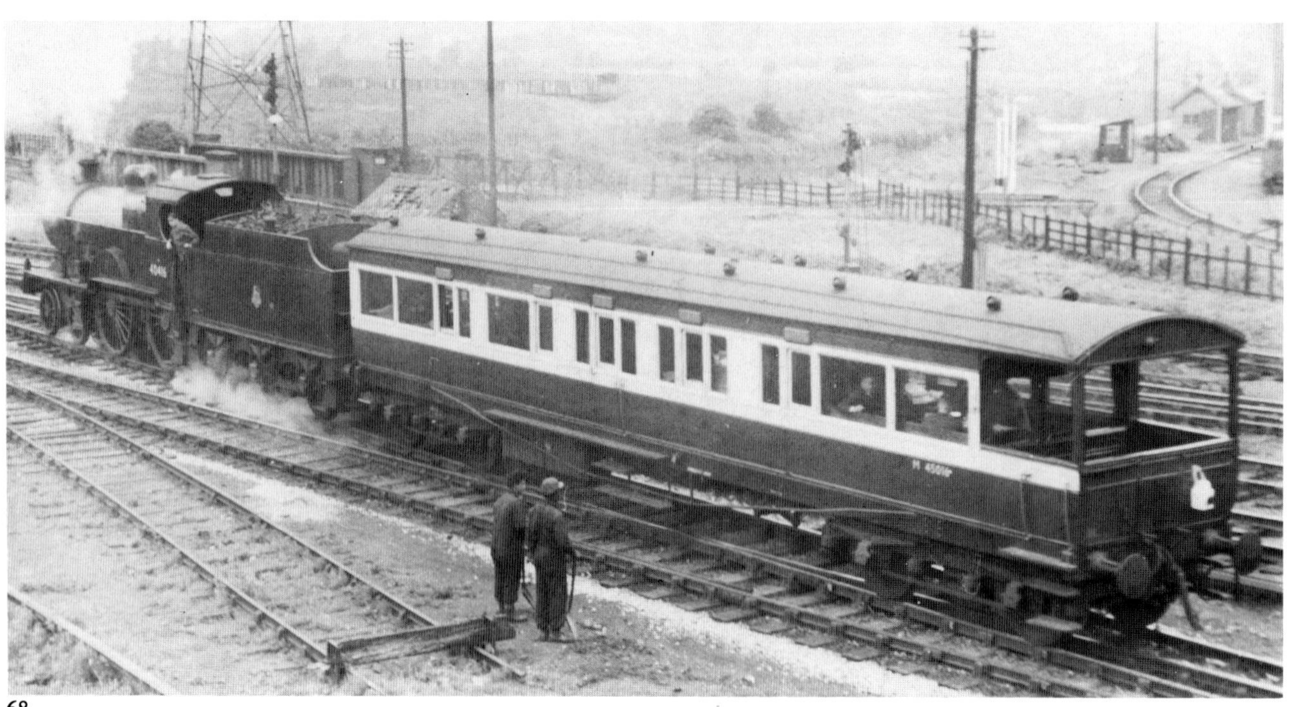

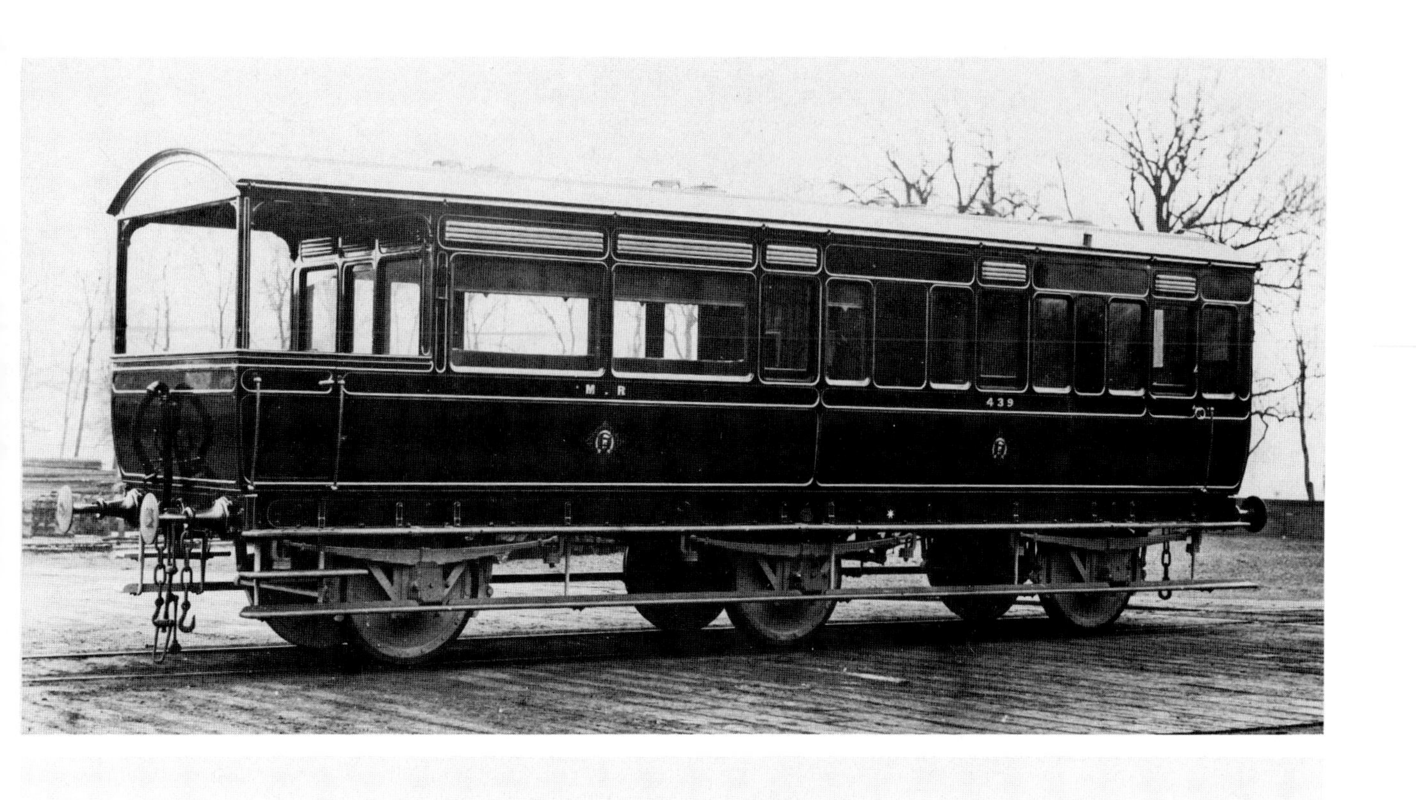
M.R
439

M.R
400

3458
M.R

FAMILY CARRIAGE.

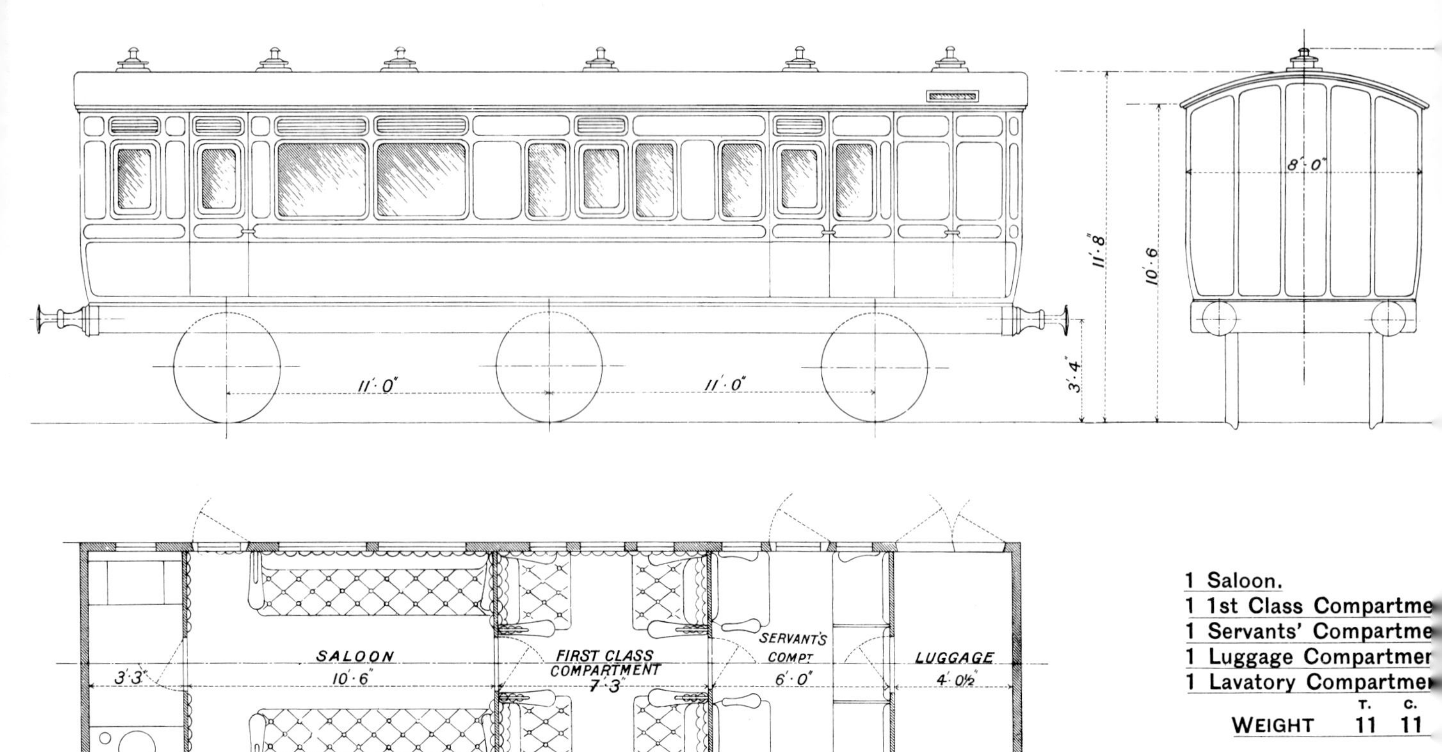

D459 *(above)*

D458 *(below)*

FAMILY SLEEPING CARRIAGE.

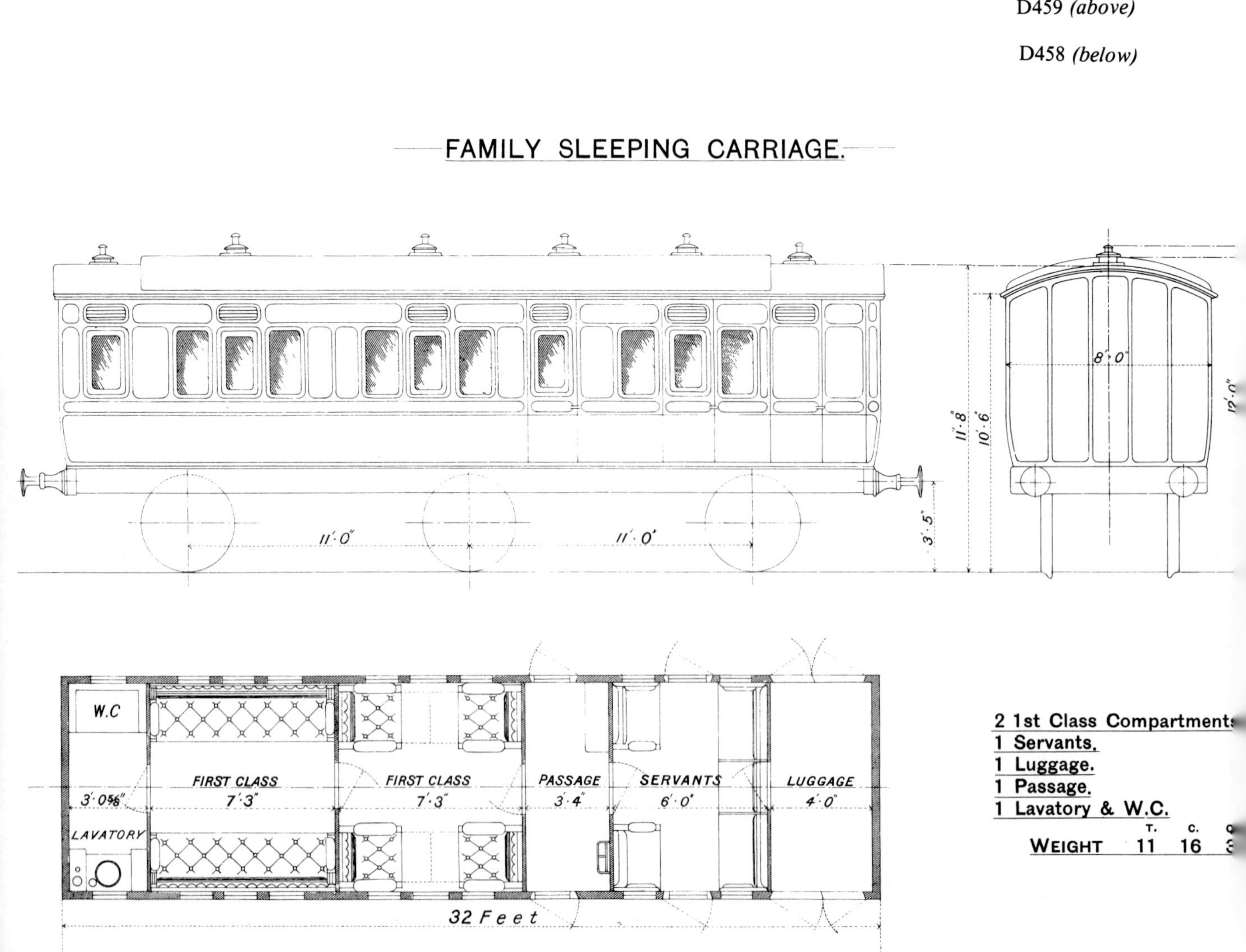

INVALID CARRIAGE.

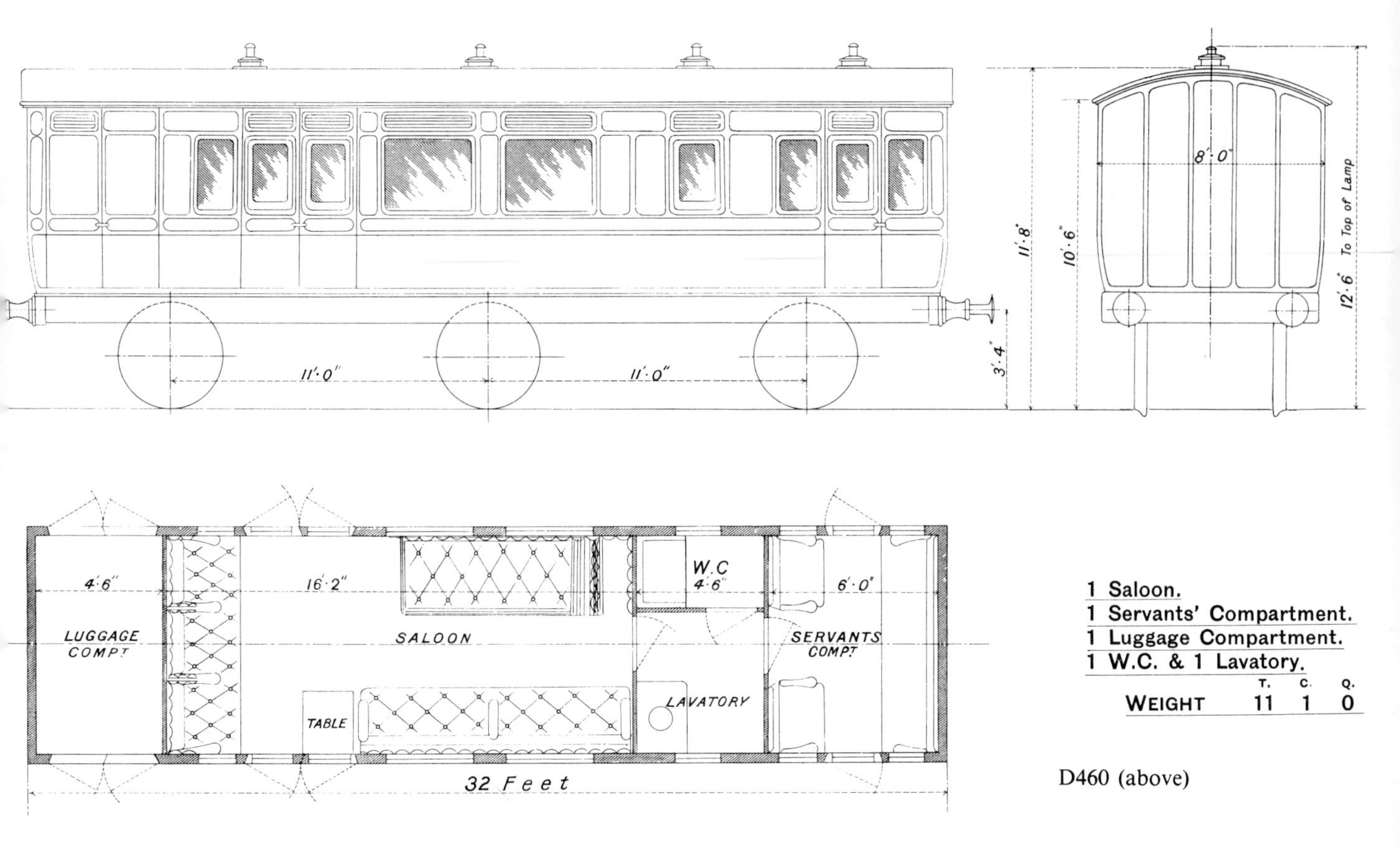

D460 (above)

Figure 23 (opposite & above) These three drawings show the basically similar saloons to *D459 (family saloon), D458 (family sleeping saloon) and D460 (invalid saloon).* The sleeping saloon can be recognized by the slightly elevated centre roof section and the invalid saloon by the double doors to the main passenger compartment. Scale: 4mm. = 1ft.

(K. C. Woodhead Collection)

Family and Invalid Saloons

Because of the relatively large number of these vehicles in service *(see page 63)* it was felt desirable to feature at least two typical types. The selection fell on D459 (six wheel) and D457 (bogie clerestory), but we have also found it possible to include details of the two other six wheel types from the 1881-7 period which were very similar to D459.

Plate 89 Invalid saloon No. 470 to D460. *(NRM)*

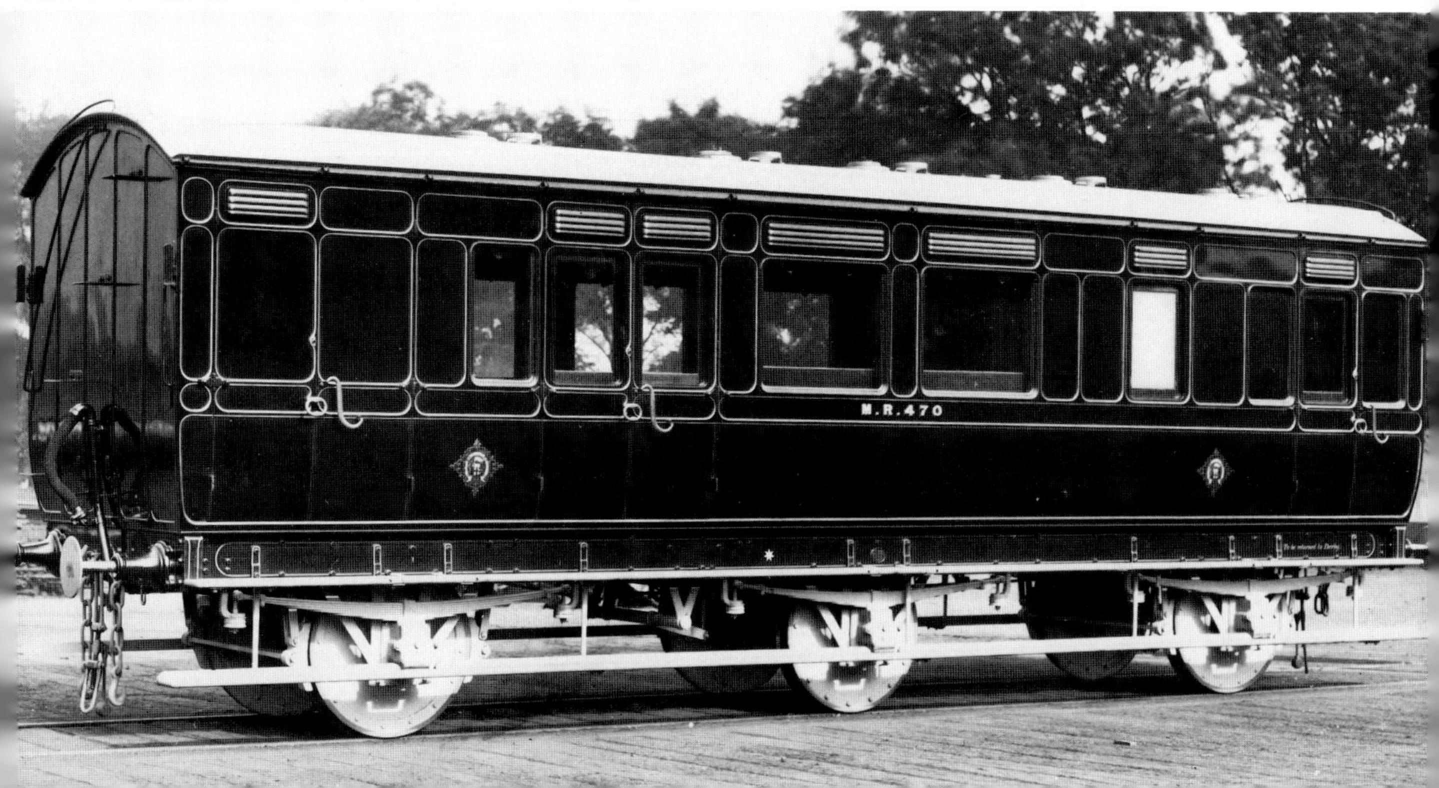

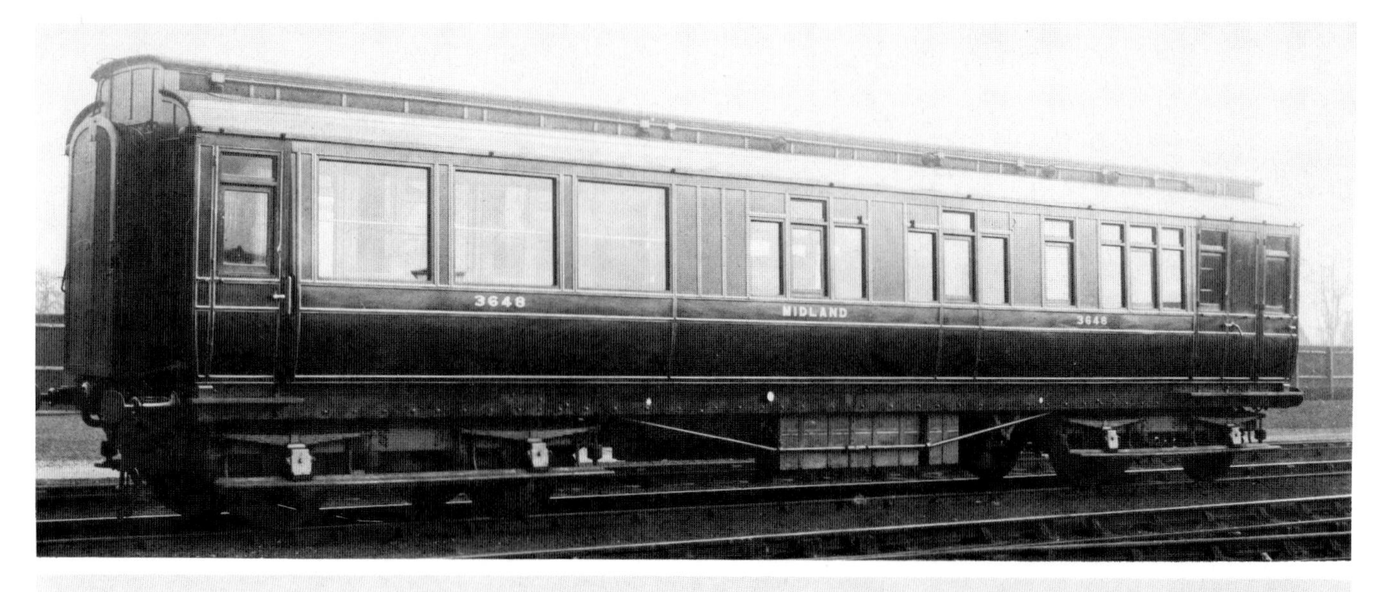

Plates 90 & 91 Opposite side views of 50ft. saloons originally to D457. No. 3648 is as built and No. 3653 shows the club car conversion to D1187 *(see Table 4)*. Saloon No. 3648 became second LMS No. 928 and No. 3653 became second LMS No. 931.

(BR/LMR)

Plate 92 Club car conversion of vehicle No. 3653. The view shows the former servants' area now converted to a second 'lounge'. The former luggage space (through the door to the left) was now a pantry. Note that the large windows on the right have replaced the former (smaller) lavatory and compartment windows of the original version - *(see Plate 91)*.

(BR/LMR)

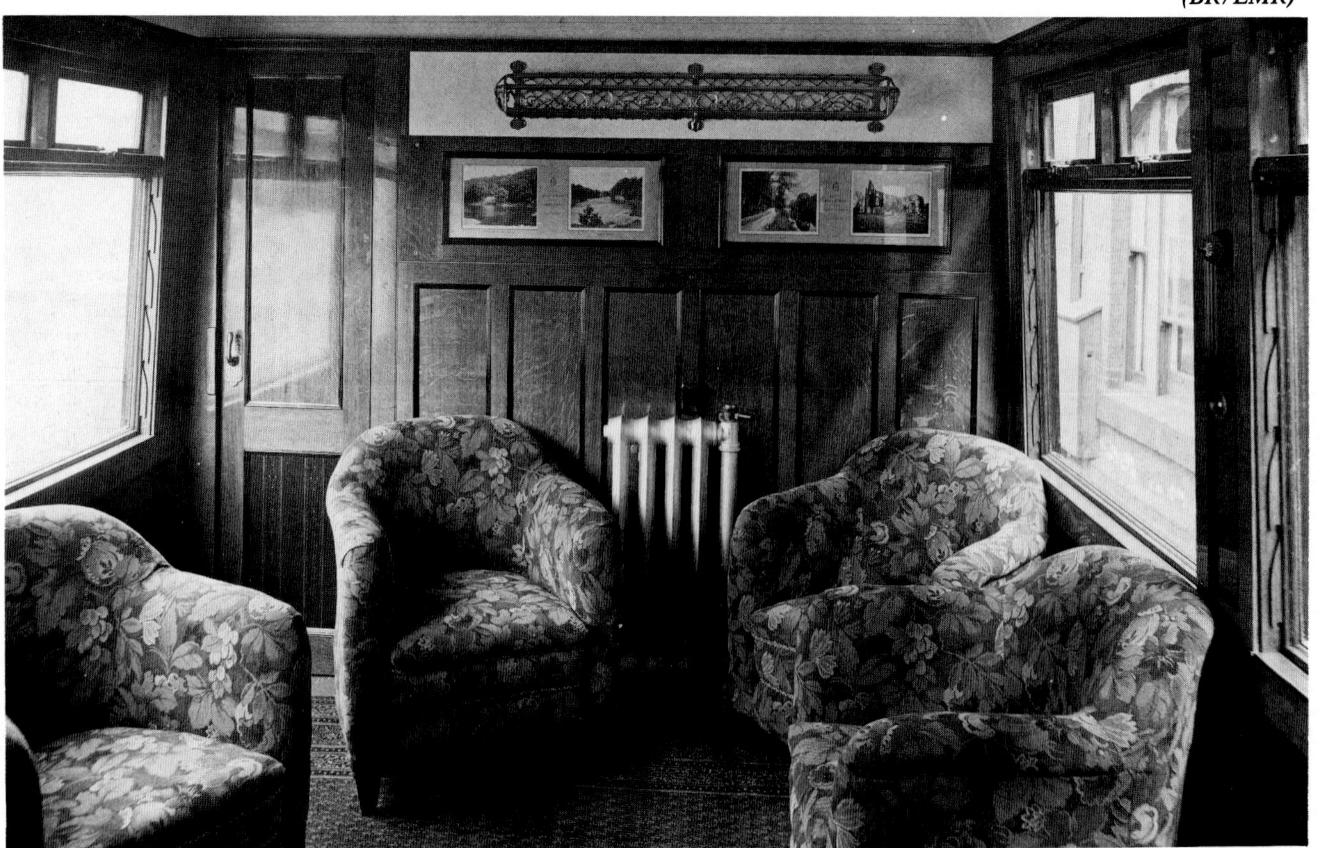

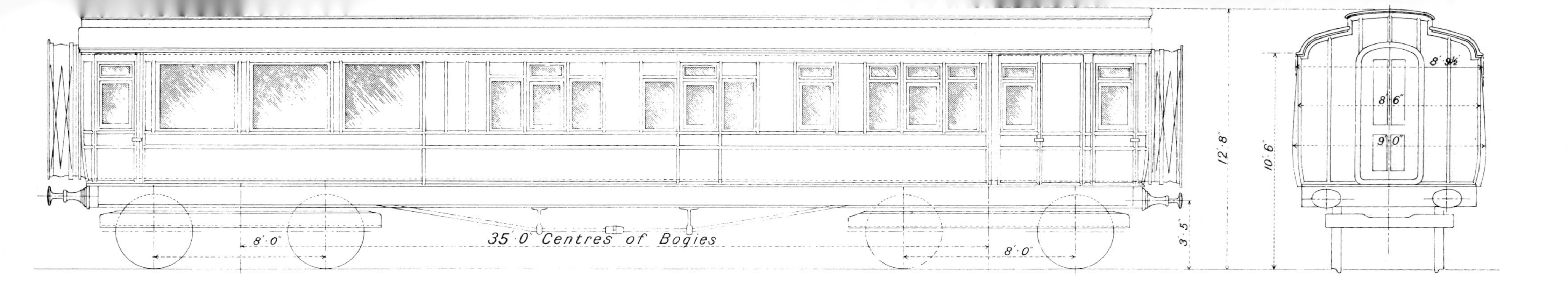

1 Double Convertible Berth.
1 Single Convertible Berth.
1 Saloon.
1 Servants' Compartment.
1 Luggage Compartment.
2 Lavatories.

	T.	C.	Q.
WEIGHT	27	19	1

Figure 24 Family sleeping carriage to D457. These were very attractive vehicles, had an average life span of some forty years, and shared many detail features in common with their contemporary sleeping and dining carriages. The exterior door handle detail reveals their early Bain origin, and they were some of the first vehicles to be carried on the new 8ft. Bain bogies. It is believed, although not confirmed, that the coaches were electrically lit from new. Scale: 4mm. = 1ft.

(K. C. Woodhead Collection)

Plates 93 & 94 Day and night arrangement of the principal saloon area of vehicle No. 3648, looking towards the servants' corridor.

(BR/LMR)

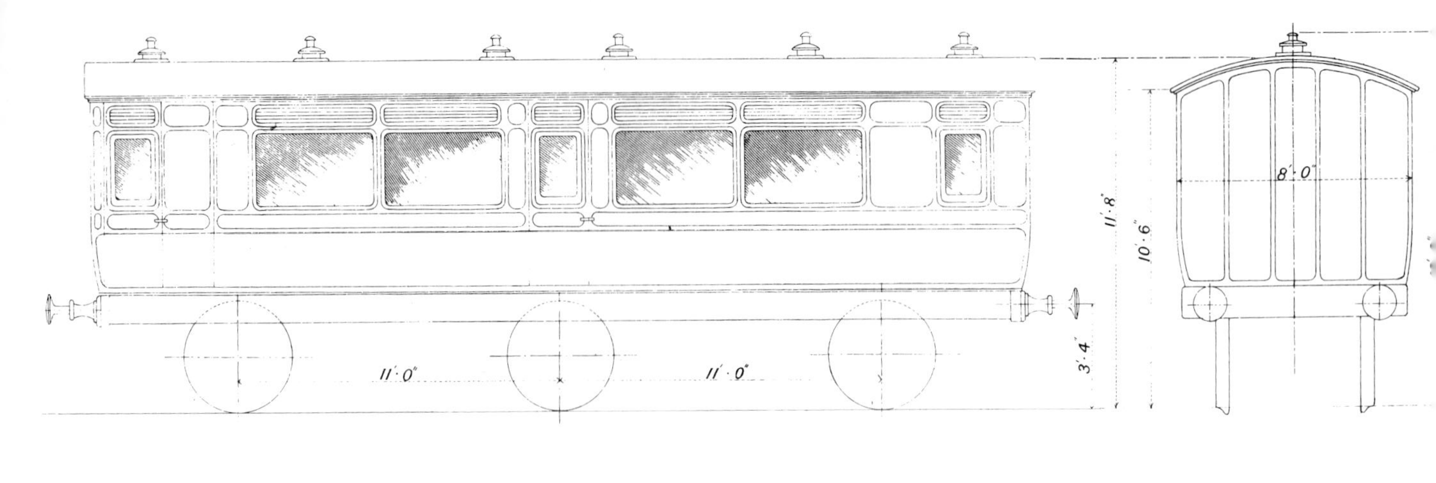

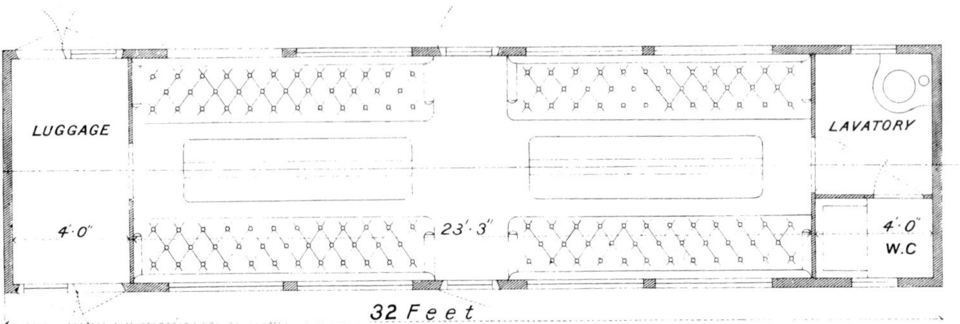

First Saloon—20 Seats.
Third Saloon—28 Seats.

	T.	C.
WEIGHT	11	1

Ordinary Saloons

By far the most common ordinary saloon (i.e. to the 'picnic' style of interior layout) was the Clayton arc roof design to D465 of which more than sixty were built - mostly third class but with one lot of first class vehicles. This, therefore, was the obvious choice for this section but we have felt justified in also providing full details of one of the bogie clerestory types.

Figure 25 First or third class saloon to D465. The only recorded difference between the two classes of vehicles was the stated seating capacity (20 first class, 28 third class) which tempts us to the conclusion that the first class version probably had better upholstery (leather rather than plush) with armrests dividing the settees into individual seating areas for each passenger, rather than the continuous bench type seat found in the third class version. Scale: 4mm. = 1ft.

(K. C. Woodhead Collection)

Plate 95 First class saloon No. 354 (D465) seen inside the still fairly new carriage works, circa 1885.

(NRM)

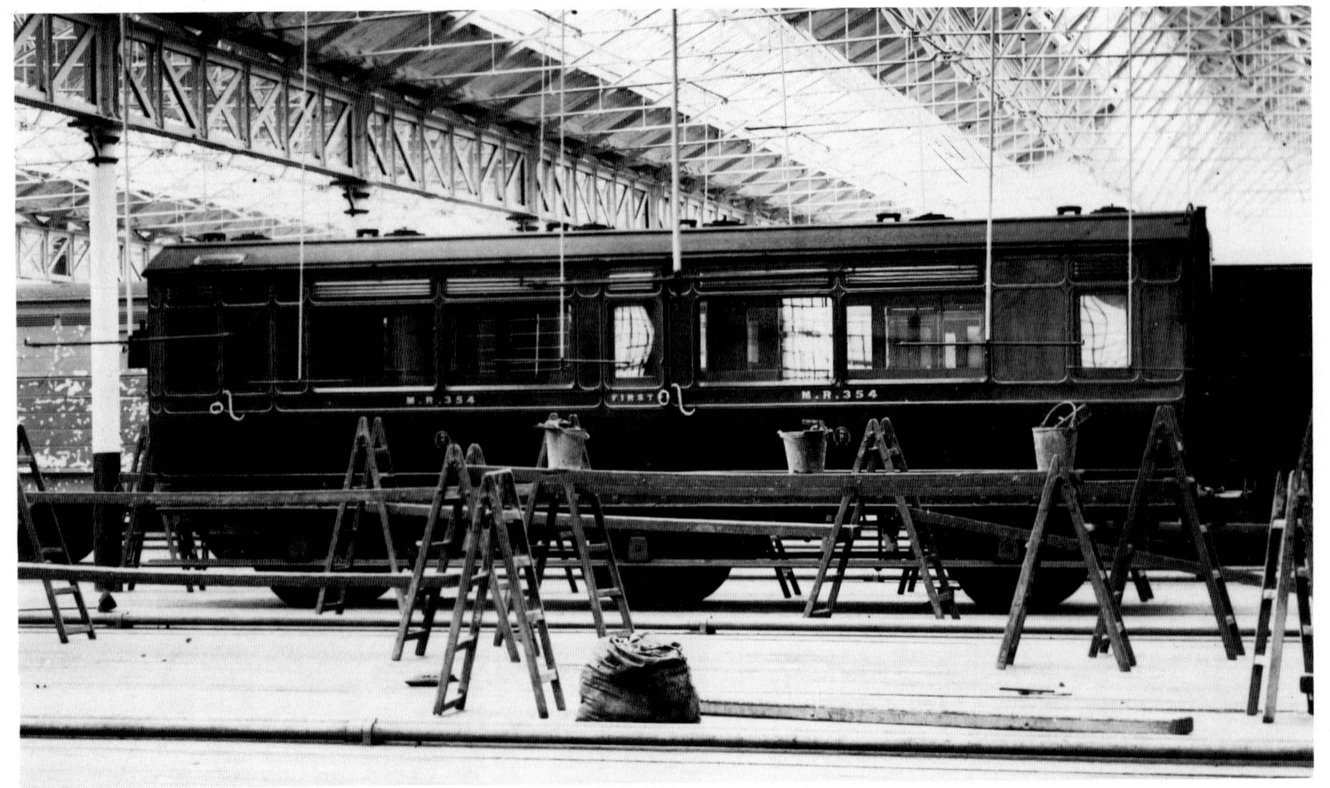

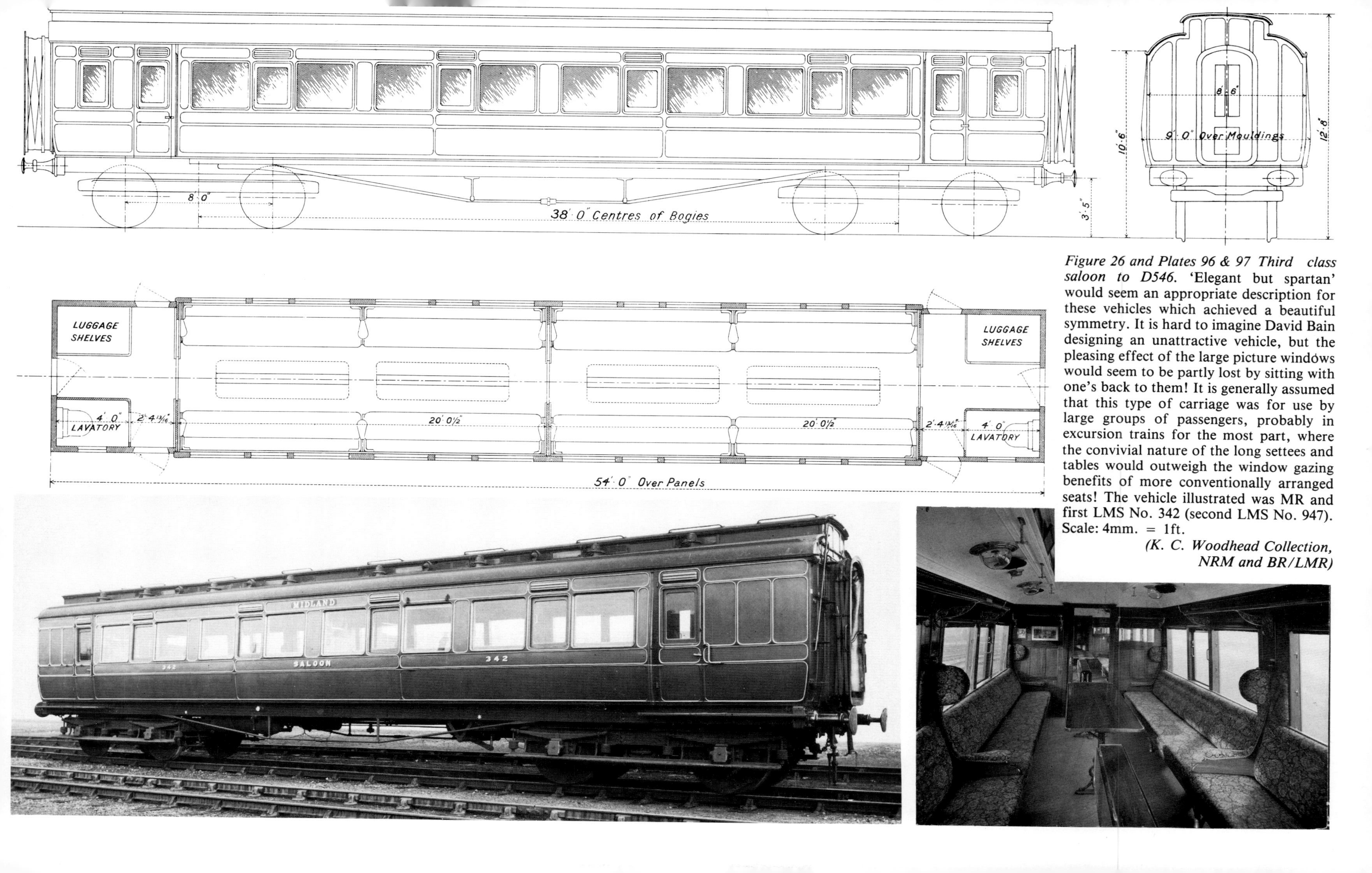

Figure 26 and Plates 96 & 97 Third class saloon to D546. 'Elegant but spartan' would seem an appropriate description for these vehicles which achieved a beautiful symmetry. It is hard to imagine David Bain designing an unattractive vehicle, but the pleasing effect of the large picture windows would seem to be partly lost by sitting with one's back to them! It is generally assumed that this type of carriage was for use by large groups of passengers, probably in excursion trains for the most part, where the convivial nature of the long settees and tables would outweigh the window gazing benefits of more conventionally arranged seats! The vehicle illustrated was MR and first LMS No. 342 (second LMS No. 947). Scale: 4mm. = 1ft.

(K. C. Woodhead Collection, NRM and BR/LMR)

TABLE 4
Summary of Midland Railway Special and Other Saloons

Diag.	Lot	Qty.	Date of Order	Dimensions	Wt.	Style	Numbering		Type Extinct	Remarks
							Midland 1st LMS	2nd LMS		
Special Saloons										
597 597A	745	1	1910	59' x 8'7"		BC4	1910	809	see remarks	In effect the *Midland 'Royal' Saloon*, generally referred to as Queen Alexandra's Saloon. The D597A relates to slight modifications to the interior. Preserved at Butterley.
462	49	1	1880	44' x 8' 0"	22T	CC1	1, later 2501/02501 (see remarks)	45034	5/57	Very long-lived. *Engineer's Saloon*, and modified from time to time (see main text). In final years allocated to District Engineer, S. Wales. MR number cyphered in 1903.
463	170	2	1887	32' x 8' 0"	13T	CA	124, later 2252 439, later 3491	to D543 45036	 1941	D463/464 only differed to the extent that D463 incorporated a lavatory. Both types were classified as *Officers' Saloon*. Conversion of 2552 to D543 dated 1908.
464	279	1	1891	32' x 8' 0"	13T	CA	400, later 3458	45035	1941	
543	170	1	1908	54' x 8' 0"	25T	CA	2552/02552?	45016	1956–7	*Officer's Saloon:* Conversion by lengthening of D463. Latterly used by D.O.M. Derby
461	558	1	1903	54' x 8' 6"	27T	BC4	2501	45052	12/52	*Directors' Saloon:* Modified clerestory (see main text) and one of first round-panelled clerestories after square-panelled period along with Lot 559. (Brake Composite – D519A). Latterly used for gas-testing purposes, hence the final LMS number in Dynamometer Car series.
478	578	1	1917	60' x 9' 0"	28T	see remarks	2234	45010		*Superintendent's Saloon:* Built by conversion of Steam Railmotor D479. Arc roof style but square cornered panelling. Preserved in National Collection – possibly to be re-instated as D479.
Family (including Invalid) Saloons										
	7	6	1877	40' x 8' 0"		CC1	731 + five others			*Family Saloon:* Type probably extinct before 1923. No diagram located.
459	61 125 147 168	10 6 6 6	1881 1885 1886 1887	32' x 8' 0"	11½T	CA	191 + many more			*Family Saloons:* Equipped with lavatories, settees, etc. but no (apparent) provision for overnight conversion to sleeping configuration. Six wheel.
458	102	7	1884	32' x 8' 0"	12T	CA	869 + five more MR, one MGSW Joint			*Family Sleeping Saloon:* Somewhat similar to D459 but not identical. Seats in one compartment convertible into single beds. Six wheel.
460	167	6	1887	32' x 8' 0"	11T	CA	446; 470 + four			*Invalid Saloon:* In similar style to D459 but bed replaced one settee and other slight changes. Six wheel.
457 including	550	12	1902	50' x 9' 0"	28T	BC3	3641–6 3648–53	922–7 928; 930; 929; 992; 931 (3652 not renumbered)	2/42 1/44	*Family Sleeping Carriage:* Gangwayed. Twelve originally built, two later conversions to D1071 & D1187. *Diagram 1071* had bathroom installed (vice luggage) and other modifications. *Diagram 1187* had servants' compartment and lavatory converted to open saloon for Club Car use between Bradford and Morecambe. The luggage space became a pantry in this vehicle which was reclassified *Club Saloon*. All twelve had *'Clipper'* profile to passenger areas.
1071	ex-550	1			28T	BC3	3645	926	2/41	
1187	ex-550	1			27T	BC3	3653	931	8/40	
542	664	10	1909	50' 9' 0"	26T	BC4	2871; 2284; 2888–9 2899 2934 2897; 2967 plus two more	917–21 932 990–1	6/49 3/61 ?	*Family Carriage:* Gangwayed. MR No. 2934 altered in 1918 to *Equerries' Saloon* for Royal Train and altered again (as LMS 932) in 1946 to *Inspection Saloon*. *'Clipper'* profile to passenger areas.
599	754	4	1912	50' x 9' 0"	26T	BC4	3637–40	993 (ex-3638)	7/56 (but see remarks)	Convertible *Invalid and Family Carriage:* Gangwayed. Stylistically very similar to D542, but, except for LMS 993, did not last as long. LMS 993 became a mobile office in 1957, was renumbered 023351 in 1962 and lasted until (at least) 1964. *'Clipper'* profile to passenger areas.
Ordinary (Picnic) Saloons										
465	103 104 153 219 261	10 5 9 10 30	1884 1884 1886 1888 1890	32' x 8' 0"	11T	CA	354 + nine 828 + four			Classified *First and Third Class Saloon*. Essentially of picnic type. Lot 103 was for first class use; remaining lots were third class but all vehicles were identical. One of them later became MR 2741 (1st MR not known) and is preserved at Foxfield. Six wheel type.
466	447 517	10 10	1898 1901	48' x 8' 6"	22T	CC2	? 1984–1993 ?		pre-1933	Classified *Third Class Saloon*, essentially of picnic saloon layout. Non-gangwayed and do not seem to have lasted long into the LMS period in spite of date of building.
545	ex-438	3	1909	60' x 8' 6"	33T	CC2	3126–7; 3130		pre-1933	Classified *Third Class Saloon* and converted in 1909 from 12 wheel composite dining carriages to D444 *(see Table 2)*. The former central kitchen was altered to a 'picnic' saloon type layout, the rest being unchanged except for downgrading. Gangwayed twelve wheelers.
546	693	4	1907	54' x 9' 0"		BC4	339; 342; 349 + one	946–8	11/47	Classified *Third Class Saloon*, essentially to 'picnic' layout. Gangwayed with *'Clipper'* profile to passenger areas.

Compiled by D. Jenkinson, December 1983

Plate 98 The richly-furnished interior of D459 *(page 70)* looking from the main saloon to the servants' compartment. The upholstery is likely to have been red leather and red plush respectively. Note the folding armrests in the saloon and the central seat in front of the luggage compartment door of the servants' area.

(NRM)

Chapter Five

General Service Corridor and Gangwayed Stock

When researching this book, the writers, like most people involved in preparing historical data, entered the subject with a degree of preliminary knowledge and some basic, indeed pre-conceived notions about the subject which we felt would only need expansion and enlargement. In the case of Midland Railway corridor stock, how wrong we were.

Everyone, we felt, would already know that because the Midland Railway had the best coaches of the LMS constituents (at least that's what all the books said!), LMS coaches were really nothing more than Midland Railway designs written larger after 1923. All we had to do, therefore, was write the Midland Railway account as the essential preliminary to the LMS story already published. However, the picture turned out to be rather different from all our earlier notions and, in fact, proved to be much more interesting. It was not that the published accounts were wrong, per se, but that they were simply too generalized to make any real contribution to the story.

The main fact is, in so far as stock records indicate, that the Midland Company was not really a corridor coach railway in the sense of the LNWR or, possibly, even the East Coast and GWR systems. Good though its carriages may have been as vehicles, the Midland Railway's total fleet of gangwayed stock was so small, relatively, to that of the LNWR that its influence had to take second place in 1923. Consequently, the story of Midland corridor and gangwayed vehicles is almost complete in itself and covers 25 years or so of development - not really a very long time.

Let us take a few comparative facts. The sum total of Midland Railway and the Midland Scottish Joint Stock was 705 *(Table 5)*, whereas the LNWR/WCJS had 2,037 of which no fewer than 244 were to one design of corridor third. The largest single build of identical Midland Railway design corridors was only 72 to Diagram 468, all for Joint Stock. Put another way, the LNWR/WCJS fleet of corridor thirds alone outnumbered the whole Midland/Midland Joint Stock gangwayed fleet, including sleeping/dining cars.

At first we found these relative ratios surprising but we soon realized that they were very significant in the light of post-1923 affairs. It seemed to us, on reflection, no surprise at all that the LMS found difficulty imposing Midland Railway ideas on the whole system, especially the West Coast lines, if the totally different balance of passenger stock provisioning in 1923 was any guide.

Nevertheless, the Midland Railway corridor coaches obviously represented a considerable portion of the Company's longer distance traffic by 1923 and the vehicles themselves were always interesting and often very elegant. *Table 5* is broken down by type and style and from this, two essential points emerge. The first and simplest is the dominance, even in 1923, of the clerestory (some 88 per cent of the total), already alluded to on *page 19*. The second fact to emerge is the very high proportion of composite coaches (i.e. first and third class) compared with all thirds; 42½ per cent and 47½ per cent respectively. Conventional wisdom assumes that in former days, a railway had considerably more third class vehicles than composite vehicles, but this was not the case with Midland Railway corridor stock. When the composites are added to the all first class vehicles, and assuming that in the composites some 30 to 50 per cent of the accommodation was first class (generally true), then it does seem that the Midland Railway carried a high percentage of first class passengers on its best trains, possibly averaging 25 per cent or more of the seats offered in many cases.

This again is a little odd. The Midland Railway certainly traversed some 'wealthy' areas but equally, was also well represented in the more industrial regions and one might have expected a heavier proportion of thirds, but this was not so. We shall return to this theme in the field of non-corridor stock but suffice to say, at this point, that it does seem to us that there is a sort of linkage with the heavy emphasis on first class saloons mentioned in the last chapter. Overall, therefore, we conclude, (by inference, it is true, but we think backed up by analysis) that the Midland Railway, for some reason, had an above average attraction for the first class traveller, compared with other lines. Perhaps this explains the high regard in which its carriages were held and also, inter alia, accounts for some of the over-simplified generalizations already mentioned, regarding Midland Railway influence on LMS practice. After all, it seems somewhat more likely that

TABLE 5
General Service Gangwayed Carriages (Passenger-Carrying)

Style / *Type*	*Square Panel Corridor Clerestory*	*Round Panel Corridor Clerestory*	*Round Panel Open Clerestory*	*Corridor Elliptical Roof*	*Total*
First Class	3	4	2	–	9
Third Class	86	96	20	30	232
Composite	72	72	–	14	158
First Class Brake	12	18	–	11	41
Third Class Brake	15	91	2	16	124
Composite Brake	62	65	–	14	141
Sub Total	250	346	24	85	705
Dining Carriages	73 (1)	35 (2)	–	6	114
Sleeping Carriages	22 (3)	13	–	–	35
Total	345 (1) (3)	394 (2)	24	91	854 (1) (2) (3)

Notes:

1) Including 12 early Clayton Clerestory (pre-square panel style).

2) Including six brake composite plus kitchen (D443) to ambulance use, c1917.

3) Including four Clayton arc roof and four Pullman style.

Compiled by D. Jenkinson, March 1984

Plate 99 Midland train marshalling and the first generation of Midland corridor stock are both exemplified by this portion of a familiar picture of a southbound express at Cotehill, circa 1910. The first seven vehicles (all square-panelled clerestories) behind the train engine are, in order: 50ft. corridor third (D564); 50ft. corridor composite (D468) - probably one of those which originally had a full set of corridor side doors *(see Figure 28)*; 50ft. corridor brake composite (D566); 50ft. corridor composite (D468) - built with only three corridor side doors *(see Figure 28)*; 54ft. corridor brake first with three compartments (D570); 65ft. first class dining carriage (D571) and 65ft. third class open dining carriage (D572). The last two vehicles are round-panelled clerestories (third and brake third) from the later Bain period. Almost certainly, the last five vehicles (brake first, first diner, third diner, third, brake third) formed the fixed part of the train, the leading vehicles being added as necessary to suit the traffic. The train, since it includes a dining 'pair' is almost certainly mostly comprised of M&GSW vehicles and is likely to have been the morning Glasgow to St. Pancras express, the forerunner of the 'Thames - Clyde Express' in LMS days *(see also Plate 118)*.

(BR/LMR)

Plate 100 Another portion of a train picture, this time taken well south of Leeds, shows off the Bain round-panelled corridors. The formation is less easy to determine at the rear but the first four vehicles are clear enough: 54ft. corridor brake composite - probably a through coach (D559); 54ft. corridor brake third (D561); 59ft. third class open dining carriage (D446); and a 59ft. first class dining carriage (D436). The fifth vehicle seems to be a 12ft. 8in. high clerestory with 'long' corridor windows, almost certainly a corridor third to D547, while the last carriage is not identified. It is likely to be a first brake or a composite brake of the 12ft. 11½in. high series. Note that the side corridor coaches are gas lit, whereas the dining carriages have electric lighting.

(NRM)

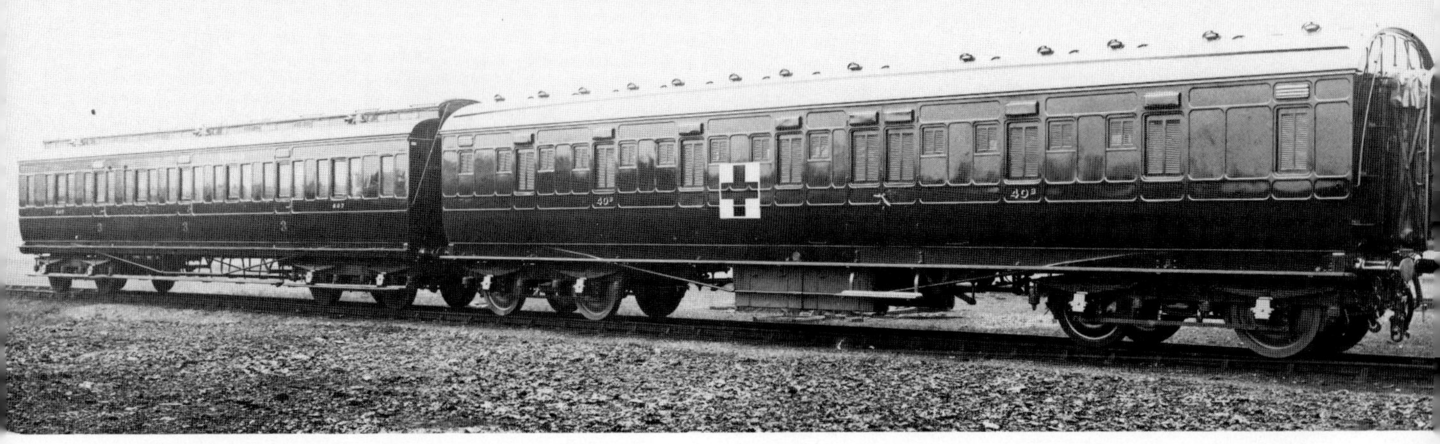

the first class passengers would articulate their views than would the humbler travellers - and the Midland Railway certainly looked after its first class patrons who would naturally appreciate matters.

This, however, is speculation. Turning now to facts, the Midland Railway corridors are not at all difficult to summarize and analyse and the rest of this chapter will deal with this topic.

The story begins in the late 1890s, during the Clayton period, with the building of 48ft. and 50ft. square light clerestory stock. The 50t. length was adopted for Joint Stock use and the 48ft. for purely Midland Railway traffic. In general, the extra length usually offered rather more spacious storage space or gave scope for rather more variations in terms of internal layout on the Joint Stock. It was during this period that the most numerous single corridor design, (composite D468, Lot 451) was built, all for Joint Stock use (42 M&GSW; 30 M&NB).

During this phase, apart from some 48ft. thirds for purely Midland Railway use, all corridor stock was for the Joint Stock, clearly reflecting a competitive situation vis-â-vis the East and West Coasts. In fact it seems probable that this factor alone provided the impetus which launched the Midland Railway into corridor coach building. Only a handful (17) of the purely Midland corridors was built (48ft. thirds to D474) and some of these must have been used on Anglo-Scottish workings, so it seems that the purely Midland Railway services were still non-corridor for the most part. All the 48ft. and 50ft. Clayton corridors ran, initially, on 10ft. bogies.

It was not until David Bain took charge that the Midland itself operated many corridors on its own exclusive routes. These were 54ft. types, initially square-panelled but, from 1905, built with round-cornered panelling. As before, composites were well to the fore and the summary of types built is complicated by the fact that the same diagram was often used for both Midland Railway and Joint Stock building. Moreover, during the Bain round light clerestory period there were several slight visible changes of detail *(see page 18)* which makes the Midland Railway round-panelled clerestory corridors amongst the more tricky vehicles to analyse and, for modelmakers, very easy to get wrong! We have included such details as we know in the summaries.

Plate 101 This picture shows two Bain 54ft. corridor thirds to D473, the nearer one having been converted to ambulance use and elliptical roof form with electric light, circa 1917. The unmodified vehicle (clerestory with gas lighting) is MR and first LMS No. 607, second LMS No. 3184 (Lot 618). Note the deep eaves panels with four element louvre vents on both varieties. Lot 618 must have been one of the last lots to exhibit these old dimensions since Lot 616 *(see Plate 119)* had the revised heights.

(BR/LMR)

During the round-panelled clerestory period, two principal size variations appeared. Firstly, was a reversion to 50ft. length, for excursion stock in the main, and secondly, some coaches were built to a reduced 12ft. 8in. height for clearing the Metropolitan line gauge. Sometimes both appeared simultaneously so one could find both 50ft. and 54ft. coaches in both heights.

The whole of the Bain clerestory corridor fleet was in service by 1913 and most had, in fact, been completed during the 1905-10 period. The summary table should clarify most of the variations, but two particular groups of carriages were to a somewhat different conception and merit a few words. In 1911 a batch of twelve third class coaches was built to Diagram 598 (Lot 752) which combined conventional compartments at one end with an open 'picnic' saloon type layout at the other. They were 50ft. long and we have been unable to

Plate 102 & 103 First class compartment of clerestory corridor brake composite No. 3328 (second LMS No. 7298) to D472 and third class compartment of the experimental elliptical roof 'one-off' corridor third No. 1348 (second LMS No. 3209) to D1047.

(NRM and BR/LMR)

Plates 104 to 106 The experimental steel-ended corridors of 1916. The upper view shows third class No. 1348 (D1047), the centre view is brake third No. 1617 (D1048) and the lower view is brake composite No. 2845, one of four to D1046 *(see also Plate 29)*. Note the recessed brake ends, the experimental 10ft. bogies and the new buffer housing pattern - the forerunner of the LMS standard type.

(BR/LMR)

Plates 107 & 108 Opposite side views of 56ft. 6in. corridor third No. 66 (later No. 3215) show one of the elliptical roof carriages to D1252, Lot 934, ordered as ambulances but delivered in the form illustrated. Note the mixture of painted and real panels between the long corridor windows.

(NRM)

establish their precise initial utilization. In 1936, however, they were all sold by the LMS to the M&GN on whose lines they continued to provide some faded elegance for several more years.

The other new development was the building, during the years 1907-9, with a repeat order in 1913 for one of the types, of a small group of gangwayed open clerestories, described as 'Vestibule' coaches. In most respects they were similar to open dining carriages but were designed for general service, predominantly excursion use. All told, there were only 24 of them, all but four of which were full thirds. At the time, they were hardly the most important vehicles built during Midland Railway days, but the idea of general service open stock clearly took root some 10-15 years later at the time of the Grouping, when the Midland Railway, at the close of 1922, issued diagrams for 57ft. third and composite vestibules to the new elliptical roof style. These were actually built by the LMS but no lots were issued! In 1924, later examples were inserted on LMS Diagrams D1353 (third) and D1744 (composite) respectively, and became the forerunners of the veritable hordes of open coaches built by the LMS during the 1920s and 1930s, which eventually paved the way to the virtual abandonment throughout British Railways of the side corridor style in the 1970s and 1980s.

The purely Midland Railway vestibules, with clerestories, were rather handsome since they displayed what several writers have referred to as the 'Clipper' profile, also used on dining/sleeping carriages. With this style, the body was widened to 9ft. between the doorways but the cantrail width remained unchanged, thus producing a more accentuated 'tumble-home' to the body sides of the passenger areas.

The final phase of Midland Railway corridor carriage building commenced in 1916/7 with the building of an apparently experimental group of six carriages (one third, one brake third and four brake composites) with full height semi-elliptical roofs on the standard 54ft. underframe. These carriages were 9ft. wide but the brakes had slightly inset flat sides at the brake ends, and all types made limited use of steel construction, principally for the carriage end panels. There is some evidence that the GWR was consulted about this form of construction, judging from odd drawings which have appeared in the Derby records, but these six vehicles were not repeated, nor did the recessed brake ends find much favour. The main build of elliptical roof corridors, such as it was, took place during 1922. The first to appear was a group of 56ft. 6in. vehicles most of which were reconversions or diverted orders for World War I ambulance coaches. Roof style and length apart they were entirely in the established Midland Railway tradition with the typical external panelling of the Bain to Reid era, including reversion to wood-panelled ends. No reason can be offered for the adoption of the unusual 56ft. 6in. length, save, perhaps, to give a little more internal space. All were 9ft. wide.

Plate 109 This is anc
56ft. 6in. ex-ambulance;
time first class brake No.
(later second LMS No. 51
Note the word 'MIDLA
well off-set in the eaves par
(N.

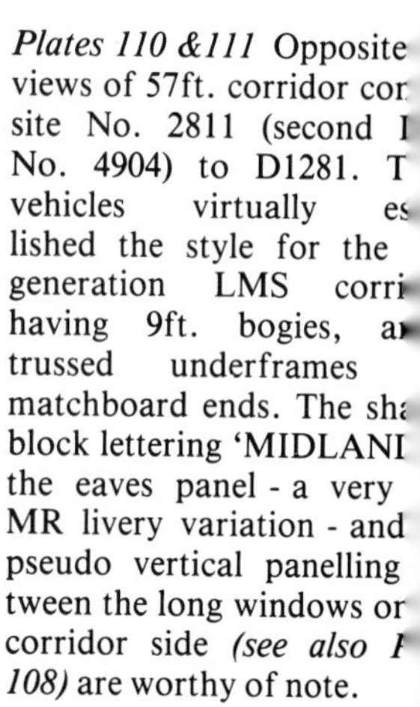

Plates 110 &111 Opposite
views of 57ft. corridor cor
site No. 2811 (second I
No. 4904) to D1281. T
vehicles virtually es
lished the style for the
generation LMS corri
having 9ft. bogies, a
trussed underframes
matchboard ends. The sha
block lettering 'MIDLANI
the eaves panel - a very
MR livery variation - and
pseudo vertical panelling
tween the long windows or
corridor side *(see also P*
108) are worthy of note.
(BR/L.

These were followed by a rather more substantial build of 57ft. corridors in which some changes took place. Most noticeable was the introduction of an angle-trussed underframe and new 9ft. wheelbase bogies, both of which features were translated without significant alteration to the first generation of post-1922 LMS standard carriages. Another mild innovation was the adoption of tongue and groove 'matchboard' panelling for the carriage ends, again adopted by the LMS in 1923.

The 57ft. length was new to the Midland Railway but had been widely adopted by the LNWR/WCJS for many years and also, to a smaller extent, by the Caledonian Railway. The latter company also adopted angle-trussed underframes in its final years so there was, even before the Grouping, a growing degree of consistency between some of the soon to be amalgamated companies. The L&YR too had also been building to a very similar dimension (56ft.) and had also issued studies for a new angle-trussed underframe so, in many ways, the LMS standard coach was not a very surprising vehicle when it emerged.

Midland Railway external detailing was adopted. The underframe/bogie was also essentially Midland but LNWR influence was very strong in terms of interior layout and, later, in electric lighting systems. The LMS, of course, adopted open carriages on an almost one-for-one basis with side corridors and the first of these were to already issued Midland Railway designs *(see page 81)*. However, it was the L&YR, amongst the larger LMS constituents, which had made by far the most use of open stock in the pre-grouping years, so it is also tempting to infer some influence from Newton Heath in the final LMS synthesis.

One thing is quite clear, the Midland Railway did not have the completely free run in post-group carriage practices as it did in locomotive and wagon matters. Reid, it is true, became the LMS Carriage & Wagon Chief so it is hardly surprising that early LMS coaches looked superficially Midland, especially in view of the continuation, unchanged, of the famous 'lake' livery. However, the types, internal layouts and mode of operation were not strictly Midland at all so a suitable degree of compromise was in fact achieved in LMS days.

One lasting legacy of the Midland Railway to LMS carriage building, was the mass production technique developed by Reid at the close of the pre-grouping period, and first used at Derby for the building of the above mentioned open stock. We have dealt in detail with this in our previous book on LMS coaches, so will not repeat matters here. Suffice it to say that it was quickly introduced at Wolverton after 1922 and proved so effective that very soon after the Grouping, Derby and Wolverton between them could cope with virtually all new construction for the whole of the enlarged LMS system, thus making for considerable economies in costs. Of the other carriage works on the LMS, only Newton Heath, and then only for a few years, was commissioned to build new LMS standard types - a foretaste, if you like, of modern day BR works rationalization.

As usual, we conclude this chapter with a full list of vehicles built *(Table 6)* and a selective 'dip' into the more important types by means of drawings and photographs.

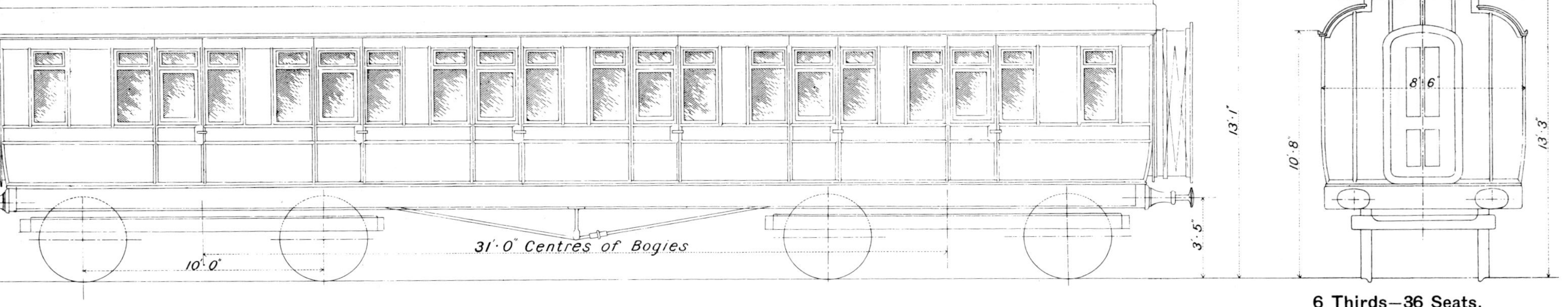

6 Thirds—36 Seats.
2 Lavatories.

	T.	C.	Q.
WEIGHT	23	10	2

Clayton Square-Panelled Corridor Stock

The Clayton square-panelled corridors were either 48ft. or 50ft. in length and we feature here three types, the two corridor third designs and the 50ft. composite. By Midland standards, all three were quite numerous but it is worth repeating that at this stage in the story, the majority of corridors were for the Joint Stock.

Figure 27 *48ft. corridor third to D474.* The very first Midland side corridor coaches to emerge were those of Lot 439 to this diagram. They embodied all the new features introduced by Clayton and some of them (probably all of Lot 439) may have had a full set of doors on the corridor side rather than as shown - *(see also the caption to Figure 28 (overleaf).* The only difference between this version and the 50ft. Joint Stock design to D564 was that in the Joint Stock versions, a narrow cupboard was located between the lavatory and the compartment at each end. Externally, there was a double plain panel between the lavatory and compartment windows. Scale: 4mm. = 1ft.

(K. C. Woodhead Collection)

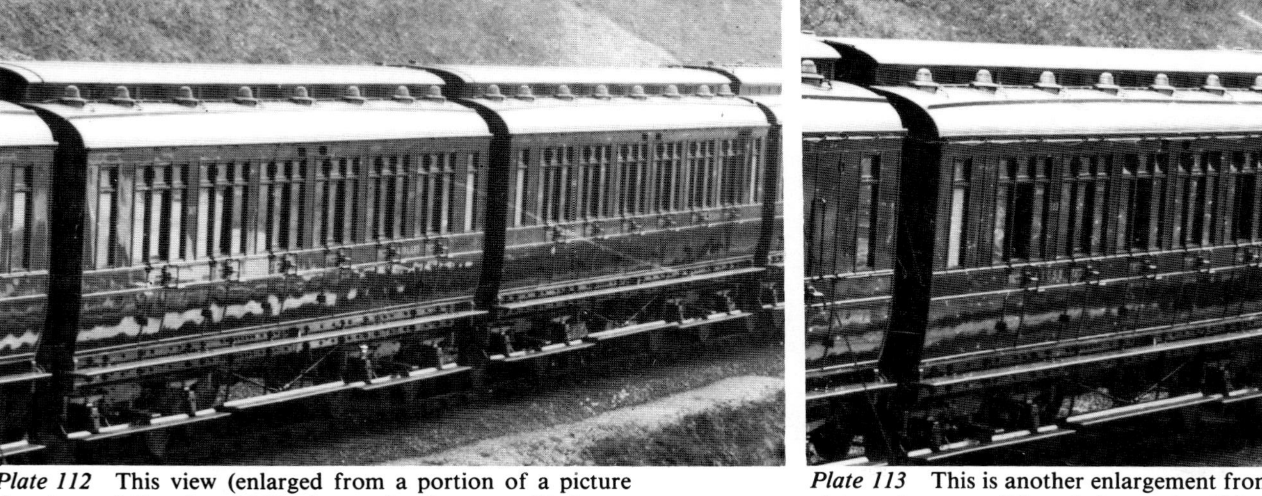

Plate 112 This view (enlarged from a portion of a picture showing a full train of MR clerestories *(see page 87* gives a clear indication of the general characteristics of the 48ft. Midland corridor thirds to D474. The running numbers are not quite decipherable but would be from the pre-1902 series.

(BR/LMR)

Plate 113 This is another enlargement from a complete train picture *(see page 87)* and shows the 50ft. corridor third to D564, M&GSW No. 203, later M&GSW No. 336. It was an early casualty (probably at Hawes Junction or Ais Gill) and was replaced in 1911 by brake third to D477, Lot 789 *(see Table 6).*

(BR/LMR)

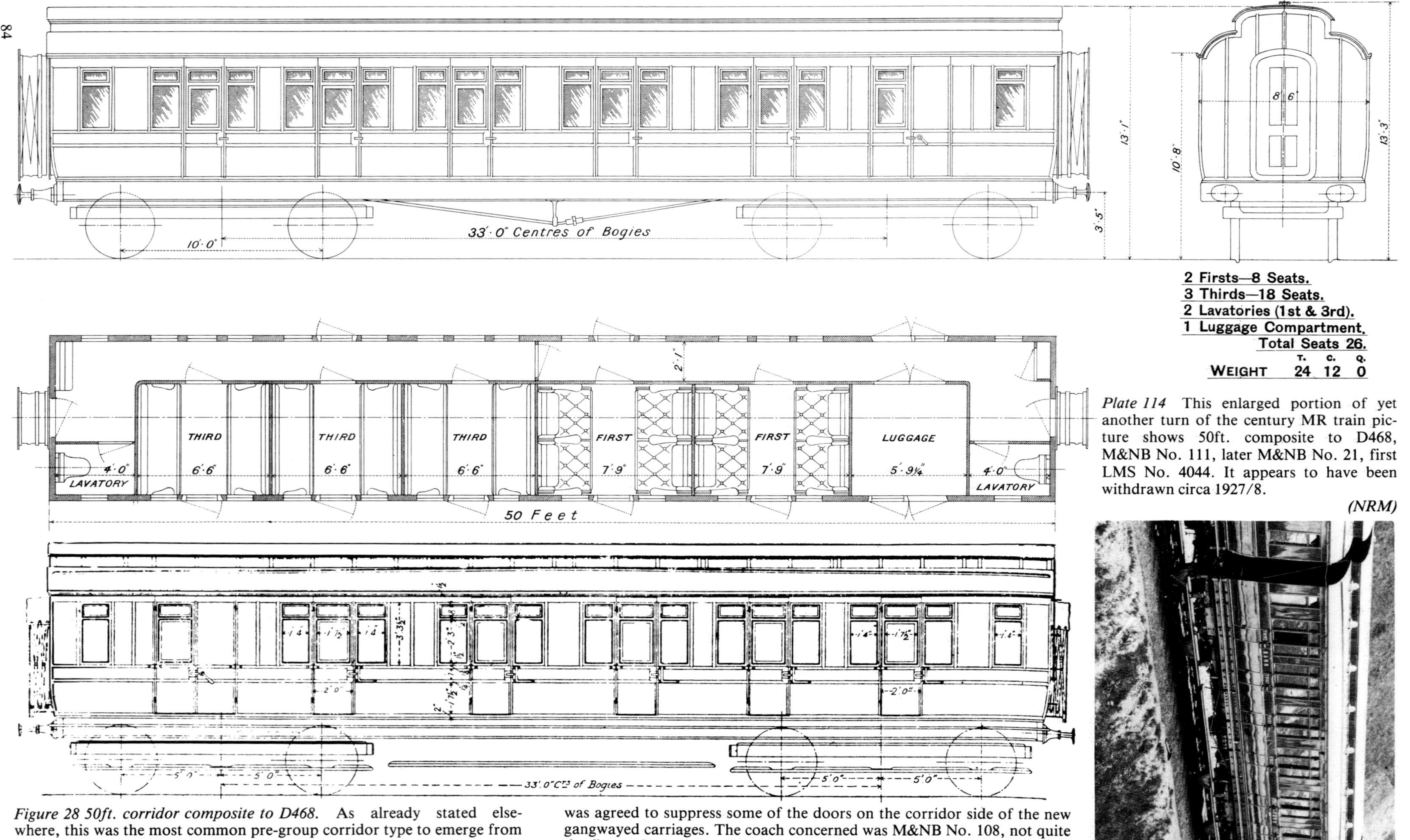

2 Firsts—8 Seats.
3 Thirds—18 Seats.
2 Lavatories (1st & 3rd).
1 Luggage Compartment.
Total Seats 26.

	T.	C.	Q.
WEIGHT	24	12	0

Plate 114 This enlarged portion of yet another turn of the century MR train picture shows 50ft. composite to D468, M&NB No. 111, later M&NB No. 21, first LMS No. 4044. It appears to have been withdrawn circa 1927/8.

(NRM)

Figure 28 50ft. corridor composite to D468. As already stated elsewhere, this was the most common pre-group corridor type to emerge from Derby. To supplement the official diagram, we have also included a contemporary drawing from the *Railway Engineer* of 1900. This latter shows a full set of doors on the corridor side whereas the diagram indicates alternating doors and droplights. It would appear that two vehicles (believed to

was agreed to suppress some of the doors on the corridor side of the new gangwayed carriages. The coach concerned was M&NB No. 108, not quite the first to be built *(see Table 6)*, so it seems quite probable that the 48ft. and 50ft. corridors built before 1900 had full sets of corridor doors (probably altered later) whereas the later versions were built with alternating doors from new *(see also Plate 118). Scale: 4mm. = 1ft.*

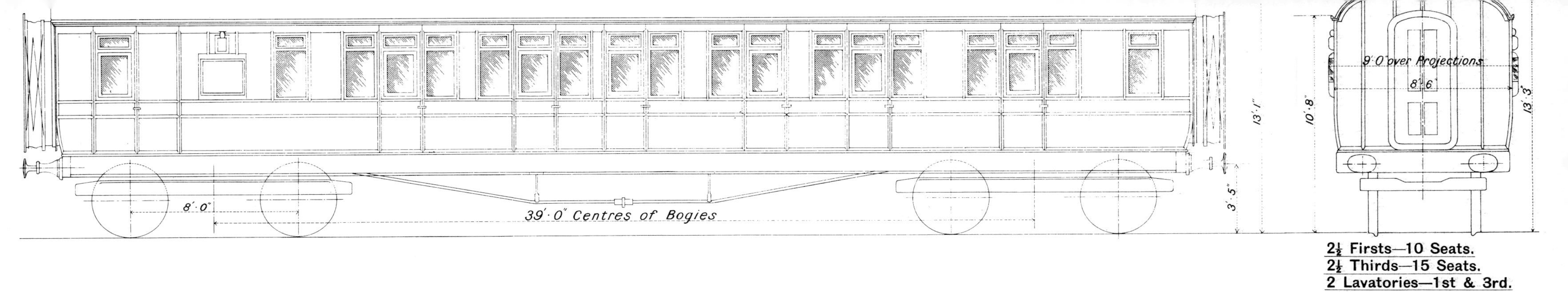

Bain 54ft. Square-Panelled Corridor Stock

The first generation of Bain 54ft. corridors retained the square-cornered panelling and most of the other Clayton body style features but with the new underframe/bogie. A subtle visible change was the lack of reinforcement beading behind the exterior door handles on the Bain carriages which were otherwise very much in the Clayton tradition.

Figure 29 Corridor brake composite to D470. We have chosen as our 54ft. square-panelled corridor, this very characteristic type of which forty were built. Unfortunately this period of MR carriage building is very badly represented by official (or other) photographs so, particularly for modelmakers, it is very much a question of making the best of what is available and assuming known standard practices for the rest! Fortunately, in the case of D470, a real life example is preserved at Butterley. Scale: 4mm. = 1ft.

(K. C. Woodhead Collection)

Plates 115 & 116 The only decent set of official photographs we have located of the Bain 54ft. square light corridors, is a group of views of the slightly-damaged third class vehicle, LMS No. 2217 to D560, Lot 568, all taken from the corridor side. The pictures do, however, give a very clear indication of the detail work applicable to all early Bain 54ft. coaches. The vehicle was scrapped before the 1933 renumbering *(see also Plate 19).*

(BR/LMR)

Plate 117 A first class coupé interior (apparently for ladies) of an unidentified example of D470.

(BR/LMR)

Plate 118 This enlarged portion of one of a celebrated series of MR train pictures, taken at Armathwaite and other locations on the Settle to Carlisle line, circa 1910, admirably illustrates the square-panelled corridor series in traffic. The leading vehicle is a Bain 54ft. corridor third (D560) followed by a Clayton 50ft. third to D564. The third vehicle is a three compartment 54ft. round-panelled third class brake to D561 (the slightly earlier square-panelled version being to D475) and the fourth vehicle is a 50ft. Clayton corridor composite to D468, clearly showing the reduced number of doors on the corridor side *(see caption to Figure 28)*. The rest of the train was a very similar five coach set to that shown at *Plate 99* and it was probably the same morning Glasgow to St. Pancras working but on a different day.

(BR/LMR)

To sum up the square-panelled corridor stock, we here take this opportunity to give the full views from which *Plates 112/113* were taken. Both pictures were specially-posed in the Derbyshire hills, at about the turn of the century, to illustrate the new Midland Railway stock.

(NRM)

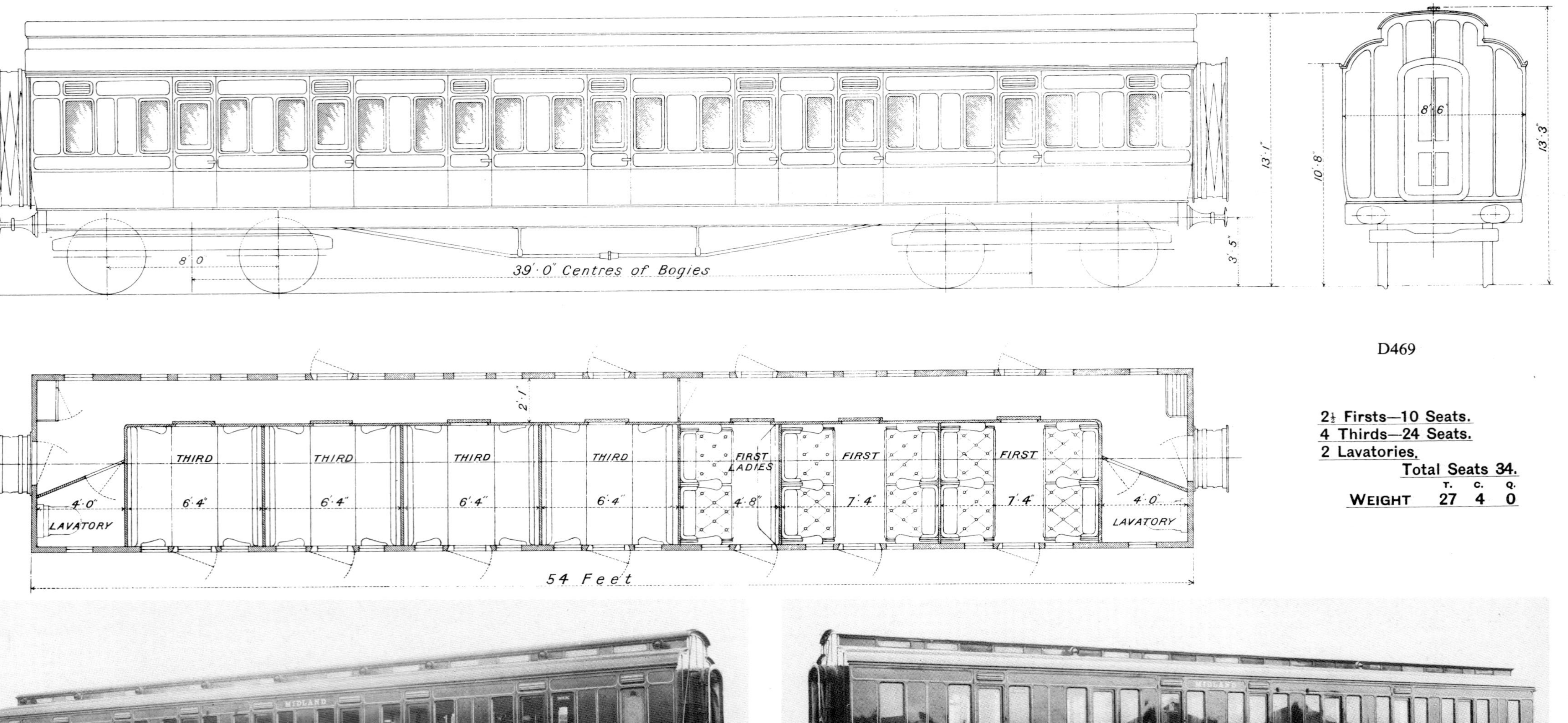

Plates 119 & 120 Compartment and corridor side views of corridor composites to D469, Lot 616. This was the largest single build of Bain period corridor composites and all exhibited the revised vertical panel dimensions with 3 element door vents, probably the first vehicles to do so - *(see Figure 33 & Plate 124 (below))*. No. 2913 became second LMS No. 4889 and No. 2874 became 2nd LMS No. 4872. Both vehicles display the post-1905 Midland livery and the pictures were taken after conversion to electric lighting.

Bain 54ft. Round-Panelled Corridor Stock

It is probably true to say that the Bain round-panelled clerestories were, in most eyes, the archetypal Midland corridor carriages, however we hope that this chapter has helped to indicate that they were but a part of a more complex story. Nevertheless, in straight numerical terms they were marginally dominant over the square-panelled corridors so we make no apology for featuring several types, additional to the design already depicted at *Figure 5 in Chapter 1.*

Figures 30 & 31 Corridor composites to D469 & D593. These highly similar designs were, by Midland standards, quite common types. Their interior layouts, apart from quite trivial dimensional differences, were identical and it was only the 'large' corridor side windows of D593 which really differentiated the diagrams. The earlier type (D469) was built across the transition from 4 element to 3 element door vents and from 13ft. 1in. to 12ft. 11in. in height, so the earlier examples *(as per diagram)* had the deeper eaves panel and greater height; while the later examples - *(see Plates 119 & 120 (opposite))* had the lower height, shallower eaves panel and slighter deeper windows. The considerably fewer vehicles to D593 all exhibited the lower height and revised vertical panel dimensions which latter, thereafter, remained unchanged until well into the LMS period. Scale: 4mm. = 1ft.

(K. C. Woodhead Collection)

Plate 121 A compartment side view of corridor composite No. 3421 to D593, Lot 727. This batch of vehicles all went to ambulance use in 1917 and the photograph was probably taken of the coach ex-works as a new vehicle in 1909/10. Note the gas lighting but the otherwise general similarity to the compartment side of D469 *(Plate 119)*. The 'long' corridor windows and handrails are just visible through some of the compartment side quarterlights. *(BR/LMR)*

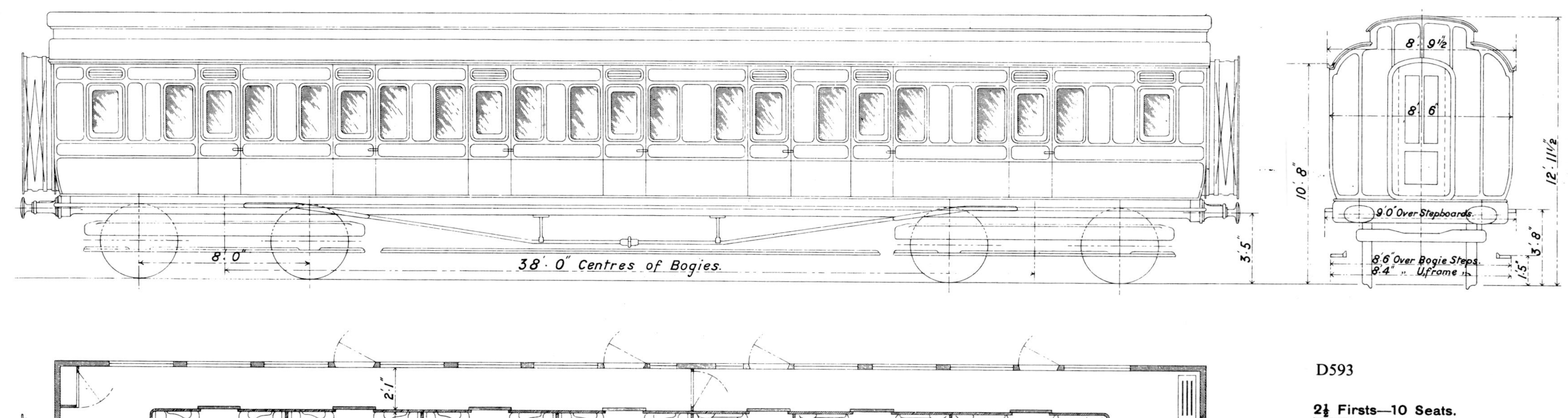

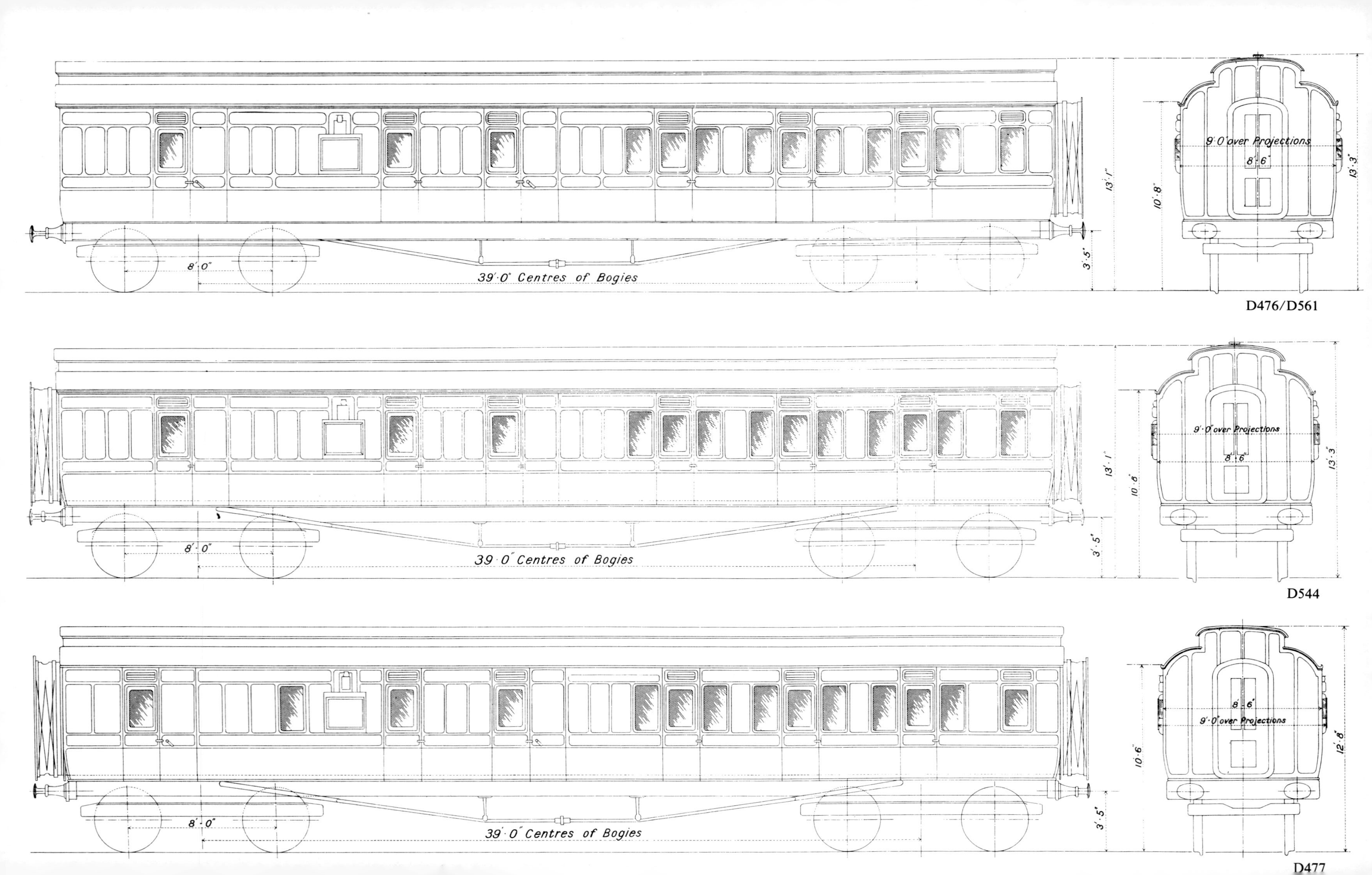
D476/D561
13'3"
10'8"
9'0" over Projections
8'6"
13'1"
3'5"
39'0" Centres of Bogies
8'0"
D544
13'3"
10'8"
9'0" over Projections
8'6"
13'1"
3'5"
39'0" Centres of Bogies
8'0"
D477
12'8"
10'6"
9'0" over Projections
8'6"
3'5"
39'0" Centres of Bogies
8'0"

the opposite page, and plans on this page. D476 was the basic type (with D561 as its equivalent with gangway at the brake end), D544 was the short-lived conversion of three vehicles (Lot 593) to kitchen form *(see Table 6)*, while D477 was the 12ft. 8in. high version with 'long' corridor windows. Note that Lots 789/828 (variously ascribed to both D561 and D477) combined the window pattern of D477 with the intermediate 12ft.11½in. height not shown on any of the diagrams! Scale: 4mm. = 1ft.

(K. C. Woodhead Collection)

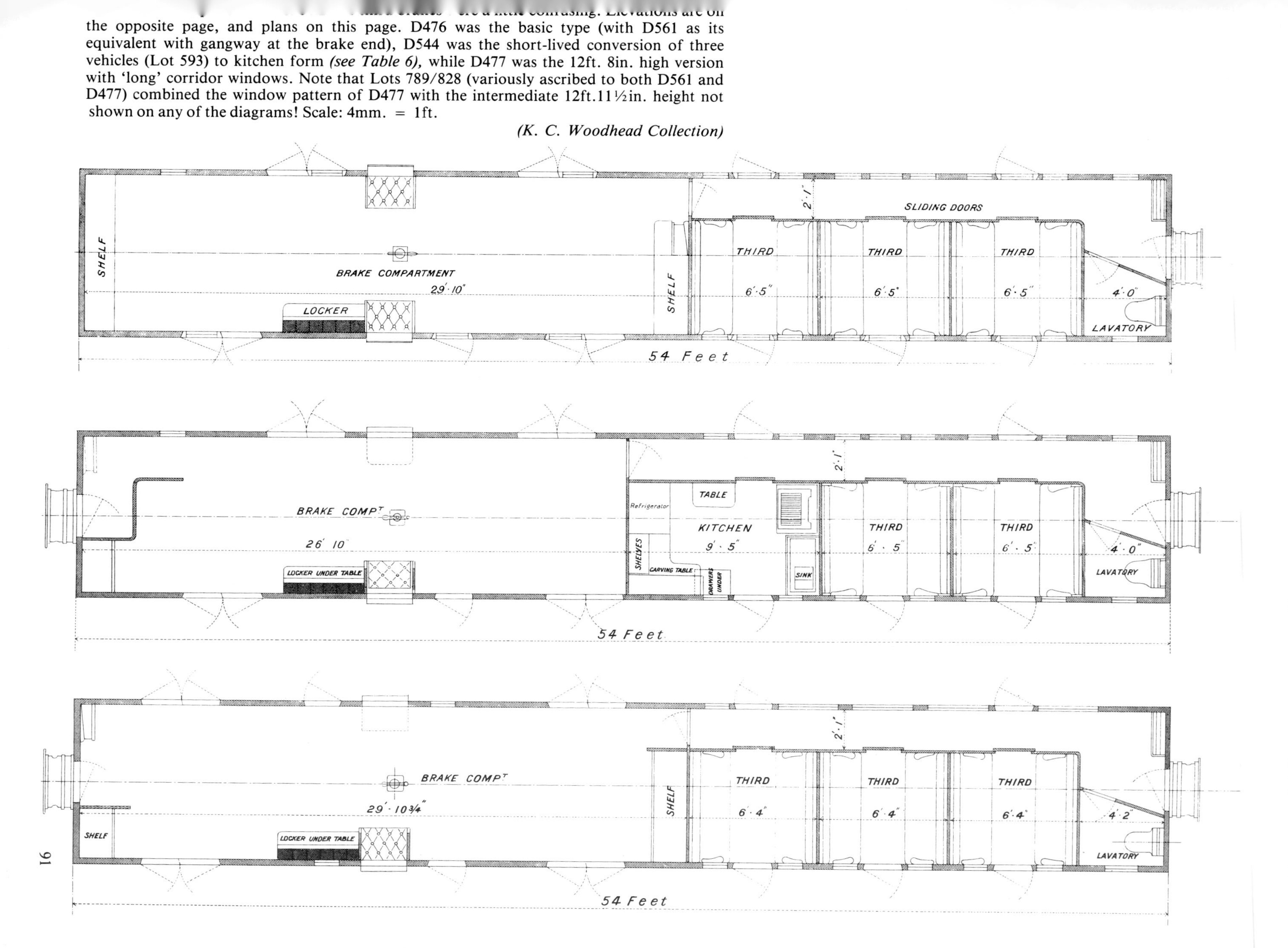

Plate 122 M&NB No.123 to D561 was one of the Ais Gill accident victims. This picture was taken after the event and is the only surviving official view of this particular type. It was one of the early series with 4 element door vents and deeper eaves panelling. The coach appears to have been repaired afterwards since it is shown as first LMS No. 4127 in 1923 and second LMS No. 6472 in 1933.

(BR/LMR)

Plate 123 This view of Midland and first LMS No. 284 (second LMS No. 6478) shows the corridor side view of the 12ft. 8in. high corridor third brakes to D477. This arrangement, more or less, set the visual style for the corridor side elevations of Midland and LMS stock until 1928-30. Note, however, that the Midland at first inserted a narrow vertical panel between adjacent large windows whereas, in later years, *(see Plates 108 & 111)* the Midland (and LMS) suppressed this feature in favour of a plain piece of beading - albeit sometimes given 'panel' style lining.

(BR/LMR)

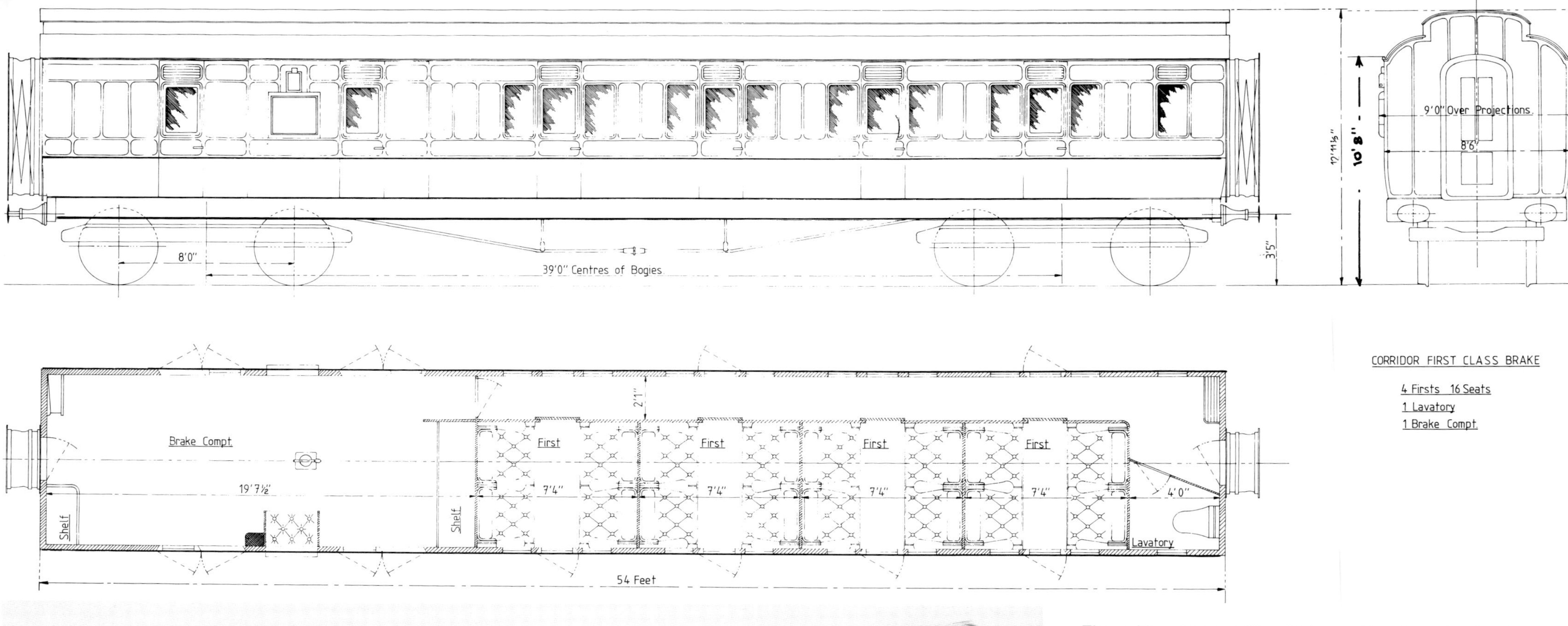

Figure 33 and Plate 124 *54ft. corridor first class brake to D576.* The Midland built far more first class brakes than full firsts - probably because, like BR today, it commonly marshalled its expresses with first class at one end and third at the other. We have selected the most numerous single type for this section and are indebted to Peter Truman for retracing the drawing from a somewhat indifferent quality original diagram. The picture shows MR and first LMS No. 2656 (second LMS No. 5184), brand-new, ex-works. All of this type were to Lot 615 and displayed the deeper eaves panel and 4 element door vents. Since Lot 616 (corridor composite to D469, *page 88*) had the revised dimensions, the point of change can be fairly precisely identified *(see also Plate 101)*. Scale: 4mm. = 1ft.

(NRM)

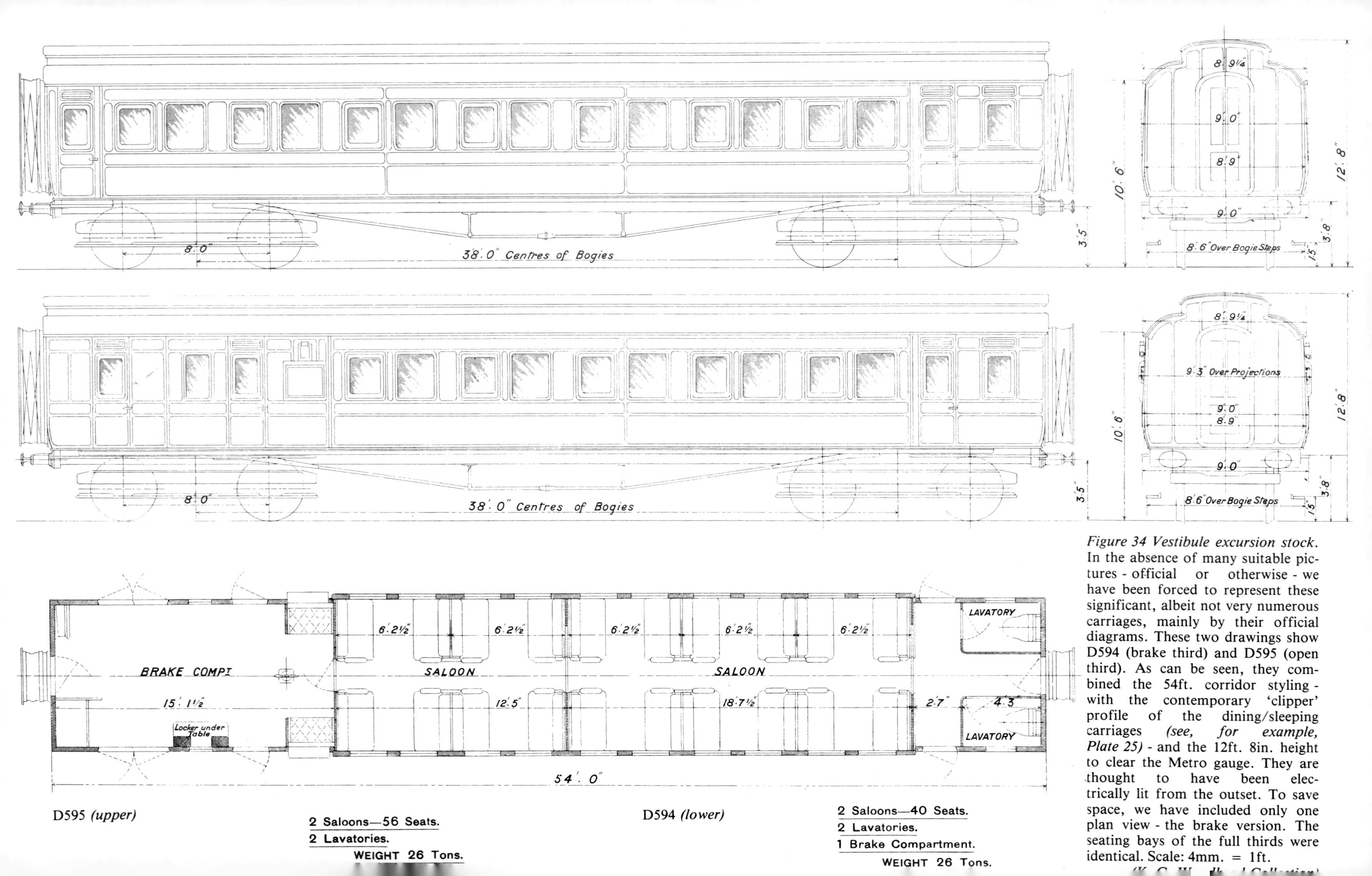

Figure 34 Vestibule excursion stock. In the absence of many suitable pictures - official or otherwise - we have been forced to represent these significant, albeit not very numerous carriages, mainly by their official diagrams. These two drawings show D594 (brake third) and D595 (open third). As can be seen, they combined the 54ft. corridor styling - with the contemporary 'clipper' profile of the dining/sleeping carriages *(see, for example, Plate 25)* - and the 12ft. 8in. height to clear the Metro gauge. They are thought to have been electrically lit from the outset. To save space, we have included only one plan view - the brake version. The seating bays of the full thirds were identical. Scale: 4mm. = 1ft.

Plate 125 The fairly utilitarian interior arrangement of the vestibule thirds to D595 is well illustrated in this view.
(NRM)

TABLE 6
Summary of Midland and Midland/Scottish Joint Stock Corridor Vehicles including Vestibuled Open Stock

Diag.	Lot	Qty.	Date of Order	Dimensions	Wt.	Style	Pre-Group Numbering: Midland	Pre-Group Numbering: Joint Stock 1st	Pre-Group Numbering: Joint Stock 2nd	Post Group Numbering: 1st LMS	Post Group Numbering: 2nd LMS	Post Group Numbering: LNER	Type Extinct	Remarks
First Class Corridor (FK)														
565	450	3	1898	50' x 8' 6"	24T	CC2	–	MGSW 210–2 (see remarks)	MGSW 212–4	3909–11	1172–4	–	2/33	An odd lot. Built as 4F + 1T composite (MGSW 201–3), then 4F + pantry (vice 3rd compartment) – c1904; finally 4F + luggage in 1921.
600	761	4	1911	54' x 8' 6"	27T	BC4	2670–3	–	–	as MR	1175–8	–	4/56	Standard Bain clerestory with 'long' corridor windows.
Third Class Corridor (TK – including Semi-TK)														
474	439 480	8 9	1898 1899	48' x 8' 6"	23½T	CC2	Various 296–323 included 2084–9	– –	– –	as MR as MR	3053–9 3060–5	– –	11/43 1/44	Standard 6 x 3rd Clayton clerestories. LMS 3054 to ARP use; 3055 to service stock – both in 1942.
564	449 449	12 12	1898 1898	50' x 8' 6"	24½T	CC2	–	MGSW 201–12	MGSW 334–45 MNB 101–8 MNB 109–10	3968–79 4105–12 –	3104–5 3109–15 3106–8/16–20 –	– – 3727/9	12/49 9/45 ?	Built between batches of D474 – 50ft. long (for Joint Stock) but otherwise identical. LMS 3105/11/19/22 all to caravan use in 1936.
560	554 568	15 30	1903 1903	54' x 8' 6"	26T	BC3	– 2203–32	MGSW 213–27 –	MNB 111–12 MGSW 346–57 –	4115–6 3980–91 as MR	3121–2 3143–53 3123–42 3162–71	– – – –	11/36 9/45 1/47 4/45	Bain development (54ft.) of D474 & D564. LMS 3132/68 to ARP use in 1942/44; LMS 3137 to caravan (1937); LMS 3154 to service stock (1944).
473 see remarks	587 592 601 618 644 791 827	4 20 4 14 6 2 10	1905 1905 1905 1906 1906 1911 1913	54' x 8' 6"	27T	BC4	– Various 15–104 – Various 575–649 – – –	MGSW 233–6 – MGSW 209 MGSW 226 MGSW 244–5 – – MGSW 225/37 –	MGSW 366–9 – MGSW 342 MGSW 359 MGSW 377–8 – MNB 125–30 MGSW 358/70 MGSW 382–91	4000–3 as MR 3976 3993 4011–2 as MR – 3992/4004 4016–25	3174–7 3154–61 3172 3173 3178–9 3180–8 – 3197–8 3199–208	– – – – – – 3894–5/9 3904/6 plus one – –	10/45 3/46 10/45 7/42 7/46 4/51 (see remarks) ? 7/53 11/55	A complicated diagram. Essentially the Bain round-panelled equivalent of D560; however, Lots 791 & 827 were built with 'long' windows on corridor side without a fresh diagram. Many early withdrawals (c1917) for ambulance conversion, all ex-MR, namely 12 from Lot 592, 5 from Lot 618. LMS 3181 (ex-MR 578) of Lot 618 was given elliptical roof c1915 and was also the last survivor. The last clerestory withdrawal from this series (Lots 587–618) was in 5/48 (LMS 3185). Not known why the LMS numbered Lot 592 in the middle of D560!
548	684	16	1907	50' x 8' 6"	25T	BC4	Various 150–1068	–	–	as MR	3088–103	–	12/51	6½ x 3rd class, reduced height (12' 8") for 'Metro' gauge and classed as excursion stock. LMS 3089 to DM 395013 in 1949 (as tool van) – scrapped 1966 from Conway.
547	687	8	1907	54' x 8' 6"	25/26T	BC4	Various 233–60	–	–	as MR	3189–96	–	4/51	As for last lots of D473 (above) but built 12' 8" high to clear 'Metro' gauge. Diagram suggests that some were to be converted to elliptical roof but not confirmed.
598	752	12	1911	50' x 8' 6"	25T	BC4	Various 3–108	–	–	as MR	3076–87	81008–19 (see remarks)	12/58	*Semi-TK* with part open 'picnic' saloon area. All transferred to M&GN in 1936 and survivors to BR became BR 60101–10 (not LNER 81016/9).
1047	912	1	1916	54' x 9' 0"	29T	E	1348	–	–	as MR	3209	–	1/52	Experimental 'one-off' – see main text.
1252	934 Part 963	12 3	1922 1922	56' 6" x 9' 0"	27T	E	Various 23–105 561; 573; 577	– –	– –	as MR as MR	3210–21 3222–4	– –	5/60 12/59	Lot 934 were 12 of 32 vehicles ordered for USA Ambulance Trains 83/4 but completed as TK for Midland use. Lot 963 were re-conversions (ex-ambulances).
1282	973	14	1922	57' x 9' 0"	28T	E	Various 632–3339	–	–	as MR	3225–38	–	5/59	Essentially the prototypes of the LMS standard series. Many disposed of to the NCC to replace war losses
Composite Corridor (CK)														
468	451	72	1900	50' x 8' 6"	24½T	CC2	– – –	MGSW 204–13 MGSW 214–45 MNB 101–106 MNB 107–115 MNB 122–32 MNB 133–6	to MR (Various) 2904–41 MGSW 231–62 MNB 12–16 (not MNB 101) MNB 17–25 MNB 32–42 MNB 43–6	as MR 3914–45 – 4040–8 4055–65 –	4794–803 4804–32 – 4786–93 4833–42 –	– – 32444–8 – – 32275/86 382/6	8/39 8/41 ? 2/39 5/46 ? ?	Largest single build of any MR corridor design and all (originally) Joint Stock (42 – MGSW; 30 –MNB). Numbering after 1923 is complicated but in 1933, the LMS numbered its own share in 1923 number order according to date built. Early withdrawals. MNB (1st) No. 101; MGSW (2nd) 244/259, all replaced by D469/D593 (below).
469	600 616 626	10 40 15	1905 1905 1905	54' x 8' 6"	27T	BC4	– Various 2816–3380	MGSW 242 MGSW 260–7 MNB 101 – MNB 144–50 MNB 160–7	MGSW 259 MGSW 277–84 MNB 11 – MNB 54–60 MNB 70–2/4 MNB 73/5–7	3942 3960–7 4034 as MR 4077–83 4093–5/7	4843 4844–51 4852 4863–902 4853–9 4860–2	– – – – – 32535–8	5/45 6/46 10/45 3/49 10/46 3/46 ?	Another large build, mostly MR but first/third lots for the Joint Stock. Building took place between 1905/7 in spite of order date. Early withdrawal: 1st LMS 4097 (ex-MNB). Lot 600 replacements for early casualties from D468 were MGSW 242 (259) and MNB 101 (11). LMS 4846 downgraded to all 3rd (No. 2235).

Diag.	Lot	Qty.	Date of Order	Dimensions	Wt.	Style	Pre-Group Numbering: Midland	Pre-Group Numbering: Joint Stock 1st	Pre-Group Numbering: Joint Stock 2nd	Post Group Numbering: 1st LMS	Post Group Numbering: 2nd LMS	LNER	Type Extinct	Remarks
593	727 790	6 1	1909 1913	54' x 8' 6"	27T	BC4	3421 + five more –	– –	– MGSW 244	– 3927	– 4903	– –	12/47	Identical to D469 except for 'long' corridor windows. Lot 727 all to ambulances in 1917. Lot 790 was a replacement for early withdrawal from D468.
1281	971	14	1922	57' x 9' 0"	28T	E	Various 2811–3483	–	–	as MR	4904–17	– LMS 4907 LMS 4913 LMS 4914 LMS 4916	7/60	Fore-runners of LMS standard type. As with matching corridor thirds (D1282), several to NCC/UTA in 1942 viz: NCC 64 UTA 270 NCC 65 UTA 272 NCC 68 UTA 274 NCC 69 UTA 276
												Other disposals: LMS 4906 – DM395553 Mess Van (1957) LMS 4908 – DM395554 Mess Van (1957)		
First Class Corridor Brake (BFK)														
569	481	3	1899	50' x 8' 6"	24T	CC2	–	MGSW 201–3	MGSW 203–5	3900–2	5157–9	–	12/33	Built as FK (4 x first plus kitchen). Altered to BFK in 1913, losing one compartment. Probably never received second LMS numbers.
467	570	6	1903	54' x 8' 6"	26T	BC3	2653–8	–	–	as MR	5174–9	–	1939	Standard early Bain square panelled style. LMS 5178 was downgraded to BTK No. 6467. Four x 1st plus brake.
570	571	3	1903	54' x 8' 6"	25½T	BC3	–	MGSW 204–6	MGSW 206–8	3903–5	5160–2	–	8/33	Three compartment version of D467 for MGSW stock.
576	615	18	1905	54' x 8' 6"		BC4	2599–601; 2655–63; 2779–84	–	–	as MR	5180–97		2/48	Round panelled equivalent of D467 (i.e. 4 x 1st plus brake) LMS 5191 to Brake 3rd (No. 6472) in 1937.
1255	Part 963	9	1921	56' 6" x 9' 0"	26½T	E	Various 2866–3329	–	–	as MR	5163–71	–	1/59	Converted ex-ambulances with 4½ compartments. LMS 5170 destroyed at Muirhead in 1933.
1285	975	2	1922	57' x 9' 0"	27T	E	3295/7	–	–	as MR	5172–3	–	9/59	Fore-runners of LMS standard series with 4½ compartments. (NB: Diagrams 1255/1258 should, in theory, have been numbered at the end of the 1933 LMS series both on grounds of length and capacity.
Third Class Corridor Brake (BTK)														
475	567	15	1903	54' x 8' 6"	25½T	BC3	2191–202	–	–	as MR	6405–16	–	9/47	Not, apparently, built until 1904.
476 561	588 593 619 628	7 30 30 12	1904 1904 1905 1905	54' x 8' 6"	25T	BC4	– Various 115–435 Various 4–1499 –	MGSW 228–30 MGSW 237–43 – – –	MGSW 361–3 MGSW 371–6 – – MNB 113 MNB 114–8 MNB 119–24	3995–7 4005–10 as MR as MR 4117 – 4123–8	6417–9 6438–43 6420–37 6444–66 6467 – 6468–73	– – – – -- 316; 3907/13 3916–7 –	10/44 12/50 10/47 1953 6/37 ? 11/47	Identical diagrams except that D476 (Lot 593 only) built without brake-end gangway – later altered. 1st MGSW 237 was early casualty from Lot 588 and replaced by TK to D473. The total built went on until 1907 in spite of order dates. Some eleven of the MR series went to ambulance use in 1917. Three of Lot 593 temporarily converted with pantries to D544 *(see Table 2)*. See also D477 for Lots 789/828.
549	685	4	1907	50' x 8' 6"	24T	BC4	210; 219; 225/8	–	–	as MR	6401–4	–	1/52	Five compartment brakes for excursion use and built 12' 8" to suit 'Metro' gauge.
477	688 789 828	5 1 2	1907 1911 1913	54' x 8' 6"		BC4	261; 271; 281/3–4 – –	– – –	– MGSW 336 MGSW 392–3	as MR 3970 4026–7	6474–8 6479 6480–1	– – –	12/46 12/47 8/48	As D476 & D561 generally but with 'long' corridor windows and reduced 12' 8" height. Lots 789/828 were identical to this new layout but had the 12' 11½" height of D561. They are variously allocated to either diagram but, height apart, more closely correspond to D477. Lot 789 seems to have replaced one of D564 (TK) – an early casualty.
1048	913	1	1916	54' x 9' 0"	27T	E	1617	–	–	as MR	6482	–	4/54	Experimental 'one-off' – see main text.
1278	Part 963	5	1921	56' 6" x 9' 0"	27T	E	113; 148; 170; 215; 231	–	–	as MR	6483–7	–	8/59	Converted ex-ambulances.
1284	974 998	9 1	1922 1922	57' x 9' 0"	27T	E	Various 135–656 224	– –	– –	as MR as MR	6488–96 6497	– –	9/61 10/59	Basis of LMS standard type. Lot 998 not built until 1924 and ordered as a replacement for old No. 224. Most of Lot 974 not built until LMS period.
Composite Corridor Brake (BCK)														
566	452	22	1898	50' x 8' 6"	25T	CC2	–	MNB 116–7 MNB 118 MGSW 246–257 MNB 137–40 MNB 141 MNB 142–3	MNB 26–7 MNB 28 MGSW 263–74 MNB 47–50 MNB 51 MNB 52	– 4051 3946–57 4070–3 – 4075–6	– 7215 7216–27 7228–31 – 7232–3	32450–1 – – – 32389 –	? 1/37 9/45 8/43 ? 9/38	Most were not built until 1900. Several conversions by LMS in 1937 to Caravan (Camping Coach) viz: LMS 7216/9/20/9.
470	569	40	1903	54' x 8' 6"	26½T	BC3	Various 2829–3783	–	–	as MR	7242–81	–	1947 (but see remarks)	Standard Bain square panelled development of D566. One of them, MR 2944 (LMS 7263) is preserved at Butterley. Three downgraded to BTK: – LMS 7261/75/80 but only 7280 renumbered (6420).
559	586 594 617 627	2 10 23 6	1904 1904 1905 1906	54' 8' 6"	27½T	BC4	– 3301 plus nine Not known –	MGSW 258–9 – – MNB 151–2 MNB 153 MNB 168–70	MGSW 275–6 – – MNB 61–2 MNB 63 MNB 78–80	3958–9 3301 – – 4086 4101–3	7283–4 7282 – – 7285 7286–8	– – – 31209–10 – –	10/44 1/48 – ? 8/40 12/50	Not many long term survivors, largely because of virtually total transfer of 9 Lots 594/617 to ambulance use (c1917). Round panelled version of D470. LMS 7288 became tool van 19854 and lasted until 1958.
471	645	8	1906	50' x 8' 6"		BC4	Various 2945–87	–	–	as MR	7234–41	–	4/52	Reduced height (12' 8") and originally for Dover/Deal through services. LMS 7235/40 to BTK 6403/33 in 1937.
472	686	10	1907	54' x 8' 6"	26T	BC4	Various 3328–734	–	–	as MR	7298–307	–	7/51	Variation of D559 with 'long' corridor windows and 3 x 3rd; 2 x 1st class compartments.
596	741	6	1910	54' x 8' 6"	26T	BC4	2803–6/8/10	–	–	as MR – not 2804	7289–93	–	1955	'Double ended' slip brakes. MR 2804 to ambulance use in 1917.
1046	876	4	1917	54' x 9' 0"	29T	E	2834; 2845/9; 2851	–	–	as MR	7294–7	–	1/57	Experimental lot (c.f. TK – D1047; BTK – D1048). Ordered as clerestory but built with elliptical roof. Layout as D472.
1283	972	10	1922	57' x 9' 0"	28T	E	Various 2893–3306	–	–	as MR	7308–17	–	10/61	Basis of the LMS standard design.
Vestibuled (Open) Stock														
540	690	2	1907	54' x 9' 0"		BC4	2508/10	–	–	as MR	7559–60 (later 26998–9)		9/48	*First Class (FO). 'Clipper'* profile; 5½ bays.
541	689	2	1907	54' x 9' 0"		BC4	285/8	–	–	as MR	9587–8	–	12/45	*Third Class (TO). 'Clipper'* profile; 6½ bays.
595	733 844	12 6	1909 1913	54' x 9' 0"	26T	BC4	1391/8 1500–10 (not 1502) Various 512–44	– –	– –	as MR as MR as MR	9589–90 9591–600 9601–6	– – –	6/51 7/52 3/55	*Third Class (TO). 'Clipper' pro*file; 7 bay design for excursion use.
594	734	2	1909	54' x 9' 0"	26T	BC4	1511–2	–	–	as MR	9971–2 (later 27971–2)	–	4/52	*Third Class Brake (BTO). 'Clipper'* profile; 5 bay design for excursion use. *Note:* For other ex-MR open 3rd class stock (LMS second series 9607–29, *(see Table 2, Catering Vehicles)*.

Compiled by D. Jenkinson, December 198

Chapter Six

Non-corridor 'Express' lavatory stock

The non-corridor compartment carriage, with lavatory accommodation, while not being peculiar to Britain was, nevertheless, a highly characteristic British type, almost until the close of the steam era; and many British companies made as much, if not more, use of this type of vehicle than they did of gangwayed stock for their more long-distance trains. Such a company was the Midland, whose fleet of lavatory non-corridors (over 850 examples) outnumbered its general service corridor stock by some 150 vehicles. Most of them dated from the late 1890s onwards and as *Table 7* indicates, the clerestory style was again dominant, representing some 72 per cent of the total - a proportion almost approaching that of the corridor stock. If one excludes the Clayton arc roof series, most of which had been displaced by the time of the Grouping, then the clerestory proportion rises to well over 80 per cent.

Turning now to the actual vehicles built, once again, as with corridor stock, it can be seen that composite coaches represented a high proportion, in fact, almost exactly half the fleet. This merely reinforces the inferences drawn in the previous chapter regarding the attraction of the Midland Railway for the first class passenger and almost suggests that during much of its history, the Midland Railway probably regarded both its corridor and its lavatory non-corridor stock as being of similar importance. In fact, the usual description adopted by the Company was 'Express Lavatory Carriage'; hence the title of this chapter.

The large scale building of lavatory-equipped coaches began in 1884 with a batch of 25 Clayton arc roof 54ft. bogie composites to Lot 105 (D512), almost certainly for the Scottish services. There was in fact a slightly earlier series of six twelve wheel 54ft. third brakes with one lavatory only (Lot 85) but these seem to have been a bit experimental and possibly even conversions from non-lavatory vehicles. There is evidence that it was the introduction of Pullmans *(see Appendix I)* which proved strongly influential in the provision of lavatories for the longer distance stock.

During this earlier Clayton period there was no great consistency in lavatory stock; almost as if the Company was feeling its way forward. A brake composite version of Lot 105 to Diagram 527, Lot 149 appeared in 1886, then a one-off 56ft. twelve wheel brake composite in 1888 for the Paris Exhibition, a design of considerable elegance, but never repeated in either style or length. Full firsts were non-existent, as indeed remained the case until well into the Bain period; and the full thirds with lavatories, which appeared in 1889/90, all seem to have been conversions from erstwhile non-lavatory stock (six wheelers to Diagram 494, ex-D493, and 47ft. bogies to Diagram 488, ex-D490).

Finally, in 1895, and just prior to the adoption of the new clerestory style, a series of twenty rather palatial 54ft. twelve wheel brake composites appeared (Diagram 522, Lot 359) which had a rather longer survival rate than the other Clayton arc roofs.

One thing seems certain. During this period, lavatory accommodation was by no means common, probably being confined to only the best trains, and even then, only representing some of the vehicles in the formations. The strong emphasis on composites suggests that the first class passenger had the prior claim to consideration, and such third class compartments as could gain access to the lavatories arose more as a result of their presence in a composite vehicle than for any more deep-rooted reason of policy.

This situation did not last. The Midland never neglected for long its third class passengers, in spite of its self-evident concern for the first class riders, and once the clerestory style became adopted, then all travellers benefited considerably.

The pioneer carriages were the three special sets of vehicles ordered in 1896 for the Bristol to Bradford services. There were only six coaches per set including a six wheel kitchen car and a six wheel full brake; but the passenger carrying twelve wheelers (all 60ft. long) were really sumptuous and as good as anything available anywhere in Britain. Four varieties were provided, none of which became 'standard' types but in all of which were established design trends which later became incorporated into the larger batches of 'common user' designs.

TABLE 7
General Service Non-Corridor Lavatory Stock (Built 1877 and subsequently)

Type \ *Style*	*Clayton Arc Roof*		*Square Panel Clerestory*		*Round Panel Clerestory*	*Bain Arc Roof*	*Elliptical Roof*	*Total*
	Six-Wheel	*Bogie*	*Six-Wheel*	*Bogie*				
First Class	–	–	–	–	–	4	4	8
Third Class	42	6	11	125	25	100	–	309
Composite	–	25	12	162	15	2	70	286
Third Class Brake	–	6	–	63	45	–	–	114
Composite Brake	–	31	–	92	22	–	–	145
Total	42	68	23	442	107	106	74	862

Note: This table does not include vehicles converted to lavatory style from non-lavatory style

Compiled by D. Jenkinson, February 1984

Plates 126 & 127 The Clayton arc roof lavatory stock was distinguished by displaying a multiplicity of length and compartment variations. Two typical examples are shown here. Midland No. 196 is a 47ft. third class to D488, Lot 224 (essentially a 43ft. seven compartment third, lengthened to provide the lavatory section), while No. 395 is a composite to D512, Lot 105, on the more common 45ft. underframe. Note the water tank on the roof. Both varieties are carried on the standard Clayton 8ft. bogies.

(NRM and BR/LMR)

There was a full third (compartment style), a third open for dining, gangwayed at one end to the kitchen car, a composite, also gangwayed to the kitchen car, and a composite brake (compartment style) with no fewer than five compartments and four lavatories as well as the brake van portion. The composite, adjacent to the kitchen car, was an odd design in that it was a mixture of open first for dining, plus compartment thirds with lavatories; but there was no access from the third class end to the first. Ten years later, these three were converted to a mixture of first and third class open plus compartment third.

Somewhat similar twelve wheel vehicles were also ordered in 1897 for the St. Pancras to Manchester and the St. Pancras to Bradford services, again in rather small quantities and again embodying excellent provisioning for both first and third class travellers.

We do not know if the Midland Railway built these early twelve wheelers specifically to test the market, as it were, or had already decided to adopt the new style for common user designs as well, but it was not long before considerable additional numbers of coaches were put into service. In late 1897 and early 1898, the large scale adoption of clerestories began with the almost simultaneous introduction of six wheel thirds and composites together with a very considerable number of 48ft. bogie composites. The latter were either given brake or luggage compartments. The six wheelers numbered less than two dozen and were built mainly for the Bradford and Manchester services. They were, presumably, not felt worth repeating but in 1898, bogie thirds and brake thirds were added, plus more composites, to a slightly different design. Thereafter until 1901, substantial numbers of all four types were added each year to the lists but full firsts were never built, either plain or brake-ended.

A measure of the quantitative significance of this construction, by Midland Railway standards, is the fact that the period from 1896 to 1901 saw the building of over half of the total lavatory non-corridors ever owned by the Company, and all were to the Clayton square-panelled style. Composites somewhat outnumbered thirds and the balance between brake-ended and non-brake vehicles, of either category, was some 1:2.

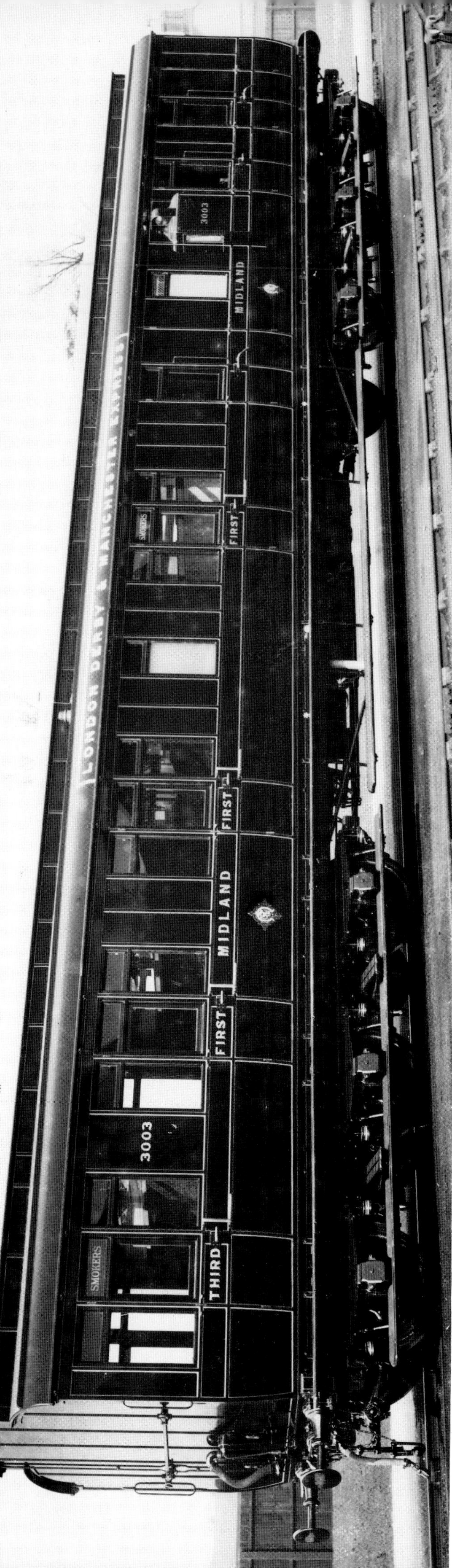

Plate 128 This superb view of one of the first generation Clayton lavatory clerestories shows 60ft. brake composite No. 3003 to D518, one of two built for the Manchester services. The original print clearly shows the lining on the clerestory side panels and solebars/headstocks. Note also the two-tone roof (black below raintstrip, grey above) and the 'smokers' indication above some of the doors. The prominent 'first generation' guard's look-out is also noticeable *(see also Plate 18, Chapter 1)*. This was later removed and ultimately substituted by a slightly less dominant fitting *(see Figure 38 and Plate 134, below)*.

(BR/LMR)

For a few years afterwards, corridor coach construction was more dominant in the long-distance field and, apart from a number of 50ft. brake composites (some of them for slip working) in 1902/3, no square light lavatory clerestories were built with the Bain modifications. However, the Bain period did see additions to the lavatory fleet at intermittent intervals. Most of these were thirds or brake thirds, now 54ft. long, and until 1913 all were round-panelled clerestories.

First were batches of brake thirds and brake composites in 1905, the brake thirds having but three compartments and a large van portion, so clearly intended for longer-distance work. Then an odd pair of 'slip' brakes in 1906 was followed in 1907/8 by an interesting new idea - fifteen pairs of lavatory coaches (full composites and brake thirds to Lots 691/2). These were destined for operation as two coach sets in the North of England and probably set the style for the, later to be familiar, 'Inter-District' lavatory sets used widely by the LMS. Interestingly, at much the same period in history, the LNWR was building somewhat similar sets but usually of three or four coaches with a rather smaller proportion of first class accommodation.

Clearly, the Midland Railway did attract a higher than average number of first class passengers and even when coaches were supplied to the Midland Division in LMS days, a higher proportion of first class was demanded than for the ex-LNWR and ex-L&YR lines. This caused some problems in rationalizing set formations after 1923 as we have already indicated in our book on LMS coaches.

As we have seen, the final Bain period saw the first moves to the full height roofs and the last Midland Railway lavatory stock was built to this profile during Reid's period of office. All but four were composites of which 58 were to Diagram 1245. They were 54ft. by 8ft. 6in. and were built for general service during the 1914-22 period, most of them probably after the war. The other twelve composites were also 54ft. vehicles but were built in small batches *(see Table 8)* and were 9ft. wide. Three separate diagrams were involved and all were built as part of new set trains for the LT&S services. These vehicles closely anticipated LMS practice but were not precisely identical to their LMS descendants.

Reverting to the Bain round-panelled carriages, the 'class' balance was somewhat redressed in 1912/3 with, by Midland Railway standards, a huge build of lavatory thirds totalling 125 vehicles. These carriages are a little confusing to analyse since they involved four separate diagrams, D1056, D1057, D1060 and D1053, in that order.

Diagram 1056 was a conventional Bain clerestory type to the 54ft. length and Diagram 1057 had an identical layout, but with Bain arc roof. The other two were 50ft. long vehicles of otherwise similar layout, also with arc roofs. Designed for excursion use, Diagram 1060 was 9ft. wide and Diagram 1053 was of 8ft. 6in. width. Further details are given in *Table 8* but it is worth noting that one or two of Diagram 1056 were later rebuilt with full elliptical roofs and some of the others went into ambulance use.

During the later Bain period, in 1914, the Midland Railway introduced a full lavatory first class design, also with arc roof, to Diagram 1049. This was a batch of four, 48ft. coaches, 9ft. wide for the Tilbury line boat trains. Finally, in 1922, another four full firsts (54ft. x 9ft.) were put into service, again as part of the re-equipment programme for the LT&S routes.

Plate 129 This is one of only two or three surviving official views of Bain round-panelled non-corridor stock - all of which feature the lavatory brake composite No. 2951 to D521 when new, circa 1906. The livery style is transitional to the new post-1906 order with unlined clerestory/underframe and the new position and style of Company ownership. However, the class markings (later to become large numerals on the lower doors). still conform to the older arrangement. The coach did not reach the LMS, having been converted to either ambulance or full brake use in 1917. Another view is given at *Plate 25.*

(BR/LMR)

Summing up the situation, therefore, it can be seen that the non-corridor lavatory coach played a significant part in Midland Railway operations both for general service and, also, for specific services (e.g. the early six and twelve wheelers and the final LT&S build). At the time of the Grouping, few of even the earlier clerestories were life-expired and much of the fleet was only 10-15 years old, so it is not surprising that the vast majority lasted well into LMS days and most received numbers in the rational 1933 series, including even some of the 1897 six wheelers.

As a consequence, the LMS, which had also inherited some other fine modern lavatory stock, particularly from the LNWR, did not find it necessary to build very many more coaches in this particular category, although it continued to make use of the type for many years. Increasingly, as more gangwayed stock came into use on the main lines in the 1920s and 1930s, there was a cascading effect upon the non-gangwayed types and some quite humdrum local services found themselves provided with spacious lavatory coaches of Midland Railway origin as years went by. Like the early Midland dining carriages, they seemed particularly popular on the Highland lines where they replaced some pretty dreadful and spartan vehicles on the local and branch line services. For modellers, therefore, an odd ex-Midland Railway lavatory composite or third would not look too out of place on almost any model based on LMS practice in the 1920s.

Plate 130 This view shows Bain clerestory lavatory third No. M18831M (ex-MR first LMS No. 383) at Stockport in 1955. This was one of over 100 lavatory thirds built during 1912/13 and alluded to on *page 99.*

T. J. Edgington

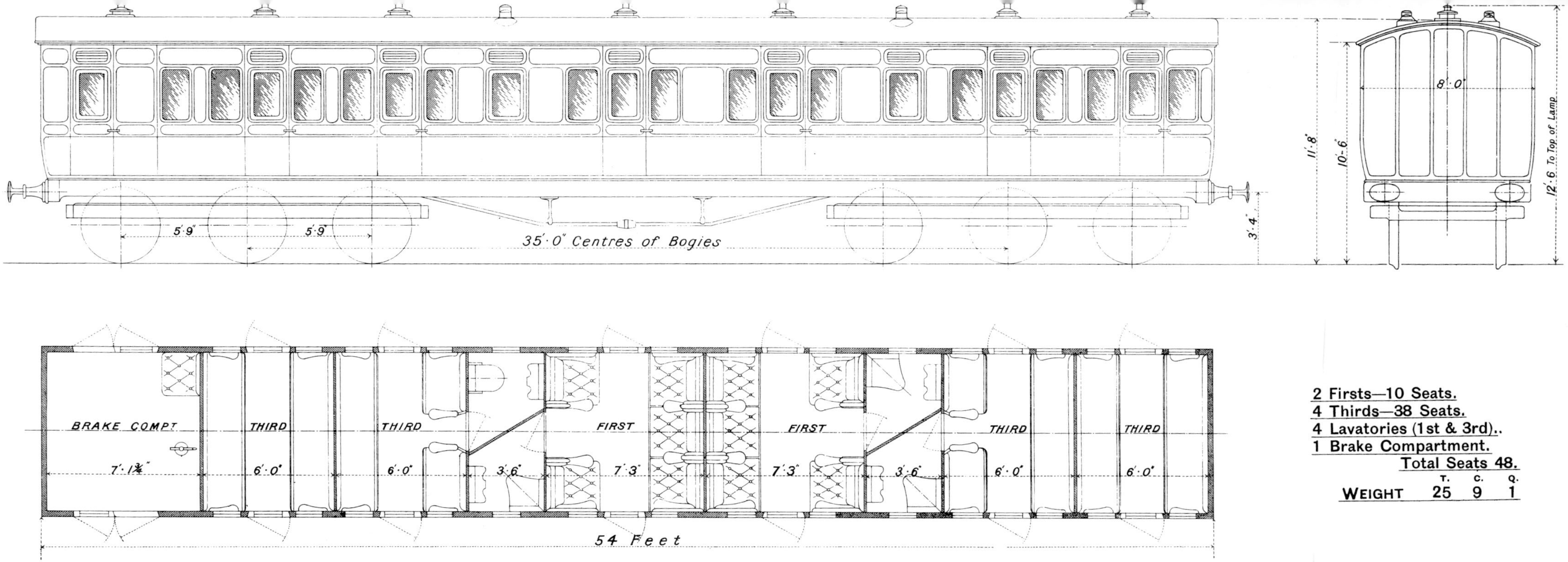

35'·0" Centres of Bogies

5'·9" 5'·9" 3'·4" 11'·8" 10'·6" 8'·0" 12'·6" To Top of Lamp

BRAKE COMPT 7'·1¾" THIRD 6'·0" THIRD 6'·0" 3'·6" FIRST 7'·3" FIRST 7'·3" 3'·6" THIRD 6'·0" THIRD 6'·0"

54 Feet

2 Firsts—10 Seats.
4 Thirds—38 Seats.
4 Lavatories (1st & 3rd)..
1 Brake Compartment.
Total Seats 48.

	T.	C.	Q.
WEIGHT	25	9	1

Figure 35 and Plate 131 *54ft. lavatory composite brake to D522.* We start our detailed survey of lavatory stock with a characteristic Clayton arc roof example. It is not very easy to select a typical type from this period since there were so many variations - especially if the later conversions of non-lavatory stock are included. We decided therefore, to show preference to modellers by featuring what were undoubtedly the longest lasting examples - the twelve wheel brake composites built to Lot 359 in 1896, a type which survived well into the LMS period, not becoming extinct until 1936 *(see also Table 8)*. The photograph of No. 484 and the diagram are self explanatory and all principal visible features conformed to the detailed drawings at *Figure 2, page 5.* Scale: 4mm. = 1ft.

(K. C. Woodhead Collection and NRM)

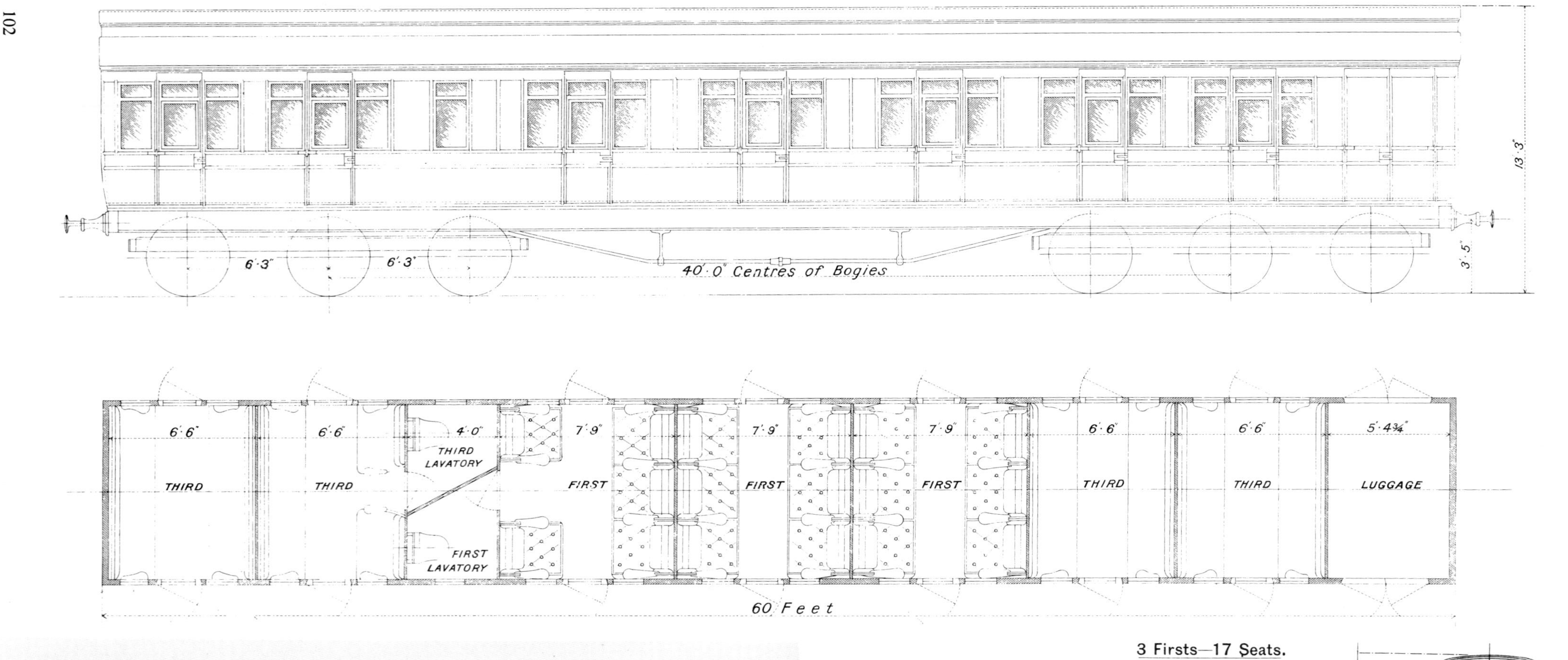

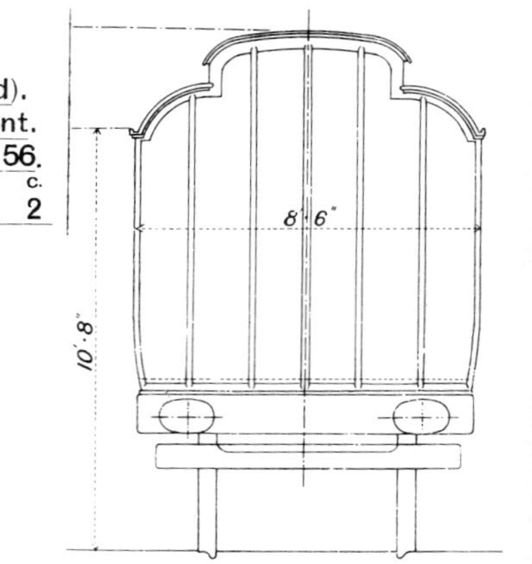

3 Firsts—17 Seats.
4 Thirds—39 Seats.
2 Lavatories (1st & 3rd).
1 Luggage Compartment.
Total Seats 56.

	T.	C.	C.
WEIGHT	30	12	2

Figure 36 and Plate 132 *60ft. lavatory composite to D506.* Although the Clayton clerestory non-corridor twelve wheelers were relatively few in number, it seemed logical to include at least one example because of their importance in setting the style for much which was to follow. The choice has fallen upon D506, mainly because it was the most common variety, but also because the type lasted well into the 1930s. The surviving official picture is of indifferent quality but, together with the diagram and the more detailed drawing at *Figure 3* should enable interested modellers to produce an acceptable representation. The coach illustrated is MR and first LMS No. 3014, later No. 03014, second LMS No. 19814. Scale:

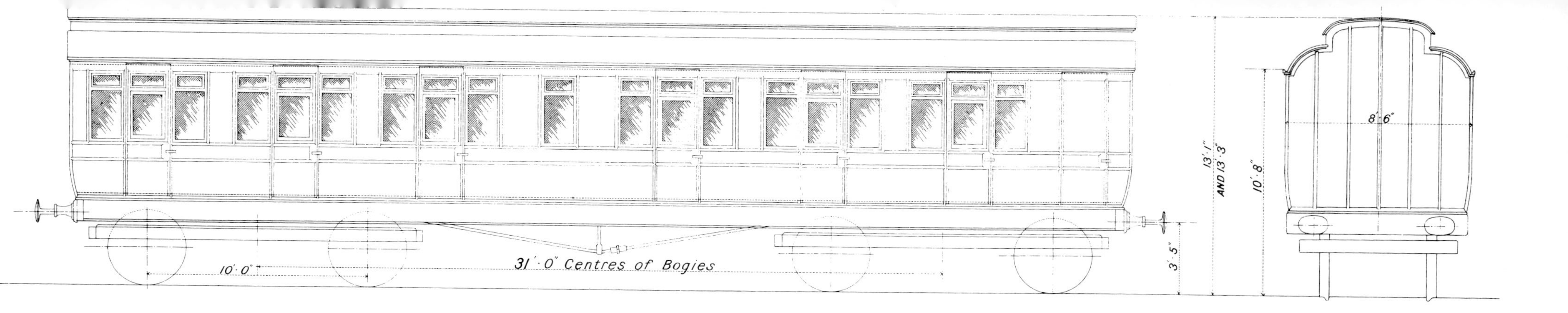

6 Thirds—58 Seats.
2 Third Lavatories.
1 Luggage Compartment.

	T.	C.	Q.
WEIGHT	22	13	3

Clayton 'Express' Lavatory Stock

The eight wheel square-panelled clerestory non-corridor lavatory coaches were undoubtedly the most typical of all MR long-distance vehicles at the turn of the century. Most were built to a standard 48ft. length and two typical types are featured. Some of the later examples were to a 50ft. length and two of these variants are also covered in this section. Reference should be made to *Figure 3, page 12,* for additional dimensional data for this series of vehicles.

Figure 37 and Plate 133 Lavatory third class to D486. This design was, marginally, the most common single 48ft. lavatory clerestory design, *(see Figure 38 (overleaf))*. We have not been able to locate an official picture but the photograph we have found is particularly interesting. It shows one of these coaches (unidentified) forming part of a train leaving Settle, during World War I, with a load of volunteers for military service. Beyond the third class carriage is a 48ft. luggage composite to D508 - *(again see Figure 38)*. Scale: 4mm. = 1ft.

(K. C. Woodhead Collection and K. & J. Kelly, courtesy C. R. Davey)

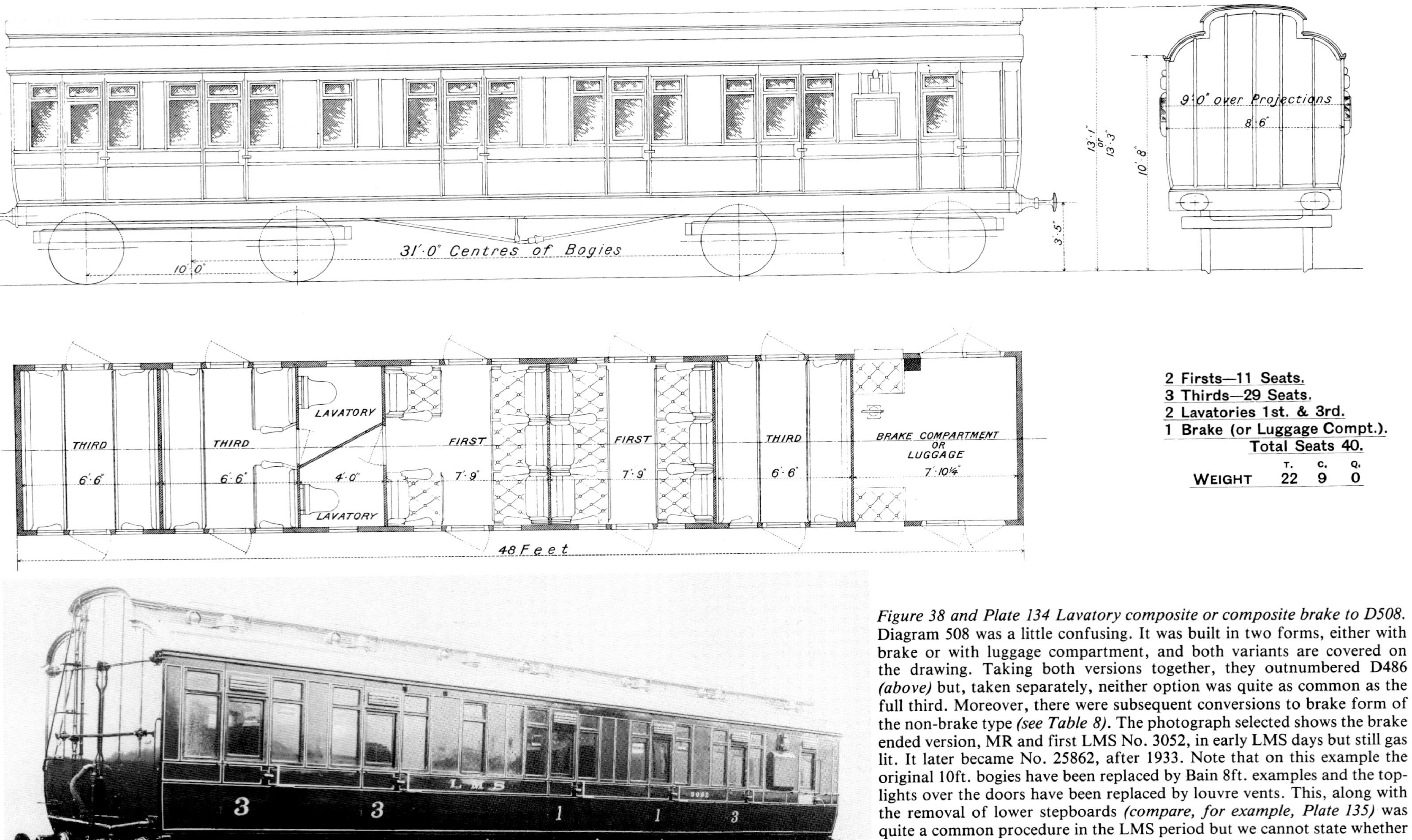

2 Firsts—11 Seats.
3 Thirds—29 Seats.
2 Lavatories 1st. & 3rd.
1 Brake (or Luggage Compt.).
Total Seats 40.

	T.	C.	Q.
WEIGHT	22	9	0

Figure 38 and Plate 134 Lavatory composite or composite brake to D508. Diagram 508 was a little confusing. It was built in two forms, either with brake or with luggage compartment, and both variants are covered on the drawing. Taking both versions together, they outnumbered D486 *(above)* but, taken separately, neither option was quite as common as the full third. Moreover, there were subsequent conversions to brake form of the non-brake type *(see Table 8)*. The photograph selected shows the brake ended version, MR and first LMS No. 3052, in early LMS days but still gas lit. It later became No. 25862, after 1933. Note that on this example the original 10ft. bogies have been replaced by Bain 8ft. examples and the top-lights over the doors have been replaced by louvre vents. This, along with the removal of lower stepboards *(compare, for example, Plate 135)* was quite a common procedure in the LMS period but we cannot state whether all vehicles were so treated. The removal of all lower stepboards (except below the axleboxes at the brake ends) and the substitution of louvre vents seems to have been well-nigh universal by the LMS, but many coaches retained their 10ft. bogies, save that the transverse leaf bolster springs were often changed to the more modern coil type bolster springs. Scale: 4mm. – 1ft.

35 This fascinating picture shows an example of D508, No. 938 (pre-1902 series) in
riage shops at Derby, circa 1900/01. It is a brake-ended version (note the sidelight) in
f the lack of raised guard's look-outs. For a short period (circa 1899 to 1902),
ing look-outs were removed from the new style clerestories to avoid fouling the load
The Clayton look-out on some of the early square-panelled clerestories was quite
ent *(see Plate 18)* and had caused clearance problems so it was omitted for a while. It
er redesigned to project rather less from the side of the carriage and, after this time,
a common enough feature - *see, for example, Plate 134 (opposite).* *(NRM)*

e 136 An unidentified
nple of brake composite to
3, *(see overleaf)* after
ng been 'slipped' at an
nown location. Note the
rvation window in the
age end.
(BR/LMR)

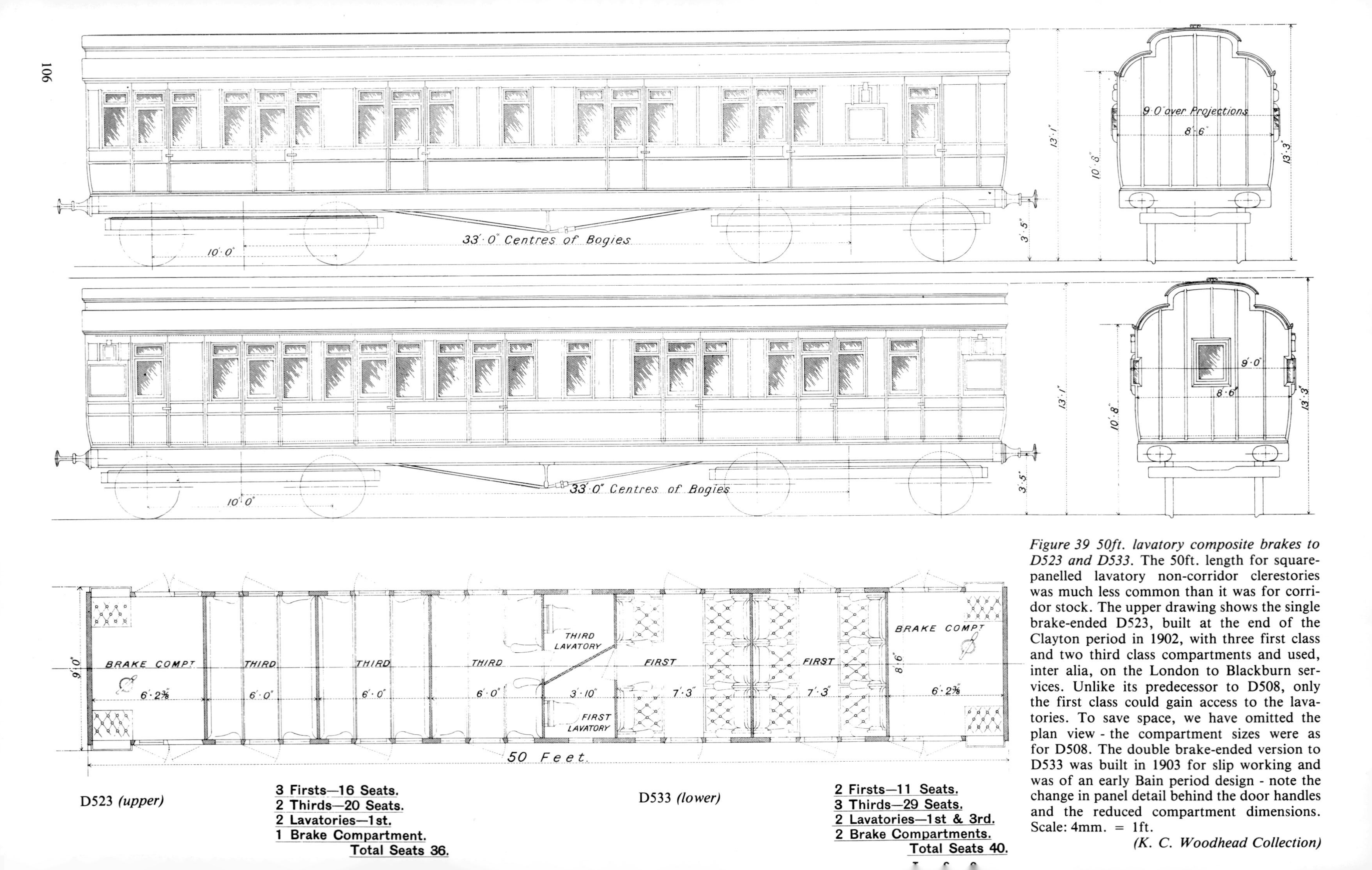

D523 *(upper)*

3 Firsts—16 Seats.
2 Thirds—20 Seats.
2 Lavatories—1st.
1 Brake Compartment.
Total Seats 36.

D533 *(lower)*

2 Firsts—11 Seats.
3 Thirds—29 Seats.
2 Lavatories—1st & 3rd.
2 Brake Compartments.
Total Seats 40.

Figure 39 50ft. lavatory composite brakes to D523 and D533. The 50ft. length for square-panelled lavatory non-corridor clerestories was much less common than it was for corridor stock. The upper drawing shows the single brake-ended D523, built at the end of the Clayton period in 1902, with three first class and two third class compartments and used, inter alia, on the London to Blackburn services. Unlike its predecessor to D508, only the first class could gain access to the lavatories. To save space, we have omitted the plan view - the compartment sizes were as for D508. The double brake-ended version to D533 was built in 1903 for slip working and was of an early Bain period design - note the change in panel detail behind the door handles and the reduced compartment dimensions. Scale: 4mm. = 1ft.

(K. C. Woodhead Collection)

Plates 137 & 138 (above & below) First and third class interior views of 50ft. brake composite to D523, MR and first LMS No. 3636, second LMS No. 25925.

(NRM)

Plate 139 An interior view of lavatory composite No. 3330 to D1245 *(overleaf)* showing the lavatory itself.

(NRM)

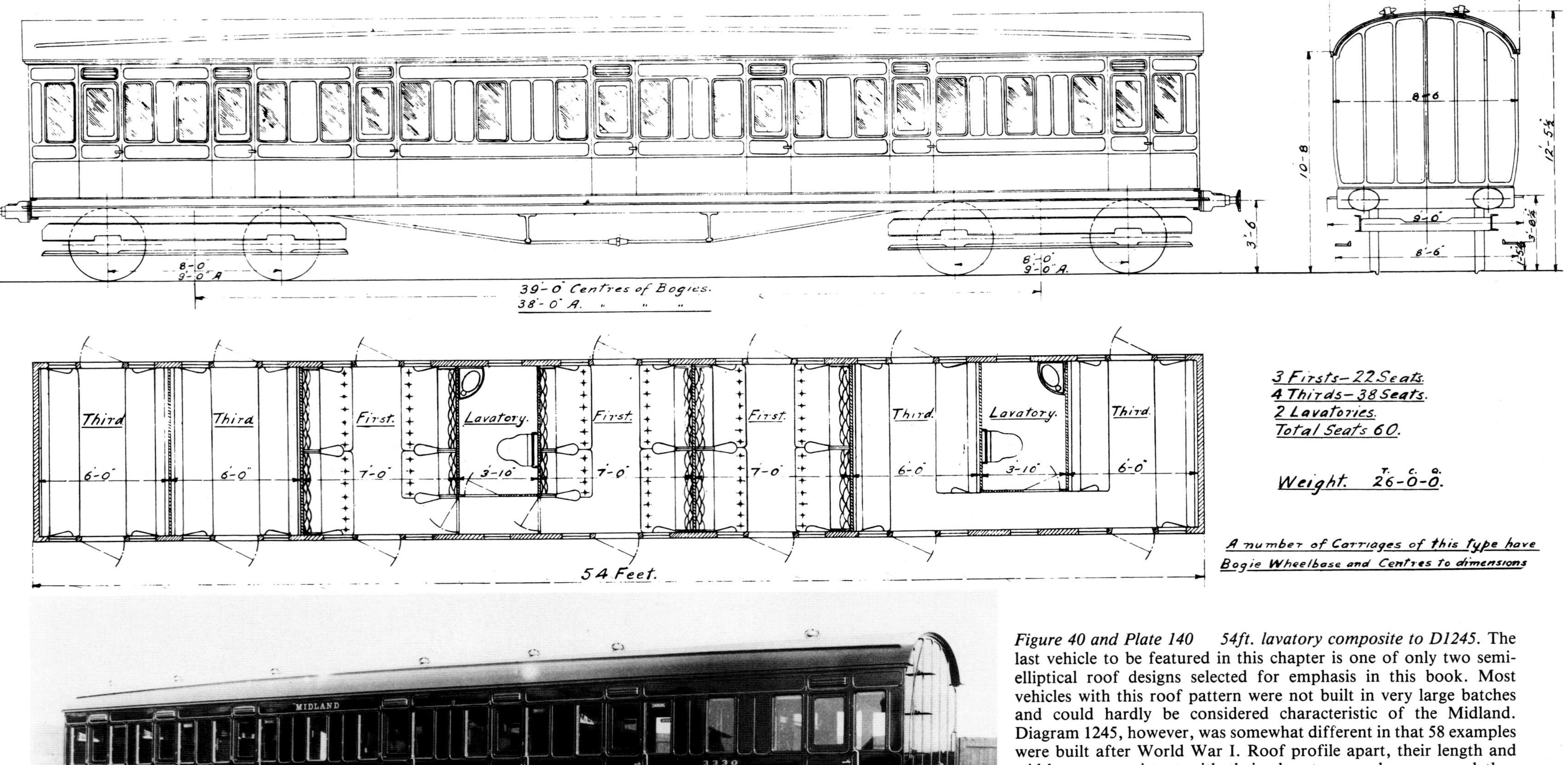

Figure 40 and Plate 140 *54ft. lavatory composite to D1245.* The last vehicle to be featured in this chapter is one of only two semi-elliptical roof designs selected for emphasis in this book. Most vehicles with this roof pattern were not built in very large batches and could hardly be considered characteristic of the Midland. Diagram 1245, however, was somewhat different in that 58 examples were built after World War I. Roof profile apart, their length and width were consistent with their clerestory predecessors and they were used in general service throughout the system. They do not seem to have been formed into sets with their contemporary non-lavatory thirds or brake thirds, and it seems likely that they were simply operated as required with older stock - probably to give more up-to-date accommodation to first class passengers. Some examples had the later pattern 9ft. bogies. The photograph shows MR and first LMS No. 3330, second LMS No. 19747, and we must apologize for the slight sub-standard quality of the official diagram. Scale: 4mm. = 1ft.

(BR/LMR)

TABLE 8
Summary of Midland Railway Non-Corridor Lavatory Stock

Diag.	Lot	Qty.	Date of order	Dimensions	Wt.	Style	Numbering		Type Extinct	Remarks
							Midland/1st LMS	2nd LMS		
First Class Lavatory (FL)										
1049	858	4	1914	48’ x 9’ 0”	25T	BA	2692; 2704/6–7	18187–90	11/60	Built for LT&S line boat trains.
1424	996	4	1922	54’ x 9’ 0”	27T	E	2505; 2512/4/7	18191–4	11/61	Anticipating LMS style but not quite the same. Nos. 18193–4 to NCC in 1942 as 5 and 7, later 353/181.
Third Class Lavatory (TL/TLZ*)										
488	224	6	1889	47’ x 8’ 0”	19T	CA	196 + five others			Essentially as D490 (7 x 3rd) but with lavatory bay (2 lavatories) added.
494*	225	22	1889	31’ x 8’ 0”	12½T	CA				Essentially as D493 (5 x 3rd) but with two lavatories replacing centre compartment. Six wheel.
	258	20	1890							
484	387	3	1896	60’ x 8’ 6”	31T	CC2	1861–3	18892–3	2/37	Originally built for Bristol–Bradford sets as part of first new style clerestory trains. Twelve wheel.
492*	414	11	1897	31’ x 8’ 6”	13½T	CC2	Various: 138–1191	27417-24	6/39	Originally built for London–Manchester and London–Bradford trains. Six wheel.
486	437	18	1898	48’ x 8’ 6”	22½T	CC2				Large ‘general service’ batches for express services. Although the type survived until late into the 1940s, the vast majority were withdrawn before the end of World War II, most of them by 1940/41.
	464	73	1899				Various: 289–2043	18664–777	7/48	
	499	31	1900							
1056	799	25	1912	54’ x 8’ 6”	27T	BC4	Various: 375–1372	18828–41	8/58	Eight were transferred to ambulance use in 1917 and there were a few more early withdrawals. At least one, 18840 (ex-1353) was given a replacement elliptical roof. Not known whether any others were so modified. No. 18828 (ex-375) became DM395031 in 1952 and is now preserved at Lakeside.
1057	804	50	1913	54’ x 8’ 6”	26T	BA	Various: 29–1393	18842–91	1/58	Internal layout identical to D1056 but built with Bain arc roof not clerestory.
1060	848	30	1913	50’ x 9’ 0”	24T	BA	Various: 764–1009	18778–807	10/58	Layout as for D10567 but shorter length and 9’ 0” wide (excursion use).
1053	850	20	1913	50’ x 8’ 6”		BA	Various: 1076–1253	18808–27	11/56	As D1060 but only 8’ 6” wide.
Composite Lavatory (CL/CLZ*)										
512	105	25	1884	45’ x 8’ 0”	18¾T	CA	395; 487 + 23 others			3 x 1st; 3 x 3rd; 2 x lavatories.
539	384	3	1896	60’ x 8’ 6”	31½T	CC2	3595–6; 3643	19807 (ex-03595)	9/40	Built for Bradford–Bristol service. Initial internal layout was TL+FO (dining section). Later converted to a combination of FO, TO and T (ordinary) plus lavatories. Twelve wheel.
506	406	10	1897	60’ x 8’ 6”	30½T	CC2	3005–14 (cyphered in LMS period)	19808–14	10/36	Built for London–Manchester and London–Bradford services. 3 x 1st; 4 x 3rd; 2 x lavatories; 1 x luggage. Twelve wheelers. First LMS numbers were cyphered to allow re-use of series for LMS built stock.
514*	424	12	1897	33’ 6” x 8’ 6”	14½T	CC2	3056–63	27443–5	11/36	Built alongside non-lavatory composites (CZ–D515) to two heights (3056–63 were 13’ 3” the rest 13’ 1”). 2 x 1st; 2 x 3rd; 2 x lavatories. Six wheel.
							3108–11	27446–8	12/36	
508	419	42	1897	48’ x 8’ 6”	22½T	CC2	Various: 3015–3251	19617–41	5/44	An unusual diagram with both CL and BCL on same diagram. Lots listed here were CL with luggage compartment. BCL version had brake compartment vice luggage – see below in BCL lots. Nos. 18659–63 were ex-Lot 497, downgraded to 3rd before 1933 and hence numbered in 3rd class series. Many were downgraded later, including all 18603–12 series. No. 19386 was Lot 419, overlooked (re-instated?) as 3102 pre-1933. Virtually all withdrawals were pre-World War II and only a few lasted until the mid-1940s.
	487	25	1900					19665–82	11/43	
	497	33	1900				3748–72	19642–64	12/46	
							plus:	18659–63 (see	12/46	
								19386 notes)	10/40	
509	428	27	1898	48’ x 8’ 6”	23T	CC2	Various: 3074–3156	19683–701	12/46	An alternative to D508 with 3 x 1st; 3 x 3rd; 2 x lavatories and no luggage compartment.
	496	16	1900				3207–22	19702–13	6/46	
	526	6	1901				Various 3603–35	19714–9	12/48	
520	691	15	1907	54’ x 8’ 6”		BC4	Various: 2814–3791	19724–38	5/52	Built alongside BTL to D550 as two-coach sets.
1245	882	58	1914 (see remarks)	54’ x 8’ 6”	26T	E	Various: 2946–3449	19739–96	6/62	Ordered as 50ft. vehicles, built as 54ft. and delivery took place between 1920 and 1922 because of cessation of activity during World War I. Last general service MR batch of this type.
1062	888	2	1915	50’ x 9’ 0”	26T	BA	3451/9	19722–3	3/57	Built for LT&S services: 3 x 1st; 3 x 3rd; 4 x lavatories.
1219	961	2	1921	48’ x 9’ 0”	24T	E	3858–9	19720–1	6/61	Built for LT&S services: 3 x 1st; 3 x 3rd; 2 x lavatories.
1280	965	6	1921	54’ x 9’ 0”	25T	E	3461–2/4/7/9–70	19797–802	6/61	Built for LT&S services, anticipating LMS type but not the same. Lots 980/989 delivered after the Grouping. Nos. 19801–3 latterly were all 3rd.
	980	1	1922				2619	19803	6/61	
	989	1	1922				2628	19804	10/57	
2085	979	1	1922	54’ x 9’ 0”	26T	E	2618	19805	6/61	Built for LT&S services and delivered in 1923.
	990	1	1922				2630	19806	2/62	
Third Class Lavatory Brake (BTL)										
	88	6	1883	54’ x 8’ 0”		CA	1369 + five others			Twelve wheel and mildly experimental. 6 x 3rd (one only with access to lavatory); 1 x Guard/Luggage.
496	392	2	1897	60’ x 8’ 6”	30½T	CC2	952 + one more	25669	9/34	Probably for Leeds and Manchester service. One destroyed at Wellingborough. Twelve wheel.
499	432	25	1898	48’ x 8’ 6”	22T	CC2	Various: 103–590	25571–94	7/46	Large ‘general service’ batches for express use. In spite of withdrawal data given, most examples had, in fact, gone before World War II. 4 x 3rd; 2 x lavatories. 1 x Guard/Luggage.
	488	25	1900				2090–2114	25596–607	7/44	
								26617–28	10/44	
	500	11	1900				164; Various: 145–1616	25595	7/46	
								25608–16	2/46	
498	610	30	1905	54’ x 8’ 6”		BC4	Various: 363–558; 1916	25630–53	6/52	Built simultaneously with BCL to D521 but not known whether designed to operate together. Six to ambulance use (1917). A strange design with only 3 x 3rd compartments and large luggage/brake area. Precise original utilization not known.
550	692	15	1908	54’ x 8’ 6”		BC4	Various: 290–375	25654–68	11/53	Built to operate in pairs with CL – D520 (above). Similar to D498 but 4 x 3rd; 2 x lavatory; 1 x brake. (NB: for LMS 25629 see BCL – D508 *(below)*.
Composite Lavatory Brake (BCL)										
527	149	10	1886	45’ x 8’ 0”	18¾T	CA				1 x 1st; 4 x 3rd; 2 x lavatories. 1 x Brake/Guard.
524	212	1	1888	56’ x 8’ 0”	25T	CA	916			Elegant ‘one-off’ for Paris exhibition. Twelve wheel vehicle to a length never repeated – 3 x 1st; 3 x 3rd; 4 x lavatories. 1x Brake/Guard.
522	359	20	1895	54’ x 8’ 0”	25½T	CA	484; Various: 3378–3594	25926–31	1/36 (see remarks)	Twelve wheel – 2 x 1st; 4 x 3rd; 4 x lavatories; 1 x Brake/Guard. Late survivors from Clayton arc roof period and one of them, LMS 25930 (ex-3587) not actually written off until May 1955 but as 3587! Probably not used for passenger purposes after mid-1930s.
517	386	3	1896	60’ x 8’ 6”	31¼T	CC2	829; 917–8, later 3654; 3717–8	25938–40	8/46	Twelve wheel for Bristol–Bradford services: 2 x 1st; 3 x 3rd; 4 x lavatory; 1 x Brake/Guard.
518	397	2	1897	60’ x 8’ 6”	30½T	CC2	3003–4	25937 (ex-3004)	4/39	Twelve wheel, similar to D517 in style but 3x 1st; 1 x 3rd; 2 x lavatories; 1 x Brake/Guard. Built for Manchester–St. Pancras (also Leeds–St. Pancras?) services.
508	420	50	1897	48’ x 8’ 6”	22½T	CC2	3026–55	25840–65	5/39	‘Express’ stock and the ‘other half’ of D508 (see CL – D508 (above)). The Lot 497 series were conversions to the BCL form of the CL version. Lot 498 were altered for ‘slip’ working c1905. Second series LMS No. 25629 had an extraordinary life. It began as CL to D508, was then converted to BCL – D508 and finally downgraded to BTL! The quoted number is in the BTL series.
							3179–38	25866–82	5/39	
	ex-497?	see CL D508	1900				3253/5	25883–4	5/38	
	498	9	1900				3256–64	25885–93	5/44	
	ex-497?	see CL D508	1900				3751/4; 3761/4; 3770	25894–8	11/43	
	527	9	1901				Various: 3597–3633	25899–907	11/43	
	ex-487	see CL D508	1900				3748	25629(see remarks)	8/37	
523	528	15	1901	50’ x 8’ 6”	23½T	CC2	Various: 3599–3636	25912–25	12/45	A variation of D508 with 3 x 1st; 2 x 3rd, hence extra length. Used (inter alia) for London–Blackburn services when first built.
533	547	4	1902	50’ x 8’ 6”	23½T	CC2	2815/24; 3348/70	25908–11	1/37	‘Double ended’ coaches for ‘slip’ working. Same amount of accommodation as D508 (2 x 1st; 3 x 3rd; 2 x lavatories) but two brake ends.
521	611	20	1905	54’ x 8’ 6”		BC4	Various: 2948–72	25932–6	7/60 (see remarks)	Built alongside D498 (BTL) with 2 x 1st; 4 x 3rd; 2 x lavatories; 1 x Brake. Ten went to ambulance use and five more to full brake. Of the five survivors, LMS 25936 was rebuilt with elliptical roof and was the last survivor. The last clerestory example went in 12/50.
535	657	2	1906	54’ x 8’ 6”		BC4				A pair of ‘double ended’ brakes for ‘slip’ working – c.f. D533 (above). Both to ambulance use in 1917. Other details not known.

Compiled by D. Jenkinson, December 1983

Chapter Seven

Non-corridor 'Ordinary' stock

During the steam era of Britain's railways, the non-corridor, non-lavatory coach was the archetypal vehicle on most systems, and the Midland Railway was no exception. Almost two thirds of its general service passenger fleet fell into this category which probably, in terms of the number of seats offered, represented some 75 per cent or more of the passenger carrying capacity of the system.

An analysis of the types introduced from 1877 onwards is given in *Table 9* from which it is immediately obvious that the balance was somewhat different both in classification and carriage style from the long-distance corridor and lavatory stock already considered.

Dealing first with style, the dominant type was, unquestionably, the Clayton arc roof vehicle, representing some 64 per cent of the total 'build' between 1877 and 1923 and of which almost two thirds were four or six wheel carriages. Most of them, of course, were built during the 1880s and early 1890s and, until the clerestory period, were the absolutely dominant type in any Midland Railway train, be it suburban or long-distance.

When the long-distance services began to be turned over to the new clerestory lavatory and corridor stock of the late 1890s, many of the Clayton arc roofs were by no means life-expired, so they were naturally 'cascaded' downwards to replace older vehicles of similar kind. Consequently, there was not the same need to build vast quantities of replacement 'ordinary' stock and new vehicles of this genre were relatively fewer than before. Those that were built during the Clayton to Bain clerestory period were, with but one solitary exception, square light clerestories, about a quarter of which were six wheelers. These mostly came into service around the turn of the century and, interestingly, a large proportion of the bogie coaches were built by outside contractors - the first time the Midland Railway had resorted to this method of procurement since the opening of the new carriage works.

Again, we are tempted to speculate that the reason for this was the fact that the works was fully occupied in building new long-distance coaches, including dining and other specialized vehicles. Equally, however, the constantly growing cities and towns served by the Midland system must have been placing ever increasing demands on suburban services as the commuting habit began to grow; so there was a short-term need for additional ordinary stock which could only be fully met by going to outside contractors.

What is certain is that after the first generation of new express lavatory and corridor stock had been put into service, the Midland Railway itself was able to turn the carriage works over to the volume production of ordinary carriages for shorter distance working. By now, Bain was well and truly established in succession to Clayton and embarked on a considerable programme of ordinary stock building which exhibited the new Bain arc roof style, mentioned on *page 17*.

Many of these carriages were, undoubtedly, replacements for the, by now, ageing six wheelers of the early Clayton period but, of course, being bogie vehicles they could seat far more passengers. In consequence, fewer absolute numbers of carriages were needed. Most were built for specific district needs such as Birmingham, Sheffield, Nottingham, etc., and exhibited subtle variations of panelling, compartment disposition, width, etc., within an overall recognizable house style. Further details are given in *Table 10* at the end of the chapter.

The final phase of Midland Railway 'ordinary' stock was represented by the fewer than 200 vehicles which displayed the semi-elliptical roof. These were predominantly, but not exclusively, built for services on the London, Tilbury & Southend line which the Midland Railway had acquired in 1912, along with some pretty ancient carriages. This re-equipment of the LT&S services tended to 'straddle' the railway Grouping of 1923 and we have already dealt with the LMS side of the story in our earlier book. Suffice it to say that the late MR/early LMS carriage replacement programme on the Tilbury line stood the test of time, most of the vehicles remaining in service until replaced by their electrified successors in the British Railways period.

TABLE 9
General Service Non-Corridor Ordinary Stock (Built1877 and subsequently)

Type \ Style	*Clayton Arc Roof*		*Square Panel Clerestory*		*Round Panel Clerestory*	*Bain Arc Roof*	*Elliptical Roof*	*Total*
	Four and Six Wheel	*Bogie*	*Six Wheel*	*Bogie*				
First Class	127	3	–	2	–	87	13	232
Third Class	834	350	100	90	–	163	105	1642
Composite	202	262	15	80	–	88	6	653
Third Class Brake	259	180 (1)	11	143	–	288	52	933 (1)
Composite Brake	30	78	–	23	1	13	–	145
Total	1452	873 (1)	126	338	1	639	176	3605 (1)

Notes: *(1) Including 30 early Clayton clerestories (pre-1880 build).*
(2) Table includes coaches built non-lavatory and subsequently converted to lavatory style.

Complied by D. Jenkinson, February 1984

Plates 141 & 142 Clayton arc roof six wheelers. These were very charcteristic vehicles and the more common types are reviewed later in the chapter. The pictures on this page represent designs not covered on *pages 116 to 118*. The full first No. 321 is to Lot 73 and was unusual in being to a 30ft. length. Brake composite No. 247 was to D534. It had the same accommodation as D516 *(see page 116)* but, being fitted with a handbrake, the van portion was moved to the end of the coach with an additional look-out window. These vehicles were often used for slip working.

(BR/LMR and NRM)

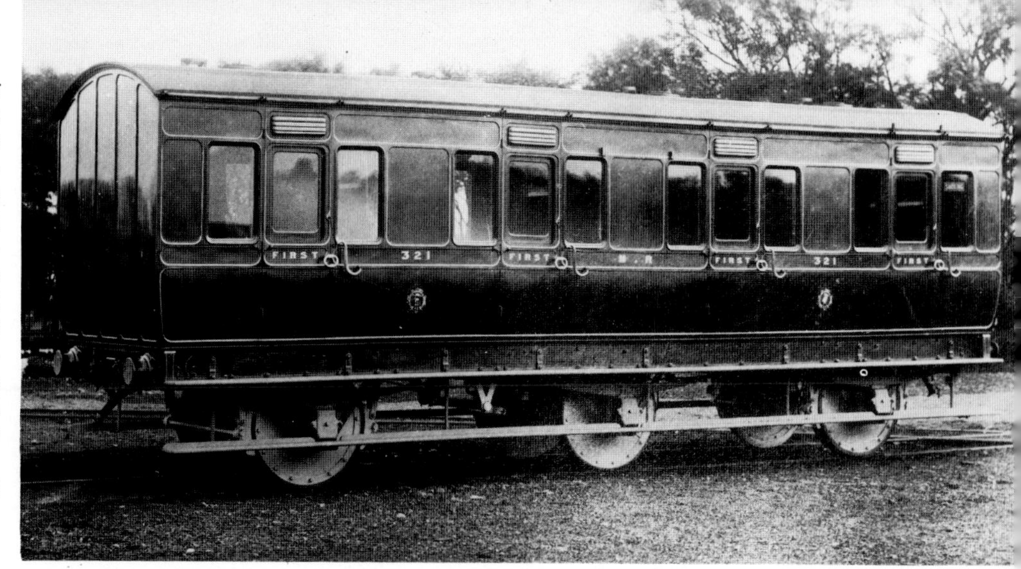

Plate 143 A small group of Clayton six wheelers were built to a lower height for use on the West Bridge branch. This picture shows brake third No. 1247 - part of Lot 201 and included on D504.

(NRM)

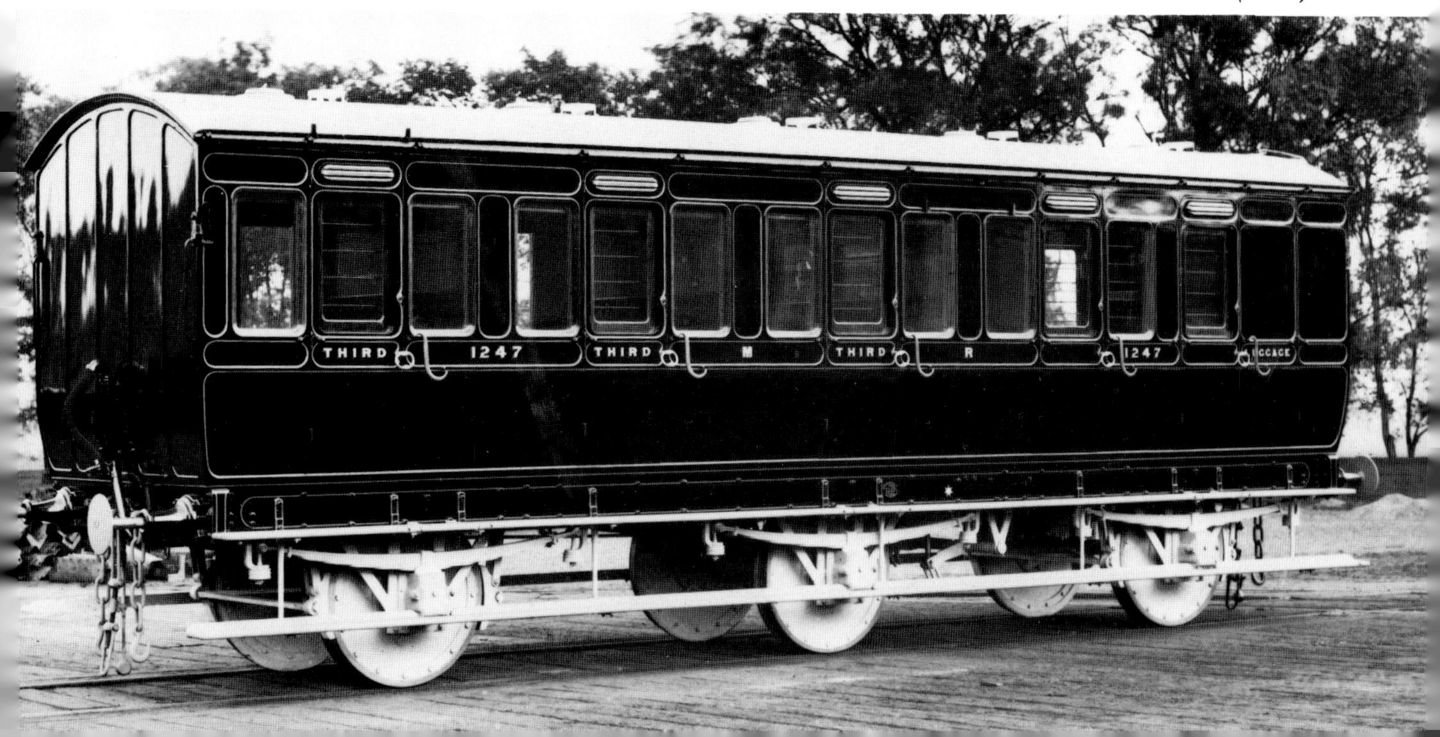

Plates 144 to 146 Clayton 40ft. stock. These views show some typical early Clayton arc roof bogie coaches. The upper picture shows brake third No. 1409 to Lot 5 - note the 'American' bogies. The two other vehicles are composites with Midland pattern bogies. The centre view depicts No. 114 to Lot 16 - a five compartment type identical to Lots 25 & 83. Lot 69 was visually also identical but classified as brake composite. Finally, the lower picture shows a four compartment brake composite No. 198 to D528.

(BR/LMR)

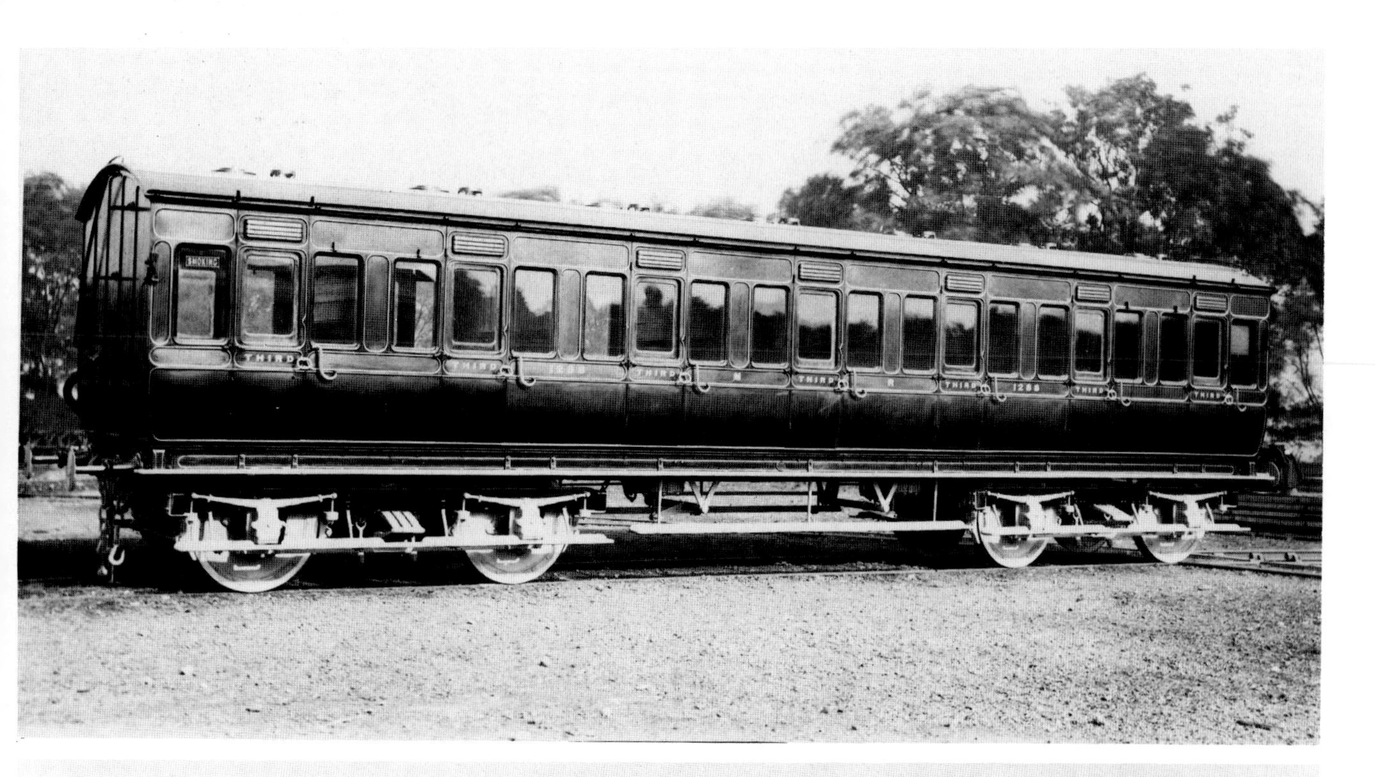

Plates 147 & 148 Clayton 43ft. stock. The next stage in evolution was to 43ft. and 45ft. length. These are additionally featured on *pages 119 to 120.* The two designs shown here are the standard 43ft. seven compartment third class to D490 (MR No. 1288) and 43ft. composite No. 316 of Lot 86. This vehicle was essentially a 43ft. version of the 45ft. Lot 79 *(see Plate 161),* with one fewer first class compartment and one extra third class.

(BR/LMR)

Turning now to the class 'balance' within Midland Railway ordinary carriages, one can immediately notice, from *Table 9*, a higher number of third class only vehicles than in the corridor and lavatory stock fleets and also a somewhat smaller total proportion of brake-ended vehicles. Ordinary stock was used over shorter distances in the main, and was utilized predominantly by travellers going to and from work, or on other similar journeys which did not need vast amounts of luggage space. There was, therefore, no great need for numerous luggage compartments of high carrying capacity. Separate through carriages incorporating their own brake/luggage compartments were rare to non-existent, so most non-corridor non-lavatory trains were undoubtedly operated with sets of coaches containing the statutory minimum number of brake vehicles.

The heavier emphasis on third class is undoubtedly a reflection of the commuter nature of much of the stock. Then, as now, more people used the train for getting to work than for long-distance travelling; and for home-to-office purposes, there was every economic incentive to travel as cheaply as possible. Moreover, the Midland Railway's third class was of a very high quality.

What is perhaps still noteworthy is that in spite of the analysis offered in the preceding two paragraphs, there was still a considerable proportion of first class and composite carriages within the Midland Railway's ordinary stock, approaching some 30 per cent of the total number of vehicles available which in seat terms, offered perhaps 15-20 per cent of the overall seating capacity to the first class traveller. We have not been able to make comparative analyses of the other contemporary railways in this respect, but we feel it probable that the proportion of first class, even on the most humble trains was probably above average for the period.

In the more detailed survey of types which follows, we have attempted to concentrate on the more numerous and, by definition, more typical 'ordinary' carriages operated on the Midland system, but the tabular summary *Table 10* includes all types we can identify from the 1877-1923 period.

Footnote: The detailed survey begins at the foot of *page 115*, following two pages of pictures to complete the general survey.

Plate 149 The arc roof Clayton twelve wheelers were rather fine vehicles and much used for long-distance work in the 'pre-lavatory' era. This picture shows full first No. 36, one of three identical carriages to Lot 89.

(BR/LMR)

Plate 150 Virtually all the non-corridor, non-lavatory clerestories built around the turn of the century were square-panelled, many by contractors. This view shows a 45ft. composite to D511, No. 3205, built by the Lancaster C. & W. Co. It became LMS No. 17272 after 1933.

Authors' Collection

Plates 151 & 152 Official views of most varieties of the Bain arc roof suburban series are notable by their absence, so it is necessary to use these less than perfect pictures to illustrate the essential differences in profile between the 8ft. 6in. and 9ft. wide series. The upper view shows an unidentified four compartment 48ft. brake third to D552, Lot 801 *(see also page 132)* of the 8ft. 6in. wide stock, while below is seen a five compartment brake third of the 9ft. wide series to D556. This was, in fact, one of the 50ft. long vehicles for the Bedford services and the carriage illustrated (LMS No. 23198 - ex-MR No. 1202) is seen after conversion as part of the experimental three coach articulated set, which paved the way for the LMS standard articulated coaches of 1937. The other two coaches in the set are third class No. 14234 (ex-MR No. 763 to D555) and first class No. 10529 (ex-MR No. 2550 to D553), also from the 50ft. x 9ft. Bedford service.

(Authors' Collection)

'late 153 (above) This is one of the few surviving official ictures of Bain arc roof suburban stock. It shows the some-'hat rare 48ft. x 9ft. full first to D1054, No. 2609 (second MS No. 10503). Only three were built, all for the LT&S ervices. They were, in essence, a 9ft. version of D481 *(see age 134).*

(BR/LMR)

Plate 154 (below) The final Midland non-corridor designs were, to all intents and purposes, indistinguishable from LMS standard stock - indeed the last to be built did not appear until 1923. Such a vehicle is shown here at the end of a train - 54ft. brake third, LMS No. 470 (second LMS No. 23269) to D2086. Only the five compartment layout reveals its Midland origin -the LMS standard versions having either six or seven.

Authors' Collection

Clayton Six Wheel Arc Roof Stock

We start our detailed survey of types *(overleaf)* with the ries of vehicles which probably characterized the Midland specially in the 19th century) more than any other carriages. fully detailed drawing of the third class version to D493/494 given at *Figure 2 in Chapter 1* and this is supplemented here diagrams of two more typical varieties. Essentially, the rriages were designed mostly to be made up into set trains ilizing two third brakes plus as many full thirds and full firsts as required. The lavatory conversions of some of them came later while luggage composites were in great demand for longer distance use, many of them being built for the Joint Stock.

Except for the outer ends of the brake thirds, vehicles regularly used in 'block' trains of six wheelers were fitted with short buffers to allow close-coupling (hence the alternatives shown on the diagrams).

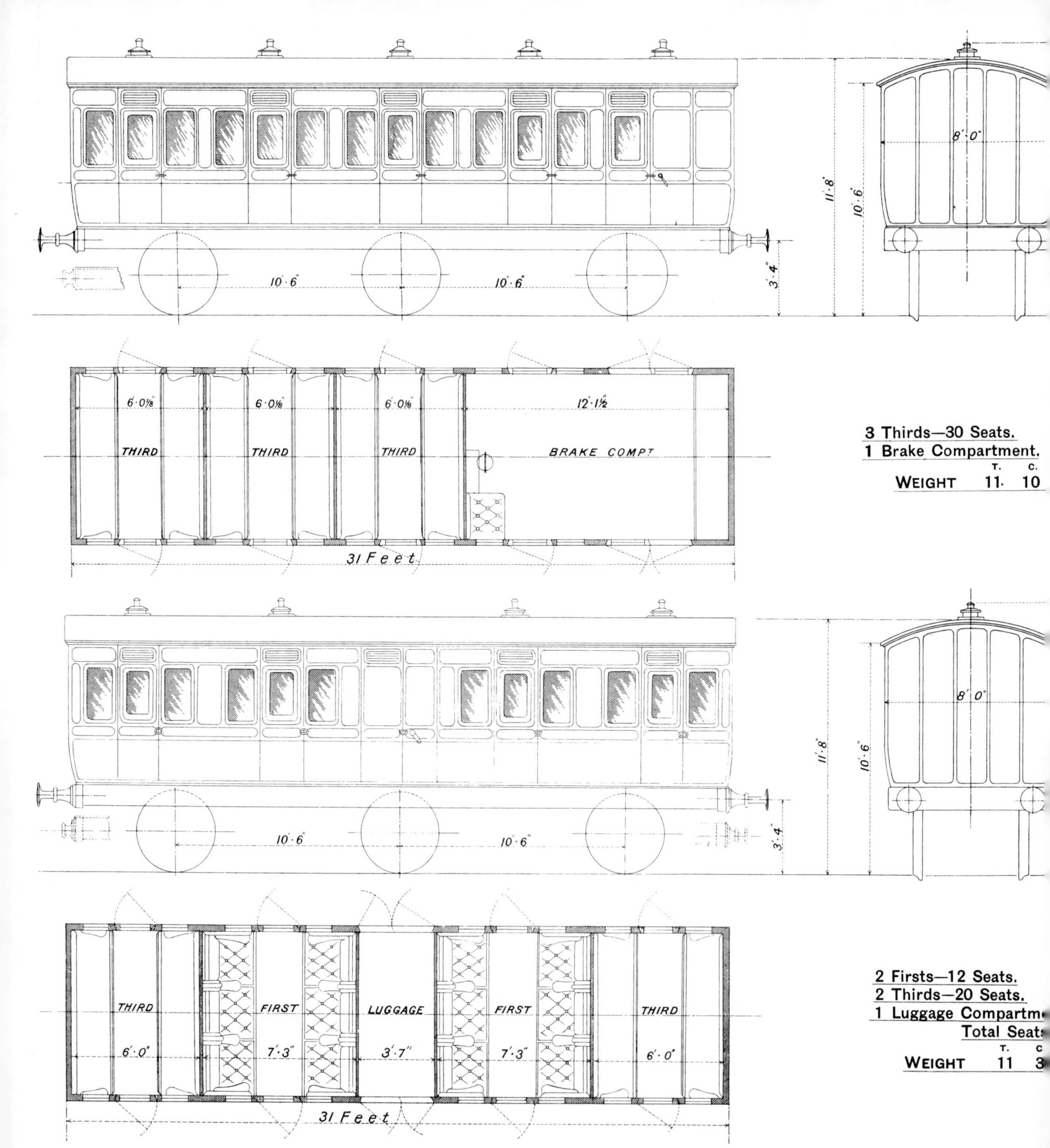

Figure 41 The upper drawing shows brake thi D504 - of which over 200 were built, some survivi reach the second LMS number series *(see Tabl* The lower drawing is the centre luggage compos D516 of the type preserved by the National Ra Museum. Some of these had the luggage compart replaced by two lavatories but no new diagram issued. Scale: 4mm. = 1ft.

(K. C. Woodhead Colle

Plates 157 (this page) & 158 (opposite) MSJS N represents the luggage composite to D516. Like No. 8 *(Plate 156)*, this vehicle was built in Scotl this time by the NBR at Cowlairs in 1883. MR Nc is the alternative version with the luggage compart converted to a central lavatory.

(BR/LMR &

Plates 155 & 156 (above) These two views show the brake third to D504, No. 865, as per the diagram, and the full, five compartment third class to D493, MSJS No. 8. The centre lavatory version of this vehicle to D494 is given in full detail at *Figure 2, page 4.* MSJS No. 8 was actually built by the GSWR at Kilmarnock in 1883.

(BR/LMR)

Plates 159 & 160 The interior view shows the sumptuous first class compartment of composite MR No. 901 to D516 as built. The preserved example at the National Railway Museum was restored by reference to this picture. The exterior view shows two D516 composites enlarged from a general picture of an Anglo-Scottish train of the 1890s. The nearer example (MSJS No. 43) shows the lavatory version and the further example (MSJS No. 24 or 34), the original form. Note that both have been fitted with replacement hooded metal door ventilators - a quite common practice.

(NRM)

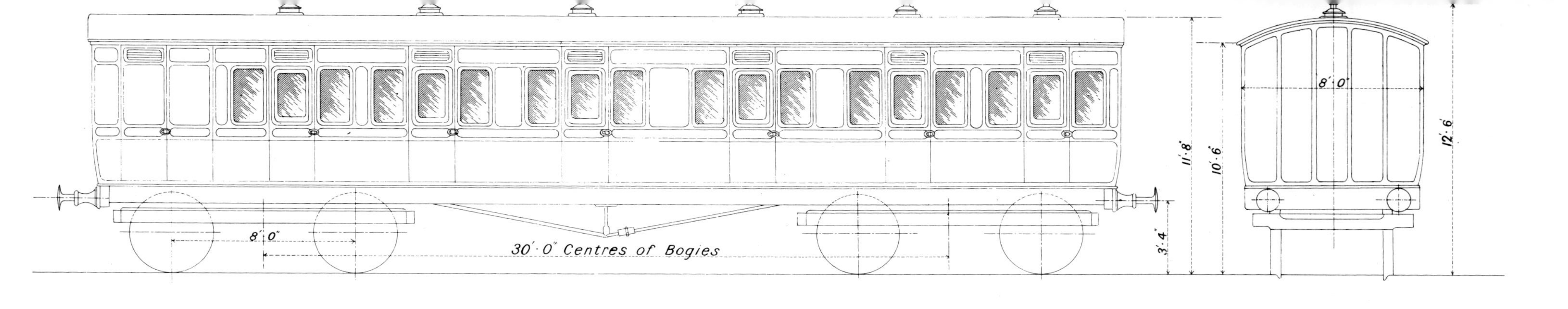

Clayton Bogie Arc Roof Stock

The Clayton bogie arc roof carriages shared their visual lines with the six wheelers. They were considerably less common and, originally, mostly used on longer distance workings. Lengths varied a little, as already explained, but since this variation was almost entirely related to the number, class and disposition of the compartments, it is not too difficult for modellers to derive other varieties from the examples featured.

Figure 42 and Plate 161 45ft. composite brake to D526. No apology is offered for featuring yet another brake composite type. The Midland had many composites but, more importantly, by using this drawing it is possible to derive a number of associated types. The full composite to D513 was built to the same drawing. Instead of the brake van portion, it had a separate luggage compartment and an extra third class compartment but otherwise displayed the same external features. In fact, the brake version shown may even have been rebuilt from D513. The 43ft. third brakes to D502 were virtually the same again but with equal sized compartments (hence the shorter length), while the 45ft. composites to Lot 79 (illustrated here by MR No. 6) were again almost identical, except that the luggage compartment was a foot or so narrower to allow for the additional first class compartment. MR No. 6 was later altered to lavatory form, by conversion of the left-hand first class compartment into two lavatories to serve both classes of passenger. Scale: 4mm. = 1ft.

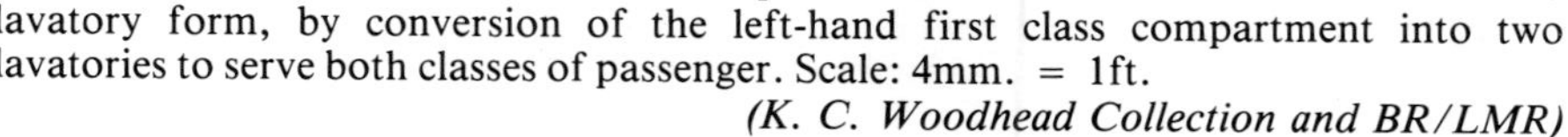

(K. C. Woodhead Collection and BR/LMR)

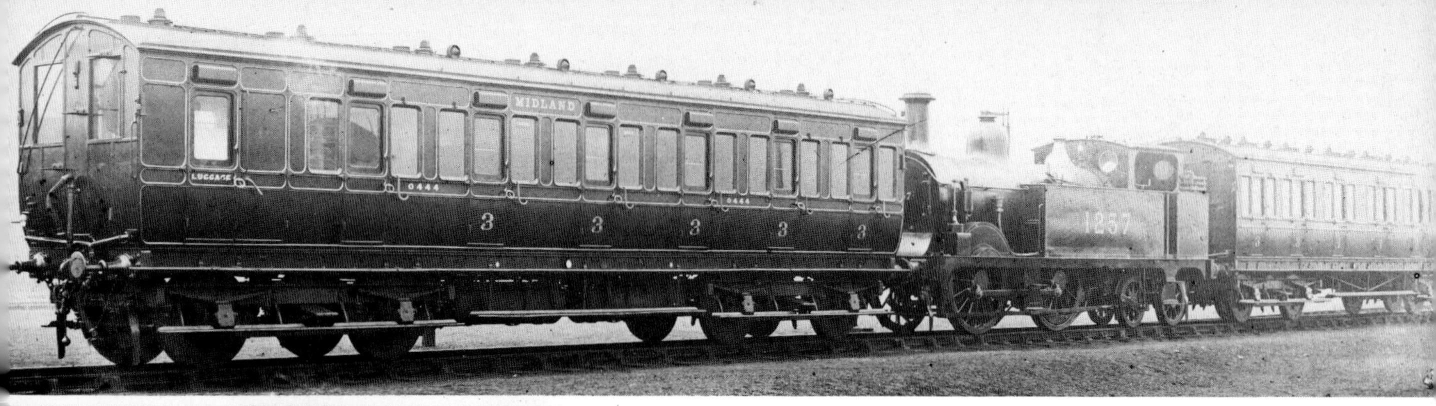

Plates 162 to 164 This group of pictures has been selected to emphasize more of the points made at *Figure 42.* The picture *(above)* shows a Midland push-pull set consisting of 0-4-4-T No. 1257 between converted examples of a 43ft. to D502 (third class brake, nearer end), and a 45ft. to D513/526 (composite, far end). Note the replacement door vents and later style livery. The vehicles are numbered 0444 and 3543 respectively. The interior view shows the driving end of one of these conversions whilst the picture of MR No. 429 shows a 43ft. brake third to D502 as built. Note the general similarity to the 45ft. to D526 at *Figure 42*, except that with the 43ft. and shorter series, the central underframe queen post and truss rods were not always fitted.

(BR/LMR)

Plate 165 Yet another variation is shown by this lavatory conversion of third class brake No. 537 to D502.

(NRM)

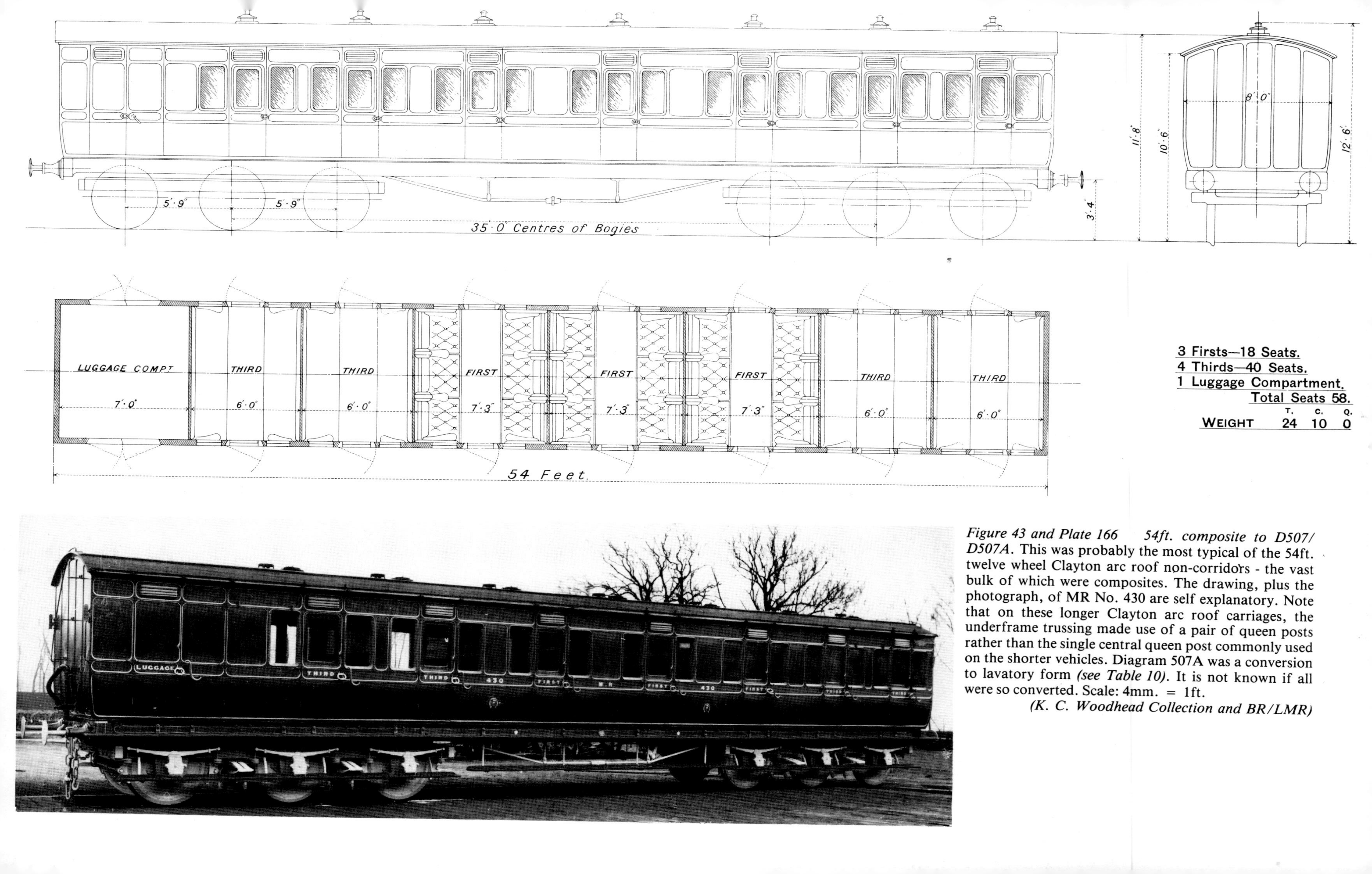

Figure 43 and Plate 166 *54ft. composite to D507/ D507A*. This was probably the most typical of the 54ft. twelve wheel Clayton arc roof non-corridors - the vast bulk of which were composites. The drawing, plus the photograph, of MR No. 430 are self explanatory. Note that on these longer Clayton arc roof carriages, the underframe trussing made use of a pair of queen posts rather than the single central queen post commonly used on the shorter vehicles. Diagram 507A was a conversion to lavatory form *(see Table 10)*. It is not known if all were so converted. Scale: 4mm. = 1ft.

(K. C. Woodhead Collection and BR/LMR)

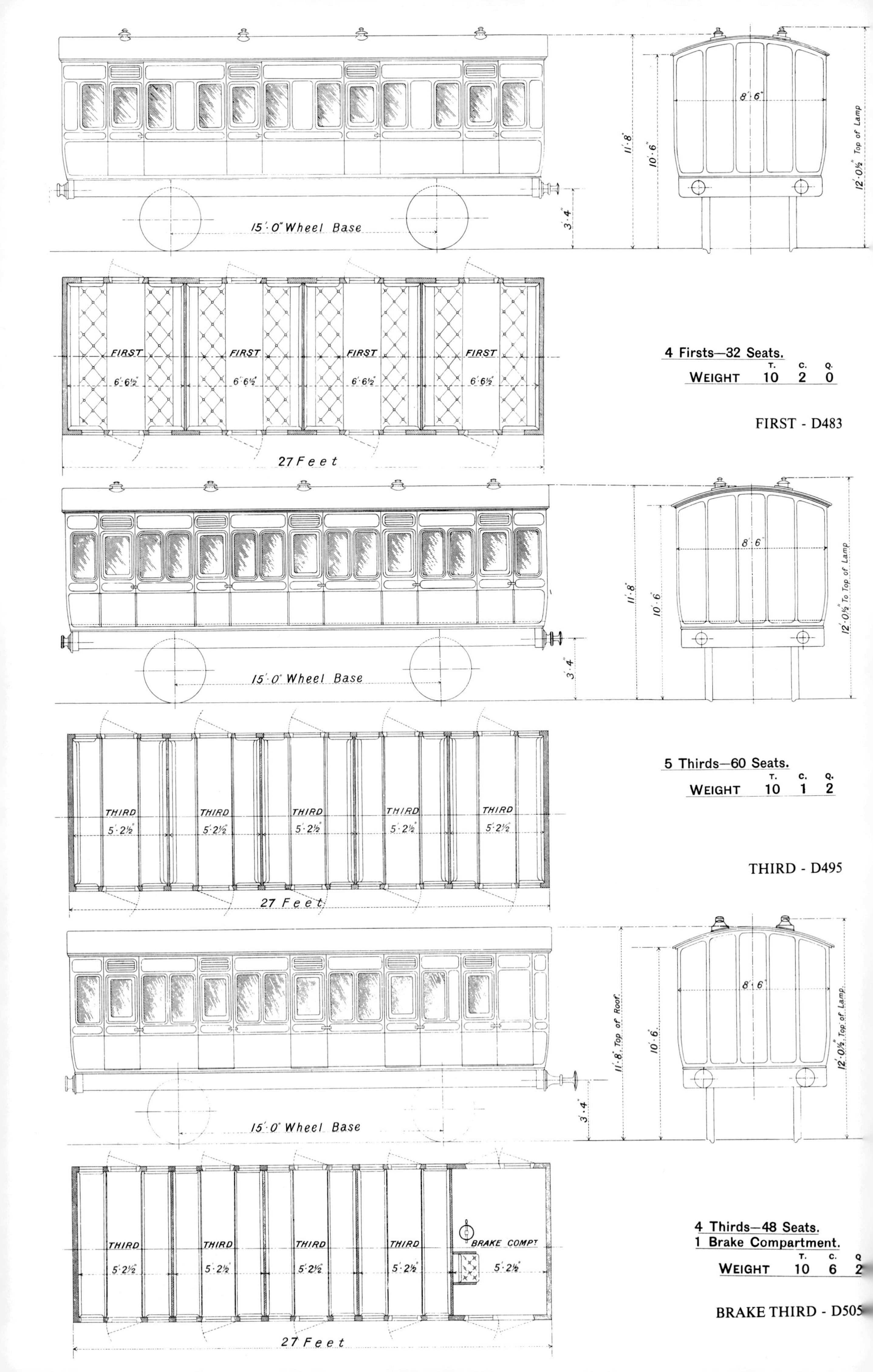

15' 0" Wheel Base
3' 4"
11' 8"
10' 6"
8' 6"
12' 0½" Top of Lamp
FIRST
6' 6½"
27 Feet
4 Firsts—32 Seats.
WEIGHT T. 10 C. 2 Q. 0
FIRST - D483
15' 0" Wheel Base
3' 4"
11' 8"
10' 6"
8' 6"
12' 0½" To Top of Lamp
THIRD
5' 2½"
27 Feet
5 Thirds—60 Seats.
WEIGHT T. 10 C. 1 Q. 2
THIRD - D495
15' 0" Wheel Base
3' 4"
11' 8" Top of Roof
10' 6"
8' 6"
12' 0½" Top of Lamp
THIRD
5' 2½"
BRAKE COMPT
27 Feet
4 Thirds—48 Seats.
1 Brake Compartment.
WEIGHT T. 10 C. 6 Q. 2
BRAKE THIRD - D505

Figure 44 (opposite) These three drawings show the types employed in the Metropolitan area. It is interesting to note that although they shared common heights and detail treatment with the general service Clayton six wheel and bogie arc roof stock, they were made 6in. wider, and thus exhibited a rather flatter roof profile. From the quoted diagram seating capacity, their extra 6in. of width was expected to allow six passengers per side in the thirds, rather than the five per side of the 8ft. wide stock! The firsts were similarly regarded as four per side (without armrests) rather than three per side. These factors, combined with the much narrower compartments, clearly made their comfort factor less than typically Midland. Scale: 4mm. = 1ft.

(K. C. Woodhead Collection)

Metropolitan Area Four Wheel Stock

Although confined, geographically, in their area of utilization, it was felt that these very characteristic four wheelers should be included in the detailed survey. Because of their generally diminutive size, space is available for all three types to be included - D483 (first), D495 (third), and D505 (brake third).

Plates 167 to 169 These three pictures give detailed views of two of the four wheel types (MR No. 315, first class and MR No. 1545, third class brake), together with a view of MR 0-4-4T No. 1427 on a full train of Metropolitan area four wheel stock at Mill Hill, circa 1908. The set is formed as follows: brake third; 2 x third; 5 x first; 2 x third and brake third. It is probably quite typical but we believe that the precise number of vehicles in any train varied according to need.

(BR/LMR and W. Stubbs)

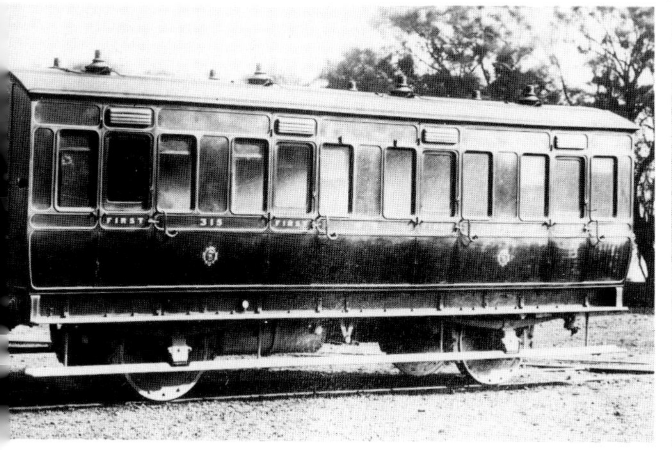

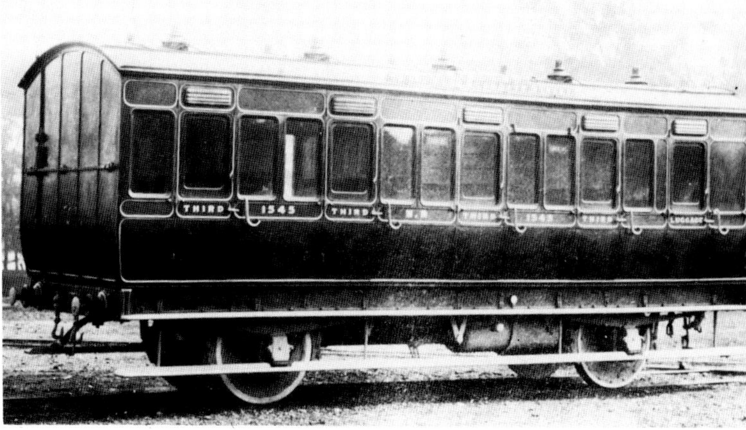

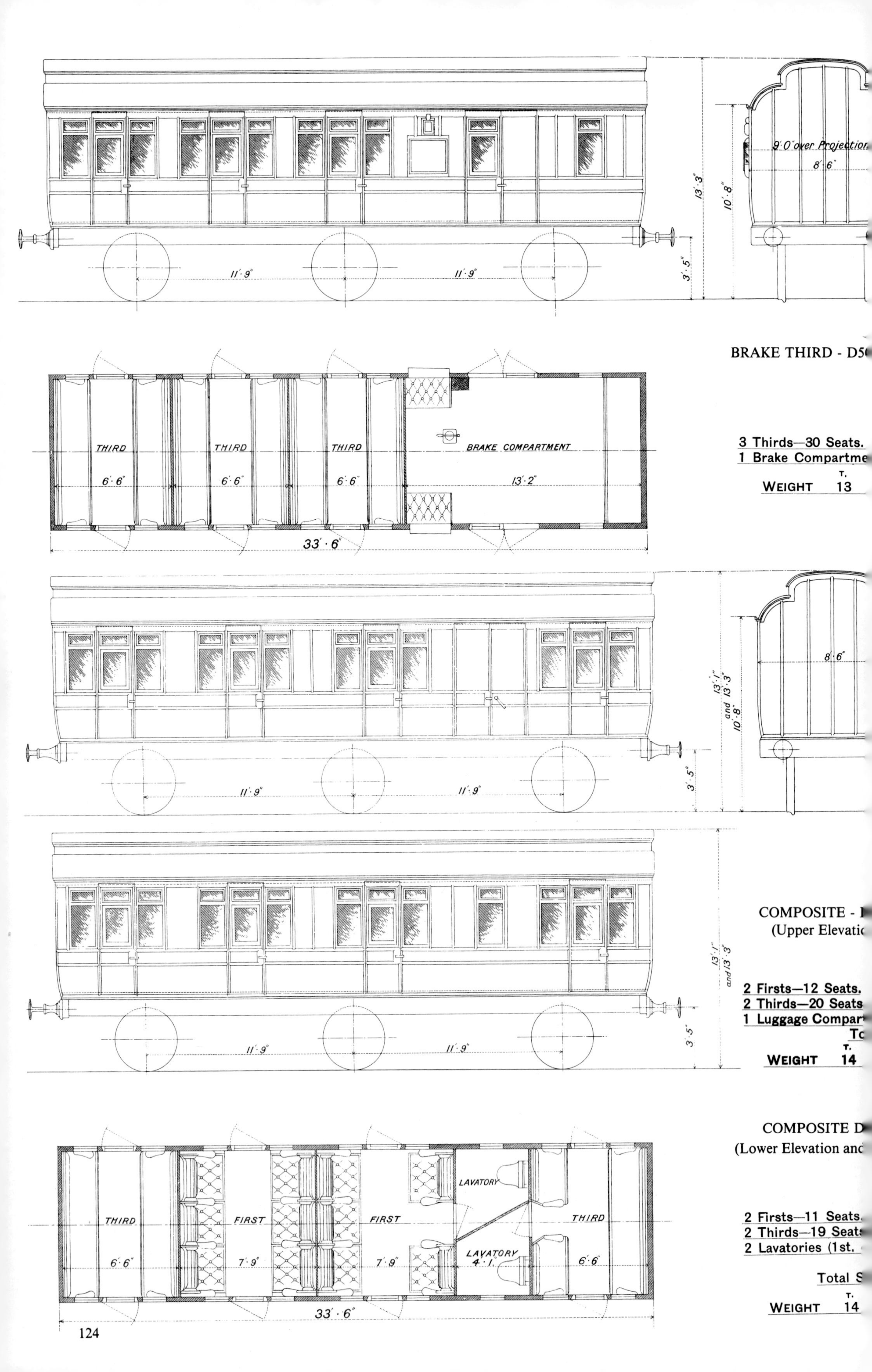
13′·3″
10′·8″
9′·0″ over Projection
8′·6″
3′·5″
11′·9″
11′·9″
BRAKE THIRD - D5
THIRD
THIRD
THIRD
BRAKE COMPARTMENT
6′·6″
6′·6″
6′·6″
13′·2″
33′·6″
3 Thirds—30 Seats.
1 Brake Compartme
T.
WEIGHT 13
13′·1″ and 13′·3″
10′·8″
8′·6″
3′·5″
11′·9″
11′·9″
COMPOSITE -
(Upper Elevati
13′·1″ and 13′·3″
3′·5″
11′·9″
11′·9″
2 Firsts—12 Seats.
2 Thirds—20 Seats
1 Luggage Compar
T.
WEIGHT 14
COMPOSITE D
(Lower Elevation and
THIRD
FIRST
FIRST
LAVATORY
LAVATORY
4′·1.
THIRD
6′·6″
7′·9″
7′·9″
6′·6″
33′·6″
2 Firsts—11 Seats.
2 Thirds—19 Seat
2 Lavatories (1st.
Total S
T.
WEIGHT 14

Figure 45 33ft. 6in. clerestory stock to D503/D514/D515. There were actually four varieties of 33ft. 6in. stock - the omitted type being the five compartment full third to D491, which can readily be derived from the brake third to D503. There was also a matching fifth type, not illustrated, a four compartment lavatory third (D492) to the standard 31ft. length which had a pair of 4ft. 1in. lavatories centrally located. The two 33ft. 6in. composite designs (D514 - lavatory; D515 - luggage) were identical except in the lavatory/luggage area. Scale: 4mm. = 1ft.

(K. C. Woodhead Collection)

Clayton Six Wheel Clerestory Stock

The Clayton clerestory six wheelers of the late 1890s were an odd group of carriages. Firstly, it was a little retrograde to be building six wheel main line stock at this time and, secondly, the length of 33ft. 6in. was a non-standard underframe dimension. However, the Company may also have perceived some weight saving advantages compared with bogie stock *(see discussion on page 15)*. What can be said is that, internally, they were fully to the new spacious main line standard of the time and their high survival rate, well into the LMS period, makes them a favourite choice for the space-starved modellers. Underframe detail was all but identical to that of the Clayton arc roof six wheelers *(see Figure 2, page 4)*, allowing for the increased wheelbase, while panel detail and overall height was entirely consistent with all other Clayton square-panelled clerestories. We could have divided them between the lavatory and non-lavatory chapters but it seemed more logical to keep them together.

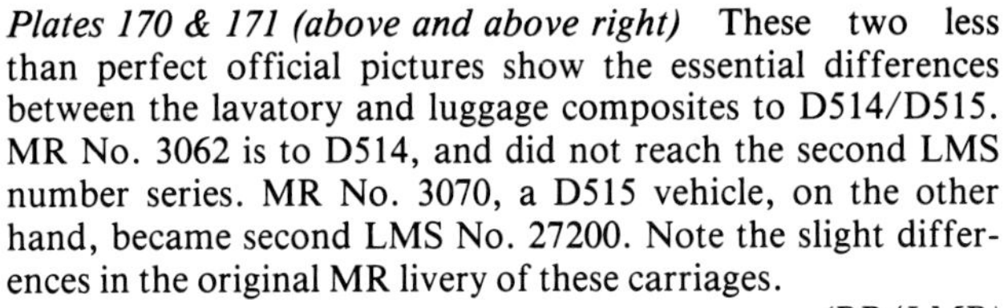

Plates 170 & 171 (above and above right) These two less than perfect official pictures show the essential differences between the lavatory and luggage composites to D514/D515. MR No. 3062 is to D514, and did not reach the second LMS number series. MR No. 3070, a D515 vehicle, on the other hand, became second LMS No. 27200. Note the slight differences in the original MR livery of these carriages.

(BR/LMR)

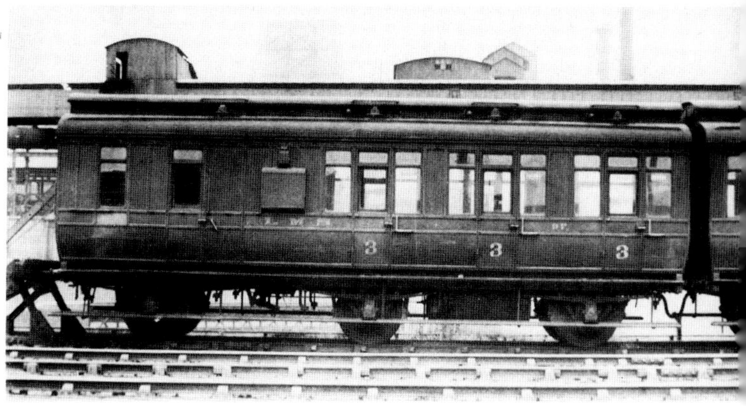

Plates 172 & 173 (right and below) These pictures, taken at Saltley in 1934, show in close up, third brake to D503, LMS No. 97 (later No. 27746), and the same vehicle at the end of a close-coupled train of matching stock. The first four vehicles can be identified as brake third (D503); 2 x luggage composite (D515) and full third (D492). Note that they are still gas lit.

R. E. Lacy

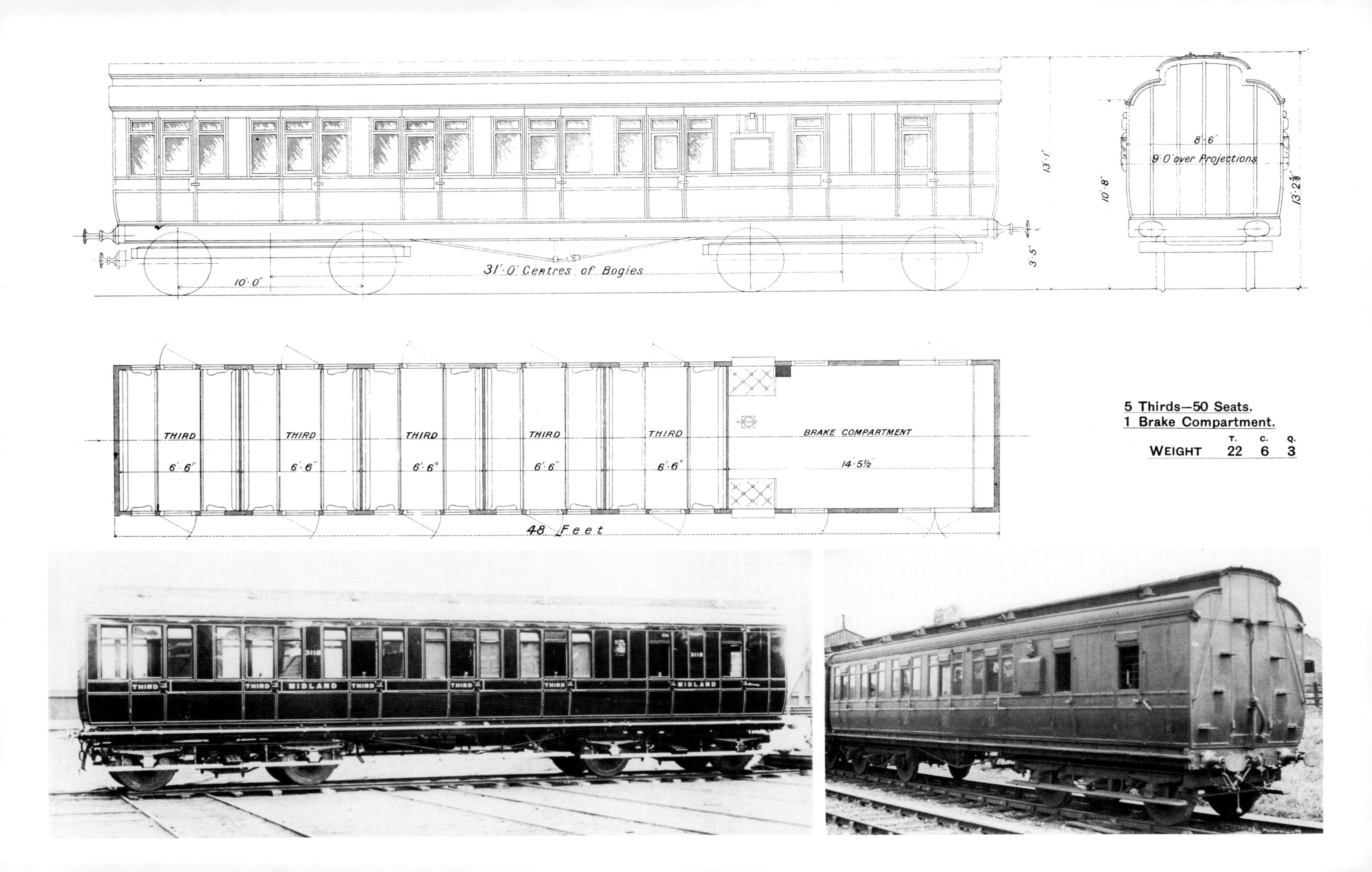

5 Thirds—50 Seats.
1 Brake Compartment.

	T.	C.	Q.
WEIGHT	22	6	3

Figure 46 and Plates 174 & 175 48ft. brake third to D500. This was the only variety to utilize a standard underframe length. Many (probably most) were originally built without guard's look-outs for clearance reasons *(see also Plate 135)*, but it seems that all were eventually fitted with the standard shallower depth look-out. The standard 46ft. 7½in. full third can be derived from this drawing by simply replacing the brake end with two more 6ft. 6in. compartments and setting the bogie centres at 29ft. 7½in. The pictures show MR No. 3118 (pre-1902 number series) as built and first LMS No. 269 (later No. 23016) with guard's look-out. Note also the retention of gas lights, the modification of the door tops, the addition of torpedo ventilators and the removal of most lower stepboards. Scale: 4mm. = 1ft.

(K. C. Woodhead Collection, Authors' Collection and R. E. Lacy)

Clayton Bogie Clerestory Stock

The non-corridor, non-lavatory Clayton bogie clerestories seem to the writers to be amongst the more forgotten Midland carriages - probably because so many were built by outside contractors. They were clearly intended principally for suburban use, in view of the short buffers on the non-brake vehicles, and one confirmed form of six coach set was as follows: brake third (D500); third (D489); 2 x composite (D511); third (D489) and brake third (D500). We have been unable positively to confirm their principal area of operation but in view of the fact that the next generation of suburban coaches (the Bain arc roof series of the early 1900s) was built for every major industrial region served by the MR, except the Leeds and Bradford district, we are inclined to think that many of the square-panelled clerestories were probably employed in the West Riding. This is confirmed, in part, by the personal recollection of reliable sources.

Clerestory construction with lavish compartment dimensions was probably regarded as a little too expensive for purely suburban use, and we feel it significant that Bain quickly went back to a less spacious arc roof form for his suburban series a few years later.

Plates 176 & 177 These views show the 46ft. 7½in. thirds to D489. Midland No. 3111 (old MR number series) is as built, by contractors, and LMS No. 13977 (ex-MR first LMS No. 2060) shows an example in post-group condition. Note, again, the characteristic LMS detail changes. Apologies are offered for the less than clear quality of these pictures.

(Authors' Collection)

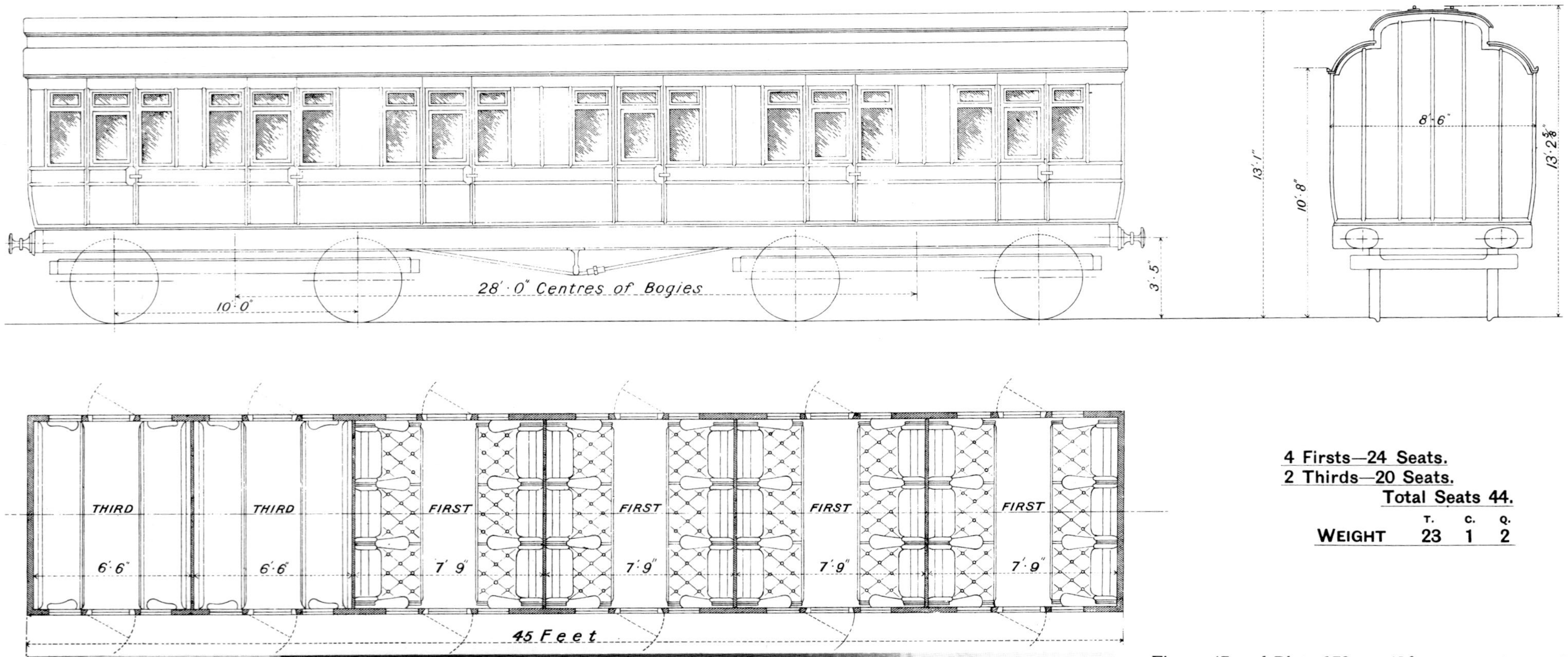
28'·0" Centres of Bogies
10'·0"
3'·5"
13'·1"
10'·8"
8'·6"
13'·2⅝"
THIRD
6'·6"
THIRD
6'·6"
FIRST
7'·9"
FIRST
7'·9"
FIRST
7'·9"
FIRST
7'·9"
45 Feet

4 Firsts—24 Seats.
2 Thirds—20 Seats.
Total Seats 44.

	T.	C.	Q.
WEIGHT	23	1	2

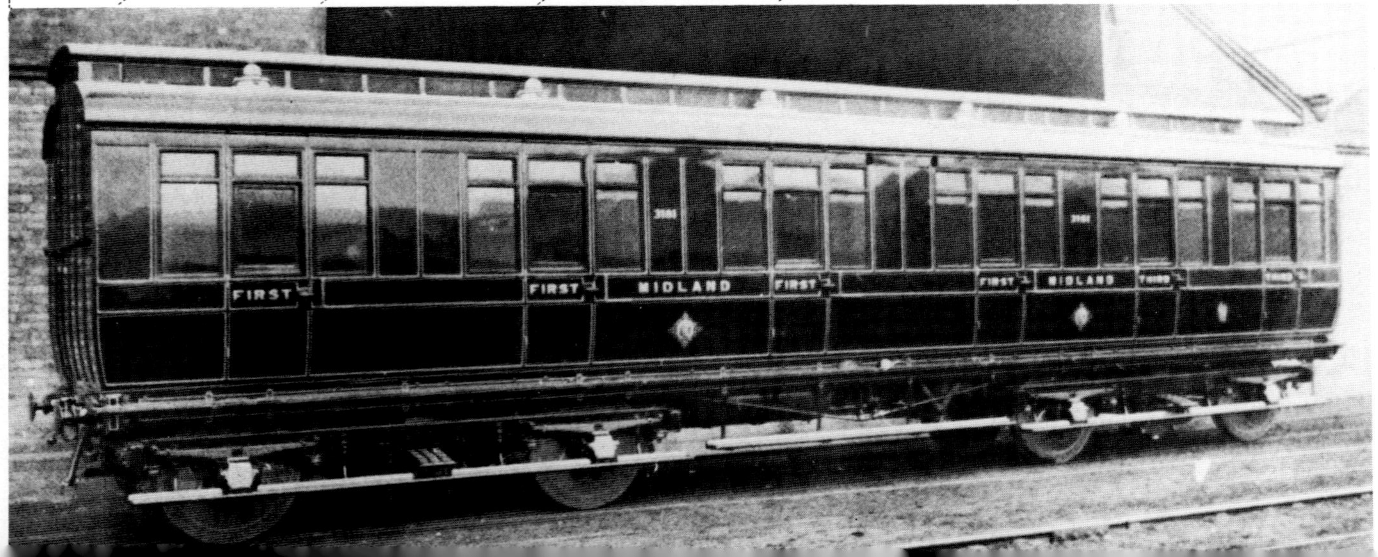
FIRST
FIRST
MIDLAND
FIRST
FIRST
MIDLAND
THIRD

Figure 47 and Plate 178 *45ft. composite to D511.* This variety shared a common underframe with some of the contemporary full brakes, but the 45ft. length was no longer a Midland standard dimension for passenger carrying stock when this type was built. Once again, the overall length was entirely a function of the compartment arrangement. The vehicle illustrated is No. 3181, the last of the Brown-Marshall batch, circa 1902. Unlike some of the other contractor-built clerestory vehicles, this example received a running number in the new post-1901 MR series, but does not appear to have survived into the 1933 LMS renumbering. Scale: 4mm. = 1ft.

(K. C. Woodhead Collection and C. R. Davey Collection)

Bain Clerestory Stock

As already stated, David Bain preferred a new arc roof style for most of his suburban coaches but, in 1903/4, three 54ft. diagrams were issued for clerestory non-corridor, non-lavatory types to replace vehicles sold to the M&GN. The numbers built do not make up into tidy sets, but it seems probable that the coaches were for inter-district rather than suburban use although some were found on the LT&S section in LMS days.

All but one of the vehicles built to this 54ft. length were square-panelled. The exception was the last brake composite (part of Lot 559), which came out with round panelling, thus dating the style change to the 1904 period. For some reason, this vehicle was assigned D519 whereas the much more common square-panelled type was D519A *(see Table 10).*

Plate 179 A 54ft. brake composite to D519A, No. 3487 (MR and first LMS), later second LMS No. 24748. The picture cannot be dated but is probably of late Midland period. Note particularly the deepening of the upper panelling at the centre of the vehicle below the gutter. This was to permit the word 'Midland' to be incorporated after the 1906/7 livery change, and was virtually universally applied to all square-panelled clerestories *(see, for example, Plate 134).*
(NRM)

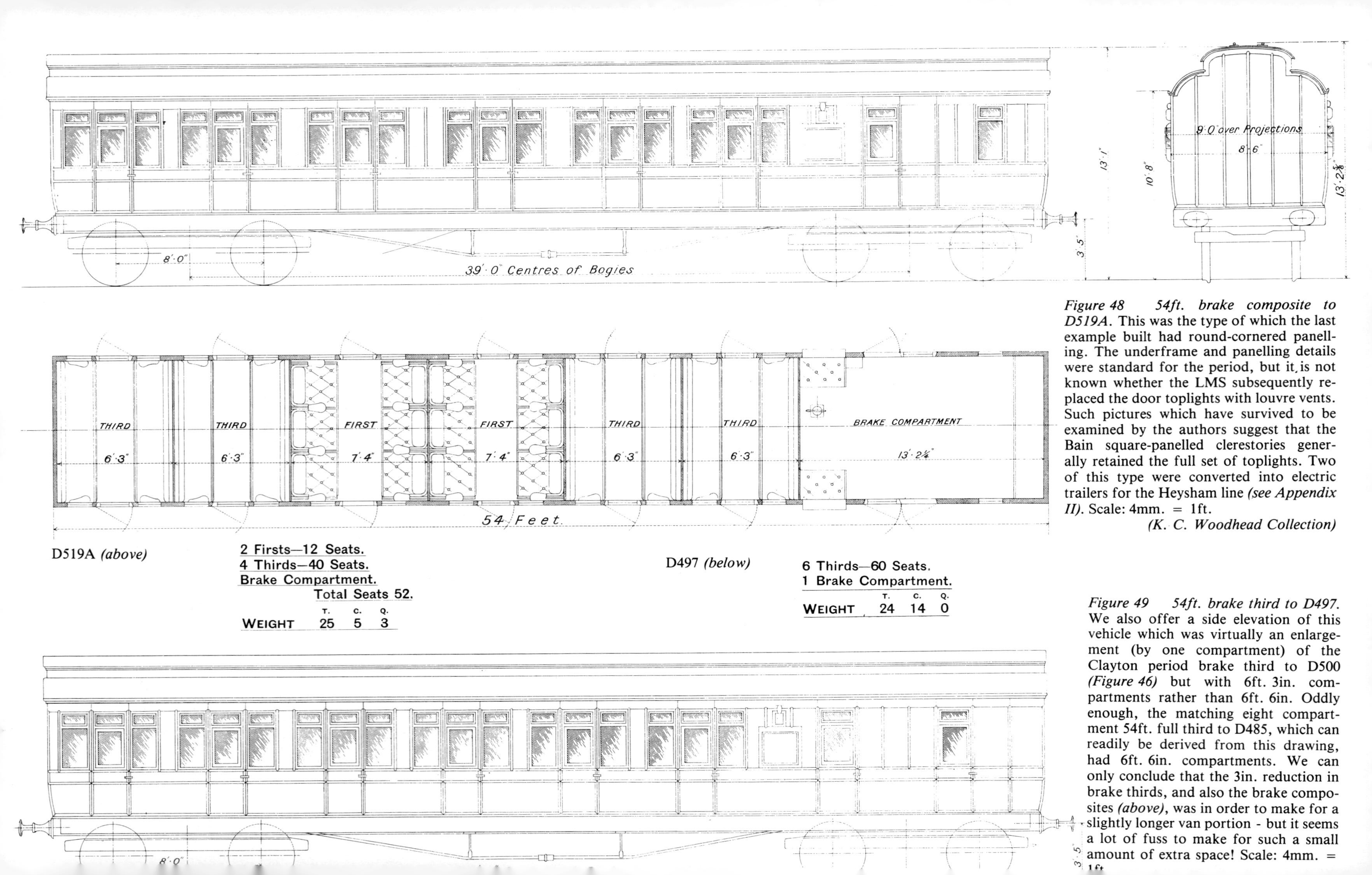

D519A *(above)*

D497 *(below)*

Figure 48 *54ft. brake composite to D519A*. This was the type of which the last example built had round-cornered panelling. The underframe and panelling details were standard for the period, but it is not known whether the LMS subsequently replaced the door toplights with louvre vents. Such pictures which have survived to be examined by the authors suggest that the Bain square-panelled clerestories generally retained the full set of toplights. Two of this type were converted into electric trailers for the Heysham line *(see Appendix II)*. Scale: 4mm. = 1ft.

(K. C. Woodhead Collection)

Figure 49 *54ft. brake third to D497.* We also offer a side elevation of this vehicle which was virtually an enlargement (by one compartment) of the Clayton period brake third to D500 *(Figure 46)* but with 6ft. 3in. compartments rather than 6ft. 6in. Oddly enough, the matching eight compartment 54ft. full third to D485, which can readily be derived from this drawing, had 6ft. 6in. compartments. We can only conclude that the 3in. reduction in brake thirds, and also the brake composites *(above)*, was in order to make for a slightly longer van portion - but it seems a lot of fuss to make for such a small amount of extra space! Scale: 4mm. = 1ft.

During the Edwardian period, David Bain instituted a massive building programme of non-corridor, arc roof suburban stock. The permutations of compartments, panel sizes, lengths and widths are a little subtle, and it is difficult to select a few examples to typify the range. All the vehicles shared remarkably similar visual lines (as did their Clayton arc roof forebears) but, in the survey which follows, an attempt has been made to analyse the principles which were followed.

For the most part, the carriages were built in sets for operation in the various suburban areas served by the Midland (Sheffield, Manchester, Birmingham, etc.), and the subtle variations of style tended to be associated with particular district allocations. As the years passed, reallocation and new building tended to confuse the issue but it is probably simpler to analyse them according to their first utilization.

a) The 8ft. 6in. wide series
Figures 50 to 52 and Plates 182 to 185

The 48ft. stock to the 8ft. 6in. width was built essentially, for the Manchester, Birmingham and Sheffield areas. Five types of carriage were built but with only four body styles. There were two types of brake third (four compartment and six compartment), a full third and a full first. The fifth type, a composite, was derived by utilizing the body of the full first but inserting false partitions in three of the compartments at one end to form third class accommodation.

Overlaying these basic layouts were two variations of panel style and underframe. The Manchester and Birmingham coaches had 10ft. bogies and displayed the first Bain round-panelled style (i.e. deeper eaves panels with 4 element louvre vents). The Sheffield sets, although built to the same diagrams, made use of the newer 8ft. bogie and displayed the later panelling (shallower eaves panel and 3 element louvre vents).

We have chosen to depict the whole series by utilizing the official diagrams which show the 10ft. bogie and earlier panelling with the only surviving official photographs - those of the Sheffield sets which embody the later stylistic variations.

b) The 9ft. wide series
Figures 53, 54, and Plates 26, 180 & 181

The 9ft. wide stock to the 48ft. length was used in the Nottingham area and on the Metropolitan lines. The panel styling was universally of the later type and they all ran on 8ft. bogies. Several types were simply 9ft. wide versions of the 8ft. 6in. designs covered already e.g. the full third (D605) and the four compartment brakes (D603). However, the six compartment brake (Metropolitan area only) and the composite (both areas) were slightly different, and these are the featured types in this section. We have been unable to find any good exterior pictures of these vehicles (there are plenty of poor ones) but, apart from the six vertical panels on the ends, they were, in all essential respects, so like the 8ft. 6in. stock that we do not think it would be a serious difficulty for model-makers; but *see Plate 24, Chapter 1.*

In passing, it is worth mentioning that a further series of Bain suburbans with 9ft. wide bodies on 50ft. underframes were built for the outer London services to Bedford and St. Albans. We have omitted these from this survey - but *see Plate 152* for a picture of some of them.

Plates 180 & 181 Interior views of a Metropolitan area 48ft. composite, No 2831 to D606. The vehicle became second LMS No. 17389 in 1933.

(BR/LMR)

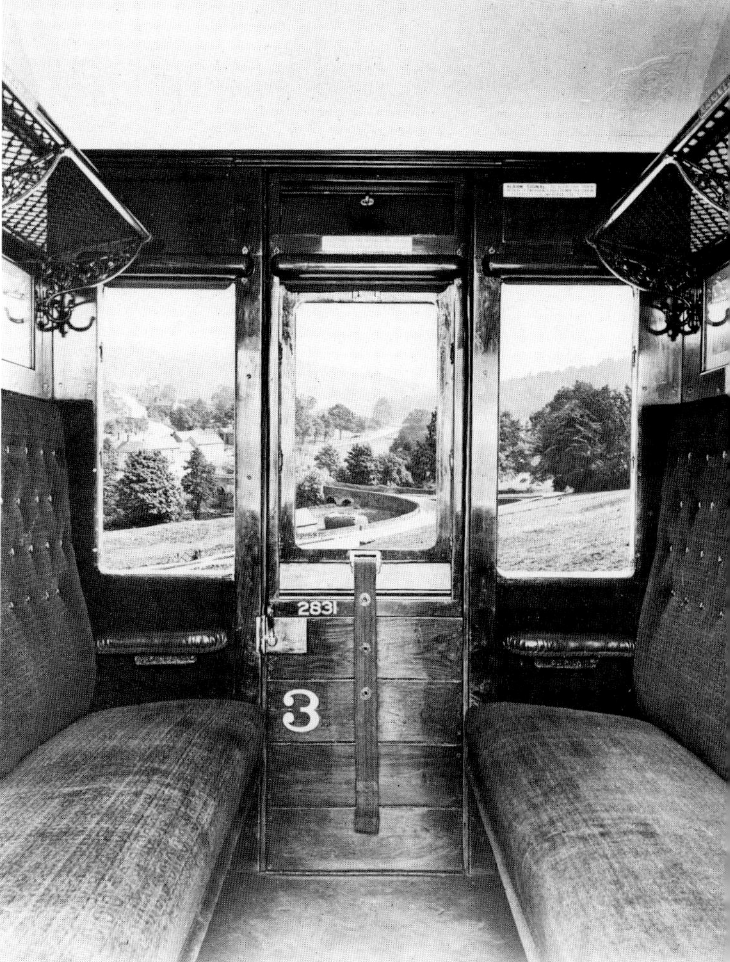

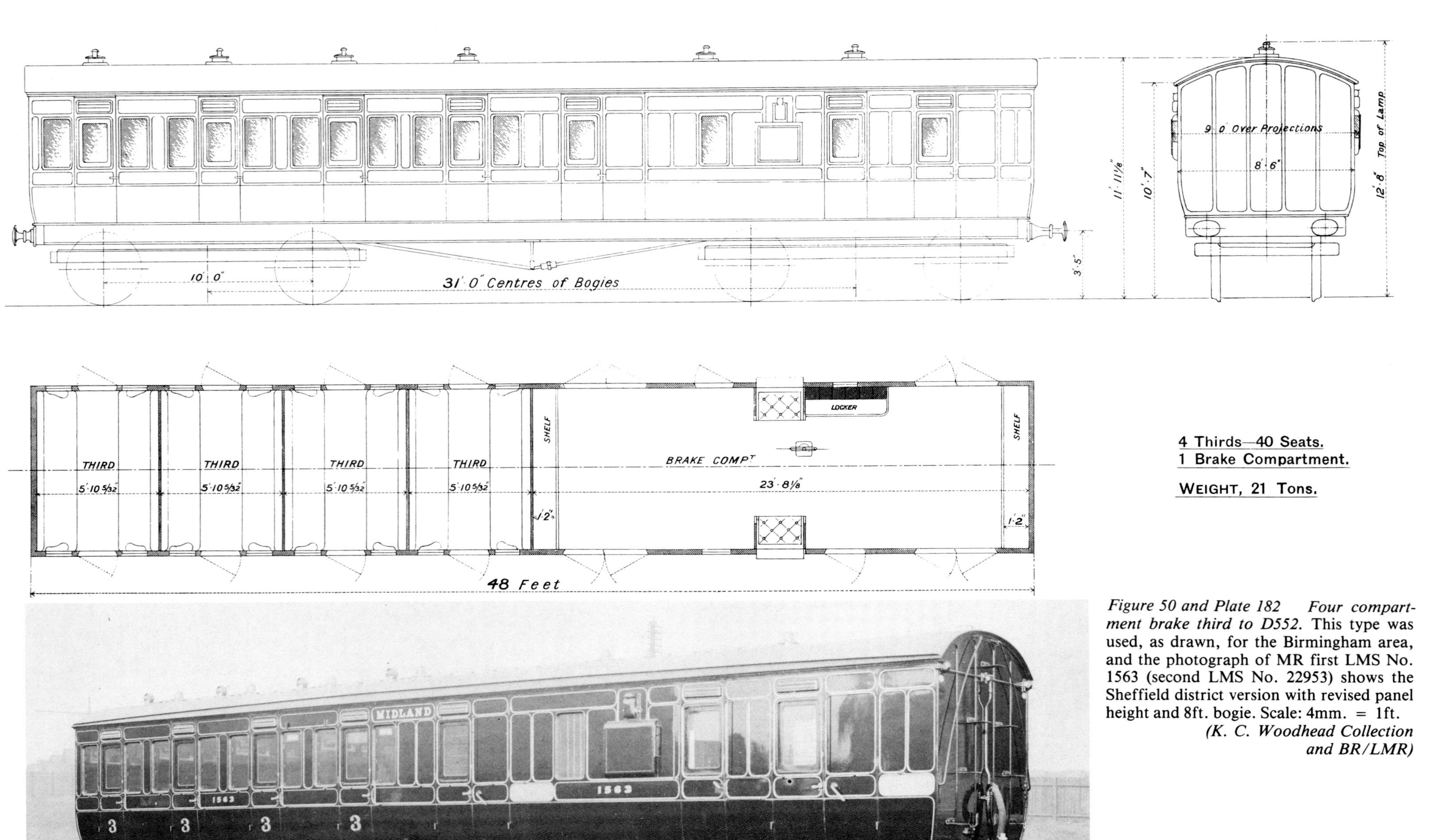

Figure 50 and Plate 182 *Four compartment brake third to D552.* This type was used, as drawn, for the Birmingham area, and the photograph of MR first LMS No. 1563 (second LMS No. 22953) shows the Sheffield district version with revised panel height and 8ft. bogie. Scale: 4mm. = 1ft.
(K. C. Woodhead Collection and BR/LMR)

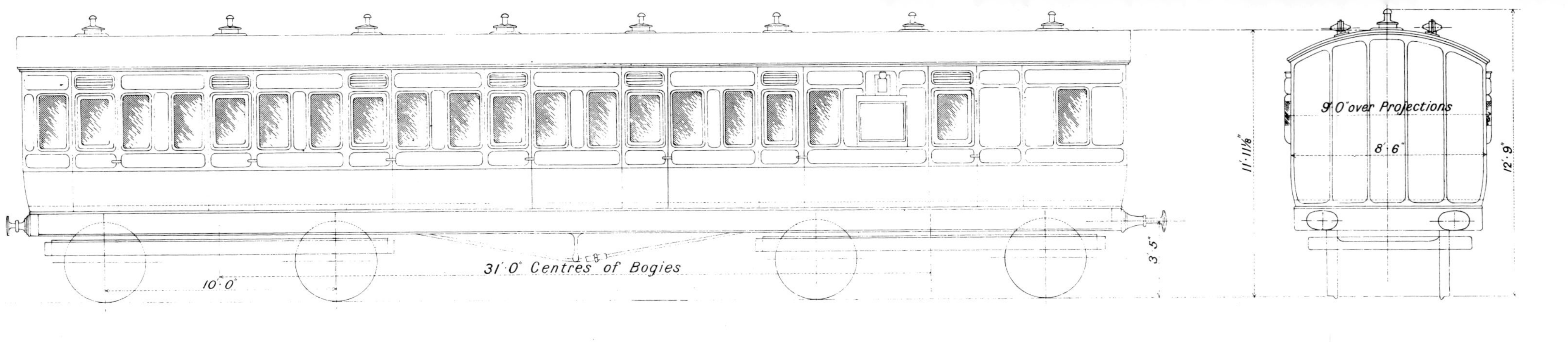

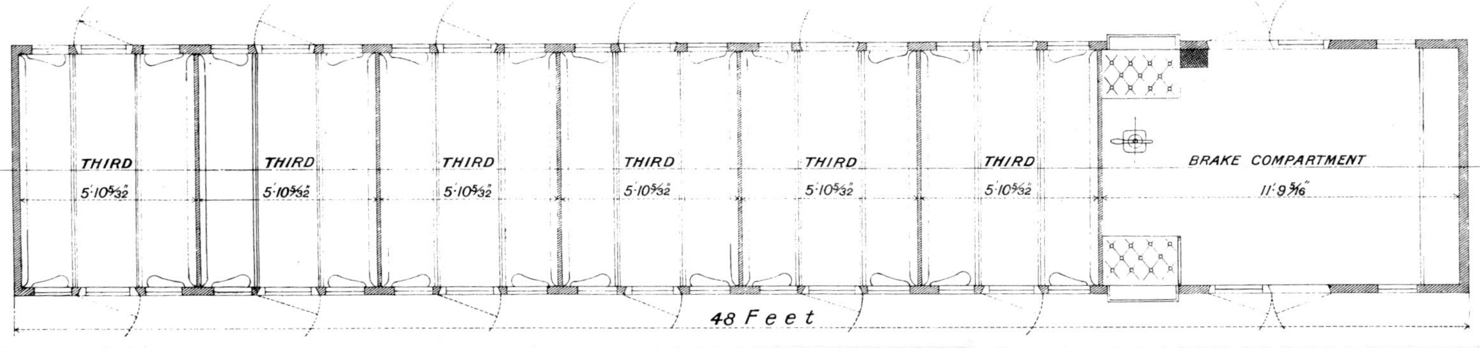

6 Thirds—60 Seats.
Brake Compartment.

	T.	C.	Q.
WEIGHT	21	18	0

Figure 51 and Plates 183 & 184 Six compartment brake third to D501 and full third to D487. The six compartment brake was used in both the Manchester and Birmingham areas as drawn but never in the Sheffield area. The eight compartment full third to D487 can be derived by repeating the passenger end of D501 about the centre line. The photograph of MR and first LMS No. 809 (second LMS No. 14138) shows the Sheffield version of the full third with 8ft. bogies and newer panelling, whilst LMS No. 23119 (MR and first LMS No. 564) shows a former Birmingham area six compartment brake third at Upminster, circa 1948. Scale: 4mm. = 1ft.

(K. C. Woodhead Collection, NRM and Authors' Collection)

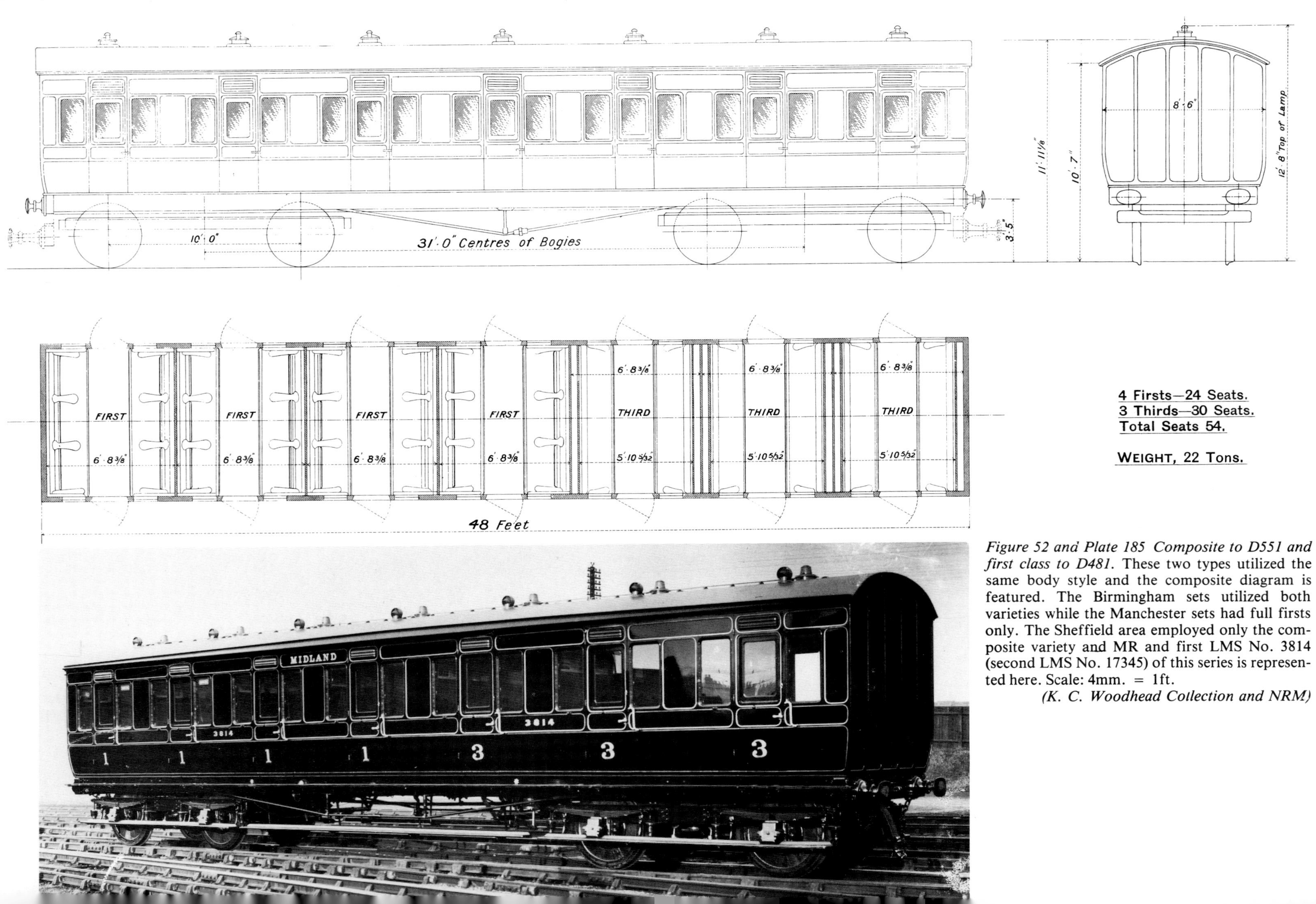

Figure 52 and Plate 185 Composite to D551 and first class to D481. These two types utilized the same body style and the composite diagram is featured. The Birmingham sets utilized both varieties while the Manchester sets had full firsts only. The Sheffield area employed only the composite variety and MR and first LMS No. 3814 (second LMS No. 17345) of this series is represented here. Scale: 4mm. = 1ft.

(K. C. Woodhead Collection and NRM)

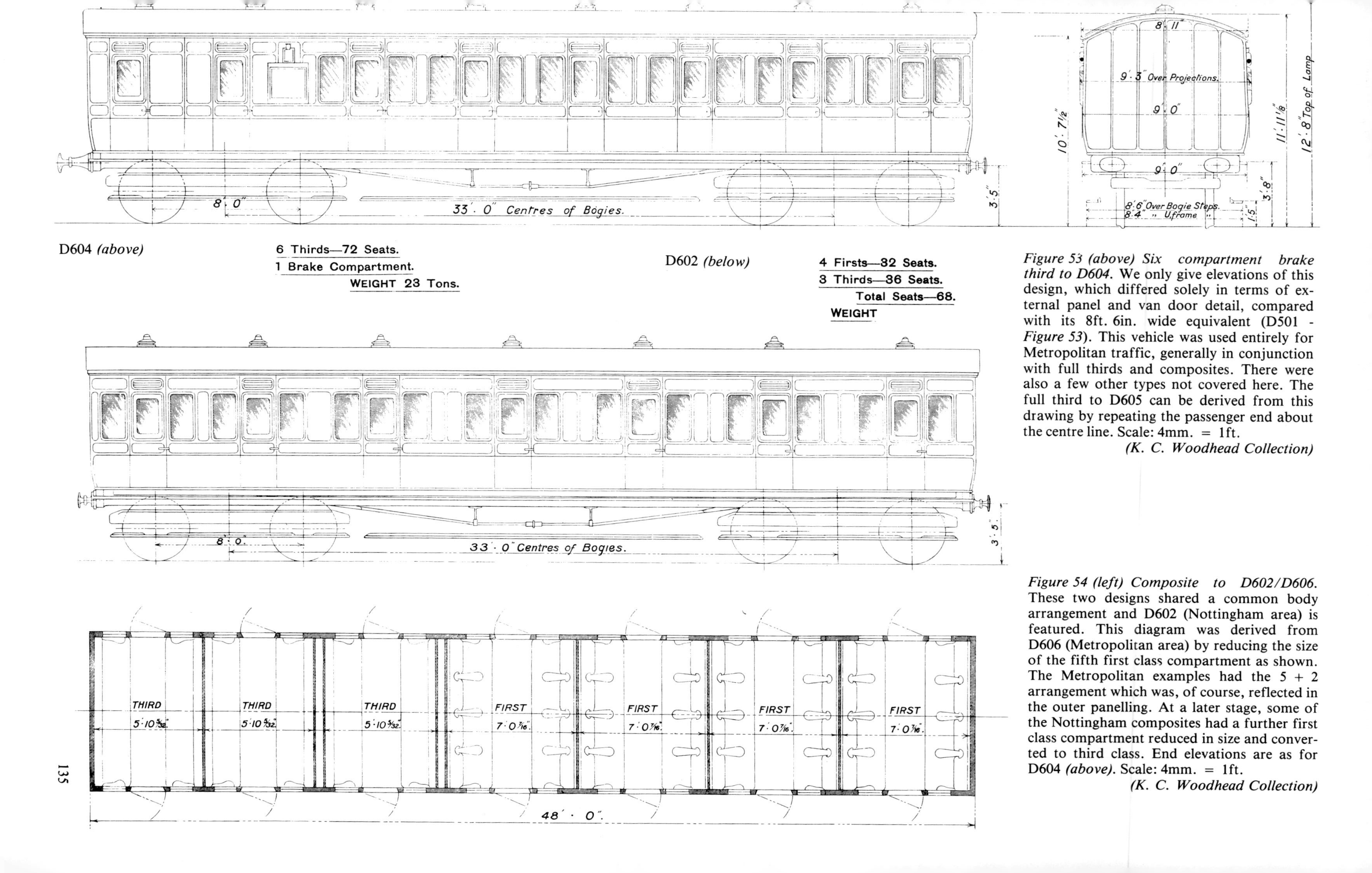

Figure 53 (above) Six compartment brake third to D604. We only give elevations of this design, which differed solely in terms of external panel and van door detail, compared with its 8ft. 6in. wide equivalent (D501 - *Figure 53*). This vehicle was used entirely for Metropolitan traffic, generally in conjunction with full thirds and composites. There were also a few other types not covered here. The full third to D605 can be derived from this drawing by repeating the passenger end about the centre line. Scale: 4mm. = 1ft.

(K. C. Woodhead Collection)

Figure 54 (left) Composite to D602/D606. These two designs shared a common body arrangement and D602 (Nottingham area) is featured. This diagram was derived from D606 (Metropolitan area) by reducing the size of the fifth first class compartment as shown. The Metropolitan examples had the 5 + 2 arrangement which was, of course, reflected in the outer panelling. At a later stage, some of the Nottingham composites had a further first class compartment reduced in size and converted to third class. End elevations are as for D604 *(above)*. Scale: 4mm. = 1ft.

(K. C. Woodhead Collection)

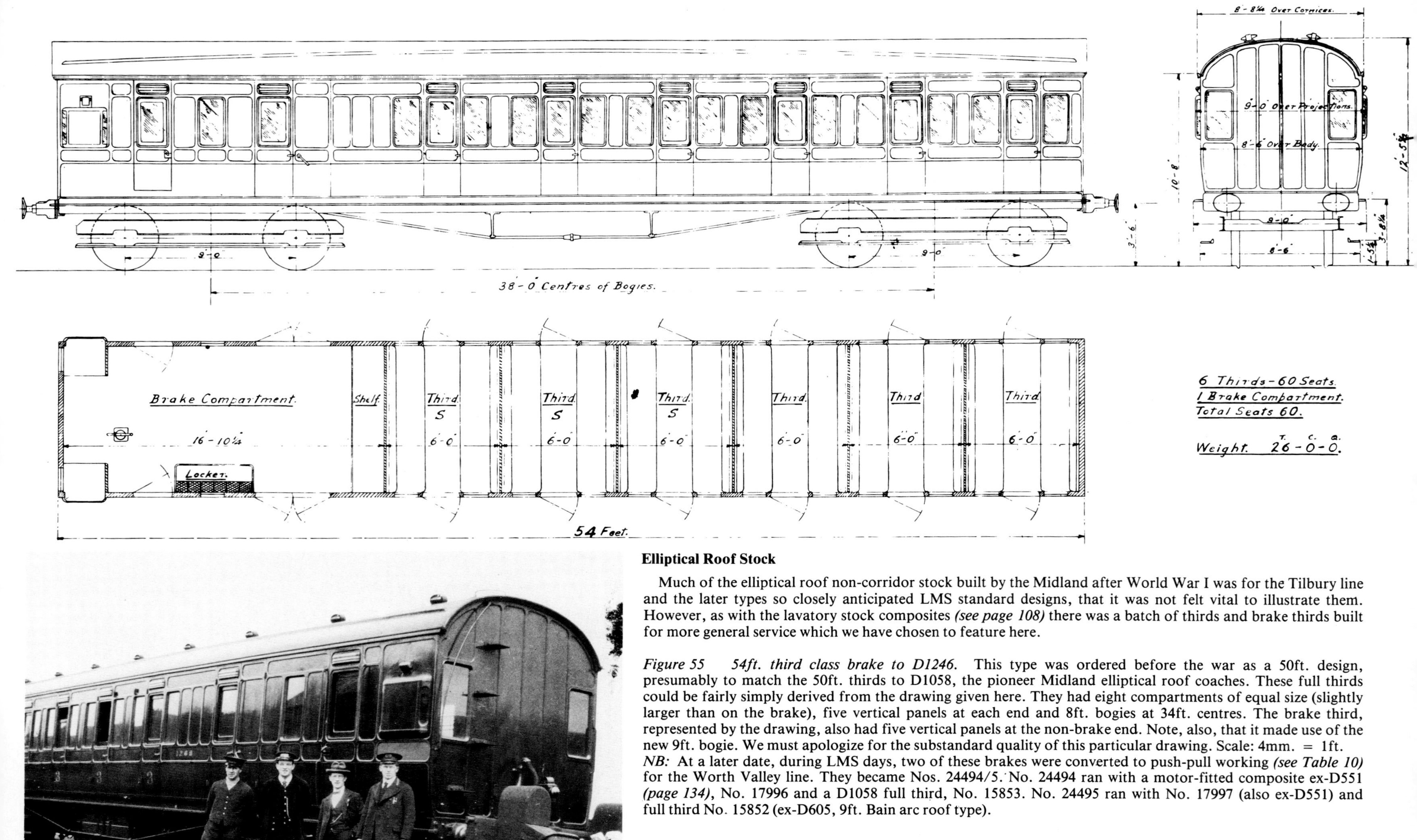

Elliptical Roof Stock

Much of the elliptical roof non-corridor stock built by the Midland after World War I was for the Tilbury line and the later types so closely anticipated LMS standard designs, that it was not felt vital to illustrate them. However, as with the lavatory stock composites *(see page 108)* there was a batch of thirds and brake thirds built for more general service which we have chosen to feature here.

Figure 55 54ft. third class brake to D1246. This type was ordered before the war as a 50ft. design, presumably to match the 50ft. thirds to D1058, the pioneer Midland elliptical roof coaches. These full thirds could be fairly simply derived from the drawing given here. They had eight compartments of equal size (slightly larger than on the brake), five vertical panels at each end and 8ft. bogies at 34ft. centres. The brake third, represented by the drawing, also had five vertical panels at the non-brake end. Note, also, that it made use of the new 9ft. bogie. We must apologize for the substandard quality of this particular drawing. Scale: 4mm. = 1ft.
NB: At a later date, during LMS days, two of these brakes were converted to push-pull working *(see Table 10)* for the Worth Valley line. They became Nos. 24494/5. No. 24494 ran with a motor-fitted composite ex-D551 *(page 134)*, No. 17996 and a D1058 full third, No. 15853. No. 24495 ran with No. 17997 (also ex-D551) and full third No. 15852 (ex-D605, 9ft. Bain arc roof type).

Plate 186 Midland and first LMS brake third No. 1268 (second LMS No. 23294) to D1246. This vehicle was the last to be built to the diagram but we do not think that was the reason for this obviously-posed group of

TABLE 10
Summary of Midland Railway Non-Corridor Ordinary Stock

g.	Lot	Qty.	Date of Order	Dimensions	Wt.	Style	Numbering		Type Extinct	Remarks
							Midland/1st LMS	2nd LMS		
: Class (F/FZ*)										
	73	85	1882	30' x 8' 0"		CA	321–45 (not LMS)			Standard Clayton six wheel (4 x 1st) but shorter than standard length for Clayton arc roof period.
	89	3	1883	54' x 8' 0"		CA	36 + two (not LMS)			Twelve wheel (6 x 1st plus two luggage compartments).
3*	98 407	30 12	1883 1897	27' x 8' 6"	10T	CA	 315 + eleven (not LMS)			Four wheel stock for working on to Metropolitan lines.
	510	2	1901	47' 6" x 8' 6"	23½T	CC2	2559–60	10441–2	7/38	Odd length pair of coaches with short buffers. Obviously part of sets built to the new style.
	536 677	28 26	1903 1908	48' x 8' 6"	23T	BA	2561–90 (not 2568/75) 2502–5 2507 2511–30 2664 Various: 2561–84	10443–63 10464–6 10467 10468–84 10485 14058–64 (see remarks)	see remarks 4/52 3/50 10/56 8/49 10/47	Standard Bain type. Lot 536 probably first reversion to round cornered panelling of any Bain type. As with many Bain 48ft. non-corridors, built for district use viz: Lot 536 – Manchester; Lot 677 – Birmingham. Nos. 14058–64 were downgraded to 3rd class before 1933, retaining original MR/1st LMS numbers and in 1933 went (in correct sequence) to 3rd class series. Many more post-1933 downgradings, both to T (including 13515–9) and C (including 16917–21) – generally the whole of the 10443 –63 series except 10445 (withdrawn 10/43). Last survivors of this group were withdrawn in 1947 (13512/3 ex-10454/10443).
	710 857	26 4	1909 1913	50' x 9' 0"	24T	BA	2531–51 2665–9 2686–7/93/708	10510–30 10531–5 10536–9	5/57 11/57 9/58	More spacious version of D481 for outer London (Bedford–St. Pancras) services. Lot 857 was for LT&S line, possibly modified slightly (details uncertain) but essentially D553. Considerable numbers downgraded to composite in the 1930s (e.g. 16931–6) and one, at least, 14296 (ex-10516) to 3rd. Some transfers to NCC, later UTA viz: 16936 (ex-10511) to NCC 23, UTA 275 and 10513 to NCC 22, UTA 351. Finally, 10529 was formed into LMS experimental articulated set in 1935 with 14234 (T – D555) and 23198 (BT – D556). NB: Withdrawal dates refer to survivors in 1st class series.
	833	3	1913	48' x 9' 0"	26T	BA	2609–11	10503–5	1957	9ft. wide version of D481 for LT&S services. No. 10505 to all 3rd in 1952, latterly all three in Eastern Region stock as 3rd class.
	960	4	1921	48' x 9' 0"	25½T	E	2612–15	10506–9	2/62	Elliptical roof version of D1054 for LT&S. All ended up as Eastern Region stock (3rd class).
	978 988	4 5	1921 1922	54' x 9' 0"		E	2635–8 2623–7	10547–50 10542–6	4/62 3/62	Final 54ft. LT&S series. All but one ended as all 3rd in Eastern Region stock. Exception was 10544, also E. R. stock, but as composite.
1 Class (T/TZ*)										
	27 36	50 50	1879 1879	40' x 8' 0"		CA	1466 + many more			Orthodox 6 x 3rd. Some (all?) had 'American' type equalised beam bogies.
	Part 60 Part 85	90 20	1881 1882	43' x 8' 0"	18T	CA	33 + many more 673 1288			7 x 3rd class. Balance of Lots 60/85 were Brake Thirds to D502.
	95 113	100 30	1883 1884							
	74 117	73 10	1882 1884	31' x 8' 0" (Short buffers)	11T	CA	Included 77, 1573–91			The commonest single type of MR carriage – six wheel; 5 x 3rd. Some additional examples built at Kilmarnock (GSWR) for MSJS use (e.g. MSJS No. 8). Numbering details very fragmentary. One or two official survivors beyond 1934 but possible that these later dates were those of the official write-off and that the vehicles were scrapped earlier. The vehicles concerned were: 26459 (ex-492–0492) – 4/37 26461 (ex-1203–01203) – 4/37 26467 – written off 5/55 (!) as 0988. Lot 201 was a low-height variant for the West Bridge service because of the restricted clearances.
	112 142 166 193 226 230 259 290 357	250 50 14 12 22 85 120 75 50	1884 1885 1885 1887 1889 1889 1890 1892 1895	31' x 8' 0" (Long buffers)	11T	CA	1st MR series Included 1217; 1709–81 2nd MR series Various: 492–1767	26459–71	11/34 (see remarks)	
	Part 201	1	1888	see remarks	11T	CA	929			
	99 205 314 339 408	22 2 13 11 24	1883 1888 1893 1894 1897	27' x 8' 6"	10T	CA	382	26457 (ex-01799)	1937	Four wheel stock for working over the Metropolitan lines. Numbering details are very fragmentary but 26457 was almost certainly this type – officially written off in 1937.
		50 25 25	1897	33' 6" x 8' 6"	14½T	CC2	1884–1933 1934–58 1959–83	1933 survivors were:- 26475–523 (T) and 27750–3 (BT)	 6/39 3/39	Contractor built coaches – lot numbers never issued; first fifty by Birmingham C. & W. Co. remainder shared between Ashbury and Lancaster C. & W. Co. Nos. 27750–3 were, apparently, later conversions (date of conversion not known) to Brake 3rd (ex-1904/11/63/46), before 1933. Six wheel.
	511 542 – –	4 4 20 30	1901 1902	46' 7½" x 8' 6"	23½T	CC2	Various: 134–1357 2044–73	13941–94 (see note)	6/46	7 x 3rd and mostly contractor built by Lancaster C. & W. Co and Metropolitan C. & W. Co. (2044–73). Originally a mixture of long/short buffer types for fixed sets (c.f. D482 – F). *Note:* LMS (1933) number series was followed by a long series (13995–14057) of ex-LT&SR coaches, then the downgraded ex-First Class to D481 (above: (14058–64).
	537 679 802	21 37 22	1902 1907 1912	48' x 8' 6"	23T	BA	1465–85 Various: 22–1259 Various: 451–863	14065–85 14086–120 14121–41	10/47 9/57 11/57	Standard Bain type and built for district use viz:- Lot 537 – Manchester; Lot 679 – Birmingham; Lot 802 – Sheffield. The Sheffield coaches had 8ft. bogies and revised height panelling. Two transfers to NCC in 1948 viz: 14102 – NCC 24 (later UTA 343); 14104 – NCC 25 (later UTA 345). Body of 14140 went to Butterley in 1977 for preservation (ex-private ownership).
	561	32	1903	54' x 8' 6"	26T	BC3	2159–90	14299–329	9/46	Essentially an eight compartment version of D489 and built to replace older coaches sold to M&GN.
	712	26	1909	50' x 9' 0"	24T	BA	Various: 681–823	14214–39	11/57	A more spacious version of D487 for outer London (Bedford–St. Pancras) services. No. 14234 was used in experimental articulated set in 1935 with 10529 (F – D553) and 23198 (BT – D556). Two transfers to NCC in 1948 viz: 14222 –NCC 26 (later UTA 349); 14226 – NCC 27 (later UTA 347).
	739 758 766 835 845	6 18 8 16 9	1910 1910 1911 1913 1913	48' x 9' 0"	24T	BA	Various: 126–2137 1588–96 2444–59 Various: 550–635	14142–62 14170–2 14163–9 14173–88 14189–97	4/57 11/58 5/57 10/58	9ft. wide version of D487 for Nottingham district and Metropolitan use viz: Lots 739/758 and one of Lot 845 – Metro; Lot 766, balance of Lot 845 – Nottingham. Lot 835 was for LT&S line. Vehicle No. 1590 (Lot 766) converted to push-pull use (LMS Motor Diagram 66) in 1931, becoming 15852 in 1933 and latterly used on Keighley & Worth Valley line (scrapped 7/56).
	856 883	25 30	1913 1914	50' x 8' 6"	24T	E	Various: 32–1399 Various: 984–2442	14240–64 14265–93 (see note)	7/61 3/62	First MR elliptical roof type. Vehicle No. 1070 (Lot 883) converted to push-pull use (LMS Motor Diagram 65) in 1931, becoming 15853 in 1933 and latterly on Keighley & Worth Valley line (scrap 8/54). *Note:* LMS 14294–8 were used for ex-LT&SR coaches.
	959	16	1921	48' x 9' 0"	25T	E	2460–2; 2469–74; 4201–7	14198–213	10/61	Elliptical roof version of D605 and all built for LT&S services.
	966 981 984 991 997	3 12 6 11 2	1921 1922 1922 1922 1922	54' x 9' 0"	25T	E	1272/86/95 2429–33/5; 2463–8 Various: 387–1395 4215–20/2–4; 4265/90 31; 203	14330–2 14339–50 14333–8 14351–62 14362–3	6/61 5/62 12/60 6/62	Forerunner of LMS standard 54ft. type (9 x 3rd) and mostly for LT&S services. Bulk of order not delivered until after the Grouping. Last of series became NCC 200 (later UTA 355).
osite (C/CZ*)										
	16 25 83	50 20 37	1878 1878 1882	40' x 8' 0"		CA	Included 114 and MSJS 30			3 x 3rd; 2 x 1st; 1 x luggage. Lot 25 was for MSJS. Lot 69 was visibly identical but classed as brake composite (below).
	24	10	1879	54' x 8' 0"		CA	Possibly MSJS 1–10			12 wheel: 3 x 1st; 4 x 3rd; 2 x luggage. Nos. 1, 2, 3 rebuilt as dining (presumably RCO style) c1895.
	79	30	1883	45' x 8' 0"		CA	Included 6; 225			45ft. version of Lot 16 etc. but with 3 x 1st. Some (e.g. No. 6) later altered to CL by removal of one first class compartment and replacing by two lavatories.
	86	10	1883	43' x 8' 0"		CA	Included 316			43ft. version of Lot 79 with 4 x 3rd; 2 x 1st (hence shorter length).
	108	80	1884	45' x 8' 0"	18½T	CA				2 x 1st; 4 x 3rd; 1 x luggage. Note that BC (D526, Lot 109) was built to same drawing.
	110	25	1884	54' x 8' 0"	24½T	CA	Included 279; 430; 481			12 wheel; 3 x 1st; 4 x 3rd; 1 x luggage. D507A had 1 x first class compartment altered to two lavatories – usually, but not always, at luggage end. All may have been converted to D507A (279 confirmed). D507A conversions are dated 1892.

Diag.	Lot	Qty.	Date of Order	Dimensions	Wt.	Style	Numbering: Midland/1st LMS	Numbering: 2nd LMS	Type Extinct	Remarks
516*	111 141 Part 201	100 100 2	1884 1885 1888	31' x 8' 0"	11T	CA	Included; MSJS49; MR 877; 901 and also 3675–712 (second MR series) 213 + one more			Built with centre luggage, 2 x 1st; 2 x 3rd. Many converted to CLZ (lavatc vice luggage space). One preserved at NRM as MR901 in luggage configura Lot 201 was built to low height for West Bridge service. All six wheel. Son examples (e.g. MSJS49) built by NBR at Cowlairs.
515*	425	15	1897	33' 6" x 8' 6"	14½T	CC2	3064–73 3112–6	27198–202 27203–4	2/38 1/35	Built alongside lavatory composites (CLZ – D514) to two heights (3064– were 13' 3", the rest 13' 1") 2 x 1st; 2 x 3rd; 1 x luggage. Six wheel.
511	509 – –	25 25 25	1901	45' x 8' 6"	23T	CC2	3265–89 3157–81 3182–206	17274–92 17251–73	2/46 11/46	Last fifty were contractor built, 25 each respectively by Brown-Marshall a Lancaster C. & W. Co. All were short buffered stock (c.f. D482 (F) and D489 (T) – above), obviously for fixed sets. The matching brakes were to D500 (BT) – below D511 had 4 x 1st; 2 x 3rd.
510	525	5	1901	48' x 8' 6"	23T	CC2	3602/9/26/30–1	17292–6 (see note)	8/46	2 x 1st; 3 x 3rd; 1 x large luggage. Visually like a BC design but not hand-braked. The LMS (1933 series) numbers 17297–317 were taken up by ex-LT&SR coaches.
551	678 803	11 29	1907 1912	48' x 8' 6"	22T	BA	Various: 3299–353 3794–822	17318–26 17327–53 plus motor conversions (see remarks)	10/56 1/58	Standard Bain series for district use viz: Lot 678–Birmingham; Lot 803– Sheffield. Lot 803 had 8ft. bogies, revised panel heights. Visually bodies v identical to D481 (F) but three compartments reduced in size (by 'false' internal partitions). Three conversions to push-pull (LMS Motor Diagram and two conversions to push-pull (LMS Motor Diagram 41) viz: *M40:*- 3323 (Lot 678) – 17995; 3804/10 (Lot 803) – 17998/17341 (n.b. 17341 kept LMS non-push-pull number). *M41:* -3344 (Lot 678) – 17996; 3803 (Lot 803) – 17997. Some of these motor conversions operated with converted BT (D552) – s below.
554	711	4	1909	50' x 9' 0"	24T	BA	3363/7; 3376; 3403	17397–400	12/55	More spacious version of D551 for outer London (Bedford–St. Pancras) services. Body style as D553 (F) but with four compartments reduced in s (internally by 'false' partitions).
602	767 834 846	8 3 8	1911 1913 1913	48' x 9' 0"	23T	BA	Various: 2837–3415 3855–7 Various: 3361–84	17354–61 17362–4 17365–72	6/57 10/59 11/57	D602/606 essentially identical with body style 5 x 1st; 2 x 3rd. However, D602 had one first class compartment reduced (internally) to become 4 x 3 x 3rd. Built for district use viz: Lot 767/846 – Nottingham; Lot 834 – LT&S line; D606 (all) – Metropolitan services. Some were later downgrad to all 3rd but withdrawal dates refer to the composite form.
606	738 757 855	6 18 1	1910 1910 1913	48' x 9' 0"			Various: 2801–3589	17373–96	2/57	
1559	985	6	1922	54' x 9' 0"		E	Various: 3482–564	17401–6	1/62	Essentially anticipating the LMS standard type but no exact LMS equivale
Third Class Brake (BT/BTZ*)										
	3	30	1878	40' x 8' 0"		CC1	Included 323			4 x 3rd Brake with 'American' equalised beam bogies. A rare example of u of clerestory on non-specialised stock at this period.
	5	40	1878	40' x 8' 0"		CA	Included 1409			5 x 3rd Brake, some (all?) with equalised beam 'American' style bogies.
504*	75 118 181	62 12 6	1882 1884 1887	31' x 8' 0" (Short buffers)		CA	Included 1490 and also 569; 1600 (second MR series)	Included 27719–20	11/34	Standard six wheel 3rd brake (3 x 3rd brake). Number series very fragmer tary but 2nd LMS series is confirmed as this type, thus giving some 2nd se MR numbers from the renumbering lists of 1933.
	151 194 220 241 257 291 Part 201	30 8 10 15 58 32 4	1886 1887 1888 1890 1890 1892 188	31' x 8' 0" (Long buffers) see remarks		CA	Included 865 (1st series) and Various: 149–1502 (2nd series) – mostly cyphered in later years 1247 + three more	27721–33	4/37	Lot 201 was to a low height for the West Bridge services.
502	Part 60 Part 85 150	10 80 20	1881 1882 1886	43' x 8' 0"	18T	CA	Included 1254; 429; 1431; 228, 537	22844–5	12/34	Built alongside T (D490) as 5 x 3rd Brake. Some later to BTL with lavatc replacing the central compartment (e.g. 537). Several conversions to pusl c1907, including 0444; 0500 and 748.
505*	100 409	44 8	1883 1897	27' x 8' 6"	10½T	CA	Included 1545			Four wheel stock for Metropolitan lines.
503*	429	11	1898	33' 6" x 8' 6"	14T	CC2	Various: 13–97	27740–6 27747–9	9/36 9/36	Built alongside D492 (TLZ) and D506 (CL), first seven for London– Manchester and last four for London–Bradford services. Six wheel.
500	512 518 524	34 30 10	1901 1901 1901	48' x 8' 6"	22½T	CC2	Various: 198–677 Various: 1–1099 Most (all?) 1132–71 1330; 1436	23010–27 23032–77	6/46 2/46 (see notes)	Built with other early bogie clerestories (F – D482; T – D489; C – D51 parts of set trains. Inner ends had short buffers and not all had guard's lo outs. All were 5 x 3rd Brake. In this case, the MR built the bulk but the fifty (built 1900) were from outside contractors (Lancaster, Gloucester a Birmingham). *Note:* 23056 (ex-1140) written off as 1140 in 5/55! *Note.* example (ex-351) converted to push-pull becoming 24493, scrapped 8/3
		50	1900				Various: 5–1796 (including most (?all?) 1407–49)	22981–23009 23028–31 also 24493 (see notes)	11/46 8/38	
501	538 680	14 34	1902 1907	48' x 8' 6"	22T	BA	1450–4/6–64 Various: 88–592	23082–95 23096–128	10/47 5/57	*6 x 3rd Brake:* for district use viz: Lot 538 – Manchester; Lot 680 – Birmingham.
497	560	19	1903	54' x 8' 6"	24½T	BC3	Various: 1705–2158	23246–64	6/52	*6 x 3rd Brake:* development of D500 by adding one extra compartment take up extra length. Built to replace vehicles sold to the M&GN system.
552	696 801	12 58	1908 1912	48' x 8' 6"	21T	BA	Various: 597–680 Various: 404–1623	22867–78 22912–66	6/53 10/58	*4 x 3rd Brake:* equivalent of D501. Lot 696 – Birmingham; Lot 801 – Sheffield. Lot 801 had 8ft. bogies and revised vertical panel heights. Thr conversions to push-pull as LMS Motor Diagram 67 viz: Lot 696 22873 (ex-653) to 24463 – converted post-1933, scrapped 3/4 Lot 801 1538 (1st LMS) to 24491 – converted pre-1933, scrapped 2/58 1554 (1st LMS) to 24492 and 1/56. Paired with LMS Motor Diagram 40 (ex-Composite D551) as follows: 24 17995 and 24491 + 17998 for Cudworth–Barnsley, later Ilkeston. 2449 17341 for Stonehouse and Nailsworth, then to Buxton in 1941.
556	713 859	26 4	1909 1913	50' x 9' 0"	23T	BA	Various: 833–1367 332/8; 616/92	23182–207 23208–11	10/57 9/58	*5 x 3rd Brake:* rather more spacious than 48' x 8' 6" stock and used for London services. Lot 713 was for Bedford & St. Albans trains, Lot 859 LT&S line.
557	714 849	9 12	1909 1913	50' x 9' 0"		BA	Various: 1369–1516 Various 1019–1059 1065–6/9	23212–20 23221–9 23231–3	4/52 4/57 12/55	*6 x 3rd Brake:* otherwise identical to D556. Lot 714 was for Bedford & Albans sets, Lot 849 designated 'Excursion' stock. No. 23216 to NCC in as NCC 20, later UTA 467.
604	740 759	6 18	1910 1910	48' x 9' 0"	23T	BA	1520–5 Various: 146–548	23140–5 23129–39 23146–52	7/55 4/56	*6 x 3rd Brake:* wide bodied version of D501 for Metropolitan line servi
603	765 780 847	16 24 16	1911 1911 1913	48' x 9' 0"		BA	1573–88 Various: 594–1036 and 1597–1613 Various: 651–757	22886–95 22879–85 22896–911 22967–80 also:- 23173–80 (see note)	6/57 2/57 2/58 11/57 12/56	*4 x 3rd Brake:* wide bodied version of D552 for use in Nottingham area. *Note:* Not all of D603 reached 2nd LMS series in original form. Some e examples were converted to 7 compartment form (without change of di and were therefore renumbered in correct sequence by the LMS as 2317 Six came from Lot 765, two from Lot 847.
1051	781 853	12 1	1911 1913	48' x 9' 0"	23T	BA	Various: 679–791 424	23161–72 23181	11/55 6/53	*7 x 3rd Brake:* for Metropolitan line services with slightly recessed brak portion.
1050	852	2	1913	48' x 9' 0"	23T	BA	778/1279	23153–4	7/55	*6 x 3rd Brake:* – virtually as D604 but with recessed brake end portion Metropolitan lines.
1055	836	4	1913	48' x 9' 0"	24T	BA	3864–7	23078–81	5/57	*5 x 3rd Brake:* for LT&S line – no precise 8' 6" wide equivalent.
1052	851	8	1913	50' x 8' 6"	23T	BA	766 Various: 1256–1327	23230 23234–40	11/56 12/56	*6 x 3rd Brake:* for 'Excursion' use – an unusual length/width combinat a Bain arc roof vehicle. In 1933, the LMS renumbered these vehicles in slightly confusing 'mix' with Lot 849 of D557 (above) – presumably be of the Excursion connotation.
1246	884	20	1914 (built 1921)	54' x 8' 6"	26T	E	Various: 1098–1268	23277–94 plus:- 24494–5 (see remarks)	8/62 2/59	*6 x 3rd Brake:* Ordered as 50ft. but delivered post World War I as 54ft. Several later conversions to push-pull becoming LMS motor diagram M6 MR/1st LMS 1113 – 24494; MR/1st LMS 1122–24495. They operatec Worth Valley branch.
1226	958	6	1921	48' x 9' 0"	25T	E	3863/8–72	23155–60	2/62	*6 x 3rd Brake:* for LT&S line.
1279	967	6	1921	54' x 9' 0"	25T	E	1296–7; 1321–2/31/46	23295–300	8/62	(*6 x 3rd Brake:* for St. Pancras–Southend services. Ordered as BTL but delivered without lavatories.
1542	982 992	4 4	1922 1922	54' x 9' 0"	27T	E	3878–81 4261–4	23301–4 23305–8	11/61 4/62	*7 x 3rd Brake:* for LT&S services.
2086	983	12	1922	54' x 9' 0"	25T	E	Various 306–1703	23265–76	1/62	*5 x 3rd Brake:* for Central District service – not delivered until 1923.

Diag.	Lot	Qty.	Date of Order	Dimensions	Wt.	Style	Numbering: Midland/1st LMS	Numbering: 2nd LMS	Type Extinct	Remarks
Composite Brake (BC/BCZ*)										
–	69	50	1881	40' x 8' 0"		CA	Included 164			3 x 3rd; 2 x 1st; 1 x brake/luggage. Visibly identical to C – Lots 16, 25, 83 above.
534*	71 127 235 256	2 6 12 10	1881 1885 1889 1890	32' x 8' 0"		CA	Included 247			The only six wheel BC type and designated for 'slip' workings. Length was non-standard for Clayton arc roof six wheel style. Described in lot book as CZ but obviously BCZ from diagram.
528	106	8	1884	40' x 8' 0"	17T	CA	Included 198			2 x 1st; 2 x 3rd; 1 x Brake.
526	109	20	1884	45' x 8' 0"	18¾T	CA				2 x 1st; 3 x 3rd; 1 x Brake. One to 'slip' use 1898. Built to same drawing as C – D513 and possibly converted by incorporating one 3rd class into brake end. At least seven conversions to push-pull use c1907.
525	434	11	1898	48' x 8' 6"	22½T	CC2	3087–97 (all cyphered later)	24722–8 plus: 24896 (see note)	1/39 2/37	Orthodox square panelled clerestory. One conversion to Driving Trailer pre-1933 viz: 03094–24896.
519 and	559	1	1903	54' x 8' 6"	25¼T	BC4	3666	24752	1/37	D519/519A represent a change of style within the same lot number and probably mark the changeover of panelling style on Bain clerestory stock. The Diagram numbers obviously post-date the vehicles otherwise D519A would be the major type. Both 2 x 1st; 4 x 3rd; 1 x Brake and built to replace vehicles sold to the M&GN (c.f. T – D485; BT – D497). *Note:* 29298–9 (ex-3439/41) were converted c1929 to Electric Driving Trailer composites for Morecambe and Heysham area. Scrapped 12/44 and 5/45.
519A	559	12	1903	54' x 8' 6"	25¼T	BC3	Various: 2978–3657	24742–51 plus:- 29298–9 (see note)	5/47	
1061	782 854	12 1	1912 1913	48' x 9' 0"	23T	BA	Various: 2853–3360 3698	24729–40 24741	6/54 see note	4 x 1st; 2 x 3rd; 1 x Brake but body style suggests originally 5 x 1st; 1 x 3rd. Several later downgraded to BT taking numbers 23309–14. Lot 854 was one such (23313) and the very last to be scrapped in 4/56. Lot 854 was actually built in 1916.

Compiled by D. Jenkinson, December 1983

On page 127 we speculated about the possible areas of operation of the Clayton non-corridor, non-lavatory, square-panelled clerestories and postulated the Leeds/Bradford area as a possibility. Just as this book was going to press, we discovered a group of four, albeit poor quality pictures, which not only re-inforced this view but also suggested a fairly standard five coach set formation; so by dint of a little minor re-adjustment of page layouts, we can include two examples here.

They show an unidentified Johnson 0-4-4T (in 1907) and an unidentified Johnson 0-6-0 (in 1905), both in the Bingley area. The tank engine is heading a five coach local set comprising 48ft. brake third (D500); 46ft. 7½in. third (D489); two 45ft. composites (D511); 48ft. brake third (D500). The composites seem to be arranged with their first class portions adjoining each other and the whole set is clearly close-coupled. The 0-6-0 goods engine heads a longer train consisting of an identical five coach set (leading) plus three strengtheners, of which two at least appear to be 48ft. square-panelled clerestory lavatory thirds to D486. The last vehicle could well be a round-panelled brake third. The train is described on the original picture as an excursion which would certainly explain the exclusively third class nature of the extra carriages.

(J. H. Wright Collection, courtesy NRM)

Chapter Eight

Full Brakes, Post Offices and Non-Passenger Coaching Stock

Introduction

For this final main chapter we have chosen to depart somewhat from the format used earlier in the book. This is mainly because there are so many categories of vehicle to consider and within each category there could at times be considerable further variety. Consequently it would be quite impossible to make generalized statements covering more than a handful of vehicles. As a result, we have elected to follow more closely the style of *Midland Wagons*, deal with each category in turn and feature some of the more numerous examples on the way. For convenience, however, we have completed what we hope is a comprehensive single summary of all non-passenger stock categories and this is given at the end of the chapter as *Table 11*.

The vehicles themselves can be subdivided into two main groups - those which appeared in the same diagram book as the passenger-carrying vehicles (Brakes and TPOs) and the 'official' Non-Passenger Coaching Stock (Horseboxes, Carriage Trucks, etc.). The first main group generally followed the visual lines of their contemporary passenger carrying vehicles, while the so-called 'Non-Passenger' group exhibited wide variations of style. Some looked very much at home in the passenger fleet, while others were more like the freight vehicles in appearance; but all shared in common the ability to be attached to and run at the same speed as passenger trains. All were painted in passenger colours but many had simplified lining, or none at all, and the numbering was, to say the least, a little bewildering. We have, therefore, prefaced *Table 11* with a brief supplementary note on the numbering systems - at least as far as we can deduce them from the often fragmentary information available.

Passenger Full Brakes

The Midland Railway's passenger brakes were tolerably straightforward to understand. Each main stylistic variation made a contribution but the vast majority dated from the Clayton arc roof and square-panelled clerestory periods.

The first standard type was a 25ft. Clayton arc roof four wheel design to Diagram 529 *(Figure 56)*. The style pre-dated the lot book and the design was, by quite a margin, the most numerous of all the full brakes. Some 49 of them reached the LMS but all but one had gone by the time of the 1933 renumbering.

These carriages were followed by a substantial build of square-panelled clerestory brakes, both six and eight wheel, gangwayed and non-gangwayed. Three principal variations were apparent, a 31ft. six wheel version, a 50ft. gangwayed bogie type (Joint Stock) and a 45ft. non-gangwayed bogie design (Midland owned). The six wheelers were built gangwayed for the Joint Stock and non-gangwayed for the Midland itself. All varieties are represented in *Figures 57 & 58*.

The 45ft. non-gangwayed square-panelled bogie brakes appeared during the early Bain period and from them was developed a 45ft. round-panelled gangwayed version, fitted with shelves for Pigeon traffic (Diagram 536). This was quite a numerous type *(see Table 11)* but apart from this diagram, only a few brakes were built between 1904 and the Grouping. Two 54ft. round-panelled clerestories (Diagram 573) and twelve 48ft. semi-elliptical roof coaches (Diagram 1067) represented the sum total of new bogie brakes and all were gangwayed. Finally there was also a batch of 24 six wheel low elliptical roof brakes ordered in 1912 (Diagram 530A). These are illustrated in *Plate 187.* There were also a few ex-ambulance brakes which we have not included.

Plate 187 Six wheel full brake No. 521 (second LMS No. 34154) to Lot 788, D530A. This neat design was, in effect, the round-panelled version of the standard clerestory brake featured at *Figure 57.* The roof profile was, in effect, identical to the lower part of the standard Midland clerestory roof. Note the unusual 'beehive'-shaped buffer housings - a not uncommon feature of some Midland non-passenger stock at this time.

(BR/LMR)

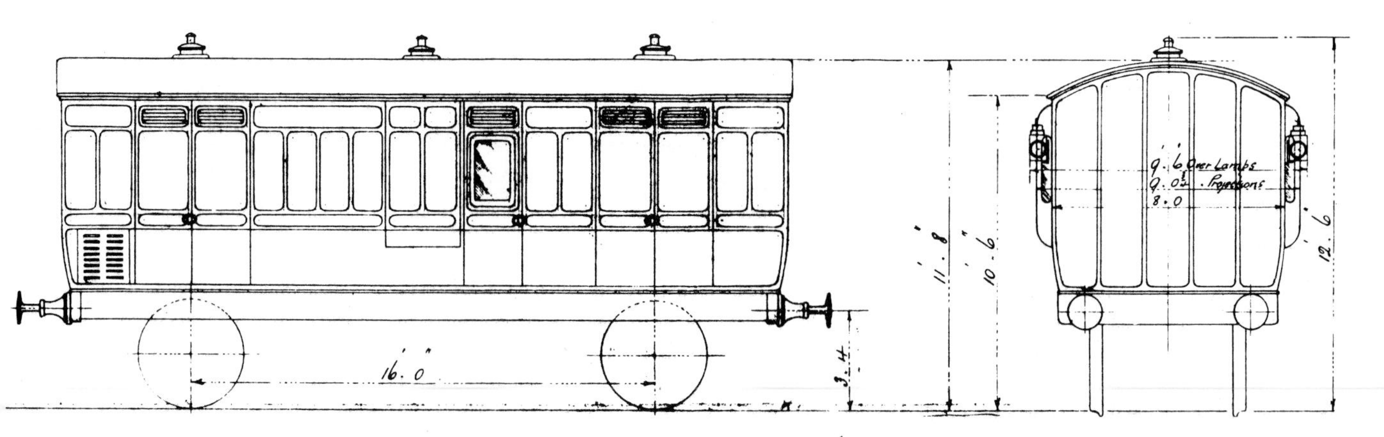

Four Wheel Full Brake to D529

Figure 56 and Plates 188 & 189 The 25ft. Clayton arc roof full brake was one of the most common Midland types, and built over a period of some twenty years. The photographs show MR No. 450, a pre-lot book example, and MSJS No. 7, one of ten built to Lot 28 for the MSJS and probably numbered, initially, MSJS 1-10. Note the roof lights on MR No. 450 - a feature not indicated on the diagram nor, we believe, ever found on the lot book vehicles at *Table 11*. Scale: 4mm. = 1ft.

(Authors' Collection, NRM and BR/LMR)

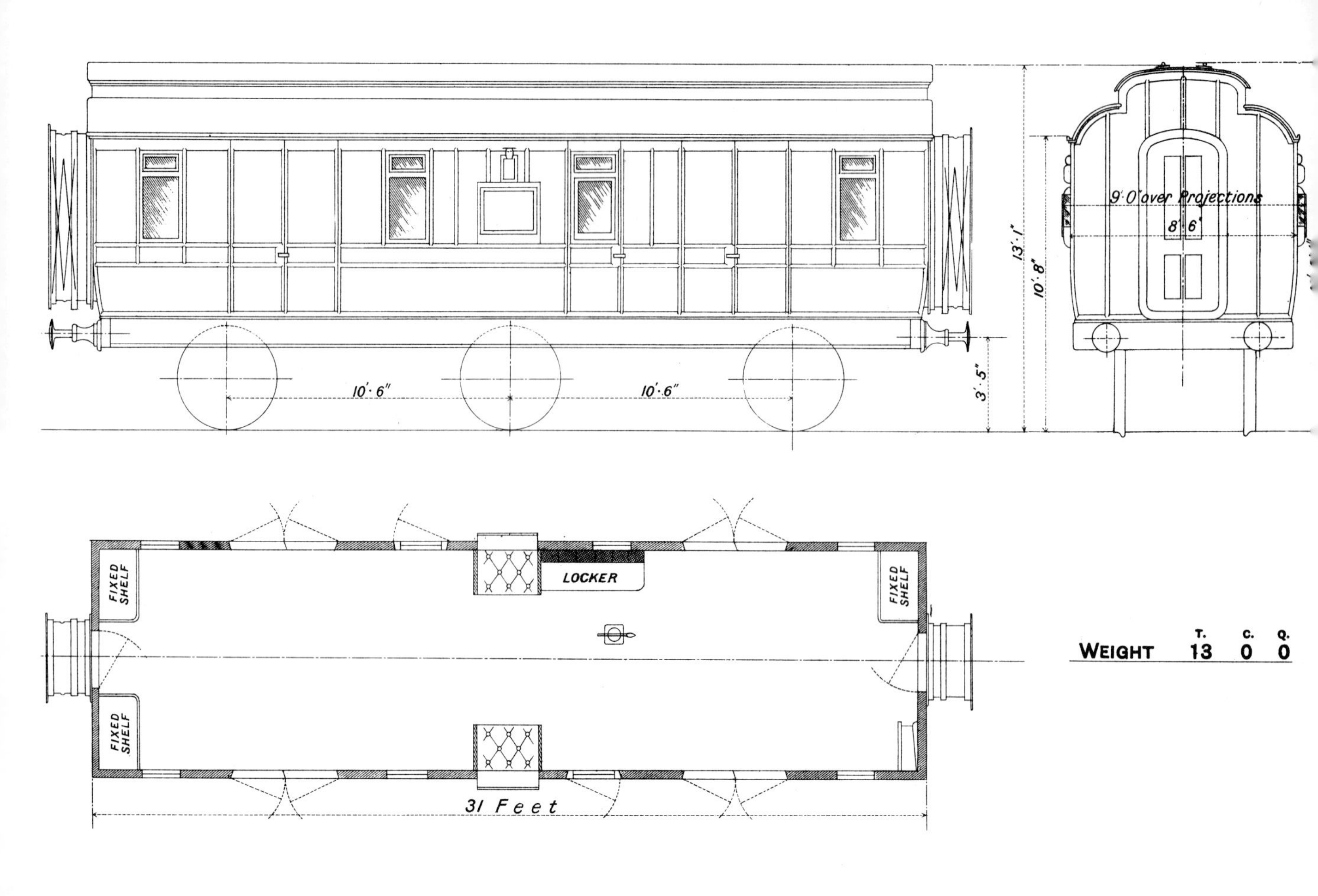

Six Wheel Full Brake to D530/568

Figure 57 and Plate 190 This was another highly characteristic type, and unquestionably the most common square-panelled clerestory design to be built, numbering almost 300 examples *(see Table 11)*. The standard type to D530 was non-gangwayed (as represented by MR No. 29 to Lot 400) and built to two heights, 13ft. 3in. and 13ft. 1in. No. 29 is of the latter variety. A gangwayed version was also built to D568 for Joint Stock use and we give the drawing of this variant. These were all to the 13ft. 1in. height. The design originated with three vehicles built for the 1897 Bradford to Bristol train to Lot 389, which were given the original large look-outs *(see Plate 18)*. They were later altered to standard form. Scale: 4mm. = 1ft.

(K. C. Woodhead Collection and NRM)

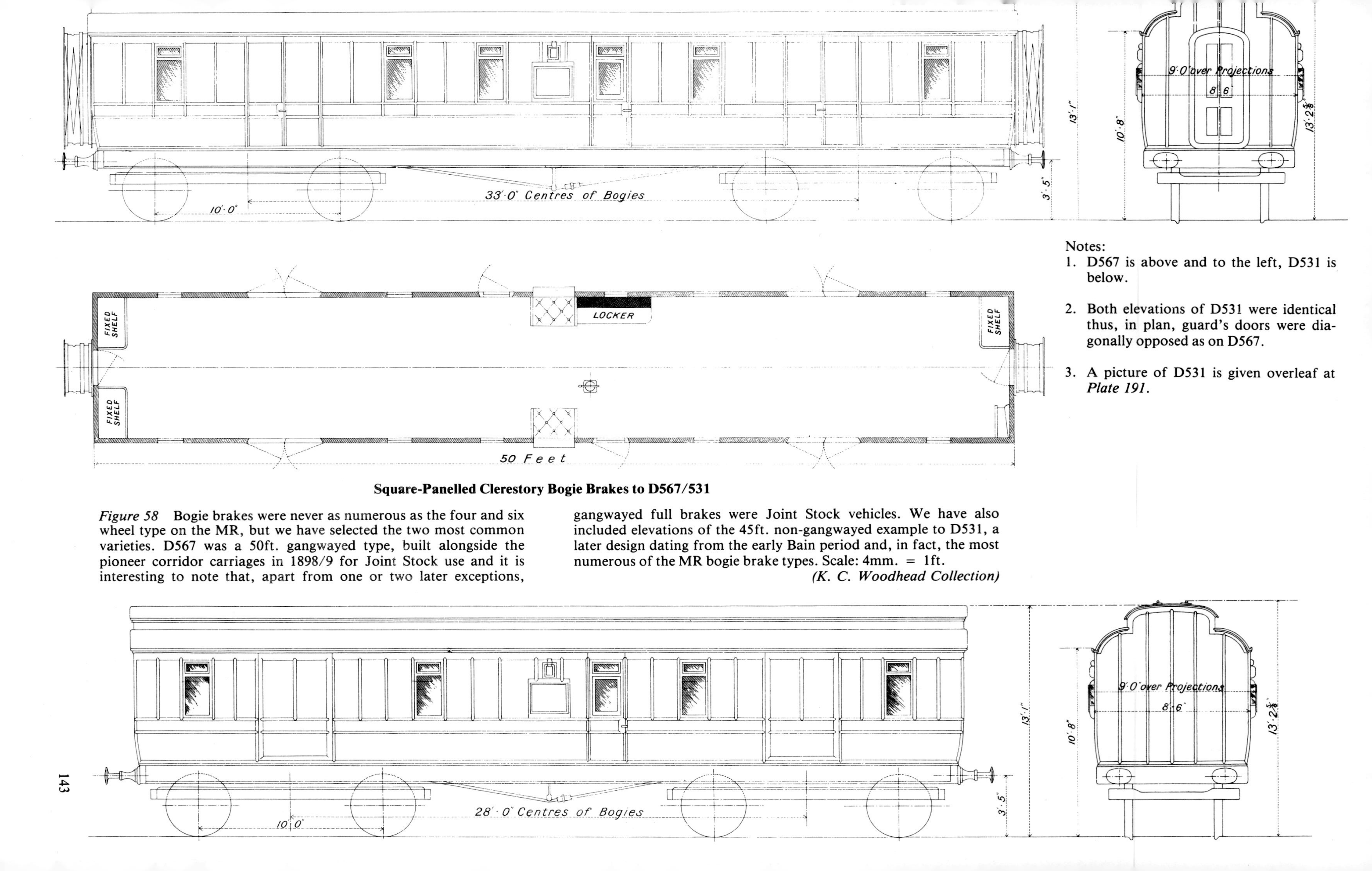

Notes:
1. D567 is above and to the left, D531 is below.
2. Both elevations of D531 were identical thus, in plan, guard's doors were diagonally opposed as on D567.
3. A picture of D531 is given overleaf at *Plate 191*.

Square-Panelled Clerestory Bogie Brakes to D567/531

Figure 58 Bogie brakes were never as numerous as the four and six wheel type on the MR, but we have selected the two most common varieties. D567 was a 50ft. gangwayed type, built alongside the pioneer corridor carriages in 1898/9 for Joint Stock use and it is interesting to note that, apart from one or two later exceptions, gangwayed full brakes were Joint Stock vehicles. We have also included elevations of the 45ft. non-gangwayed example to D531, a later design dating from the early Bain period and, in fact, the most numerous of the MR bogie brake types. Scale: 4mm. = 1ft.

(K. C. Woodhead Collection)

Plate 191 A 45ft. bogie brake, No. 157, to D531. This number was retained in 1923 and it became LMS No. 33595 in 1933. Note the coil springs to the bogie bolster on the otherwise standard 10ft. bogie.

(NRM)

Post Office and Associated Vehicles

The Midland Railway carried nothing like the volume of postal traffic as did some of its rivals, notably the LNWR/WCJS routes, and its travelling post offices were few in number. In spite of the fact that many of them lasted well into the post-1922 period, we have been quite unable to locate diagrams for most of them, save for the Bain clerestories of 1907, featured in *Figure 59.*

Prior to these carriages, all the postal-associated vehicles emerged during the Clayton period, always in small batches. Fortunately, many of them were photographed so we can give quite a comprehensive pictorial coverage even though we cannot offer any suitable drawings. Visually, most fell into two categories, the old style Clayton clerestories and the standard Clayton arc roof vehicles. They were mostly fitted with offset gangways to run with each other but, of course, were not capable of being gangwayed to the main train, even after corridor coaches were in use. There were also two 48ft. square light clerestories to Lot 455 *(see Table 11).*

Most of the Midland Railway's travelling post office services were on the north-east to south-west route in collaboration with the NER and the majority of vehicles built, albeit of wholly Midland Railway design, were jointly owned by both companies. The Midland Railway had sole ownership of some vehicles *(see Table 11)* but we cannot offer confirmed details of the routes which they served. Moreover, some of the vehicles which were originally owned by the Midland Railway were transferred to M&NE later *(see Table 11).*

Plate 192 - caption opposite

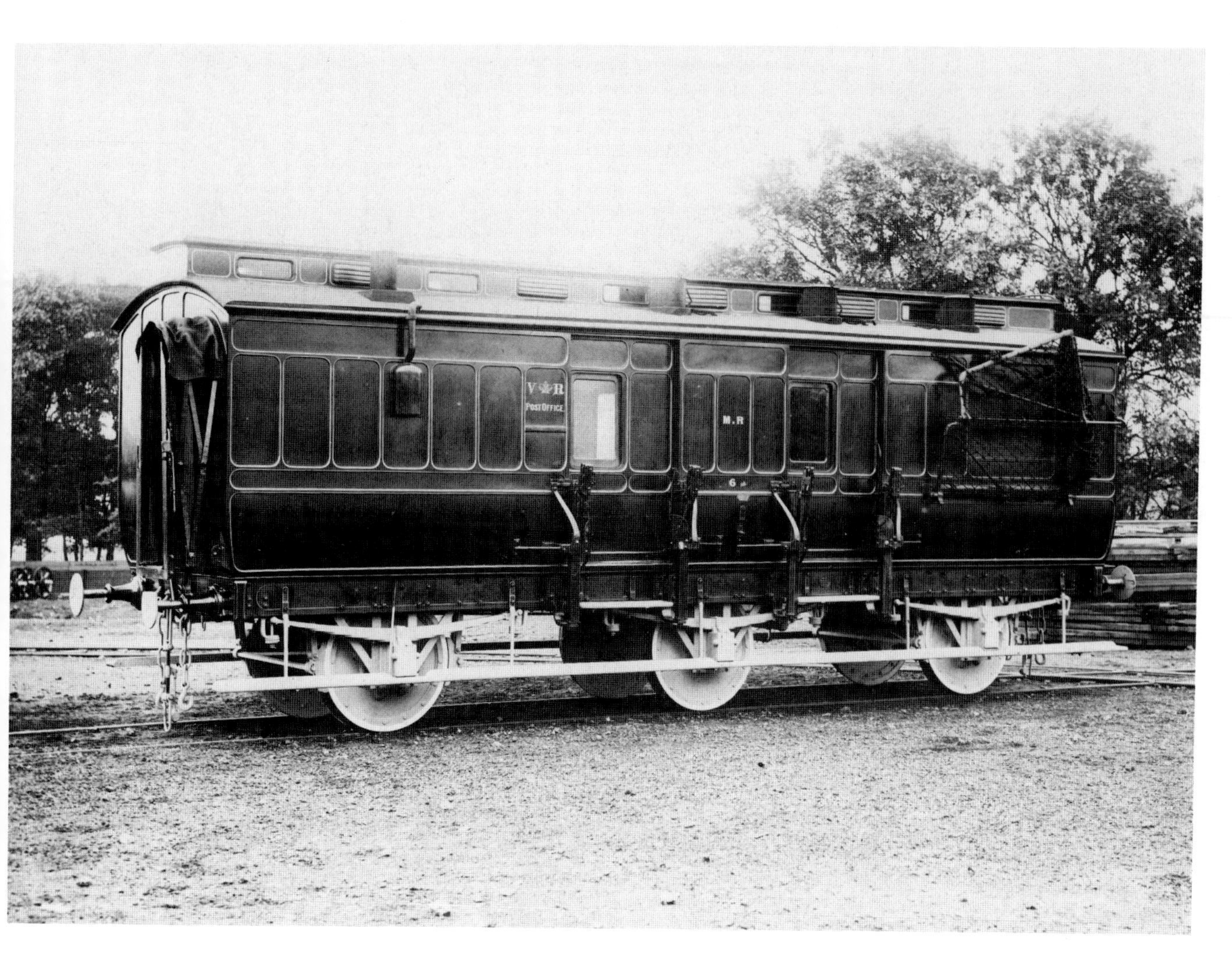

Plates 192 to 194 (this page and opposite) These three pictures illustrate typical early clerestory Clayton post office vehicles. MR No. 1 *(opposite)* was built as one of three sorting carriages to Lot 12. One source suggests that the group later became M&NEJPS Nos. 1-3. The other two views show opposite side views of two different examples from Lot 13 - described as post office tenders and fitted with pick-up nets. There is some doubt about the number of vehicles built, three or six, to this lot *(see Table 11)*. The upper view shows MR No. 6, in late Victorian days, whilst in the lower view M&NEJPS No. 5 is seen in the Edwardian period. Whether there were three MR and three M&NEJPS vehicles, or whether the three M&NE coaches were ex-MR is not clear.

(BR/LMR)

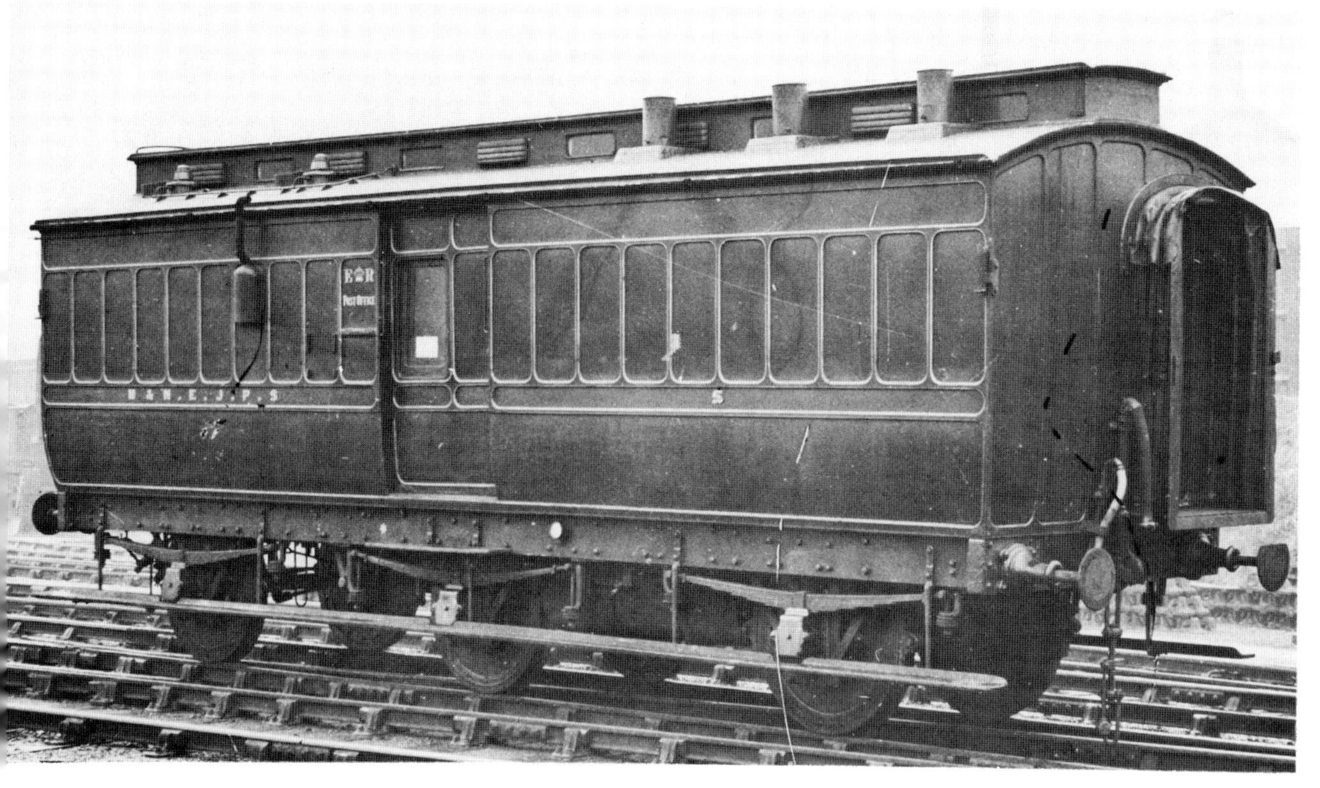

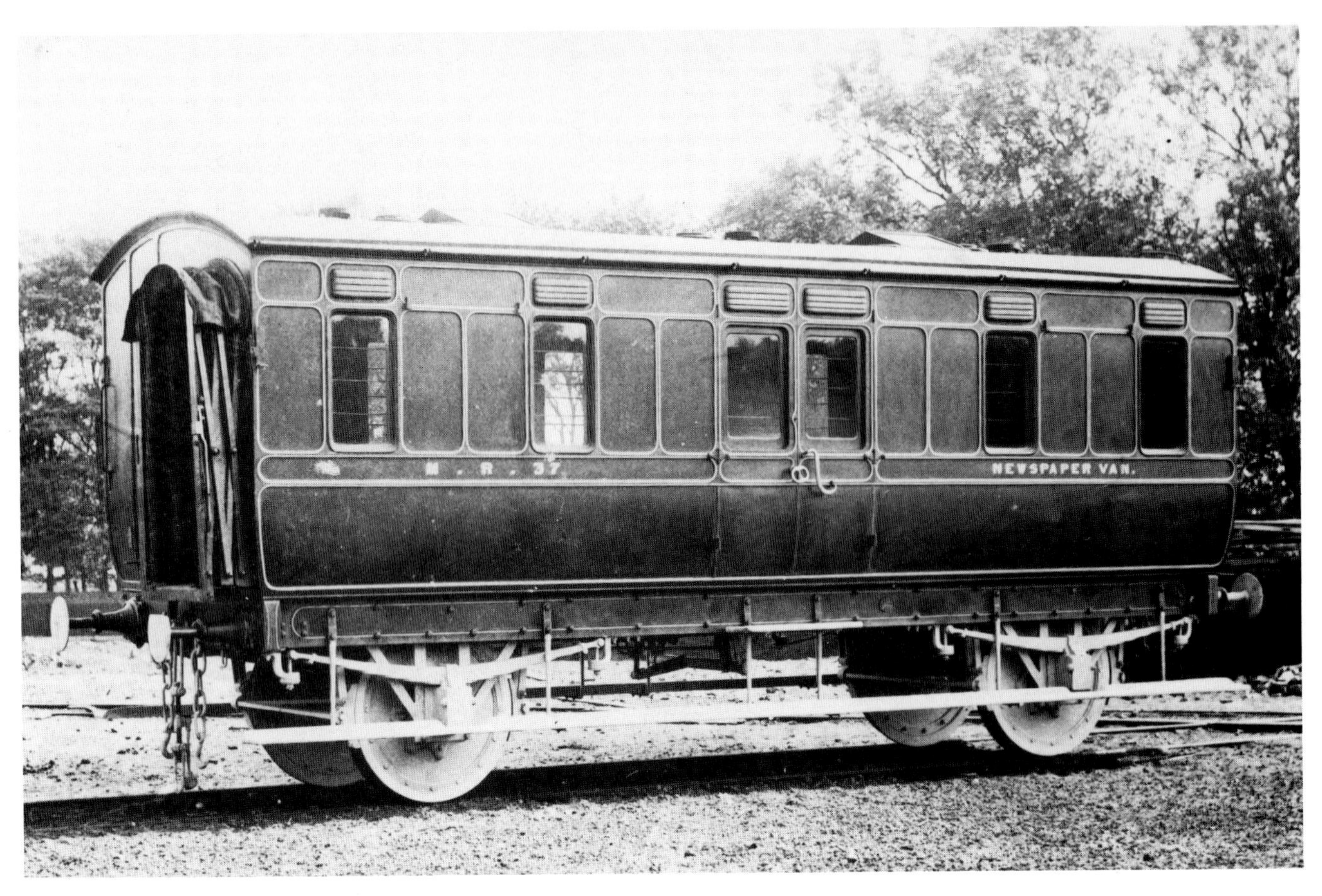

Plates 195 to 197 (this page and opposite top These views show a typical collection of arc roof postal vans of different types. The view *(above)* shows 25ft. newspaper van No. 37, one of three built to Lot 33 and derived from a pre-lot book type with a single central door. The two other views show parcels sorting vans - 32ft. six wheeler No. 74 to Lot 131 (one of three), and a handsome 43ft. bogie version, No. 80, one of two built as part of Lot 113. The rest of the lot were full thirds! The two parcels designs survived well into the LMS period *(see Table 11).*

(BR/LMR)

Plates 198 & 199 (opposite, centre and lower) A group of ▶ four, good looking 43ft. postal carriages built to Lots 191, 307 and 344, between 1887 and 1894. These pictures show opposite side views of the two examples (MR Nos. 7 & 8) to Lot 191. It is believed that they were later transferred to the M&NJEPS.

(BR/LMR)

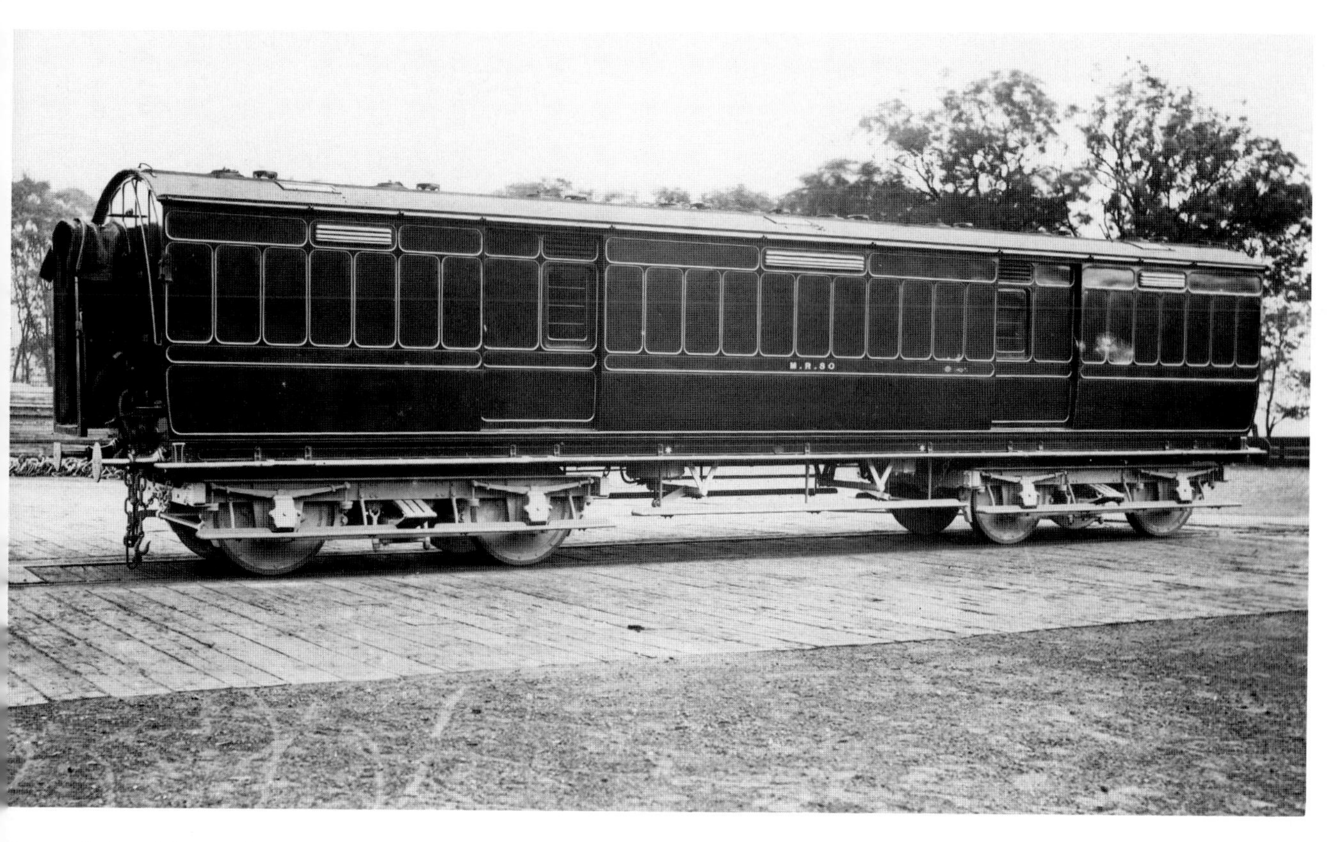

Plates 197 to 199 - captions opposite

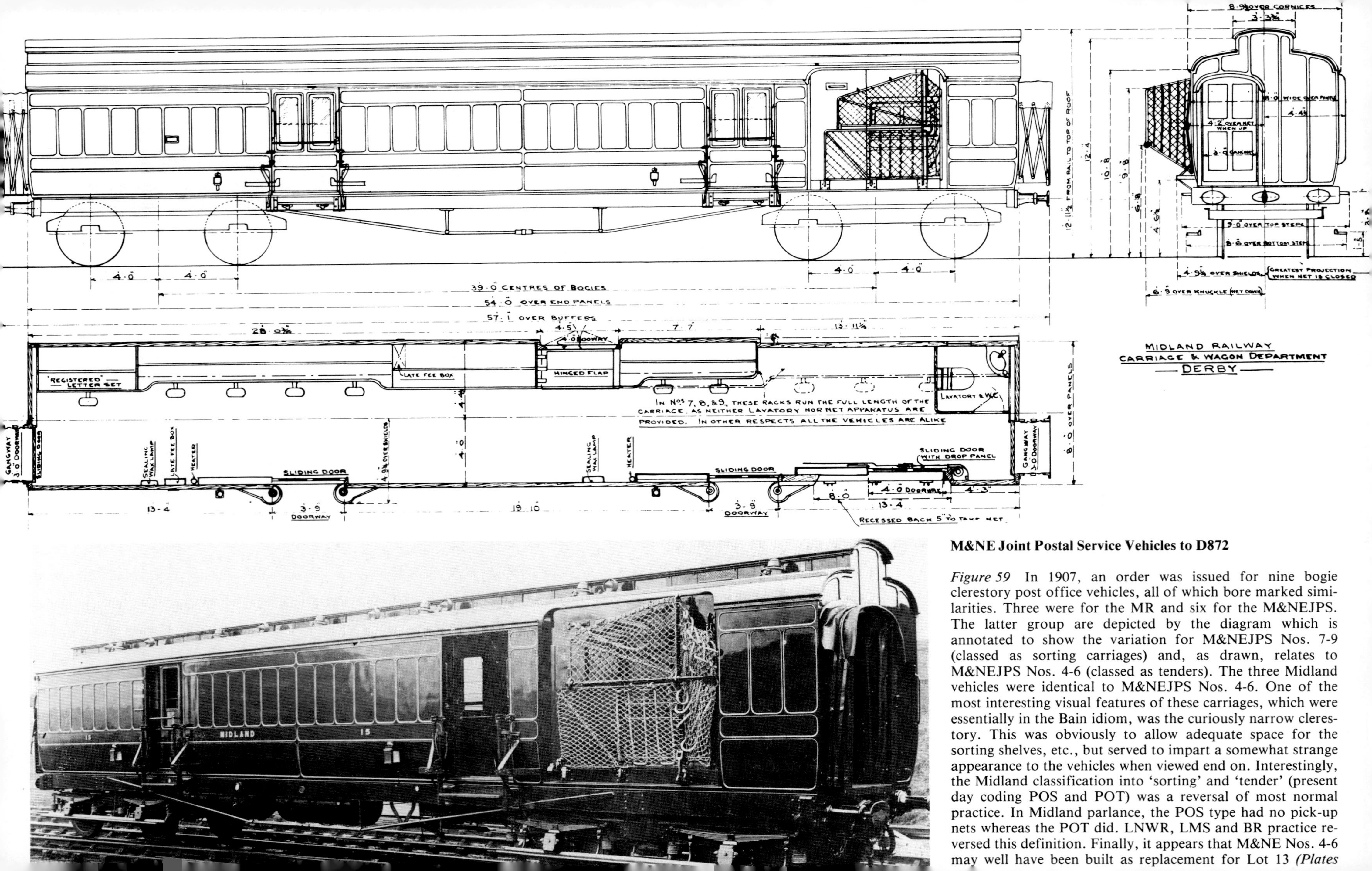

M&NE Joint Postal Service Vehicles to D872

Figure 59 In 1907, an order was issued for nine bogie clerestory post office vehicles, all of which bore marked similarities. Three were for the MR and six for the M&NEJPS. The latter group are depicted by the diagram which is annotated to show the variation for M&NEJPS Nos. 7-9 (classed as sorting carriages) and, as drawn, relates to M&NEJPS Nos. 4-6 (classed as tenders). The three Midland vehicles were identical to M&NEJPS Nos. 4-6. One of the most interesting visual features of these carriages, which were essentially in the Bain idiom, was the curiously narrow clerestory. This was obviously to allow adequate space for the sorting shelves, etc., but served to impart a somewhat strange appearance to the vehicles when viewed end on. Interestingly, the Midland classification into 'sorting' and 'tender' (present day coding POS and POT) was a reversal of most normal practice. In Midland parlance, the POS type had no pick-up nets whereas the POT did. LNWR, LMS and BR practice reversed this definition. Finally, it appears that M&NE Nos. 4-6 may well have been built as replacement for Lot 13 *(Plates*

Plates 200 to 203 (opposite and this page) This group of pictures has been selected to complement *Figure 59*. The two ex-works views of Midland No. 15 show both sides of the tenders with pick-up net apparatus. M&NEJPS Nos. 4-6 were identical. The third view, of M&NEJPS No. 30286 (ex-M&NEJPS No. 7, later No. 1981) shows the non-sorting side (without nets) of the 'sorting' carriages (M&NEJPS Nos. 7-9). We cannot locate an opposite side view of this variant. Finally, Nos. 30283/5 are seen awaiting scrapping in 1952. The picture has been selected to emphasize the 'narrow' clerestory and the curious proportions it gave to the end elevation. Note that the vehicles remained branded M&NEJPS throughout their lives.

(BR/LMR and Authors' Collection)

Livestock Vehicles

This group consisted of horseboxes and prize cattle vans, the former being much more numerous. Both types of vehicle, with but one exception (prize cattle Diagram 412), shared a feature in common, namely a compartment for the travelling groom or attendant, the only 'official' non-railway staff passengers ever to ride regularly in non-passenger vehicles.

Dealing first with the horseboxes, there were 552 such vehicles built between 1879 and 1915 to three lengths and five diagrams. A total of 448 of these survived to the Grouping, symptomatic of the considerable importance of horse-drawn traffic in the pre-grouping railway period. Most of the horseboxes were 16ft. long but batches of 19ft. 6in. and, finally, 20ft. vehicles interspersed the 16ft. series *(see Table 11)*.

Length apart, the main visual differences were in body profile. The 16ft. diagrams were 7ft. 9in. wide and straight-sided (Diagram 397), or 8ft. 3in. wide with curved-in lower panels (Diagram 398). The 19ft. 6in. series, featured in *Figure 60* were again 7ft. 9in. wide and straight sided and, built between the two 16ft. diagrams, but the two 20ft. varieties (Diagrams 400 & 401) were 8ft. 6in. wide with a much more curvaceous profile *(see Plate 206)*. Diagram 400 had square-cornered panelling and 401 had round-cornered, with minor internal dimension changes; but they were otherwise very similar. Both of the 20ft. types were panelled in the style of passenger carriages whereas the earlier series had more of a freight vehicle look. Some late examples of Diagram 401 were reduced to 8ft. 3in. wide.

Turning now to the Prize Cattle Vans (PCVs), two diagrams only were officially regarded as non-passenger stock, namely Diagram 412 (18ft. 8in. long) and Diagram 413 (23ft. long). This is one of those awkward areas where the non-passenger stock/freight stock differentiation becomes confused, for there was also another diagram (D298) for a calf van which was classified as a freight vehicle and very similar to Diagram 412. It appears in *Midland Wagons, Vol. II* (page 3). In passing we should additionally point out that Lot 546 was wrongly ascribed to Diagram 298 in that survey. It was in fact built to Diagram 413 so we rectify the mistake by offering D413, the genuine non-passenger vehicle, in *Figure 61*

As far as we can judge, the determining factor appears to have been wheel diameter. The short PCV to Diagram 412 was, in most essentials, all but identical to the Calf Van (Diagram 298) in the freight series, save for its larger wheels. It certainly had no groom's compartment, the absence of which would otherwise possibly suggest 'freight' classification. The only pictures we know which illustrate Midland Railway PCVs appear in *Midland Wagons, Vol. II* (page 4) and both of the views depict Diagram 412, Lot 204. For this reason we do not repeat them here.

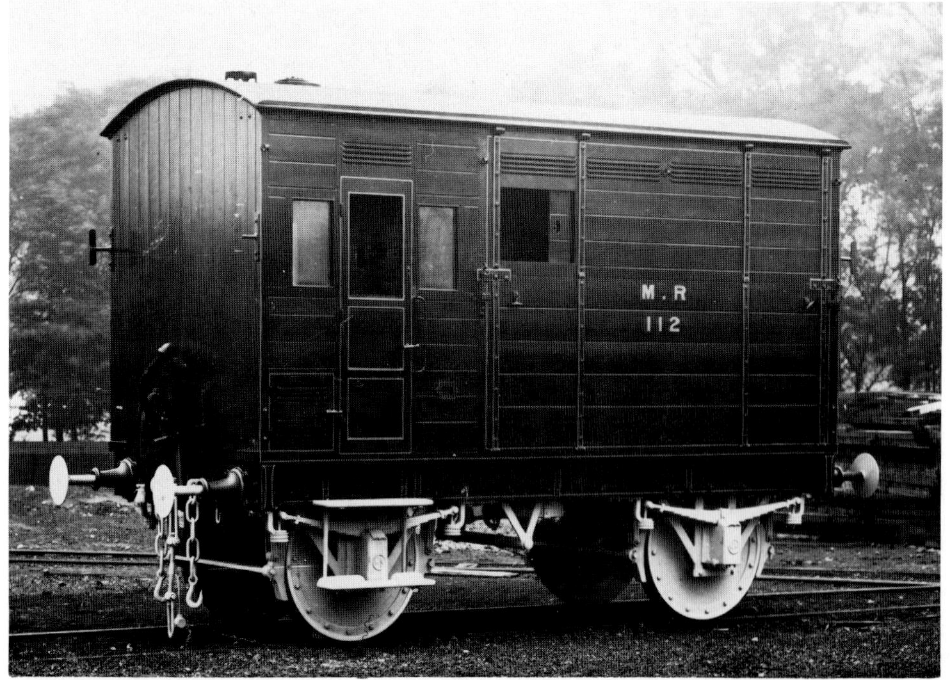

Plates 204 to 205 These views show the two standard MR 16ft. horse-box designs. No. 112 is to D397 and, like all the early examples of the diagram, was built with grease axleboxes. No. 438 is the later style to D398 and, although much detail remained the same, the changed proportions give it an altogether more modern appearance. Note, on both vehicles, the lack of outside handbrake levers - a situation which was remedied on all non-passenger stock in 1904 (and, subsequently), at an estimated cost of £3 per vehicle!

(BR/LMR)

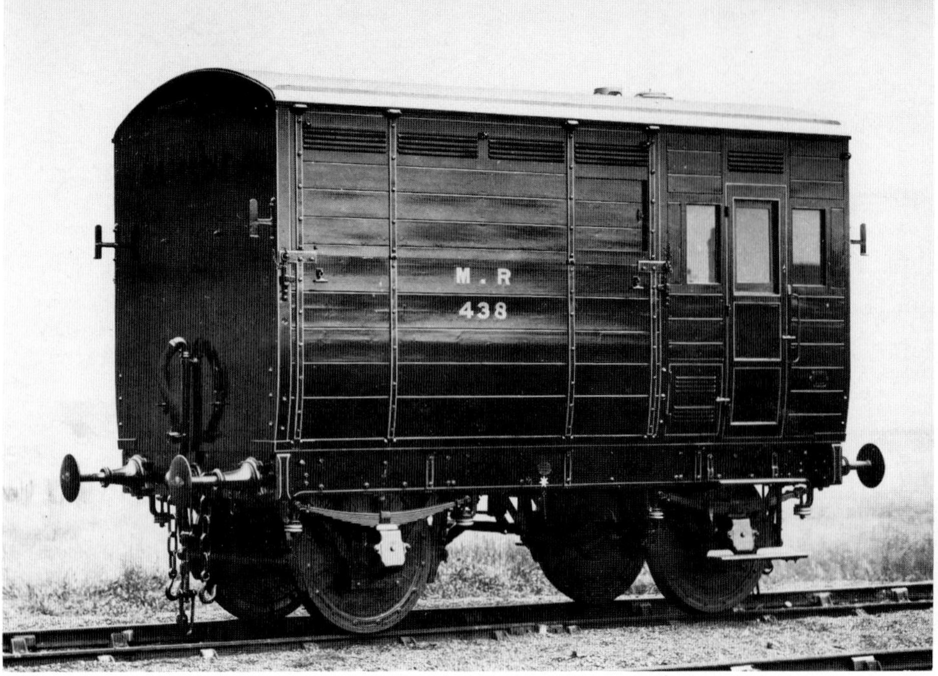

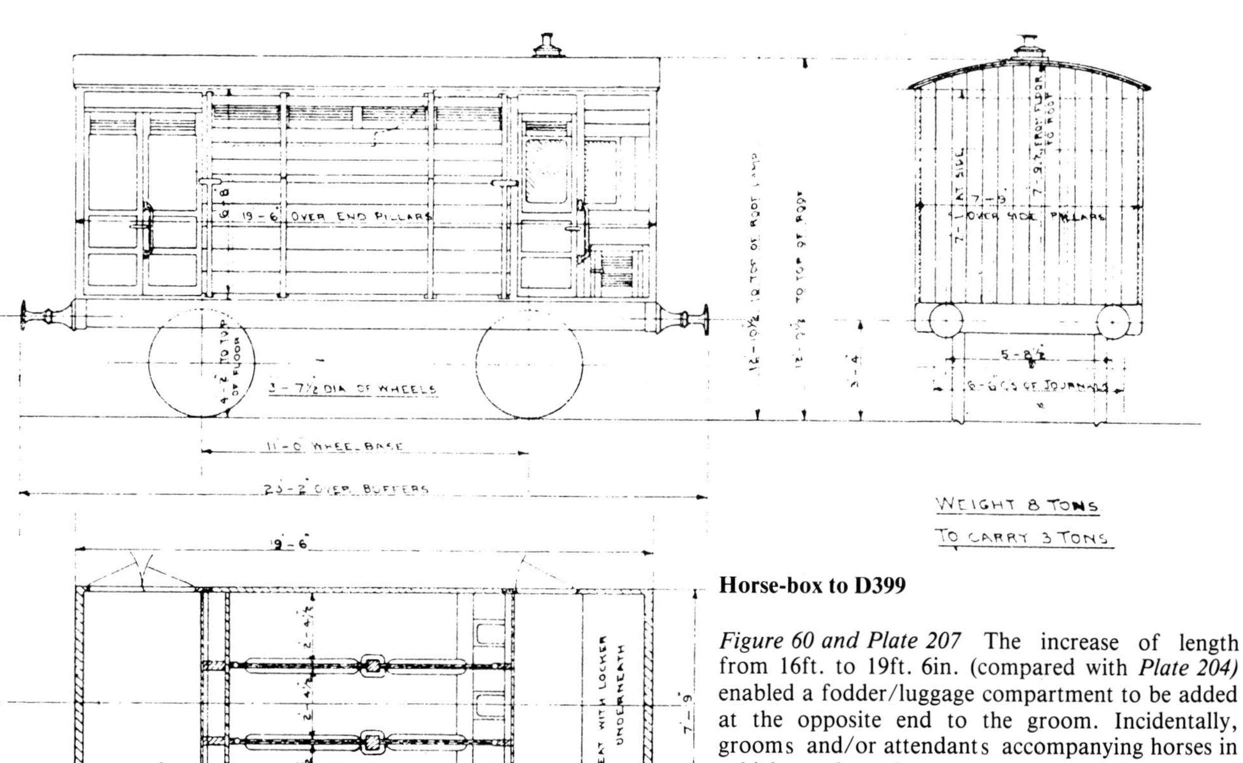

Horse-box to D399

Figure 60 and Plate 207 The increase of length from 16ft. to 19ft. 6in. (compared with *Plate 204)* enabled a fodder/luggage compartment to be added at the opposite end to the groom. Incidentally, grooms and/or attendants accompanying horses in vehicles such as these were not regarded as passengers by the MR. We do not know quite how they were classified! Note the lack of a handbrake lever, later rectified after 1904. Scale: 4mm. = 1ft.

(Authors' Collection and BR/LMR)

Plate 206 This enlarged view, from a Midland train at Cotehill in 1910, is the only picture we have found of the 20ft. horse-boxes to either D400 or D401. Two examples of D400 are shown and, fortuitously, both sides of the design are shown. Note the outside handbrake lever, fitted after original construction.

(BR/LMR)

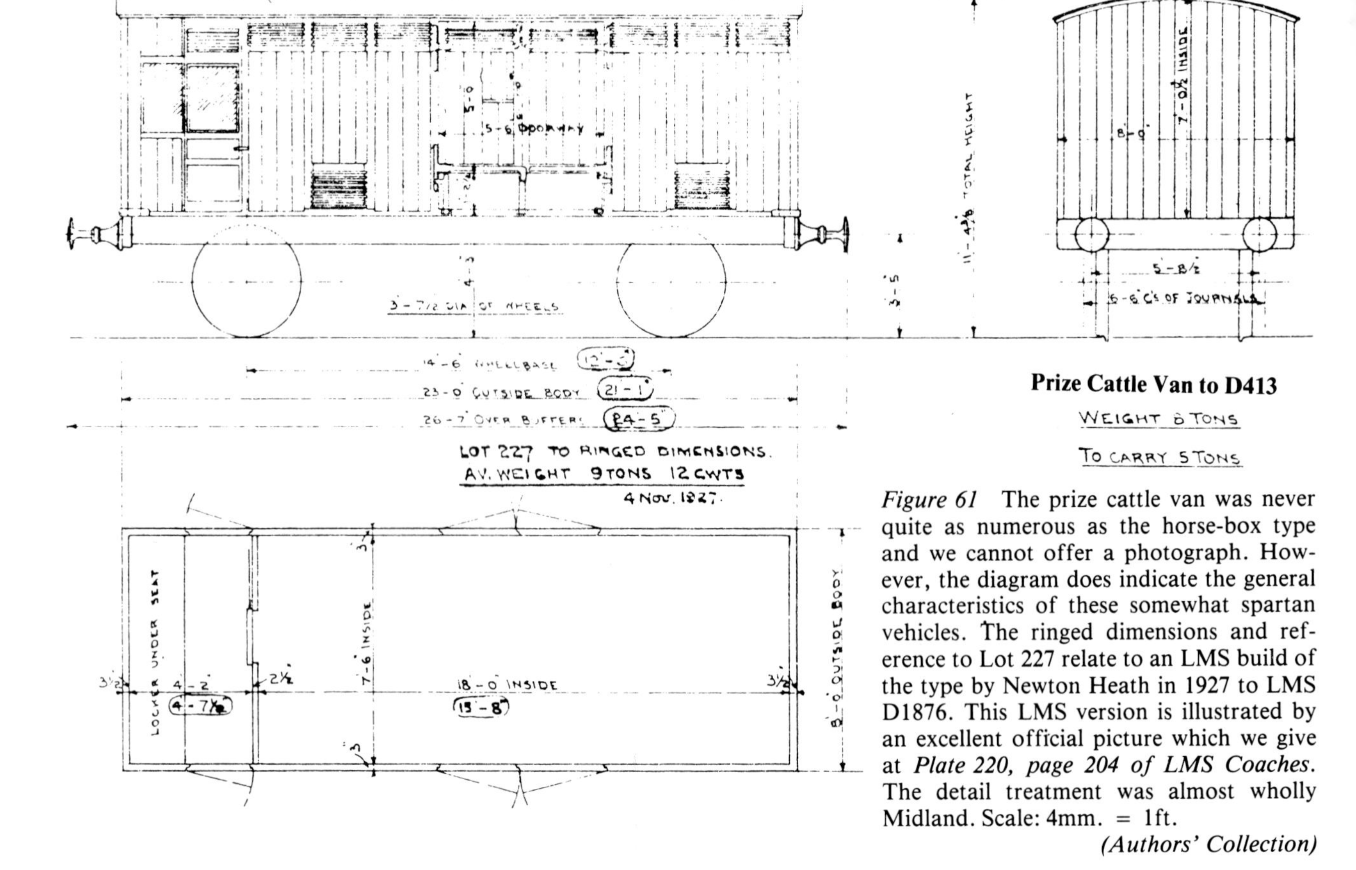

Prize Cattle Van to D413

Figure 61 The prize cattle van was never quite as numerous as the horse-box type and we cannot offer a photograph. However, the diagram does indicate the general characteristics of these somewhat spartan vehicles. The ringed dimensions and reference to Lot 227 relate to an LMS build of the type by Newton Heath in 1927 to LMS D1876. This LMS version is illustrated by an excellent official picture which we give at *Plate 220, page 204 of LMS Coaches.* The detail treatment was almost wholly Midland. Scale: 4mm. = 1ft.
(Authors' Collection)

Covered Carriage Trucks and Similar Vehicles

This group of vehicles was characterized by high roofs and end doors. Most were, indeed, designated as Covered Carriage Trucks (CCT), a type originally designed for conveying horse-drawn vehicles, usually those of higher monetary value, under weatherproof conditions; but we have felt it sensible to include the essentially similar motor car vans (MV) and scenery vans, plus a curious hybrid as well.

The 'proper' CCTs were in three main series, differentiated by length, namely 20ft., 25ft. and 30ft. 11in., the last-named being a six wheel type, the others four wheel. All shared common visual features and two heights were used namely 13ft. 3in., for normal use, and 12ft. 8in. to clear the Metropolitan line gauge. We feature in *Figures 62 & 63* the 20ft. and 25ft. versions each built in both heights. The six wheeler (Diagram 404) was built only to the lower height.

Derived from the CCTs were the MVs, two dimensionally identical 31ft. six wheel designs to Diagram 414 (square-panelled and Diagram 414A (round-panelled). The division of lots between the two diagrams is not certain and our deductions are given in *Table 11*. Visually both types looked very much at home in passenger trains. We illustrate Diagram 414A in *Plate 208* and Diagram 414 appears in *Plate 225* of *Midland Wagons, Vol. I.*

The remaining vehicles in this particular 'family' were six in number, all of bogie type and with one exception classed for 'Theatrical Scenery'. The first to appear was a fully-panelled 50ft. vehicle to Diagram 405, Lot 623, classified as a 'truck' and an obviously experimental one-off *(Plate 209)*. The other four were outside-framed vehicles designated as 'vans' and built on second-hand 44ft. 10in. underframes to Lot 950 in 1920/1. These were shown on page 38 of the non-passenger book but were never given a diagram number.

The last of the six bogie CCTs was a real maverick. Built as an experimental one-off to Diagram 415, it shared its cross-profile with the Diagram 400 Horsebox but was described as a combined Horsebox/CCT. We suspect it may have been intended to carry a complete equipage, carriage and pair as it were, and the idea seems a sensible one for use by well-to-do clientele. However it was clearly not a success and was never repeated. Perhaps the lack of a groom's compartment made it less attractive in use than it was in appearance *(Plate 210)*.

Plate 208 Motor car van D414A, No. 657, (D414 illustrated at *Plate 225 Midland Wagons - Volume* Note that No. 657 has the style buffer housings *Plate 187)* and shorter springs compared with square-panelled D414.
(BR/LM

ıtes 209 & 210 (above) These two pictures show the experimental 'one-off' bogie
:T type vehicles mentioned in the main text. No. 128 is the 50ft. scenery van to D405
d No. 16, the combined horse-box/CCT to D415. The latter shared a similar
e/roof junction with the horse-boxes to D400 *(Plate 206)*, but the central roof arch
s taller.

(NRM)

Plate 211 (below) This view shows the outside-framed scenery van No. 764, one of four built to Lot 950 on second-hand underframes.

(NRM)

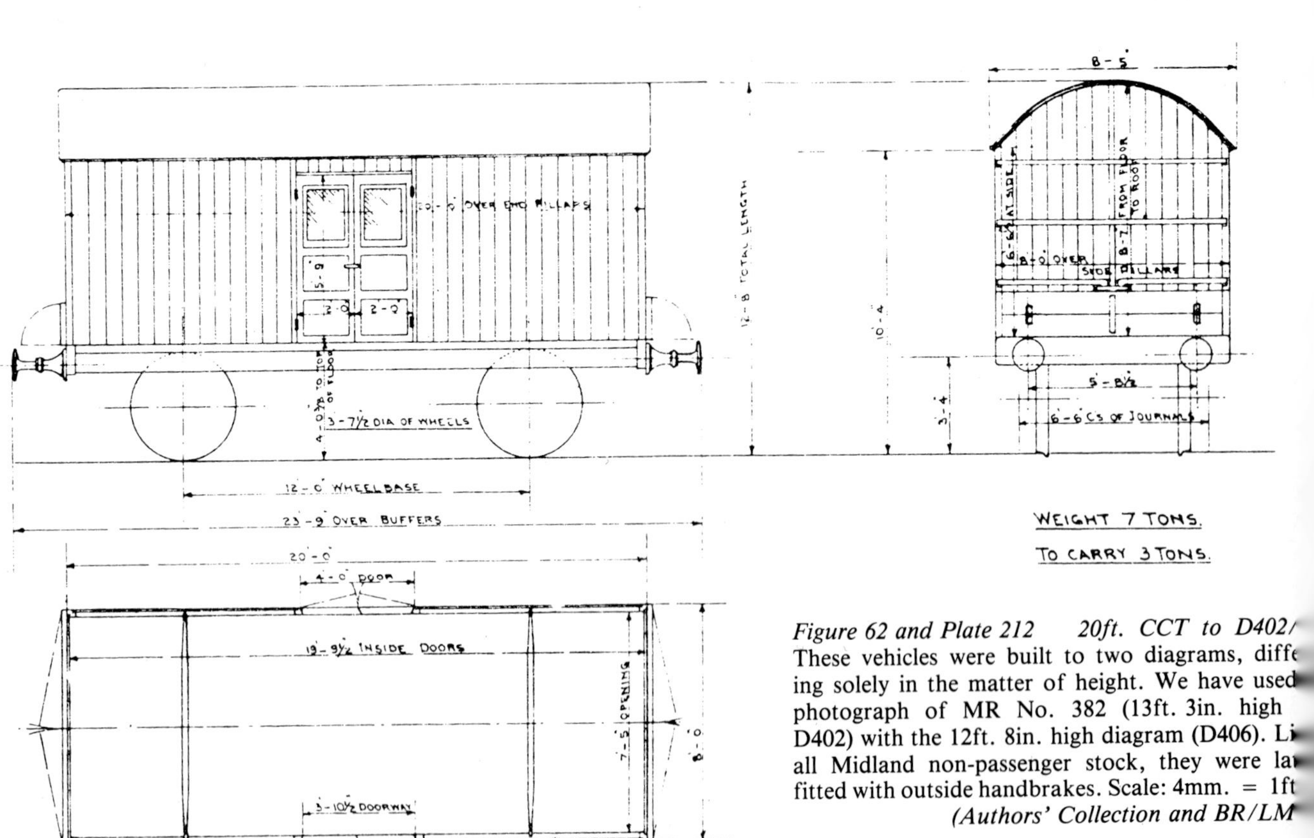

Figure 62 and Plate 212 20ft. CCT to D402/ These vehicles were built to two diagrams, diffe ing solely in the matter of height. We have used photograph of MR No. 382 (13ft. 3in. high D402) with the 12ft. 8in. high diagram (D406). Li all Midland non-passenger stock, they were la fitted with outside handbrakes. Scale: 4mm. = 1ft
(Authors' Collection and BR/LM

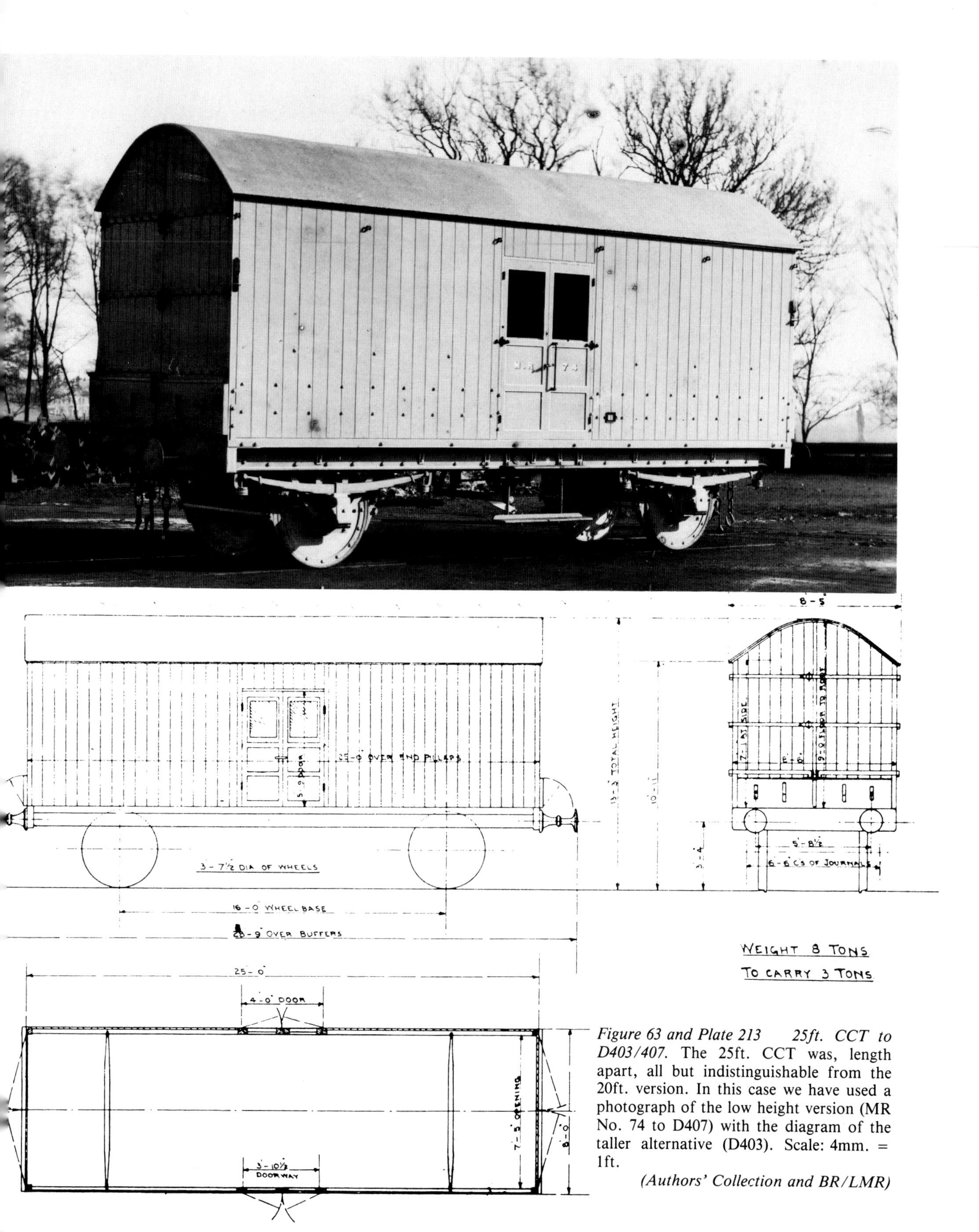

Figure 63 and Plate 213 *25ft. CCT to D403/407.* The 25ft. CCT was, length apart, all but indistinguishable from the 20ft. version. In this case we have used a photograph of the low height version (MR No. 74 to D407) with the diagram of the taller alternative (D403). Scale: 4mm. = 1ft.

(Authors' Collection and BR/LMR)

e Open Carriage Truck family

This group of some 340 vehicles, with the exception of eight gie examples to Diagram 431, can all be described as open riage trucks (OCT). Basically utilized for similar but con- ably less valuable vehicles than CCTs, the OCTs were ewise built in three lengths, 16ft., 20ft. and 30ft. 5in., the er being six wheeled and appearing in service between the four wheel designs.

All three types shared a visual family likeness and the t of the series to appear, the 16ft. type to Diagram , seems to have been derived from a still earlier pre- book design. We have illustrated both Diagram 408 and six wheel type (Diagram 410) but have chosen to feature *(Figure 64)* the intermediate length 20ft. design (Diagram 409) which was almost as numerous as Diagram 408 but lasted much longer into LMS and BR days. Derived from Diagram 409 was a 'Fire Engine Truck' version to Diagram 430. Only two were built *(see Table 11)*, one of which was actually a conversion from Diagram 409.

The eight similarly-styled bogie vehicles in this category (Diagram 431) were styled as 'Long Open Trucks for Scenery' rather that OCT. They were 46ft. 10½in. long and ran on 8ft. bogies.

Finally there was a solitary 'well-bottom' four wheel OCT to Diagram 411. It is illustrated in *Midland Wagons Vol. I* (page 33).

Plates 214a & 214b These two pictures show the 30ft. 5in. six wheel CCT to D410, No. 456, and the 16ft. four wheel OCT to D408, No. 178. The handful of six wheelers all reached the LMS as did less than half of the much more numerous D408. Both types were introduced well ahead of the 20ft. variation at *Figure 64.*

(NRM)

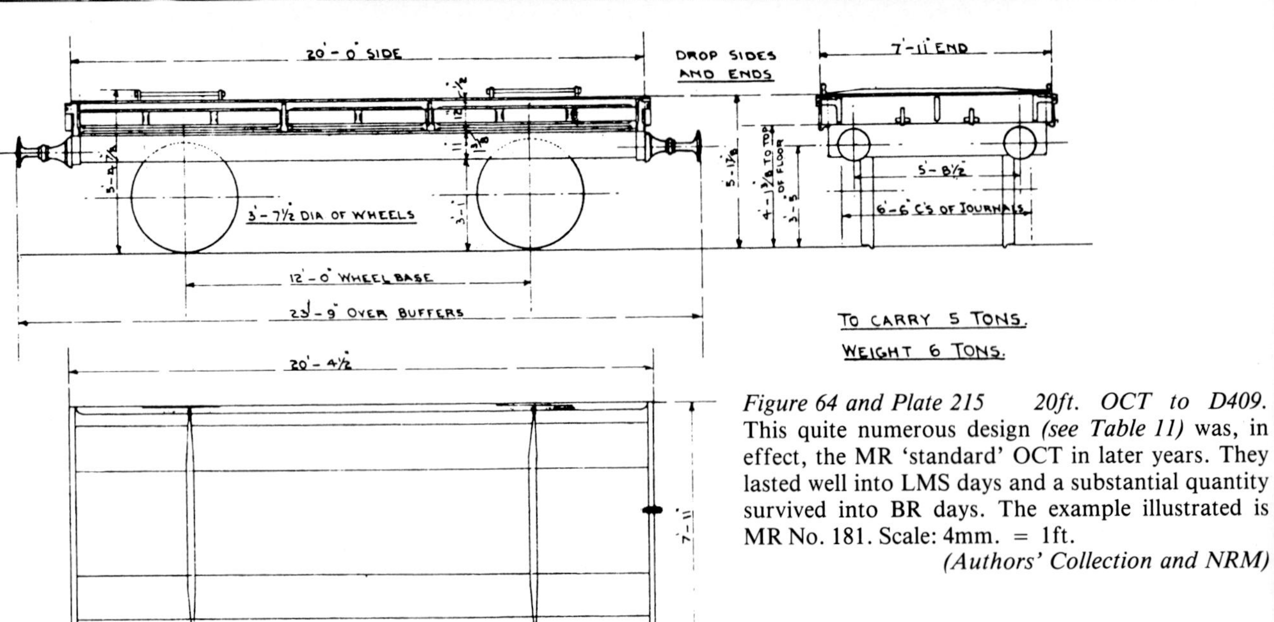

Figure 64 and Plate 215 *20ft. OCT to D409.* This quite numerous design *(see Table 11)* was, in effect, the MR 'standard' OCT in later years. They lasted well into LMS days and a substantial quantity survived into BR days. The example illustrated is MR No. 181. Scale: 4mm. = 1ft.

(Authors' Collection and NRM)

Plate 216 This second view of an OCT to D409 has been included to give modellers additional underframe/solebar detail. The picture was taken at Cardington in 1940 and shows LMS No. 41759 (1933 series), first LMS No. 869.

(Authors' Collection)

Iilk, Fruit and Parcels Vans

This group of associated vehicles was a particularly neat and omogeneous family, all sharing standard body details with he contemporary passenger carrying coaches. Most of them arried full lining, albeit in yellow rather than gilt, with the red very.

There was a degree of confusion in nomenclature which we ave tried to resolve in *Table 11*. Terms like 'Milk', 'Fruit and Iilk', 'Milk and Parcels' and 'Parcels' seem to have been anded about somewhat indiscriminately but it seems that if ney incorporated slatted side panels they were considered iitable for perishable goods.

In visual terms the most common characteristics of this roup were either the Clayton arc roof form or the square-anelled style without clerestory but with low elliptical roof. There was, of course, less intrinsic need for the expense of a clerestory in a purely non-passenger vehicle and it is believed that the Midland Railway was contemplating abandoning the clerestory on all stock for some time before it eventually did so. Consequently, these low elliptical roof vehicles may have been something of a try-out for more widespread application. However, this roof profile was never used for passenger carrying stock and remained a distinctive feature confined entirely to the non-passenger series and one group of full brakes (Diagram 530A, *Plate 187)*.

Plate 217 A 25ft. parcels van, No. 56, fairly well typifies this group of vehicles. It is actually a pre-lot book example with grease axleboxes and old type buffers. Although generally similar to D420 *(Figure 68)*, this type had only three pairs of doors and, presumably, only three compartments.

(BR/LMR)

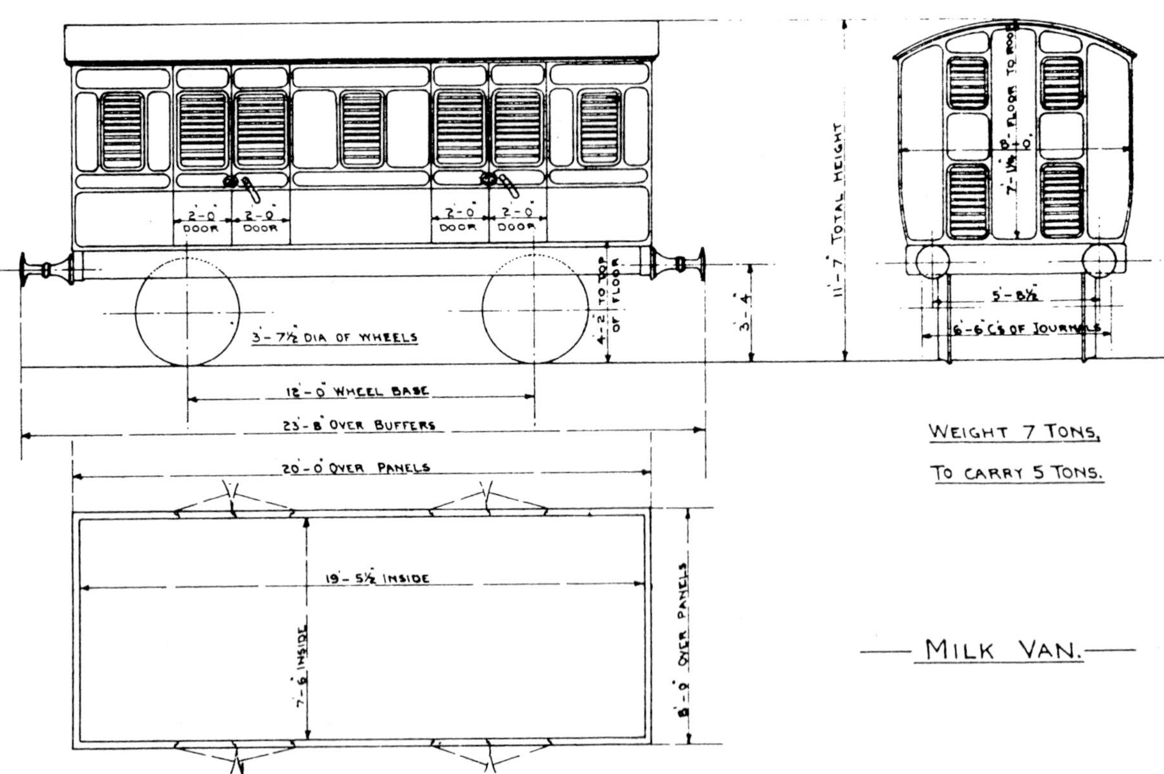

Figure 65 and Plate 218 *20ft. milk van to D416* These were numerous and designed (and presumably used) almost entirely for milk churn traffic. It does not seem to have been a dual-purpose (i.e. milk/parcels) type. The slatted end and side panels were meant to keep the air moving through the vehicle whilst in transit by creating a sort of 'ram' effect. However, in 1904, the MR decided to fit many of its fruit and milk vans with torpedo ventilators to improve matters. We have no evidence that any of D416 were so treated. Scale: 4mm. = 1ft.

(Authors' Colletion and NRM)

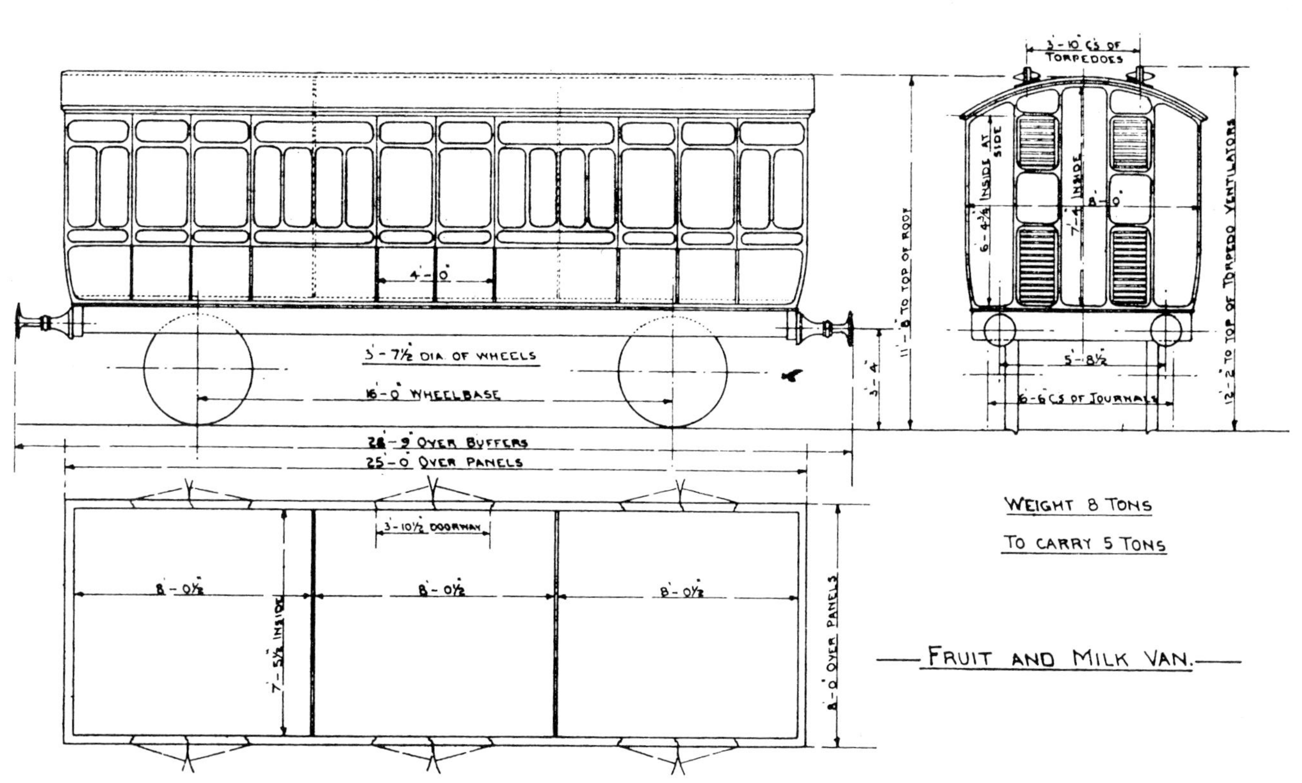

Figure 66 and Plate 219 25ft. fruit and milk van to D418. This type was an elongation of D416 with three pairs of doors, and divided internally into three compartments. Note that the diagram itself is marked with torpedo ventilators - dating the actual drawing later than 1904. Presumably the internal partitions reduced the free air circulation inside the vans, so the torpedo vents were added to compensate. The photograph of MR No. 525 was taken before it was fitted with roof ventilators which were positioned centrally over double doors, either side of the oil lamps. Scale: 4mm. = 1ft.

(Authors' Collection and BR/LMR)

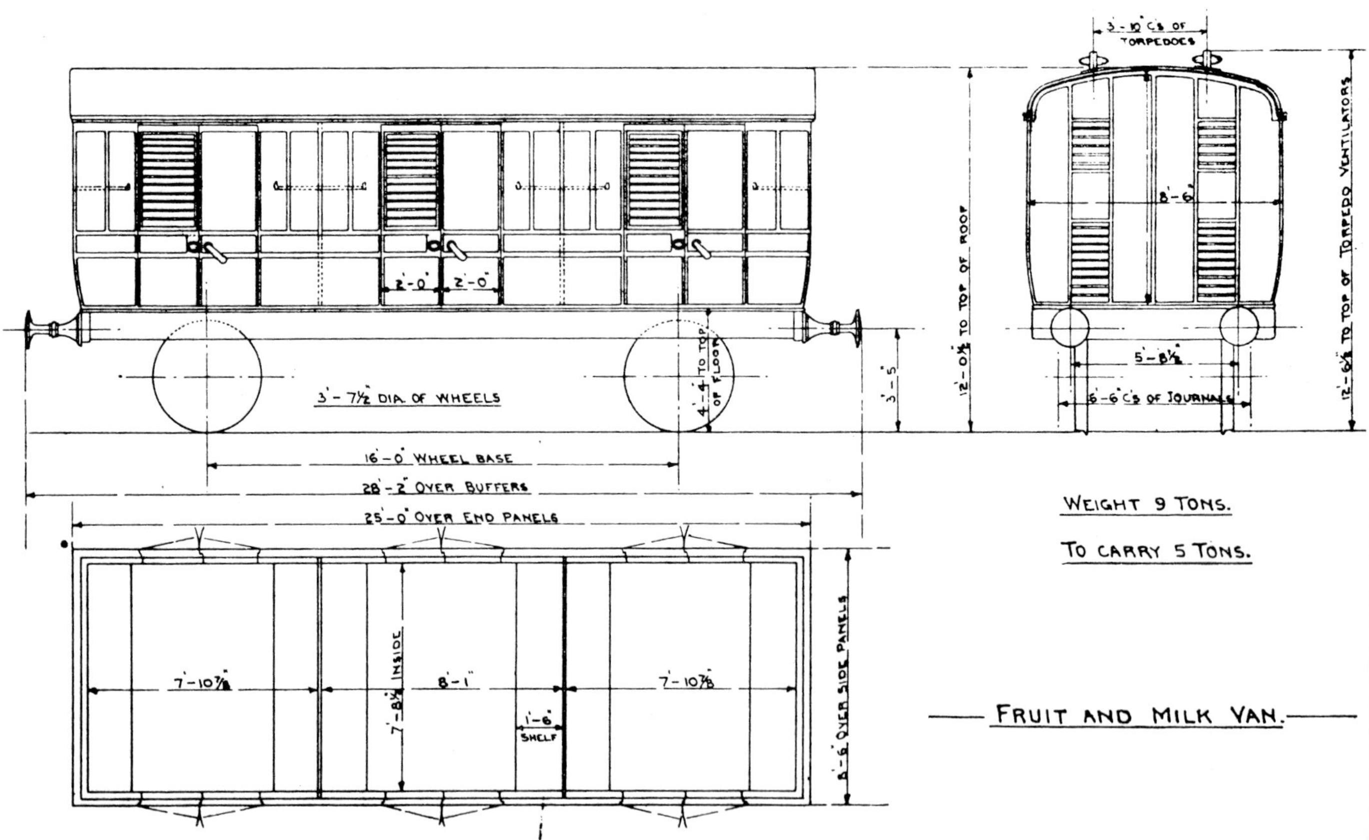

Figure 67 and Plate 220 25ft. fruit and milk van to D419. This design was virtually the square-panelled derivation from D418. The roof profile, however, was identical with the lower roof of the contemporary clerestory stock, and the picture clearly shows the general style. This vehicle was a conversion from a D419 van, the only significant visual change being the replacement of all the slatted panel areas as shown and, we believe, the removal of the internal partitions. Scale: 4mm. = 1ft.

(Authors' Collection and BR/LMR)

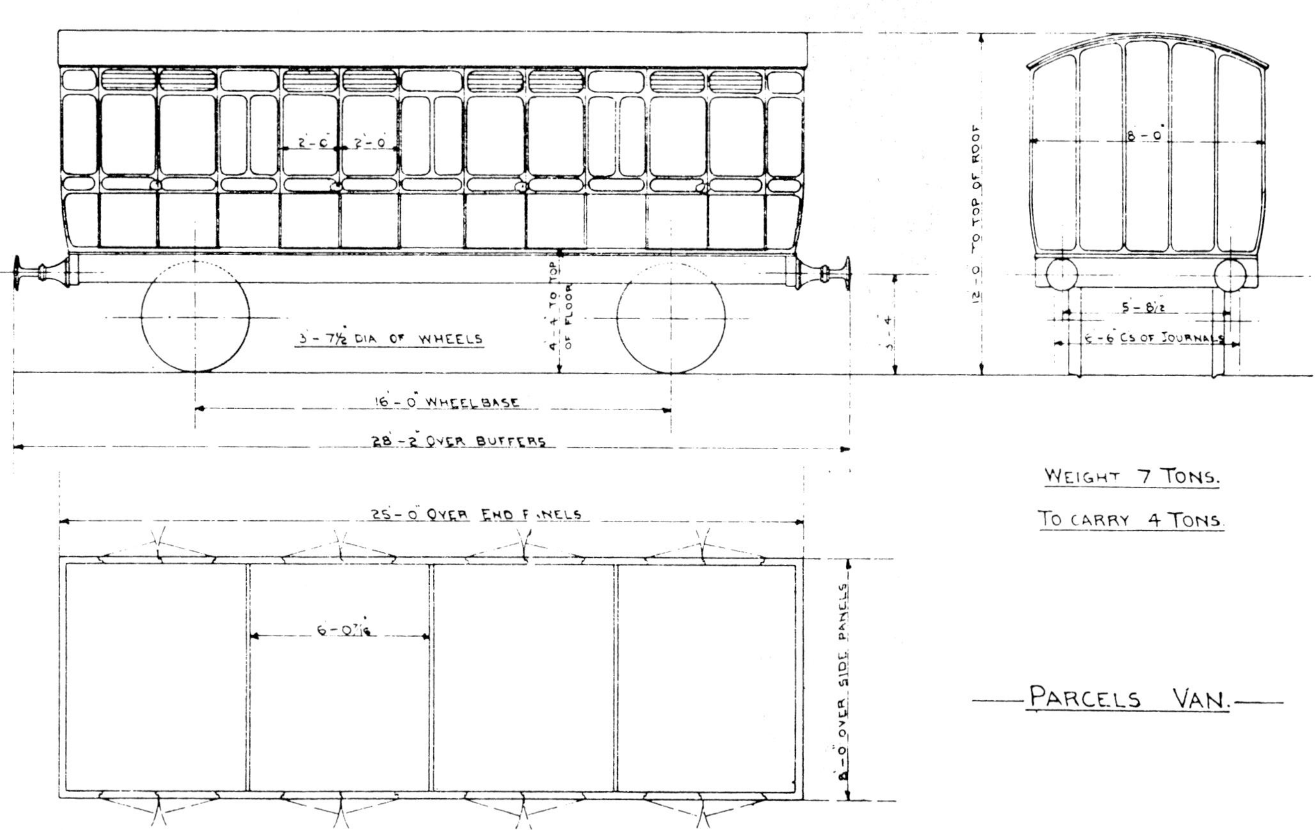

Figure 68 and Plate 221 25ft. parcels van to D420. This design was virtually a four compartment derivation of the type shown at *Plate 217.* Like many vehicles in this group, the interior was divided into compartments, the idea being that each compartment carried traffic for one particular destination, or group of destinations. Although not a very numerous design, it was a very long-lived type *(see Table 11).* Scale: 4mm. = 1ft.

(BR/LMR)

Plate 222 MR No. 126 to D428 was known as a fish tank truck although, clearly, the tank is actually labelled 'Fish Box'! Note, particularly, that the box itself was separately numbered (No. 17), and divided into four sections, themselves numbered 1-4. In the fully lined livery, these vehicles presented a colourful (if smelly) spectacle! The box itself is labelled to be returned to Grimsby. This particular type did not long survive the Grouping.

(BR/LMR)

Fish Traffic Vehicles

Fish traffic was an important part of railway operation in former days and several companies handled considerable quantities. The Midland Railway was no exception and, like its rivals, regarded fish traffic as justifying high speed transit, hence the inclusion of fish vehicles in its passenger-rated stock. We feel it is not entirely insignificant that some of the open fish vehicles were amongst the earliest types to appear in the non-passenger book.

Essentially, two main categories of vehicle were provided, open or covered and, apart from the fact that most of the covered trucks appear to have been a later innovation, we cannot readily distinguish the difference in utilization between the two types.

There were two open designs, Diagrams 427 and 428, the former being featured in *Figure 69*. Many more were built to the earlier design (Diagram 428) which embodied a removable 'fish box' carried on a wagon somewhat similar to an OCT; an early form of containerization *(Plate 222)*.

Few of the open trucks survived long after the Grouping *(see Table 11)* but the covered examples fared rather better. All had open slatted sides, of one form or another, and a total of three diagrams was issued - a four wheel type (Diagram 425) and two somewhat similar six wheelers (Diagrams 426 & 1272).

The four wheelers were to an unusual length, for the Midland Railway, of 17ft. 11in. over headstocks. They were the most numerous of the Midland Railway fish vehicle designs and although dating back to 1887, had a high survival rate after 1923. Clearly, covered vehicles were preferred to the open variety.

The two six wheel designs, of which we feature Diagram 1272 in *Figure 70*, were superficially very similar outside-framed types. However, the detailed dimensions were slightly different and the outside framing of each type was quite distinctive.

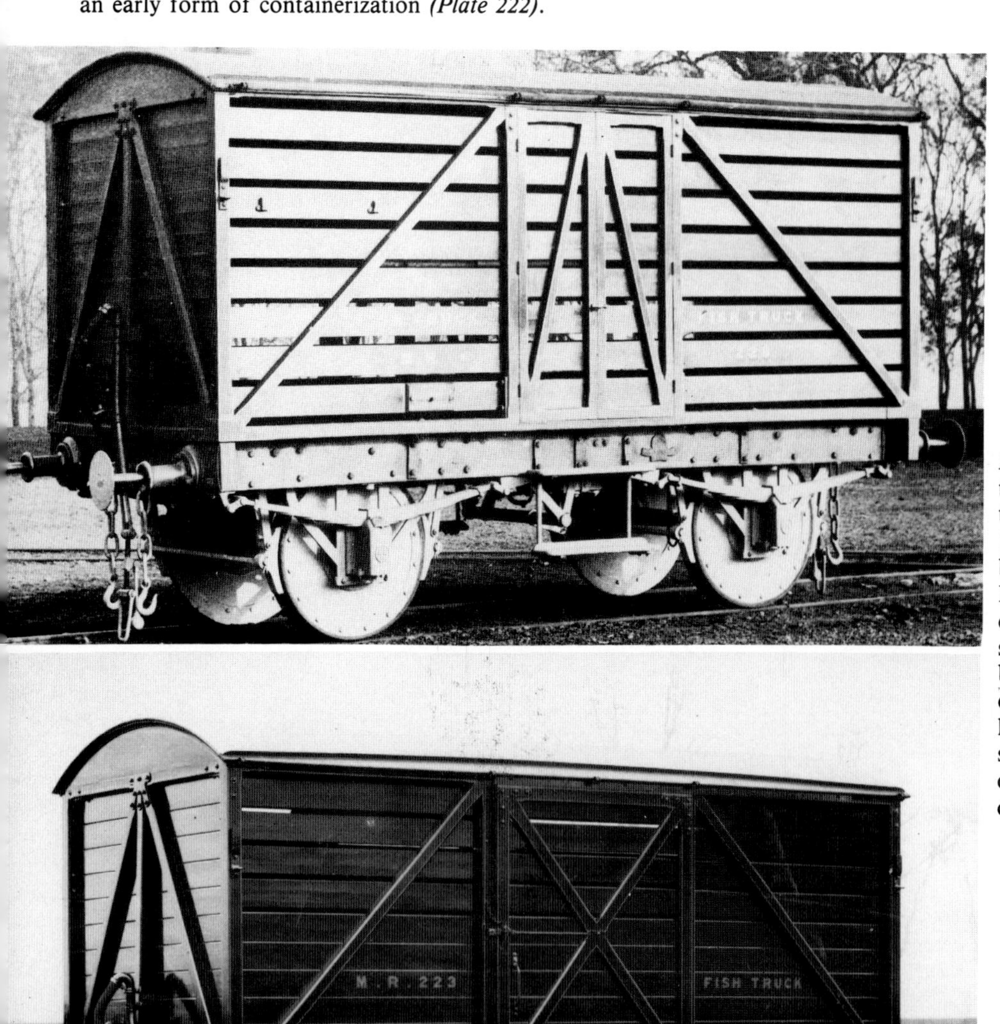

Plates 223a and 223b Covered fish truck No. 228 *(above)* was built in the pre-lot book days, at Oldbury, in 1876. It was fitted with grease axleboxes and clearly an ancestor of D425 *(below)*. The main visible difference was that D425 had a single, central sliding door (X-braced), somewhat wider than the double-hinged doors of No. 228. It had a more modern underframe and stronger springing, oil axleboxes, etc., all of which points are brought out in the view of No. 223.

(BR/LMR and NRM)

Plate 224 Six wheel covered fish truck, No. 634, to D426. This design was superficially similar to D1272 *(overleaf)* in overall dimensions but comparison of the two clearly shows the totally different body framing.

(Authors' Collection)

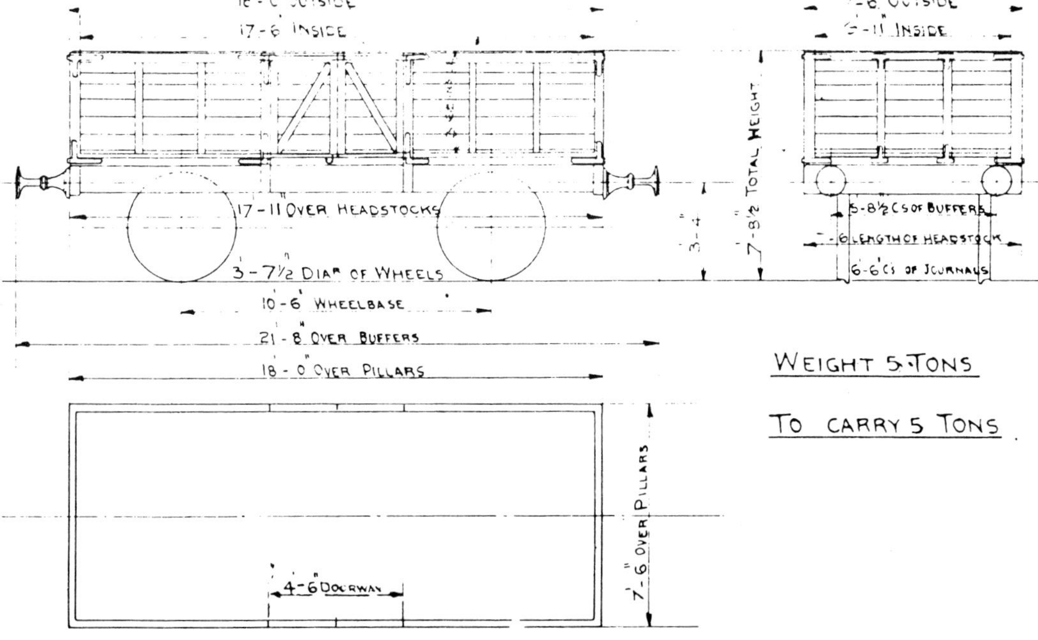

Figure 69 and Plate 225 *18ft. fish and poultry truck to D427.* This type of vehicle, essentially a rather elaborate open goods wagon, was quite a common sight in pre-grouping days, but the Midland itself did not make great use of them, only building ten and scrapping them all before 1923. The picture of MR No. 204 shows the elaborate full lining *(compare Plate 222)* and this particular example was marked for return to Ramsden Docks, Barrow-in-Furness. Note that unlike the fish tank trucks, the lining on these vehicles was confined to the vehicle side. Scale: 4mm. = 1ft.

(Authors' Collection and BR/LMR)

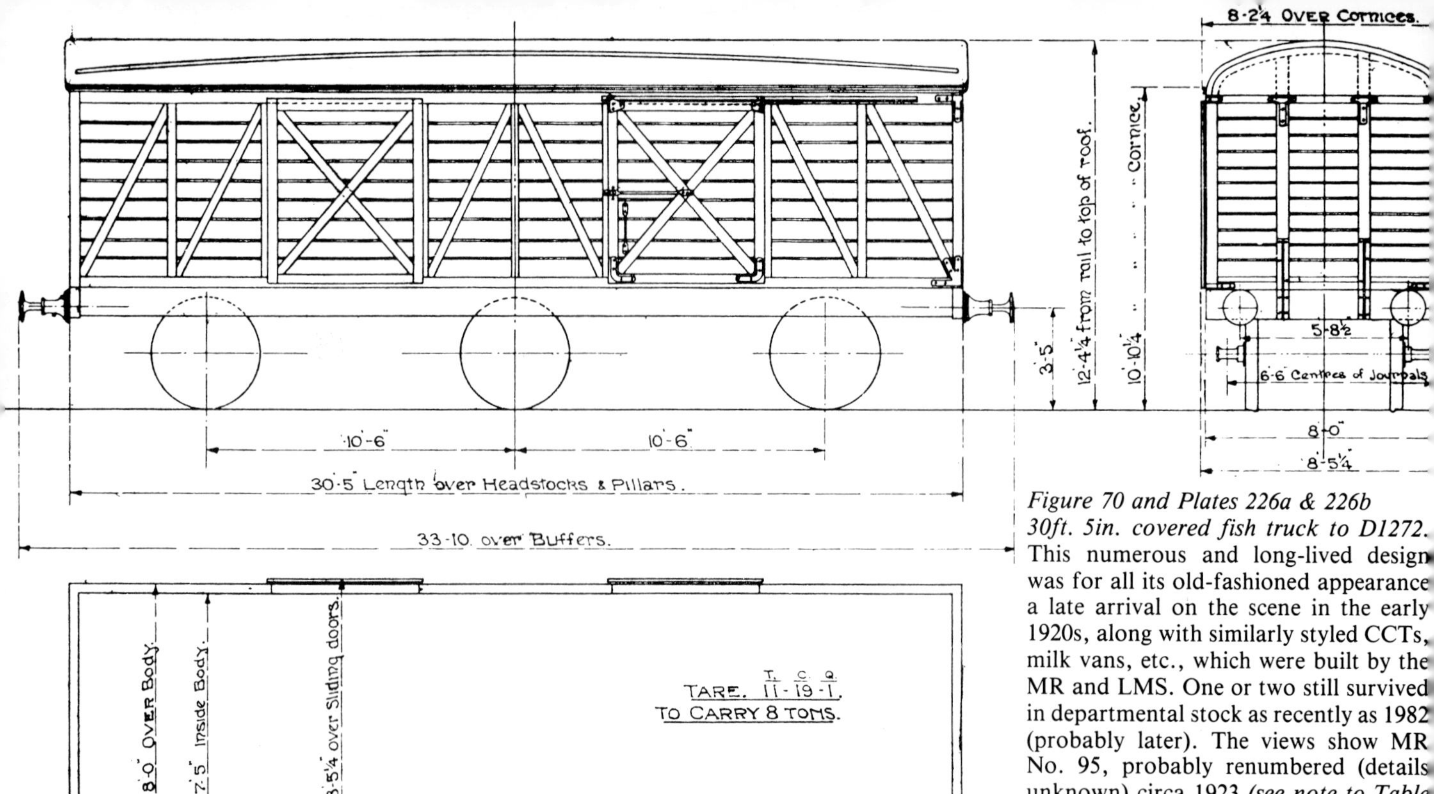

Figure 70 and Plates 226a & 226b
30ft. 5in. covered fish truck to D1272. This numerous and long-lived design was for all its old-fashioned appearance a late arrival on the scene in the early 1920s, along with similarly styled CCTs, milk vans, etc., which were built by the MR and LMS. One or two still survived in departmental stock as recently as 1982 (probably later). The views show MR No. 95, probably renumbered (details unknown) circa 1923 *(see note to Table 11)*. Scale: 4mm. = 1ft.
(Authors' Collection and BR/LMR)

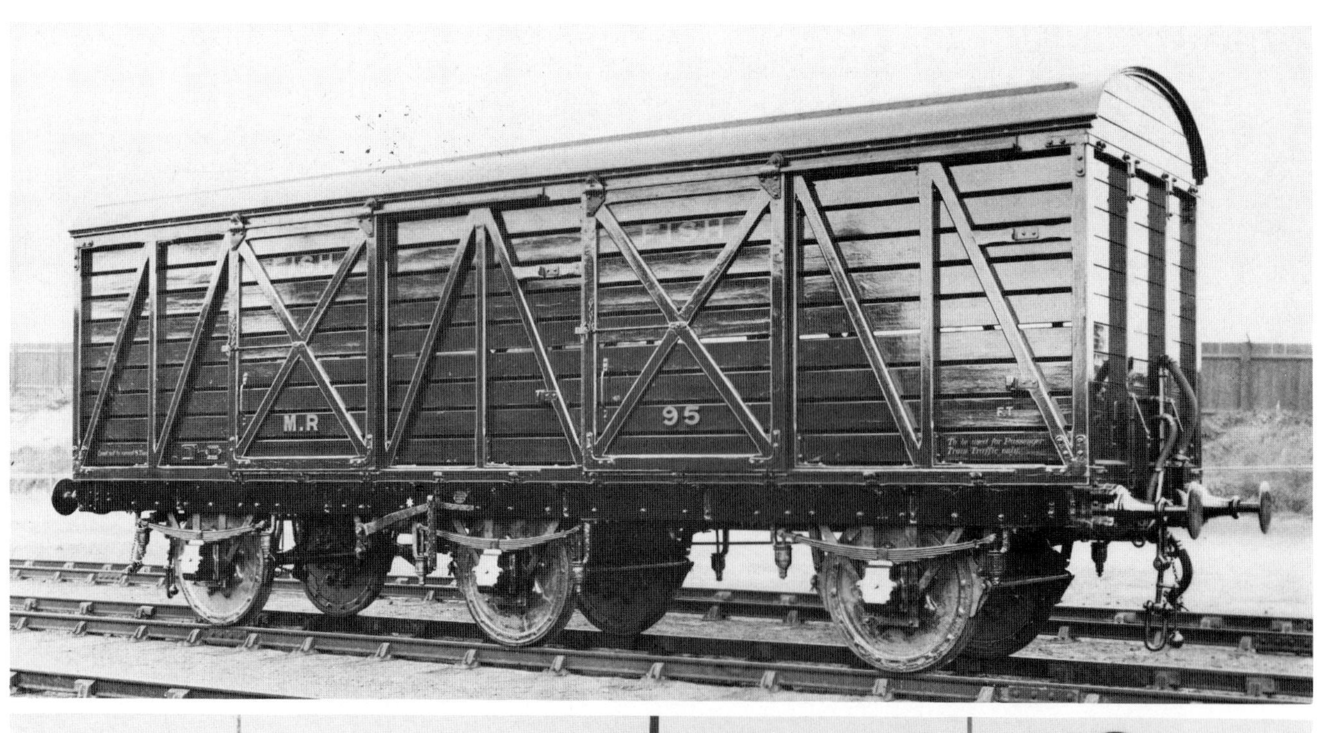

Other Vans

The final group of non-passenger stock consists of a miscellaneous group of covered vans, none of which were built in any great quantity *(see Table 11)*. All the diagrams, but one, were of Clayton arc roof style and we illustrate them all here, featuring particularly the Hound Vans to D429.

The exception was a group of three bogie baggage vans to Diagram 1198, Lot 969, built for the LT&S section boat train services. They had a marked visual resemblance to the outside-framed theatrical scenery vans to Lot 950 *(see page 152)* but their lack of end doors disqualified them from the CCT classification. Like Lot 950, they utilized second-hand underframes.

Finally, we feel we should again mention the four wheel Clayton arc roof meat vans to Diagram 379, already featured in *Midland Wagons Vol. I*. Although these were always classified as freight vehicles, they were in effect 'passenger rated' and some were turned out in passenger livery *(Plate 232)*. They fully typify the difficulty in precisely resolving the fitted freight/non-passenger demarcation line and seem to us therefore, to be a totally appropriate vehicle type with which to conclude this survey!

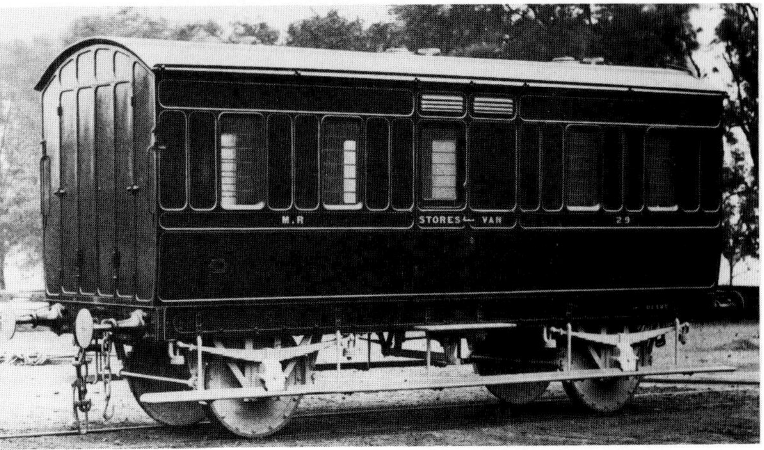

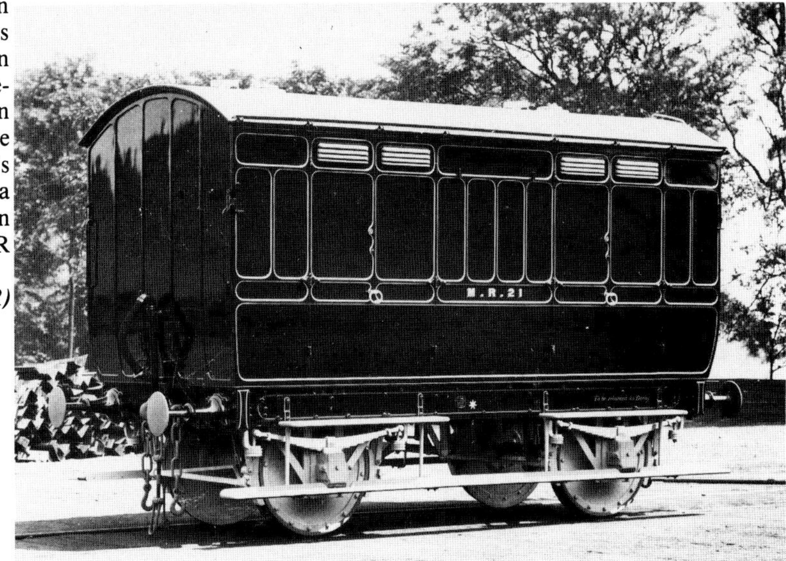

Plates 227 to 229 This group of three different types typifies the miscellaneous non-passenger carrying vans built in small quantities during the Clayton arc roof period. MR No. 29 was a stores van to D423, built to the unusual and unique length of 22ft. Note the end doors, fitted at one end only, thus necessitating considerable modification to the normal panelling. MR No. 21 seems, at first, to be a diminutive parcels van *(compare Figure 68)*, but was in fact, one of four 16ft. 7in. corpse vans to D424 in 1888. We do not know how this macabre traffic was handled but there were still three of them left in 1933! The final view of MR No. 60 shows the 'one-off' 21ft. bullion van built in 1879 for the London to Liverpool traffic to Lot 31. It is shown with the strong room door open and it also had a guard's compartment. It was some 3½ tons heavier than a normal vehicle of this dimension. We have not been able to discover a diagram for it - perhaps the MR did not want anyone to know too much!

(BR/LMR)

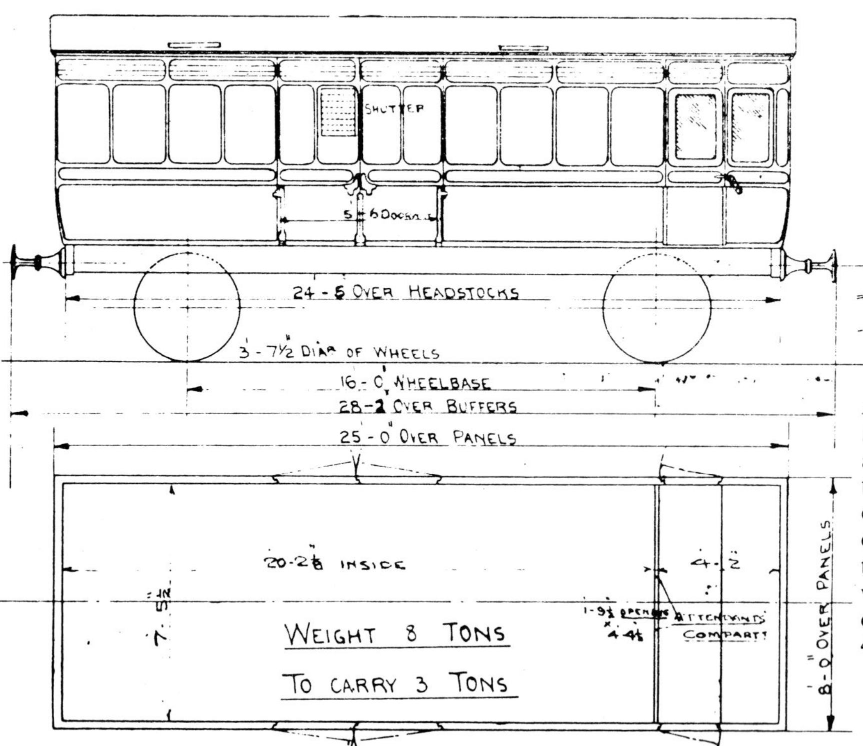

Figure 71 and Plate 230 *25ft. hound van to D429.* These vehicles, built in 1894, lasted at least forty years and were, in our view, particularly attractive. Very similar in general configuration to the horse-box but less well equipped, we cannot help but wonder whether their slightly more 'up-market' appearance was designed principally to convey some sort of social message to potential users! Scale: 4mm. = 1ft.

(Authors' Collection and BR/LMR)

Plate 231 Midland No. 279 was one of three baggage vans to D1198 for the LT&S section. Compare the style with the vans to Lot 950 *(Plate 211, page 153).*

(NRM)

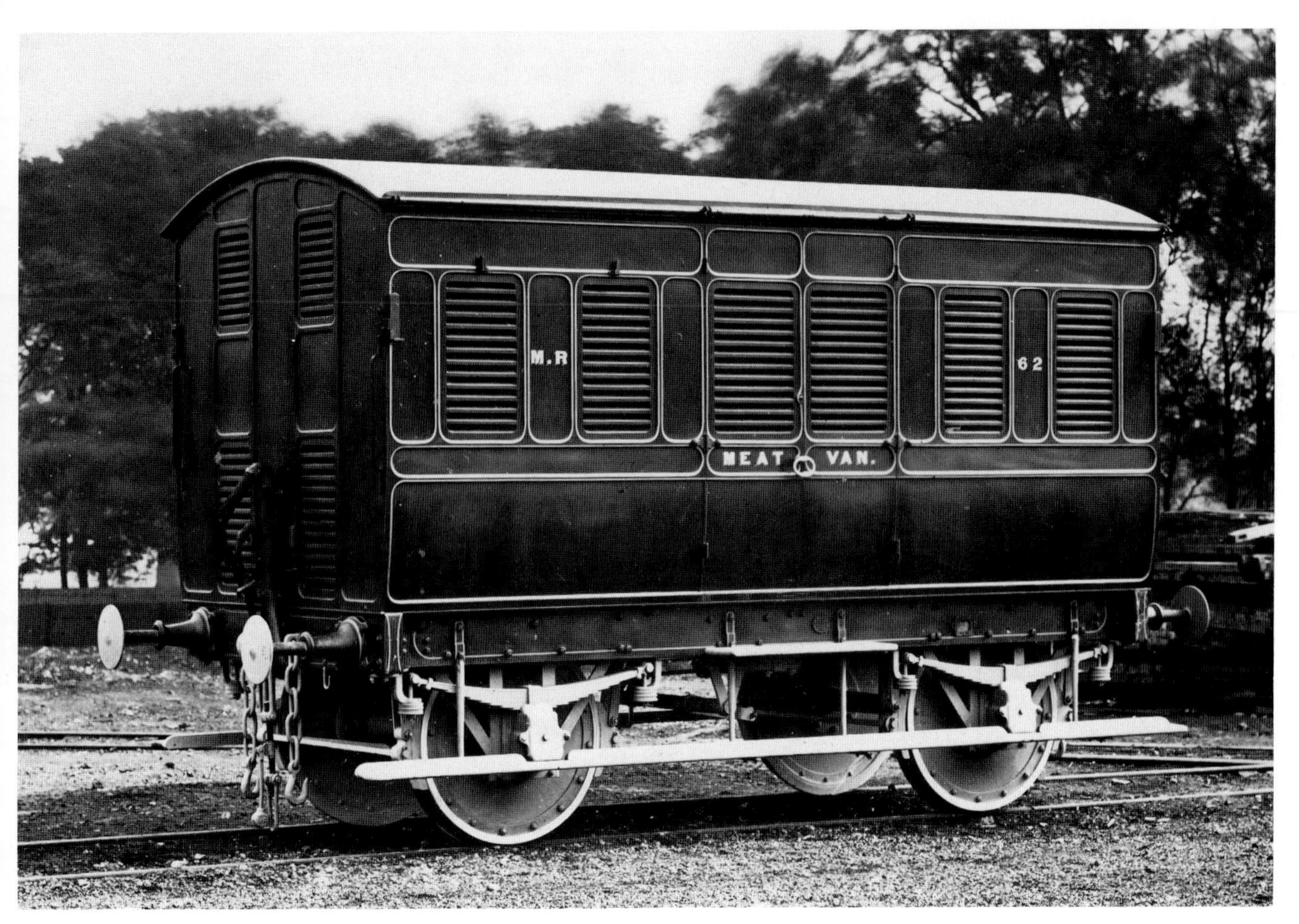

Plate 232 Meat van, No. 62, to Lot 47, D379 in full passenger livery, circa 1887. Note the communication cord 'eyelets' along the roof edge. *(BR/LMR)*

TABLE 11
Summary of Midland Railway Full Brakes, Postal Vehicles and Other Non-Passenger Coaching Stock

Preliminary Notes on Numbering

1. Before the Grouping, the MR numbered its non-passenger stock in a variety of lists, each probably starting at No. 1 but with more than one class of vehicle in each list. At some time around the Grouping – and we believe in 1923 – all the non-passenger stock was numbered into a single series by the LMS, although it may have been the MR's intention so to do. Thus, apart from brake vans (and a few others) which retained their old numbers at the head of the new consolidated list, the first LMS series *does not coincide* with the final MR series as was normally the case. Although we have not been able to fully reconcile the precise start/finish points of the various categories, we have been able to resolve matters sufficiently to be able to offer a fair selection of numbers for most vehicles covered in this table.

2. Before the Grouping, the Midland occasionally re-numbered its non-passenger stock within the various separate lists but we have not been able to resolve this, except intermittently. In consequence we cannot give precise periods for which the pre-group numbers quoted were valid. We believe that in most cases, the numbers remained unchanged until LMS days – unlike passenger carrying vehicles *(see page viii)* which were renumbered entirely c1901/2.

3. We would remind readers again that from 1923–33, the first LMS numbers for non-passenger stock were still in a separate series (starting at No. 1) from the passenger carrying vehicles. It was not until 1933 that the LMS resolved to give distinct (and unique) numbers to all its passenger rated vehicles.

Lot	*Qty.*	*Date of Order*	*Dimensions*	*Wt.*	*Style*	*Pre-Group Numbering*			*Post-Group Numbering*		*Type Extinct*	*Remarks*
						Midland	*Joint Stock*					
							1st	*2nd*	*1st LMS*	*2nd LMS*		
…ger Full Brakes												
11	100	1877	25' x 8' 0"	9T	CA	Including MR 129						*Four wheel, non-gangwayed:* Number details very poor indeed for this type.
19	50	1878	(9' 0½" over lookouts)									
28	10	1879					Believed MSJS 1–10					
37	25	1879										
96	100	1883										
140	30	1885							324	33932	3/35	
165	9	1887										
195	3	1887										
260	30	1890										
292	10	1892										
345	4	1894										
389	3	1896	31' x 8' 6"	13T	CC2	576–8	–	–	576	33933	1/38	*Standard six wheel clerestory type:* D530 was non-gangwayed, D568 had gangways. All lots were to D530 except Lot 454 (Joint Stock) which was D568.
400	116	1897				Various: 1–631	–	–	as MR	33934–34014		
454	30	1898				–	not known	not known	included: 1922–36	33480–99		
501	70	1900				Various: 44–155	–	–	as MR	34015–68		
519	82	1901				Various: 85–574	–	–	as MR	34069–144		

Diag.	Lot	Qty.	Date of Order	Dimensions	Wt.	Style	Midland	Pre-Group Numbering Joint Stock		Post-Group Numbering		Type Extinct	Remarks
								1st	2nd	1st LMS	2nd LMS		
567	453	18	1898	50' x 8' 6"	21¾T	CC2	–	MNB 101–3	MNB 162–3	to LNER as	33, 36	1941	*Gangwayed bogie style:* All Joint Stock coaches, and th
								MNB 107–11	MNB 167–71	1968–72	32844-8	5/40	somewhat accident prone, four being destroyed before t
								M&GSW 207–16	M&GSW 439–41	1914–6	32839–43	9/40	Joint Stock renumbering (in 1914) and another (2nd M
									M&GSW 443–6	1918, 1920–1 }		10/45	444) in 1918.
531	549	50	1902	45' x 8' 6"	20T	BC3	Various: 49–632	–	–	as MR	33589–633		*Non-gangwayed bogie style:* the most numerous MR bog brake design.
573	602	2	1905	54' x 8' 6"	23½T	BC4	–	MNB 101	MNB 161	LNER 32		12/47	*Gangwayed bogie style:* One copy of the diagram sugges
								M&GSW 212	M&GSW 442	1917	32850	5/46	the M&GSW example was altered to elliptical roof form this may only have been a proposal.
536	652	16	1906	45' x 8' 6"	20T	BC4	Various: 181–636	–	–	as MR	32789–804		*Gangwayed bogie style:* Virtually the gangwayed version
	675	23	1907				Various: 203–635	–	–	as MR	32805–26		D531 with rounded panelling and fitted with pigeon she Numbering details for Lot 652 not confirmed but very p able.
530A	788	12	1912	31' x 8' 6"	?	see	Various: 120–530	–	–	as MR	34145–156		*Six wheel, non-gangwayed:* Low elliptical roof with stan
	805	12	1912			notes	Various: 188–637	–	–	as MR	34157–68		Bain rounded panelling. Bain period equivalent of D530 without clerestory.
1067	880	12	1914	48' x 8' 6"	?	E	Various: 12–634	–	–	as MR	32827–38		*Gangwayed bogie style:* Ordered 1914 as clerestory but built until 1919 and then with steel ends and elliptical r
Postal Vehicles													
–	12	3	1879	30' x 8' 0"	?	CC1	Believed MR 1–3, later M&NEJPS 1–3						Designated *Post Office Sorting Carriages*. Six wheel.
–	13	6	1878	30' x 8' 0"	?	CC1	Believed MR 4–6 plus M&NEJPS 4–6 (see notes)						Designated *Post Office Tenders*. Lot Book shows six ord but some sources think only three built. In which case M 4–6 became M&NEJPS 4–6 as per Lot 12. Six wheel.
–	33	3	1879	25' x 8' 0"	?	CA	12, 37, 41	–	–	–	–		Designated *Newspaper Van*. No. 41 believed to be trans to LT&SR as milk van c1912. Four wheel.
–	Part 113	2	1885	43' x 8' 0"	?	CA	79, 80	later M&NEJPS 79, 80		1984–5	–	c1926	Designated *Parcels Sorting Van*. Bogie eight wheel.
–	131	3	1885	32' x 8' 0"	?	CA	73–5	–	–	1902–4	30380–2	12/33	Designated *Parcels Sorting Van*. Six wheel and ordered ' with Sorting Post Office', but no indication which type intended.
–	191	2	1887	43' x 8' 0"	?	CC1	7, 8 believed later M&NEJPS 7, 8 then MR 1 and 2!!			1895–6	30379	2/33	Designated *Post Office Sorting Carriages*. Bogie eight wh effectively an elongation of Lot 12 type.
	307	1	1892				3			1897		12/31	Lot 191 is confirmed as originally MR 7, 8; rest of infor
	344	1	1894				not known			1898		1931	believed correct.
–	455	2	1899	48' x 8' 6"	?	CC2		M&NEJPS No. 111	–	1986	30281	9/44	Designated *Parcels Sorting Vans*. Bogie eight wheel and
							112	–	–	1905	30282	7/44	book suggests one was originally for M&NB. Possible tha M&NEJPS No. 111 began life as MR 111.
872	665	3	1907	54' x 8' 4½"		BC4	–	M&NEJPS 7–9	–	1981–3	30286–8	2/55	Designated *Post Office Sorting* (Lot 665) or *Post Office Tender* (Lots 666–7). All built to same style *(see Fig. 5*
	666	3	1907				14–16	–	–	1899–1901	30260–2	5/51	Note that although renumbered in 1923/33 in the LMS
	667	3	1907				–	M&NEJPS 4–6	–	1978–80	30283–5	12/53	Lots 665/7 were always prefaced M&NEJPS even after I days!
													Footnote: The lot book contains three orders (Lots 507 and 653) for *48ft. Newspaper Vans*. We have no details these vehicles which, as built, would have been square pa clerestories (Lots 507/548) or round panelled clerestory vehicles were ordered on each lot and the LMS 1933 list six numbers (37994–9) for ex-Midland bogie corridor v deduction, therefore, we conclude that 37994–7 were probably Lot 507/548 (style BC3) and 37998–9 were L (style BC4). If readers can confirm/deny we will be grat
Horseboxes													
397	39	12	1879	16' 2" x 7' 9"	7T	–	349			–	–	–	Early lots (39/91) built with grease axleboxes, remainde
	91	40	1883				112			–	–		oil. Last survivor retained its pre-1933 number (1200) a
	144	100	1885				85			Various 1039–	43437–	5/41	destroyed in an air raid at St. Pancras. All the others had
	183	109	1887							1376	43466		by 1937.
398	268	30	1891	16' 2" x 8' 3"	7T	–	438 (?413–42)			1433/44/50	43467–9	2/36	Wider version of D397 with incurved lower body sides.
	374	25	1896							Various 1327–66	43470–81	1/39	
399	161	1	1886	19' 6 " x 7' 9"	8T	–				Various:	43483–581	1/39	The first 'long' horsebox with luggage compartment, oth
	176	100	1887				288 plus ?363–412?			1042–1422	(see note)		wise as D397. After 1923, some became reclassed as pri cattle, renumbered LMS 43974–84 in 1933. *(NB. LMS series) Horsebox No. 43482 was ex-LTSR).*
400	413	50	1897	20' x 8' 6"	9T	–	Included			Various:	43502–57	1/43	
	458	20	1899				443–71			1041–1487			
401	629	18	1905	20' x 8' 3"	9T		not known			Various: 1055–1205	43558–75	10/52	The final design and basis of the first LMS standard typ
	728	10	1909							Various: 1026–1130	43576–85	8/53	907 had matchboard ends (replacing panelling) which w
	807	12	1912							Various: 1074–1335	43586–97	5/53	adopted by the LMS.
	907	25	1915							Various: 1080–1458	43598–622	8/60	
Prize Cattle Vans													
412	204	25	1888	18' 8" x 8' 0"	7T	–	102			1503–11	43970–3	12/34	Original version without groom's compartment.
413	546	5	1902	23' x 8' 0"	8T					1524–8	43985–8	4/48	
Combined Horsebox/CCT													
415	630	1	1905	45' x 8' 6"	18T	–	52			946	37101	8/39	Experimental type. At one time also numbered 16 in th Horsebox series *(see Plate 210)*.
Covered Carriage Trucks and Similar													
402	59	2	1881	20' x 8' 0"	7T	–	90, 97			–	–	–	;The 13' 3" high version of the basic 20ft. CCT. The wi
	Part 187	14	1887				Various: 4–122			Various: 653–684	37077–8	6/65!!	drawal date of 6/65 is the write-off date for 37077 but others had gone by 5/34.
406	Part 187	10	1887	20' x 8' 0"	7T	–	Various: 21–125			Various: 653–684	37076	6/34	The 12' 8" high (Metro gauge) 20ft. CCT version of D4
	228	20	1889				370–389			Various: 703–18	37079–83	3/36	
403	121	4	1884	25' x 8' 0"	8T	–	22, 44, 101 plus one				–		The 13' 3" high version of the 25ft. CCT. Last withdra
	148	2	1886				74, 96			Various:	–		was No. 37095 which, latterly ran as 37667.
	277	4	1891				206/15/22, 491			656–722		3/35	
	351	2	1895				544–5			721	37084	10/34	
	373	4	1896				213/6/8, 546			692	37085	12/50	
	683	2	1908				16, 29			656/61	37094/5	11/46	The 12' 8" high (Metro gauge) 25ft. CCT version of D4
407	516	10	1901	25' x 8' 0"	8T	–	Various: 1–221			Various: 651–696	37086–93	6/46	Six wheel and 12' 8" high (Metro gauge).
404	637	5	1906	30' 11" x 8' 0"	10T	–	33, 90/7, 626–7			662/72/5	37096–100		
										723–4		4/48	Experimental one-off – fully panelled body style.
405	623	1	1905	50' x 8' 5½"	20T	–	128,			949	37697		*Theatrical Scenery*.
												7/55	Outside framed type for *Theatrical Scenery*. Visually si
1311 (?)	950	4	1920	44' 10" x 8' 5½"	?	–	?			950–3	37693–6		to D1198 but with full end doors. Built on second hand
												10/47	*Motor Car Vans* (MCV): Square panelled D414, Round
414/414A	609	25	1905	31' x 8' 6"	12T	–	601–25			955–79	37384–407		panelled D414A. Division of styles is not 100% certain
	699	1	1908				–	M&GSW 226		1961	37408	7/45	699/705/755 all described 'as Lot 609' in lot book but
	705	1	1908				47			954	37409	8/51	699 additionally annotated 'round light'. Lots 755/806
	755	12	1910				?			980–91	37410–21	1/52	to different drawings. On balance, round light series pr
	806	12	1912				?			992–1003	37422–33	4/55	started with Lot 699 – this would be in accordance wi similar styling on passenger stock in terms of date built

Lot	Qty.	Date of Order	Dimensions	Wt.	Style	Midland	Pre-Group Numbering Joint Stock 1st	2nd	Post-Group Numbering 1st LMS	2nd LMS	Type Extinct	Remarks
arriage Trucks and Similar												
38	25	1879				79						Predecessor of D408, other details not known.
53	50	1880	16' x 7' 11"	5T	–							Standard 'short' OCT. Lot 185 may have only had 21 examples but lot book shows 25. The late built Lot 638 is described as 'Fish Tank trucks converted to OCT' – presumably ex-D428 (below) – and believed classified after conversion as 'Fire Engine Trucks'..
145	50	1885										
185	25	1887							Various: 732–1883	41689–705	5/55	
266	41	1891										
art 638	9	1906										
551	22	1902	20' x 7' 11"	6T	–				Various: 728–72	41706–23	12/47	The later four wheel OCT. Twenty of Lot 565 were Westinghouse brake fitted. Lot 908 had later style of buffer body. Apparently 2nd LMS 41376 was overlooked at the re-numbering and was eventually put into the LMS standard series. One of Lot 551 converted to D430 (below). Many of these were delivered much later than order date viz: Lot 808 – 1915, Lot 908 – 1920.
565	50	1903							834–83	41724–73	10/51	
700	1	1908							795	41774	7/45	
808	12	1912							Various: 729–819	41775–86	8/57	
908	40	1915							Various: 727–921	41787–825 plus 41376	2/59	
284	6	1891	30' 9½" x 7' 11"	7T	–	456 plus five			Included 928–9	41826–7	2/43	Six wheel OCT, essentially a 'double' length version of the contemporary D408.
242	1	1890	29' 9" x 8' 7"	7T	–	390			–	–	–	Experimental 'well-bottom' OCT, never repeated.
551	1	1902	20' x 7' 11"	7T	–	17			–	–	–	Strengthened version of D409, designated '*Fire Engine Truck*'.
709	1	1909				118			–	–	–	
475	4	1899	46' 10½" x 8' 0"	14T	–				939–42	41089–91	12/35	Bogie vehicles, classified as'*Open Scenery Truck*'.
584	4	1904							944–8	41092–5	1/45	
ruit and Parcels Vans												
51	30	1880	20' x 8' 0"	7T	CA	250 plus 29 more			–	–		*Milk Vans* – a numerous and long-lived design. Lot 175 had internal handbrake for use by guard. Except for Lot 188, 1st LMS number series were largely continuous between samples quoted.
175	40	1887				Included 135, 323/5			Various: 1617–29	38376–9	12/35	
188	15	1887							Various: 1566–1653	38380–1	9/35	
265	10	1891							Various: 1637–42	38382–3	9/35	
315	25	1893							Various: 1657–79	38384–92	12/39	
492	25	1900	20' x 8' 6"	8T	see notes				1730–54	38393–403	8/41	End door *Fruit and Milk Vans* – square panelled, low elliptical roof.
316	25	1893	25' x 8' 0"	8T	CA	525 plus 24 more			1680–1704	38404–14	9/44	*Fruit and Milk Vans* with three compartments.
476	25	1899	25' x 8' 6"	9T	see notes				1705–29	38415–36	7/43	*Fruit and Milk Vans* with three compartments – square panelled, low elliptical roof design. However, Lot 881 was to a different drawing and not actually built until 1918 – probably round panelled but not confirmed. S&DJR examples all went to Southern Railway in 1930.
523	12	1901					for Somerset & Dorset Joint		–	–		
531	6	1902							1569–74	38437–41		
592	30	1903							1575–1604	38442–71		
881	20	1914							Various: 1555–1698	38472–91		
143	10	1885	25' x 8' 0"	7T	CA	27 plus nine						*Parcels Vans* with four compartments. Numbering details very poor but most are believed to have reached the LMS in 1923.
163	2	1886				277/9						
489	25	1900	25' x 8' 6" (see notes)	9T	see notes	–	M&GSW 201–25		1937–60	38607–27	3/45	*Milk and Parcels Vans* – square panelled, low elliptical roof. Built for M&GSW with outside sliding doors – width overall 8ft. 11in. and no interior partitions.
730	13	1909	31' x 8' 6"	11T	see notes	Various: 34–522			as MR	34988–99	2/51	*Parcels Vans* with five compartments – round panelling, low elliptical roof. Six wheel.
969	3	1921	44' 5" x 8' 2¼"	17T		228, 277, 279			as MR	37797–9	6/55	*Bogie Baggage Vans* – outside framed on second hand chassis for LT&SR boat traffic. Later numbered 37867–9, finally 38268–70! Preserved example at Foxfield is probably this type.
affic Vehicles												
192	20	1887	18' x 8' 0"	7T	–				1758–77? (most of these)	39804–10		*Fish Vans*. Long-term survivors almost certainly all from Lot 402 which were to a different drawing with sliding doors. Lots 192/267 may have had hinged doors.
267	30	1891										
402	20	1897										
659	15	1907	30' 6" x 8' 0"	11T	–	?628–42?			1825–39	40443–57	4/52 (but see note)	*Fish Vans* – six wheel. 1st LMS 1838 was for MR 641 but never renumbered. Allocated 40443 in 1933 it was written off in 1955 still as No. 641!
942	20	1920	30' 5" x 8' 0"	12T	–	Included 95, 362			Various:1755–1820	40458–77	6/60	*Fish Vans* – six wheel. Lot 995 not actually built until 1925 All used second hand chassis. LMS 40458 (still as MR 362) was still in stock 1963–7 by which time it was transferred to wagon stock!
995	20	1922				–			Various: 766–1893	40478–97	7/60	
197	10	1888	18' x 7' 6"	5T		Probably 196–205			–	–		
159	48	1886	16' x 7' 6"	6T	–	121			–	–	–	Open *Fish and Poultry trucks*.
638	15	1906									–	Open trucks *to carry fish tanks*. Nine of Lot 638 to OCT D408 probably almost from new if not actually built as such.
aneous Vans												
133	4	1885	22' x 8' 0"	7T	CA	29 plus twelve			–	–	–	*Stores Vans* with end doors at one end only. Not divided internally into compartments. Most reached the LMS but no number details available.
162	2	1886							–	–	–	
186	7	1887							–	–	–	
199	4	1888	16' 7" x 8' 0"	6T	CA	21 plus three			–	–	–	*Corpse Vans*. All reached the LMS but number details not available.
331	3	1894	25' x 8' 0"	8T	CA	543 plus two			1844–6	44497–9	8/38	*Hound Vans*. Very long survival rate for such a specialised type.
31	1	1879	21' x 8' 0"	10½T	CA	60			–	–	1912	*Bullion Van*. Replaced in 1912 by ex-LTSR vehicle. Built for Liverpool service.

Compiled by D. Jenkinson, December 1983

Plate 233 This fascinating picture shows one of the pioneer 1874 Pullmans some ten years or more after building. Built as an eight wheel parlour car *Britannia* it was rebuilt as a twelve wheel dining saloon in 1882 and renamed *Windsor* then, in December 1883, it was purchased by the MR, becoming No. 15.

(NRM)

Plate 234 This well-known view shows one of the 1876 parlour cars built originally as *Albion* and renumbered as Midland drawing room car No. 8 in December 1883. Note the considerable difference in decorative embellishment and the four wheel bogies compared with the otherwise rather similar car in the previous picture.

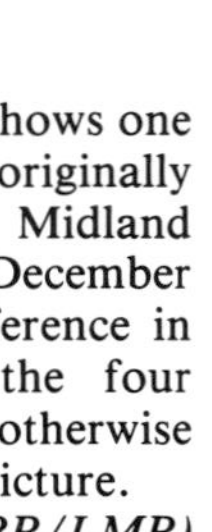

(BR/LMR)

Appendix I ~ The Pullman Contribution

This book concerns itself, essentially, with those carriages which appear in the Midland Railway diagram and lot lists from 1877 onwards. For the most part, these vehicles were not only designed by the Midland Railway but were also built by the Company. However, in the field of long-distance travel it is not possible to fully comprehend the late 19th century building programme of the Midland's standard carriage stock without some understanding of the role of Pullman carriages during the period. This is particularly true in the overnight sphere where the Midland Railway's own production of sleeping and similar carriages is noticeable by its virtual absence until the mid-1900s. The presence of Pullmans may also account, in some measure, for the somewhat later introduction of Company-built dining and corridor stock compared with, say, the LNWR. Accordingly, it is thought useful to give an outline account of the Midland Railway's involvement with Pullman cars during the 25 years or so of the Victorian period and the authors are particularly indebted to Mr Peter Truman for much of the original research on which this Appendix is based.

The Midland Railway's interest in Pullman carriages almost certainly dates from a visit by its general manager, Sir James Allport, to the USA in 1872. During his visit he travelled widely in the parlour and sleeping cars operated on the US Railroads by the company headed by George Mortimer Pullman. Pullman's carriages were of a most superior nature and Allport reported as much on his return to England.

In February 1873, George Pullman was introduced to the Midland Railway shareholders and described his cars. He then undertook to design and build similar vehicles to fit the British loading gauge and send them to this country for assembly by the Midland Railway. A contract was entered into for as many sleeping and parlour cars as the demand warranted for the 15 years until 1888. Supplementary charges, as in the USA, were envisaged from the outset and these would, inter alia, not only provide Pullman with an income but also provide the finance for the two attendants per car which Pullman promised as part of the deal. Additional to the parlour and sleeping cars, which would remain Pullman's property, George Pullman also contracted to build similar outline 'day cars' for non-supplementary fare passengers of all classes. These 'day cars' were to be the Midland Railway's property from the outset. The cost of the vehicles was substantial for the time; a typical parlour car coming in at £3,000.

The first vehicle to emerge under the deal was the sleeping car *Midland* in January 1874. However this was kept out of regular service and used more as an exhibition/demonstation vehicle until 1877. The second sleeping car *Excelsior* emerged in February 1874 and thereafter sleeping and parlour cars followed in quick succession. All were shipped in kit form and reassembled at Derby in two purpose-built sheds. Cars were also assembled for other British companies which had contracted with Pullman.

The vehicles themselves were heavily-built for the time and very large by British standards (58ft. 5in. long, 8ft. 9in. wide and 12ft. 11in. high). The interiors were arranged 'American' fashion with central longitudinal aisles down the full length. The sleeping cars had the so-called 'Pullman Sections', an arrangement of pull-out seats and drop-down top bunks to provide the night berths, screened at the aisle by 'respectability' curtains. The parlour cars, which, confusingly, the Midland Railway called 'Drawing Room Cars' as being more British, had individual swivelling armchairs. Both types had water closets and wash basins served by force pumps from low level tanks, this being an innovation for general service stock in Britain where, hitherto, lavatory facilities had been confined to special saloons and the like.

The spring of 1874 saw some experimental running of the new carriages to test reaction, which was accompanied by much Pullman hospitality; and by the end of the year there were 14 cars available, three sleepers, three parlours and eight

Plate 235 Original Pullman sleeping cars could be distinguished, externally, by the considerably higher waist rail and consequentially less tall windows, and shallower letterboard below the roof. This view shows an unidentified Pullman sleeping car at St. Pancras in the 1880s, and illustrates all the visible variations. *(P. Truman Collection)*

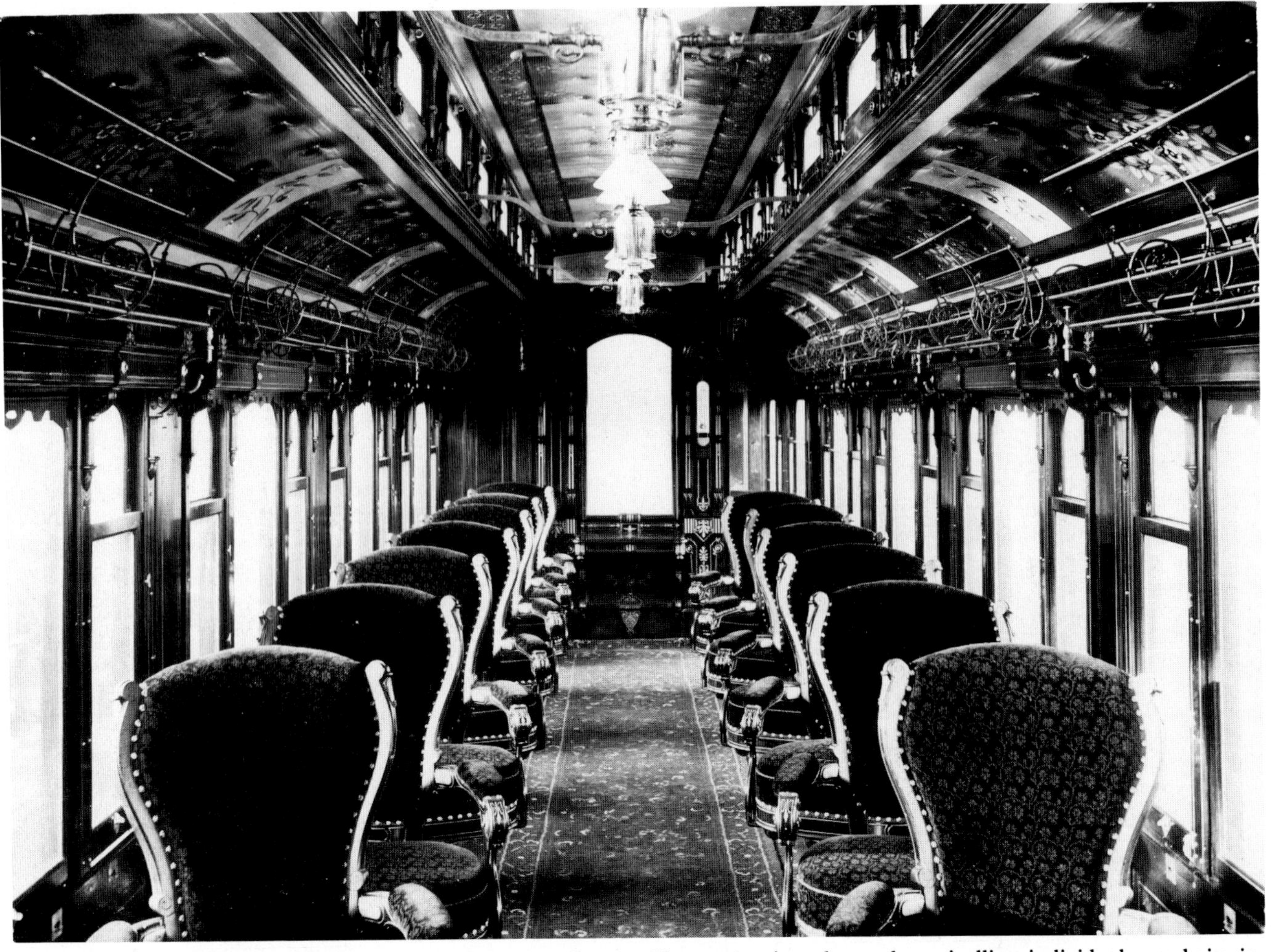

Plates 236 & 237 Typical interior views of Midland Pullmans. The upper view shows the swivelling individual armchairs in drawing room car No. 8 *(Plate 234)* and the lower view shows an unidentified sleeping car, with the sleeping sections in process of being made up for night use.

(BR/LMR and Authors' Collection)

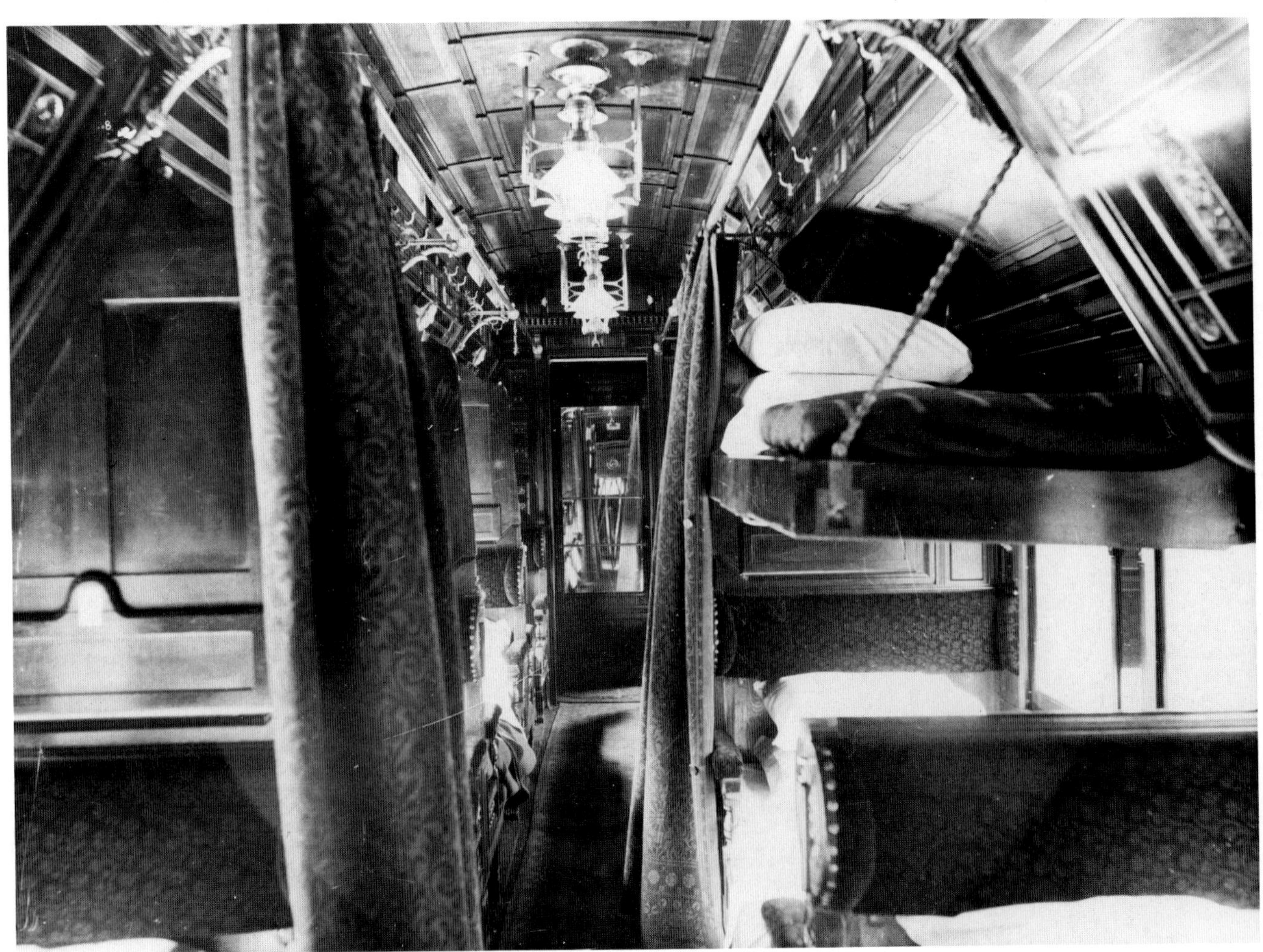

Plate 238 Midland picnic saloon No. 30, pictured at Heysham in 1906, began life in 1883 as six wheel Pullman sleeping car *St. Denis*. The rebuilding with bogies was circa 1885.

(P. .Truman Collection)

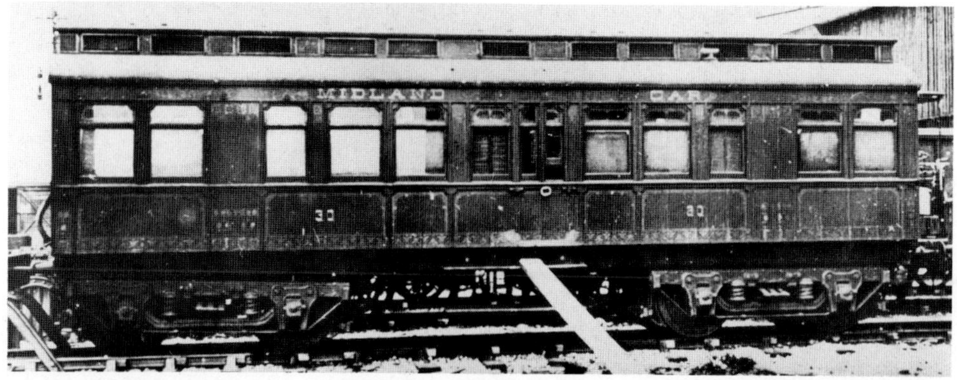

Midland Railway owned 'day cars'. **During this first year, on** 1st June, the Midland Company made history by operating the first train in Britain to be properly heated throughout and in which, should they need to, passengers could walk the full length of the train, albeit via the outside veranda platforms. It was a five coach set including one parlour, one sleeper and three 'day cars' (two with baggage space) and operated from Bradford to London by day and back the same night.

By the close of the first year, the inconvenience had been appreciated of using American pattern centre couplings with specially-modified locomotives with suitable drawgear. Consequently the Pullmans were refitted with British type buffers and couplings and the modified locomotives were re-equipped with normal drawgear.

In 1875, Pullman trains were introduced from St. Pancras to Merseyside and in May 1876, first class Pullmans were incorporated into the initial Anglo-Scottish trains via the new Settle to Carlisle line but this time accompanied by Midland Railway-built 12 wheel ordinary stock of the type shown in *Plate 2*.

Surprisingly, after some two years or so of operation, it was becoming clear that the ordinary passenger was not as interested as had been expected and preferred conventional compartment coaches. The Midland Railway had, of course, by now abolished second class and its third class was very good; but even so the 'ordinary' Pullman-built 'day' cars were better than anything hitherto offered so the lack of public appreciation must have seemed surprising. The drawing room cars and sleeping cars were, however, popular so from 15th May 1876 the Midland Railway quickly replaced the day cars with ordinary stock and concentrated its Pullman efforts on the more 'up market' section of the travelling public.

The pioneer car *Midland* itself entered service in 1877 and in 1878 the Midland Railway again tried an 'all American' train but with no better results than in 1876, so the day cars were relegated to occasional use for special parties and the like.

The next significant event was the introduction of two first class Pullman dining cars on the Midland Railway in 1882, *Delmonico* and *Windsor* (rebuilds from parlour cars *Leo* and *Britannia*). They went on to the Liverpool service and were obviously inspired by the pioneer Pullman diner *Prince of Wales* introduced on the GNR in 1879. In 1883 and 1888 respectively, the Midland Company purchased the parlour cars and sleeping cars from Pullman. Thereafter, the parlour cars no longer carried a supplement but the Midland itself continued to levy the sleeping car supplement, on its own behalf now, of course. The Company also experimented, in 1882/3, **with lighter weight six wheel sleeping cars built from American** components. Two of these went to the Highland Railway and two remained on the Midland Railway. In 1885, the Midland Railway pair were rebuilt with 6ft. 6in. Pullman pattern equalized beam bogies.

From the mid-1880s and over the next twenty years or so the Midland Railway gradually reduced its use of Pullman pattern vehicles, selling some to other companies and transferring others to more special use. Particularly interesting in this context were four of the erstwhile drawing room (parlour) cars, now numbered 1, 2, 5 and 10, which were converted for push-pull use, circa 1905 with 4-4-0T locomotives borrowed from the M&GN. They ran on the Wirksworth, Higham Ferrers, Ripley and Hemel Hempstead branches until circa 1912.

The last Pullman style cars to enter service on the Midland system were the four sleeping carriages to Diagram 453 *(see pages 53 to 57)*, built in America but Midland Railway-owned from the outset.

Many of the original 1870s and 1880s Pullmans ended their life by conversion of the bodies to lineside huts. Their immense strength enabled many to survive as huts almost until the present day and three of them have actually been 'rescued' by the Midland Railway Trust at Butterley, including the original *Midland* of 1874, a first/second 'day car' and a third class 'baggage and day car'.

The American carriages, whether Pullman or Midland Railway-owned, were never a widespread feature of the Midland's service pattern but for a quarter of a century or so they offered considerably enhanced features, compared with much ordinary stock of the time. They unquestionably introduced many new ideas later incorporated into the Midland Company's own carriage designs and were undoubtedly responsible for the late introduction to the system of Company-built sleeping carriages.

They also provided the pioneer examples of a type of carriage operation later to be adopted with great enthusiasm by other British companies, if not the Midland itself, so they deserve their place in history.

The summary which follows gives basic details of all American-built coaches associated with the Midland Railway from 1874 to 1883 and was also compiled by Peter Truman, to whom our grateful thanks are again due. The last four (to Diagram D453) are summarized in *Table 3*.

Plate 239 This familiar picture shows one of the four push-pull conversions, car No. 10, attached to M&GN 4-4-0T No. 8. The car began life in 1876 as *Apollo*, becoming No. 10 in 1883, and this particular locomotive/Pullman pairing ran on the Wirksworth branch from Derby.

(BR/LMR)

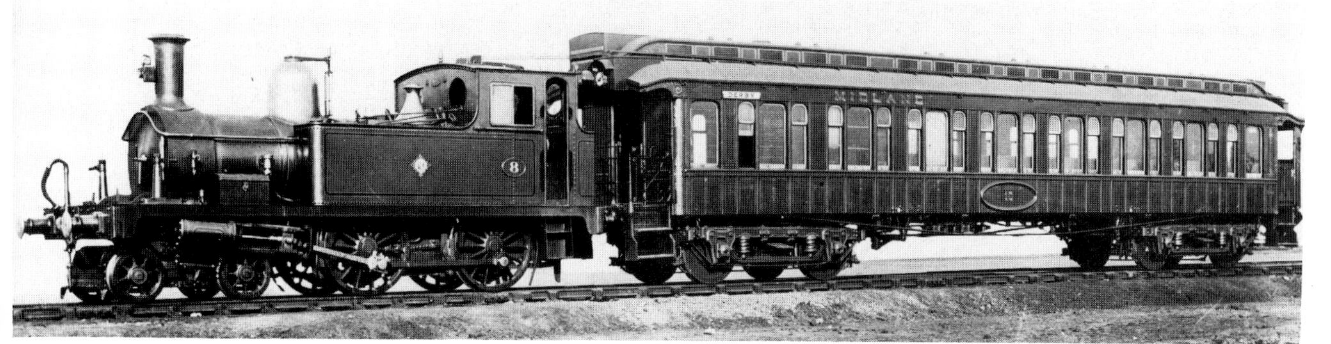

TABLE 12
Summary of Pullman Vehicles

Name/Number	*Date*		*Type*	*Comments*
	Introduced	*Withdrawn*		
No. 1	1874	c 1884	3rd class brake parlour	32 seats per car.
No. 2	1874	c1884	car	32 seats per car
No. 3	1874	c1884	3rd class brake parlour	32 seats per car
No. 4	1874	c1884	car	32 seats per car
No. 5	1874	before 1898	1st/2nd parlour car	18 1st class seats, 32 2nd class. 2nd class section converted to 1st class in 1875. Renumbered to No. 19 in late 1884.
No. 6	1874	1900	1st/2nd parlour car	18 1st class seats, 32 2nd class. 2nd class section converted to 1st class in 1875. Renumbered to No. 18 and rebuilt to 12 wheel dining car in 1884.
No. 7	1874	1900	1st/2nd parlour car	As above, except became No. 17.
No. 8	1874	1900	1st/2nd parlour car	As above, except became *London* in July 1884. Became No. 16 in autumn of same year.
Midland	Jan. 1874		Sleeping car	Used on Continent as exhibition car until bought by MR in March 1888. See history of cars for details. Became MR No. 20.
Excelsior	Feb. 1874		Sleeping car	Became MR No. 21 in March 1888.
Enterprise	1874	28 Oct. 1882	Sleeping car	Burnt out at Hunslet (Leeds).
Victoria	1874	1880	Parlour car	Transferred to LSWR, remodelled, and became *Alexandra* in 1880.
Britannia	1874		Parlour car	Rebuilt as 12 wheel dining car and renamed *Windsor* in 1882. Became MR No. 15 in December 1883.
Leo	1874		Parlour car	Rebuilt as a 12 wheel dining car and renamed *Delmonico* in 1882. Became MR No. 14 in December 1883.
St. George	1875		Sleeping car	Became MR No. 22 in March 1888.
Princess	1875		Sleeping car	Became MR No. 23 in March 1888.
Jupiter	1875	May 1882	Parlour car	Transferred to LCDR in May 1882.
Saturn	1875		Parlour car	Became the new MR No. 1 in December 1883.
Transit	1875		Sleeping car	Became MR No. 24 in March 1888.
Saxon	1875		Sleeping car	Became MR No. 25 in March 1888.
Mercury	1876		Parlour car	Became the new MR No. 2 in December 1883.
Juno	1876		Parlour car	Became the new MR No. 3 in December 1883.
Castalia	1876	Jan. 1883	Sleeping car	Sent to Italy in 1883.
Scotia	1876		Sleeping car	Became MR No. 26 in March 1888.
Venus	1876		Parlour car	Became the new MR No. 4 in December 1883.
Norman	1876		Sleeping car	Became MR No. 27 in March 1888.
Australia	1876	Jan. 1883	Sleeping car	Sent to Italy in 1883.
Vesta	1876		Parlour car	Became the new MR No. 5 in December 1883.
Minerva	1876		Parlour car	Became the new MR No. 6 in December 1883.
India	1876	Aug. 1878	Sleeping car	Transferred to GNR in August 1878.
Germania	1876	Aug. 1878	Sleeping car	Transferred to GNR in August 1878.
Planet	1876		Parlour car	Became the new MR No. 7 in December 1883.
Albion	1876		Parlour car	Became the new MR No. 8 in December 1883.
Comet	1876		Parlour car	Became MR No. 9 in December 1883.
Ariel	Aug. 1876	Oct. 1881	Parlour car	Renamed *Louise*, and transferred to LBSCR in 1881 after rebuilding.
Apollo	1876		Parlour car	Became MR No. 10 in December 1883.
Adonis	1876	Oct. 1881	Parlour car	Renamed *Victoria*, and transferred to LBSCR in 1881 after rebuilding.
Aurora	1877		Parlour car	Became MR No. 11 in December 1883.
Ceres	1877	Oct. 1881	Parlour car	Renamed *Maud*, and transferred to LBSCR in 1881 after rebuilding.
Eclipse	1877		Parlour car	Became MR No. 12 in December 1883.
Alexandra	1877		Parlour car	Became MR No. 13 in December 1883.
St. Andrew	1882		Sleeping car	Became MR No. 28 in March 1888.
St. Mungo	1882		Sleeping car	Became MR No. 29 in March 1888.
St. Louis	1883		Sleeping car 6 wheeled	Became MR No. 30 in March 1888. Rebuilt as bogie vehicle c1885.
St. Denis	1883		Sleeping car 6 wheeled	Became MR No. 31 in March 1888. Rebuilt as bogie vehicle c1885.
Missouri	1883		Sleeping car	Replacement for *Enterprise*, became MR No. 32 in March 1888.
Michigan	1883		Sleeping car	In store until June 1886, became MR No. 33 in March 1888.

Compiled by P. Truman

Appendix II ~ Self-Propelled and Associated Stock

The Midland Railway's brief essays into forms of self-propelled passenger-carrying coaches were short-lived, being confined to the mid-Edwardian period. The vehicles built were but few in number, only two ideas were attempted (one steam, one electric), neither idea was repeated and no serious attempt seems to have been made to develop either concept other than spasmodically and half-heartedly. They did not play a particularly significant role in either Midland Railway or LMS passenger-operating strategy, nor in the evolution of carriage design, so in most respects they can be considered as a somewhat maverick part of the story. Nevertheless they are interesting enough to merit mention.

The Steam Railmotor Experiment

In 1904, the Midland Railway ordered two steam railmotors to be built, originally for the Heysham services (Diagram 479). Numbered 2233 and 2234, each was 60ft. long and had a vertical-boilered prime mover but neither was very successful. They were supplemented by one only non-powered trailer, No. 2235 (Diagram 480), 43ft. long.

Of the two powered carriages, No. 2233 lasted until 1926 but No. 2234 was converted in 1917 to a Superintendent's Saloon, by removal of the power unit and complete refurbishment of the interior, and given a new diagram, D478 *(see page 63)*. By one of the curious twists of fate which sometimes befalls non-standard railway vehicles, No. 2234 has survived in its saloon form, having been purchased in the mid-1970s by the National Railway Museum from the retired senior railway officer who had originally purchased and preserved it for his own private use. Its particular significance for posterity rests not in its saloon configuration, nor in the fact that it is of Midland Railway design. Its importance lies in the fact that it is virtually the only surviving vehicle in Great Britain of steam railmotor origin. Its present condition is somewhat poor but it affords the only opportunity for the National Collection to exhibit, restored to steam railmotor form, a British company example of a type of vehicle with which several railways experimented early in the 20th century, to try and stave off growing competition on marginal or less-used routes.

Plates 240 & 241 Exterior and interior views of steam railmotor No. 2233 (D479) as built. This vehicle was withdrawn in 1926 as a steam railmotor and represents the condition to which it would be proposed to reconvert the preserved No. 2234.

(BR/LMR)

Plates 242 & 243 Electric motor cars Nos. 2236 and 2237 to D537 showing pantograph and bow collectors respectively.
(BR/LMR)

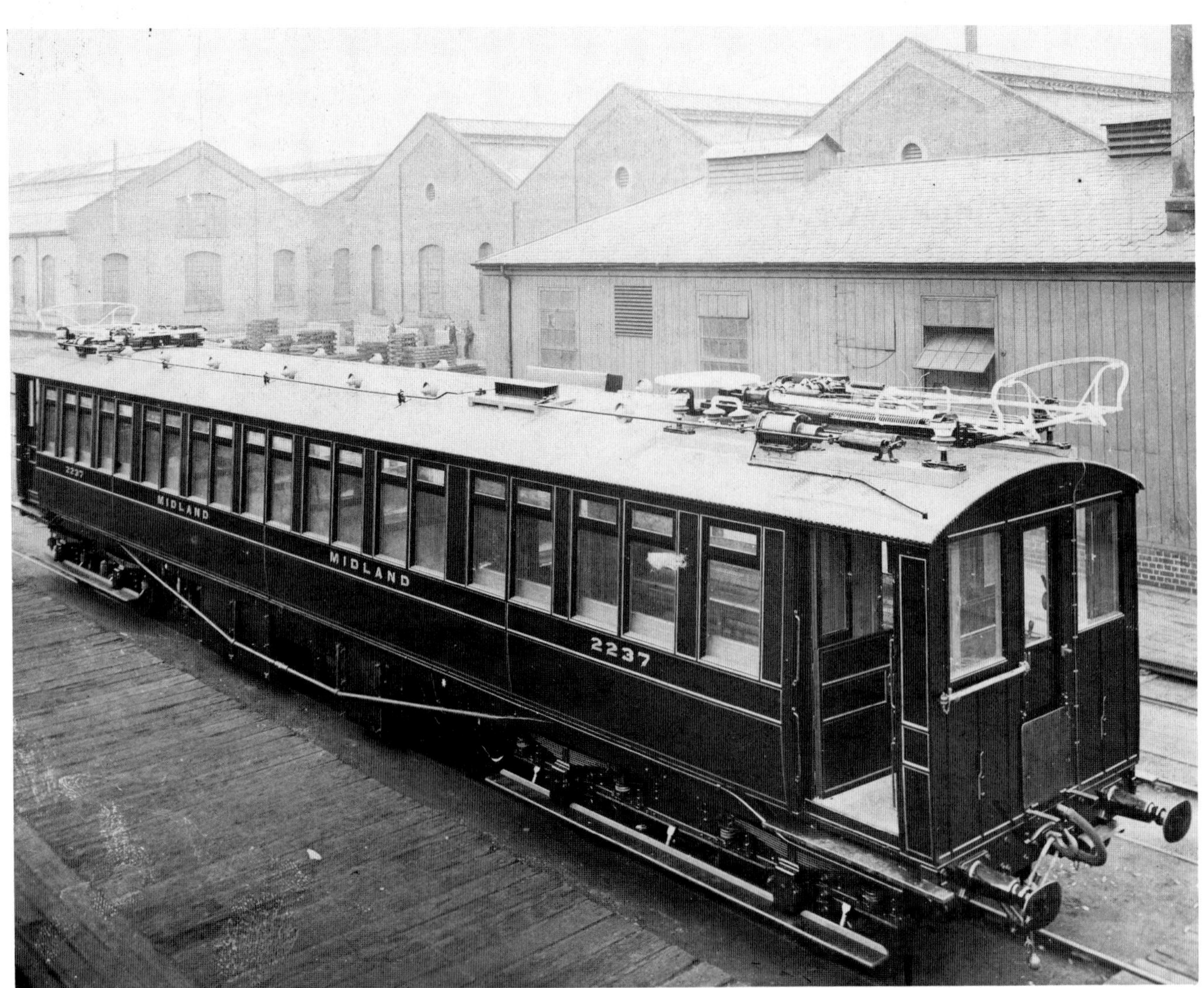

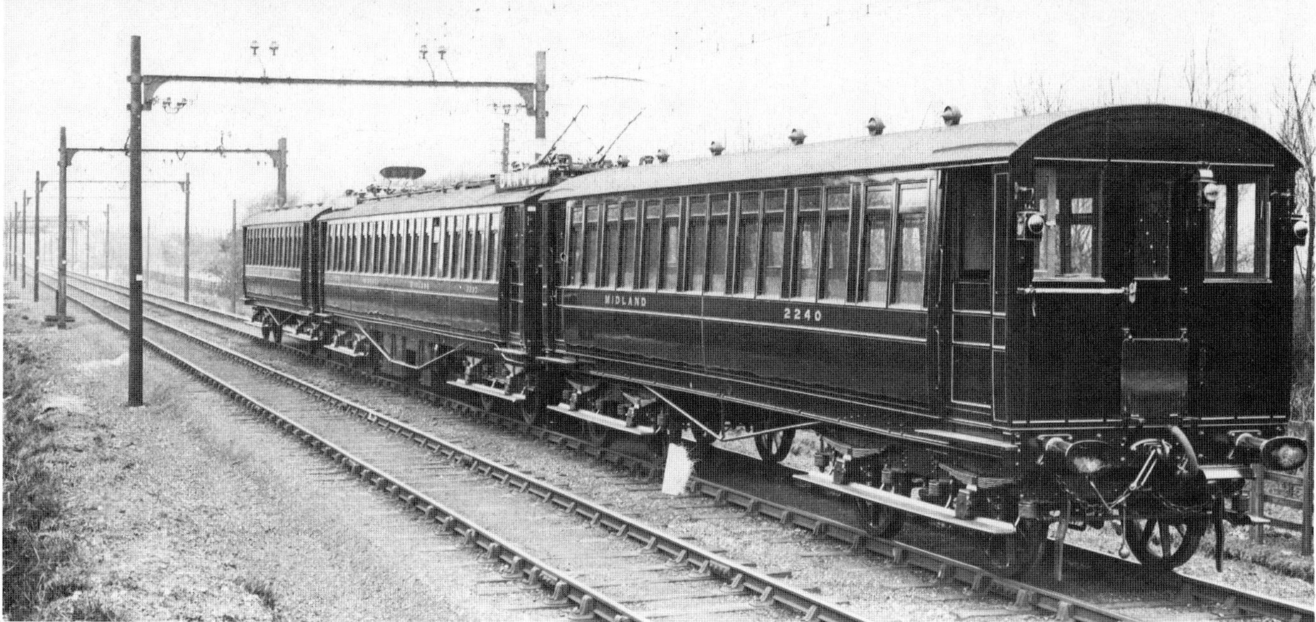

Plates 244 & 245 The two, three unit trains of purpose-built stock. The upper view is trailer No. 2239, motor No. 2238 and trailer No. 2241, while the lower is trailer No. 2242, motor No. 2237 and trailer No. 2240.

(BR/LMR)

At the time of writing (1984), it is not known whether the financial or technical resources of the National Railway Museum will permit the rebirth, even in non-working configuration, of a British steam railmotor, but it is to be hoped that it might one day so transpire. The original idea may not have been wildly successful, either on the Midland Railway or on other lines, but it was an interesting episode in British railway development which merits recording in tangible form for posterity.

The non-powered trailer was converted by the LMS to a bogie third class brake (Diagram 1059) for motor-train (push-pull) working, retaining much of its original appearance. However, it too was scrapped quite soon, being withdrawn circa 1930. The area of utilization of the steam railmotors after their replacement on the Heysham lines by electric units is not known to the authors.

The Electric Train Experiment

A few years after the steam railmotors were built, the Midland Railway ordered an alternative experimental system for the Morecambe to Heysham line. This time, the outcome was more successful. In 1908, the route was electrified on a 6,600 volt, 25 cycle, single phase system with overhead collection and, for the services, three motor cars and four trailers were constructed to D537 and D538 respectively.

In visual terms they were practically a repeat of the steam railmotors (square-cornered panelling reminiscent of the late Clayton style, with arc roofs of the Bain suburban profile); while inside they shared the spartan, perforated plywood seats of their steam-driven predecessors.

The motor cars, 60ft. long, were of two types. One, No. 2236, had Westinghouse electro-pneumatic control with a pantograph collector while the other type (Nos. 2237 & 2238) had electrical control and bow collectors. The four trailers (Nos. 2239-42) were 43ft. long and visually very similar to the previous one-off steam railmotor trailer.

Operation began experimentally early in 1908 and thereafter became the regular form of local service on Morecambe to Heysham, Heysham to Lancaster (Green Ayre) and the Lancaster (Green Ayre) to Lancaster (Castle) routes. The method of operation was for a single motor car to be flanked by two trailers with, presumably, the third motor car standing as a spare unit. During the Midland Railway period, at least

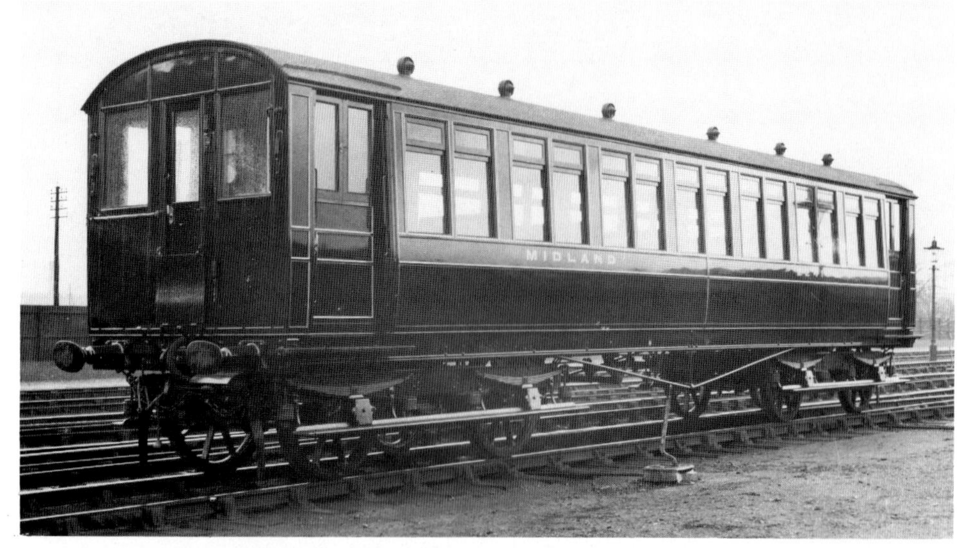

Plate 246 An electric trailer car to D538, No. 2241.

(NRM)

Plate 247 A 'scratch' set in late Midland days with motor No. 2238 running between an unidentified trailer to D538, at the far end, and Clayton arc roof third No. 01174 (ex-D490) at the near end.

(Real Photographs)

one Clayton arc roof bogie third (ex-Diagram 490), No. 01174 was converted to an electric driving trailer whilst during the LMS days, two Bain 54ft. square-panelled clerestory brake composites to Diagram 519A (Nos. 3439 & 3441), were also converted. These two later became second LMS Nos. 29298 & 29299 and the type is described on *page 130*. It has not been ascertained whether or not this conversion was to permit a third train to be assembled with the spare motor carriage. The ex-Midland Railway clerestory composites lasted until 1944/5.

All the original seven vehicles lasted until LMS days and became, in 1933, Nos. 28610-2 (motors) and Nos. 29290-3 (trailers). Except for Nos. 29290 & 29293, they survived until 1952/3 when they were withdrawn as life-expired. En-passant, it is worth recalling that the Heysham line was later converted to 25kV for yet another electrical experiment, this time in connection with the proposed new standards, since adopted, for BR main line electrification.

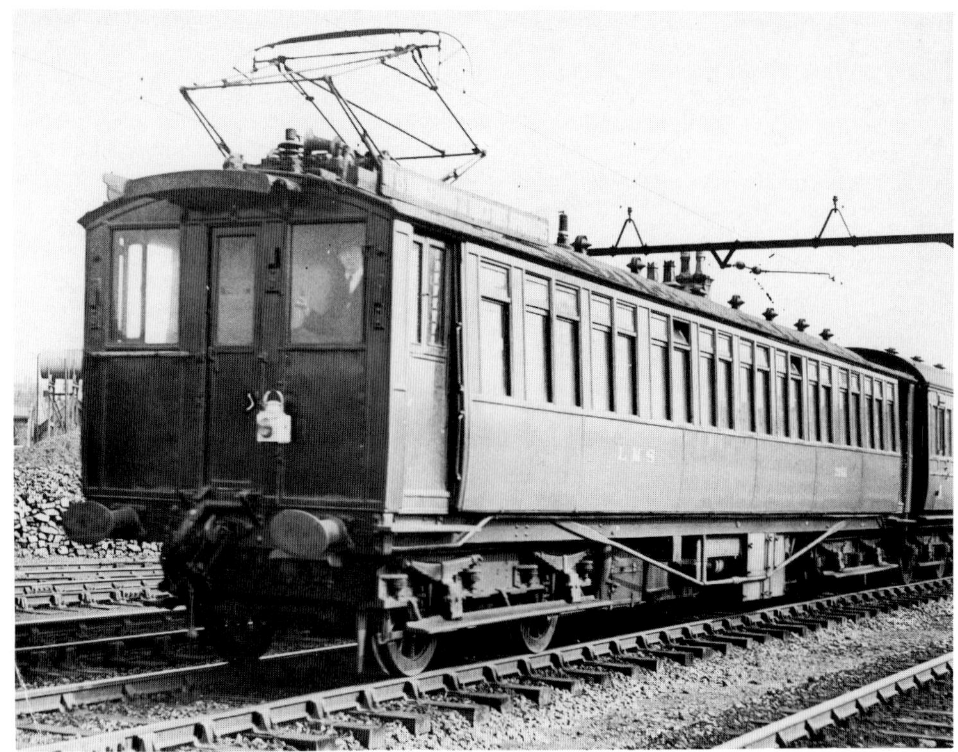

Plate 248 An electric motor car, seen in LMS days, shorn of much of its panel beading and seemingly devoid of lining. The vehicle is No. 28611 (ex-2237) and is attached to an LMS standard non-corridor coach.

(Authors' Collection)

Appendix III ~ Livery notes and other drawings

As we stated towards the end of *Chapter 1*, the subject of Midland carriage livery and that of its LMS successor has already been covered comprehensively in two previously published works - *Midland Style*, published by the Historical Model Railway Society in 1975 and *L.M.S. Coaches - an Illustrated History* by our two selves and published by OPC in 1977. In this work, therefore, we confine our attention to some additional insignia drawings *(overleaf)*, previously unpublished and specially commissioned for this work, along with an outline semi-tabulated resumé of the basic Midland carriage livery and its most significant variations *(below)*. We must stress that this resumé gives only the basic details.

We also stated in our introduction, that this book was not designed to be a technical work of history but that modellers' interest was high on our list of priorities. For this reason, we are also including in this appendix, some supplementary bogie drawings. We have put them here because they are not to the same standard of quality as the drawings offered in the main part of the work, but they should enable interested modellers to produce most of their requirements. Regrettably, we have been unable to locate a reproducible drawing (in any form) of the Clayton 8ft. bogie; but it shared many features in common with the 10ft. bogie *(Figure 76)* and the early six wheel bogie *(part of Figure 2)*. It is also well illustrated in many of the pictures in this book.

Basic Carriage Livery 1877-1923 - Principal Trends

Sides and Ends
Midland Red (Crimson Lake) - shade remaining consistent from 1883 to 1923 (and during the LMS period to 1939), save for any variation in manufacture. There was never an official instruction to alter the colour itself until 1946 when the LMS changed it to 'Maroon'.

Roof
Always lead grey between rainstrips (lower rainstrips where applicable), frequently all over grey. Later, particularly on 20th century clerestory and semi-elliptical roof stock, gloss black was almost universally applied between lower rainstrip and cantrail, the rainstrip itself being black. Clerestory sides were Crimson Lake, generally unlined in later days.

Lining and Details (Sides)

1. Mouldings black, lined each side with gold (gilt). Gold line carried a fine vermilion edging both sides down to 1885, adjacent to black only from 1885. Double vermilion edging reappeared later (date not known) but was again universal by the LMS period.

Note: Gold lining became yellow for non-passenger stock before the turn of the century and yellow was also used for economy on much ordinary stock, circa World War I. By the LMS period, (1923), the following arrangement was usual:

a) Gangwayed stock - gold lining, double-edged vermilion.
b) Non-gangwayed stock - yellow lining, double-edged vermilion.
c) Non-passenger stock - generally as non-gangwayed, but on some types with 'freight vehicle' visual charcteristics, the black was suppressed and the framing and/or moulding was given a simple 'yellow line only' treatment.

Since the LMS never, as far as we know, deviated from standard MR livery practice during the 1923-32 period, we assume that this initial LMS policy was a straight copy of the final MR scheme.

2. On fully lined vehicles, a fine horizontal vermilion line was always located at the extreme lower edge of the carriage side, immediately above the solebar and, sometimes, a second such line may have been placed immediately below the roof overhang. On non-arc roof vehicles, a horizontal vermilion line was also placed along the lower part of the gutter moulding.
3. On carriages without a bottom horizontal side moulding (e.g. most of those built or modified after circa 1908/9) the side was painted as if this moulding was present. The LMS continued this policy until 1933.
4. Raised window frame mouldings (bolections) were painted in a 'mahogany' colour (Indian Red or Teak?), which was continued, until 1933, by the LMS. This did not apply to square-panelled clerestories which did not carry bolection mouldings.
5. Droplight frames were painted Crimson Lake.
6. Carriage destination boards had either gold letters on a Crimson Lake ground, or white letters on a china blue background.

Lining and Details (Ends)
Raised mouldings and most end details (steps, lamp irons, etc.) were painted black without lining. The metal parts of corridor gangway housings (including the 'scissor' beams) were more commonly Crimson Lake but occasionally may have been black.

Underframe

1. Until 1902, solebars and headstocks were Crimson Lake, fully lined (including step brackets) in yellow only. Detailed treatment varied *(see pictures)*.
2. From 1902-14, solebars and headstocks were plain red (shade indeterminate, possibly a little browner than body lake).
3. From 1914, and copied by the LMS, all below the body side/ends became plain black.

Note: During the 'coloured' solebar/headstock period, all below this level was black, except, sometimes, the wheels. Wood-centered wheels often had their timber segments painted a sort of Indian Red shade but this treatment seems to have lacked total consistency, even under the LMS period.

Insignia

1. *Passenger Class Markings:* Fully lettered in waist panel (sans serif) until circa 1906/7, thereafter by large figures on the doors.
2. *Company Identity:* Usually, MR or M.R during the Clayton arc roof period. Thereafter, 'Midland' in full either in the waist panel(s) (sans serif) or, later, at eaves level (serif pattern against a black background). The Midland's diamond-shaped heraldic emblem appeared on saloons, first class and composite carriages, and on a very few third class vehicles, until the time of changeover to large figures on the doors, at which period its use was terminated.
3. *Designatory lettering:* Sans serif style usually on the waist panel(s).
4. *Running numbers:* Sans serif, position variable *(see pictures)*.

Note: Insignia placing was highly-varied and pictures afford the best means of analysis. However, there was always a conscious attempt to impart balance and symmetry to the finished carriage side.

A Selection of Midland Railway Carriage Insignia.

1 MIDLAND 3

MIDLAND

The drawings above (scale 1½" to 1 ft) show the later style eaves panel lettering (gold on black) and the style of shaded gold lettering. Shading left was red with white highlights, and right, black. The selection below (scale ¾" to 1 ft) shows items in 4", 3", 2½" and 2" heights, which were normally shaded like "MIDLAND" above, except that the white was omitted on the large size "FISH".

MIDLAND DINING CARRIAGE

M & G S W MOTOR CAR VAN M . V .

M & N B SLEEPING FIRST THIRD

1234567890 M . R 95 FISH

M . S . J . S M . R 1 2 3 4 5 6 7 8 9 0 3

MEAT VAN. HOUND VAN STORES VAN

FIRST THIRD LUGGAGE PASSENGERS LUGGAGE

M . R . 223 FISH TRUCK

Figure 72 (above) Midland Railway insignia drawings. *(Peter Chatham)*

Figure 73 (below) Four wheel 'American' pattern bogie as used on both Pullmans and the earliest MR built bogie stock. Scale: 7mm. = 1ft. *(P. Chatham Collection)*

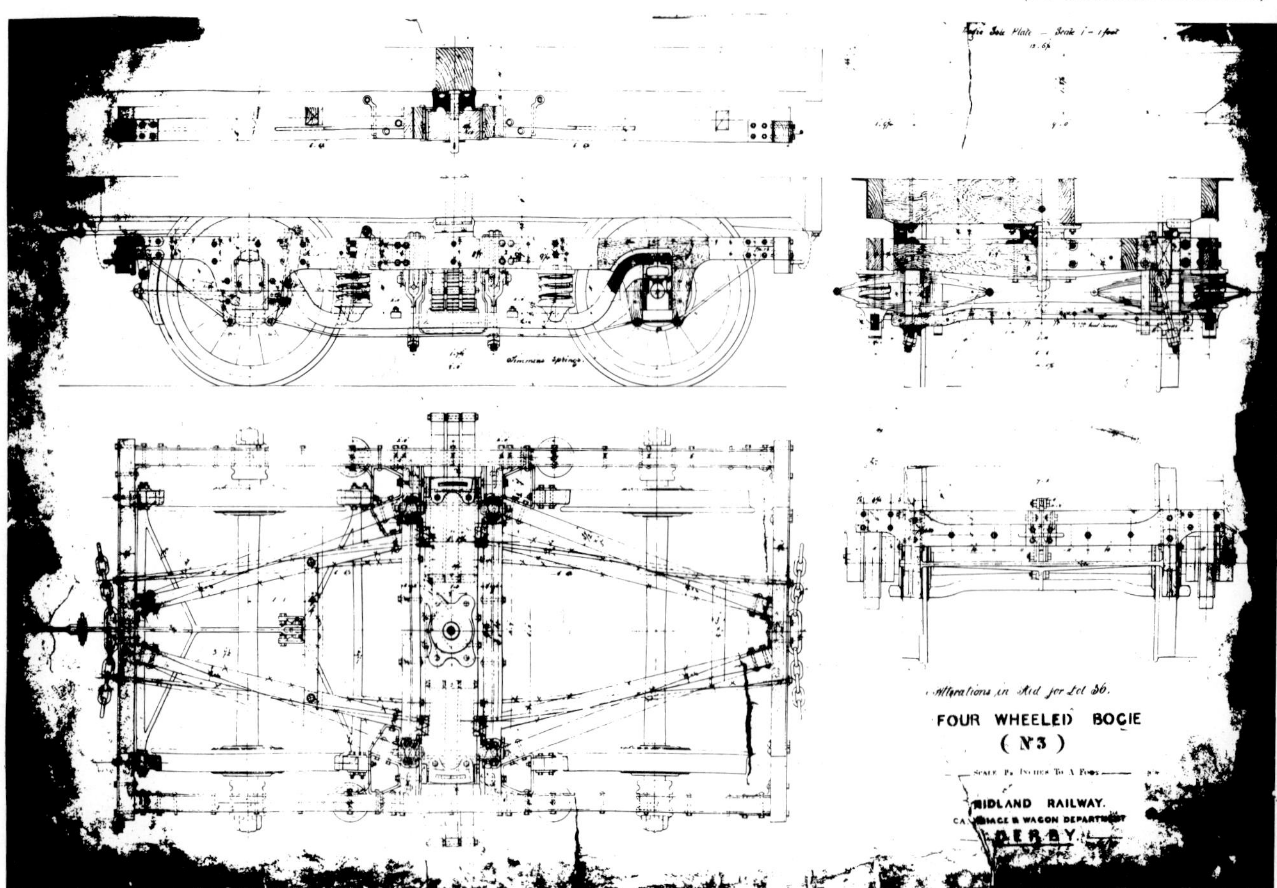

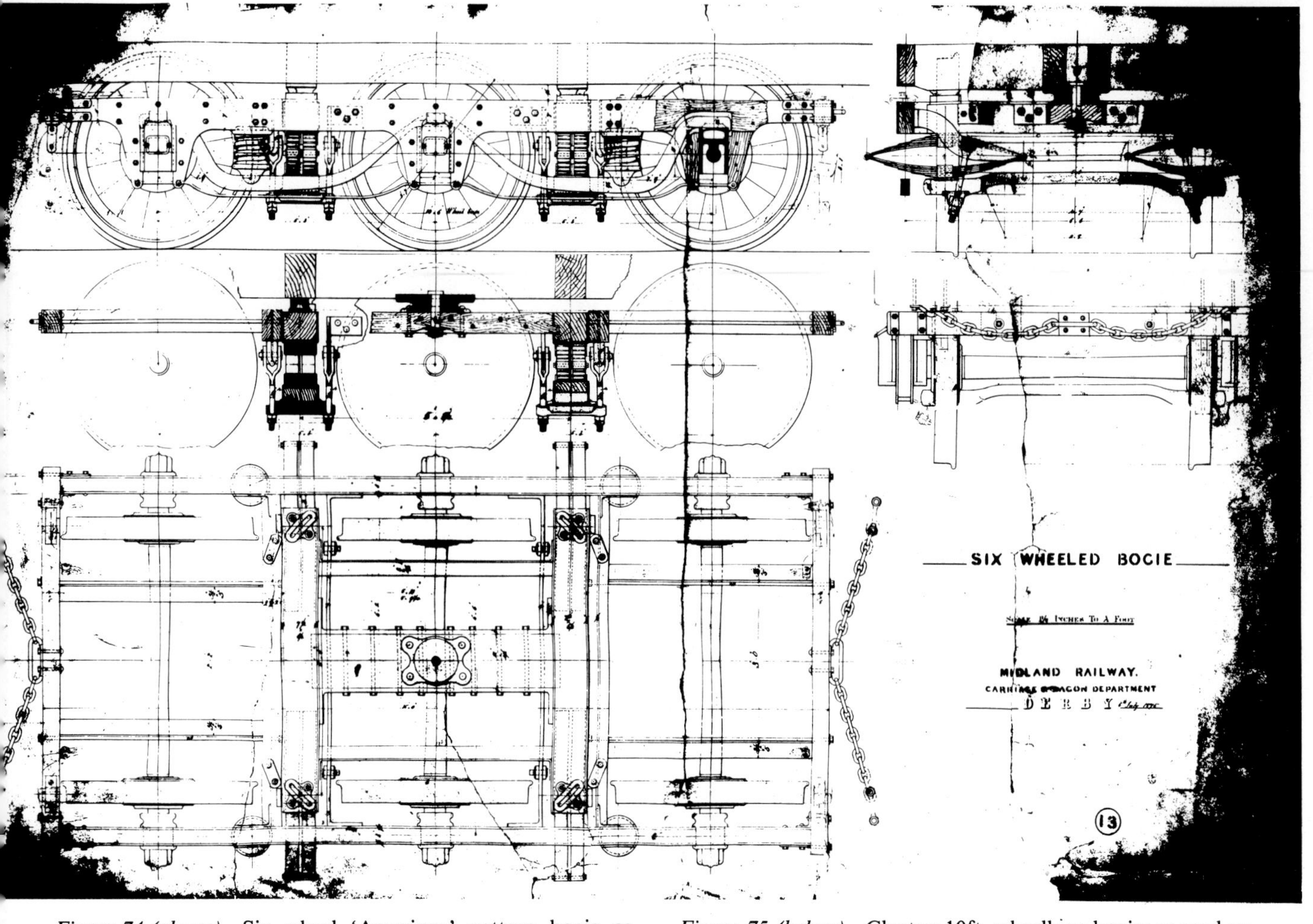

Figure 74 (above) Six wheel 'American' pattern bogie as used on both Pullmans and the earliest MR built twelve wheel stock. Scale: 7mm. = 1ft.

(P. Chatham Collection)

Figure 75 (below) Clayton 10ft. wheelbase bogies as used on square-panelled clerestory and much Bain suburban stock up to 50ft. length. Scale 7mm. = 1ft.

(P. Chatham Collection)

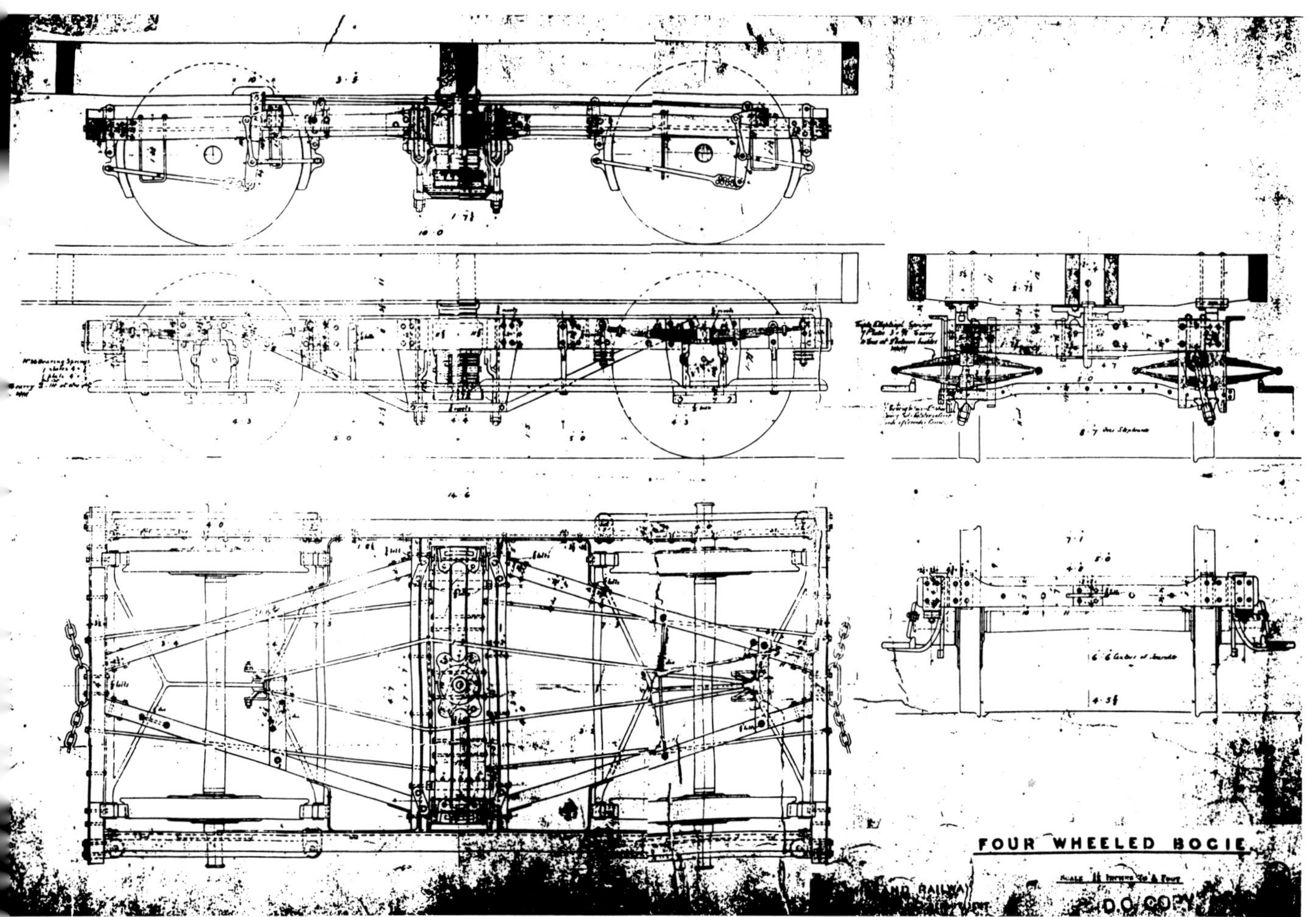

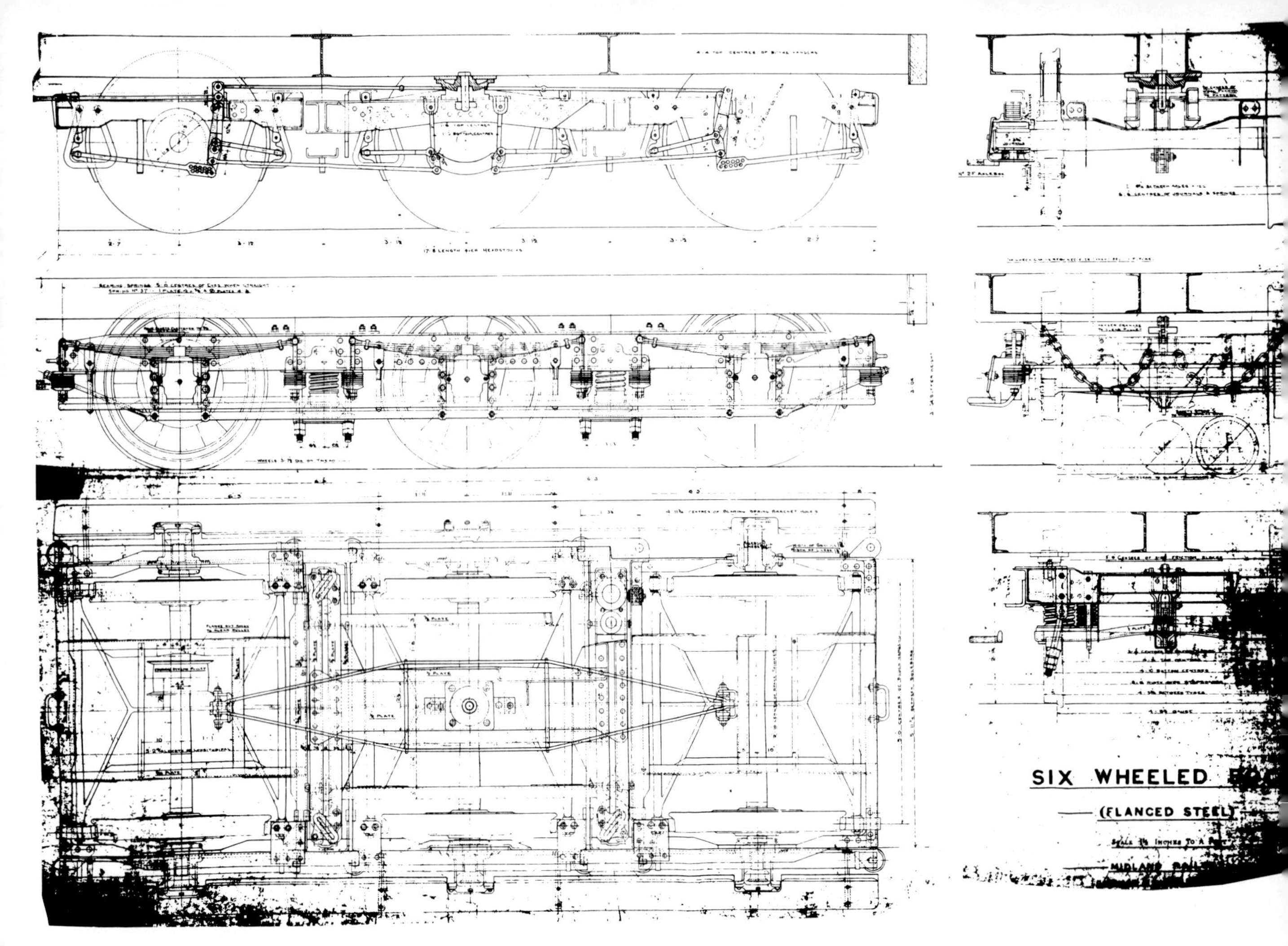

Figure 76 (above) Six wheel bogie for 20th century stock. This bogie superseded the version given as part of *Figure 2* when twelve wheel carriages became heavier. It was itself finally superseded by the version as at *Figure 7*, which was also adopted by the LMS. Scale: 7mm. = 1ft.

(P. Chatham Collection)

Figure 77 (below) Four wheel pressed-steel bogie for 59f dining carriages. This bogie was designed for the dining car at *Figure 15* (and their associated open thirds). It did no become a standard Midland type. Scale: 7mm. = 1ft.

(P. Chatham Collection

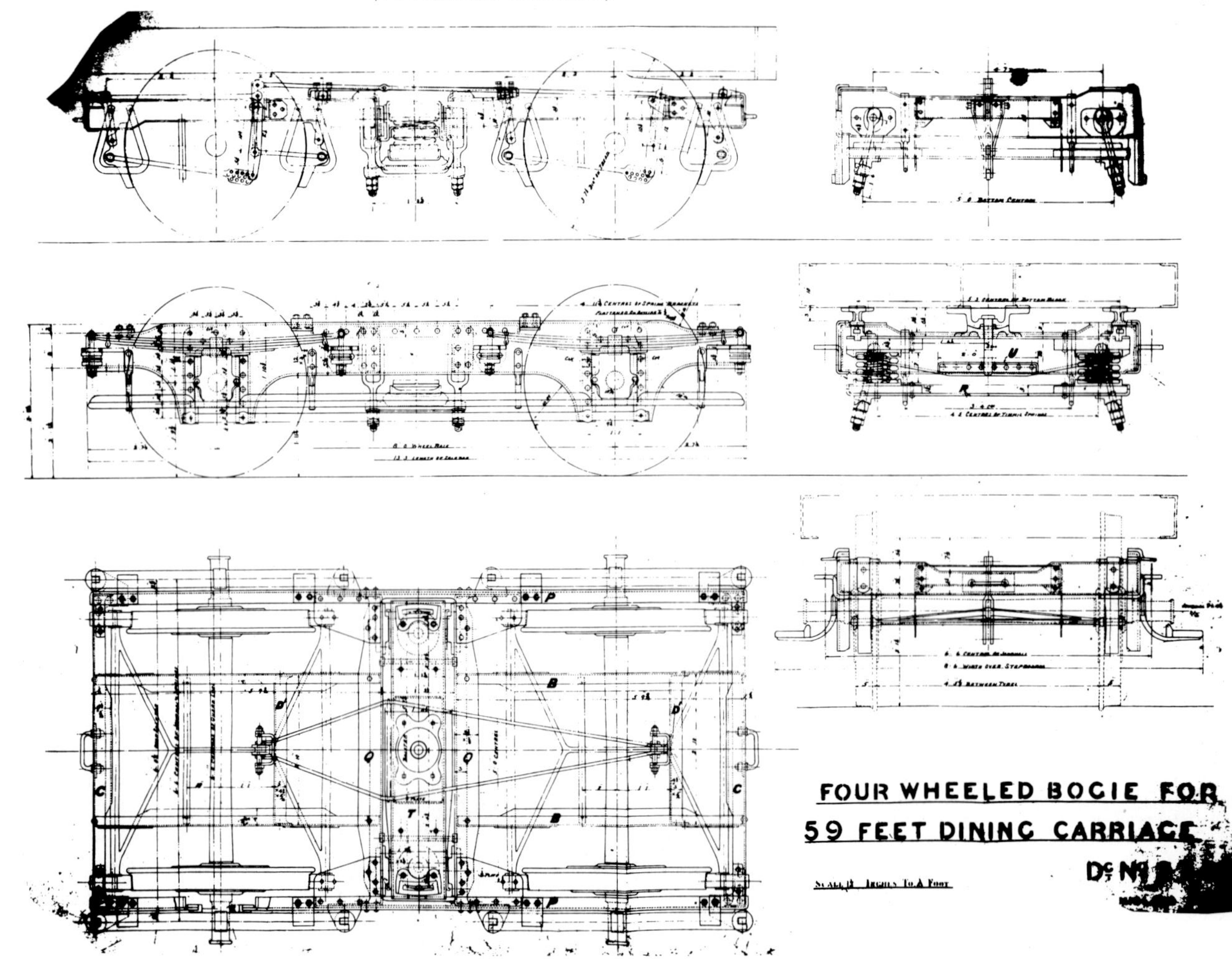

Appendix IV ~ Notes on Midland Passenger Train formations and working

'The Midland Railway ran small trains and pulled them with little engines' is the accepted generalization which appears in many books. 'Any reasonably-sized load was always double-headed' is another, oft-repeated cliché. Like all popular statements, both these have a grain of truth in them, but whilst we were compiling this book, and examining hundreds of pictures in the process, it dawned on us, with great clarity, that Midland trains were nothing like as simple to sum up as many might suppose. Indeed, we ourselves were surprised at the variety in length, make-up, style of coaches and so forth, which Midland trains exhibited, when we looked more closely into the matter. This is not the place at which to conduct a detailed analysis of train workings (although we have this in mind for the future) but it did seem to us appropriate to conclude this book with a few pictures of Midland trains, some of which tend to give the lie to the more accepted simplifications. Each view is accompanied by a brief analysis of its more interesting points and identification details of the carriage types where possible.

Plate 249 This view of what, to many, represents a typical Midland train is not quite as typical as it may seem. For one thing, it is for the period (circa 1910) far too tidy - being comprised entirely of square-panelled clerestory vehicles, a very rare state of affairs. The train, an 'up' express approaching Elstree behind 4-4-0 Class 3 No. 719, is headed by a pair of 48ft. newspaper vans which we mention in our footnote to the postal vehicle section of *Table 11*. This is the first and only picture we have found, so far, which shows these elusive carriages. The rest of the train can also, with one partial exception, be positively described. The formation is, in order from the front, as follows: two newspaper vans (either to Lot 507 or 548); a six wheel lavatory composite to D514; a 46ft. 7½in. third class to D489; a 48ft. luggage and lavatory composite to D508; (almost certainly) a 54ft. corridor composite brake to D470, the only gangway coach in the train; a 48ft. lavatory third class to D486 and a six wheel brake to D530. The high proportion of first class in the five passenger carrying vehicles accords with our comments earlier in the book.

(Bernard Matthews Collection)

Plate 250 We have chosen this circa 1929 LMS vintage picture to illustrate how little the 'Midland' look changed for many years after the Grouping. It shows another version of what many regard as a typical Midland train (two small engines pulling a handful of carriages) but it took some time for us to locate such a picture. The train is headed by a rebuilt Johnson 2-4-0, No. 194, assisting the train engine, an unidentified 483 class superheated 4-4-0. Although running under express headlamps the train is a real mixed bag. A Clayton clerestory brake third to D500 and still gas lit; an LMS standard period I (i.e. Midland-styled) non-corridor third class to LMS Diagram 1700; an MR semi-elliptical roof lavatory composite to D1245; a six wheel clerestory brake to D530; a gas lit 45ft. non-lavatory clerestory composite to D511; and three non-passenger vehicles, of which the centre one is a Midland covered carriage truck to either D402 or D403. Again, note that two of the four passenger carrying vehicles are composites.

(Bernard Matthews Collection)

Plate 251 An interesting picture showing a rebuilt 179 class 4-2-2, No. 667, in sole charge of no fewer than fourteen vehicles, and running under express headlamps, southbound, near Elstree. The original picture claims it to be a Bradford to St. Pancras express, but we doubt this. The proprtion of first class is too low and the carriage types are too suburban for the period (circa 1909 or later), which makes us believe it is far more likely to be a Bedford to St. Pancras fast train classified as an express. The identifiable carriages, from the locomotive are: milk van to D419; LNWR brake van; 50ft. Bain brake third to D556; 50ft. Bain third class to D555; 50ft. first class to D553; 48ft. Clayton lavatory third class to D486; 54ft. Bain clerestory brake third to D497; 48ft. Clayton lavatory third class to D486 and six assorted non-passenger vehicles, including a six wheel clerestory brake to D530. Note that the Bain 50ft. arc roof suburban carriages do not constitute a complete set of Bedford to St. Albans pattern, and are supplemented by clerestories which makes us think that this may have been an 'extra' working. We are somewhat intrigued by the presence of the LNWR brake van.

(Author's Collection)

Plate 252 We apologize for concluding our survey with this well-known picture of a southbound local passenger train near Colehill on the Settle to Carlisle line, circa 1910. But apart from the two leading horse-boxes to D400, (featured in close-up at *Plate 206*), it represents a varied, and lengthy, formation for a stopping train through this thinly-populated region. The locomotive is rebuilt 1738 class 4-4-0 No. 367, and behind the horse-boxes are the following coaches: Bain corridor composite to D469; Clayton 43ft. arc roof third class to D490; Clayton 40ft. arc roof composite to Lot 16, 26 or 83 (no diagram); six wheel clerestory brake to D530; 48ft. clerestory lavatory and luggage composite to D508; Clayton arc roof six wheel third class to D493; another Clayton composite to Lot 16, 26 or 83 and 25ft. Clayton arc roof four wheel brake van to D529. We can only conclude that the presence of, by 1910 standards, a modern corridor composite was to offset the somewhat elderly nature of the remaining first class accommodation in the 40ft. composites, built 1878-82. Even so, a ten vehicle stopping passenger train has to be a little different.

(BR/LMR)